The Trials of Abraham

The Trials of Abraham

♦

The Making of a National Patriarch

Martin Sicker

iUniverse, Inc.
New York Lincoln Shanghai

The Trials of Abraham
The Making of a National Patriarch

All Rights Reserved © 2004 by Martin Sicker

No part of this book may be reproduced or transmitted in any form or by any means, graphic, electronic, or mechanical, including photocopying, recording, taping, or by any information storage retrieval system, without the written permission of the publisher.

iUniverse, Inc.

For information address:
iUniverse, Inc.
2021 Pine Lake Road, Suite 100
Lincoln, NE 68512
www.iuniverse.com

ISBN: 0-595-33753-8

Printed in the United States of America

Contents

Introduction vii
CHAPTER 1   The Early Life and Career of Abram 1
CHAPTER 2   The Odyssey Begins. 10
CHAPTER 3   Detour to Egypt 34
CHAPTER 4   Abram and Lot: Irreconcilable Differences. 47
CHAPTER 5   Abram the Warrior 61
CHAPTER 6   The Covenant Between the Pieces 74
CHAPTER 7   The Birth of Ishmael 87
CHAPTER 8   Abram Becomes Abraham 98
CHAPTER 9   A Question of Justice. 117
CHAPTER 10 The Birth of Isaac 142
CHAPTER 11 Abraham's Greatest Trial and Its Aftermath 161
CHAPTER 12 Abraham's Odyssey Comes to an End 183
Selected References 207
About the Author 221
Endnotes. 223

Introduction

In Israel's narrative of its own pre-history as a nation, its origins are attributed to a divine covenant with Abraham, originally known as Abram, to whose life and work the biblical Book of Genesis devotes some fourteen chapters.[1] By contrast with the epitome of the twenty generations between the creation of the universe and the emergence of Abraham on the scene of history that is presented in the first eleven chapters of the biblical work, which I dealt with in an earlier work, *Reading Genesis Politically: An Introduction to Mosaic Political Philosophy*, the biblical author's approach to the saga of Abraham is to attempt to place the events described in a more readily recognizable historical and geographical context. This should not be understood as asserting the historicity of all or any of those events from an objective modern historical perspective, events that can be corroborated by archeological evidence or other ancient literary sources, even though an increasing number of modern scholars believe this to be the case. Writing in this regard in the mid-twentieth century, William F. Albright observed:

> Until recently it was the fashion among biblical historians to treat the patriarchal sagas of Genesis as though they were artificial creations of Israelite scribes of the Divided Monarchy or tales told by imaginative rhapsodists around Israelite campfires during the centuries following their occupation of the country…Archeological discoveries since 1925 have changed all this. Aside from a few die-hards among older scholars, there is scarcely a single biblical historian who has not been impressed by the rapid accumulation of data supporting the substantial historicity of patriarchal tradition.[2]

Whether or not things actually happened in the way they are depicted in the biblical texts is really quite beside the point, which is that the saga of Abraham has been a critical component of Israel's national historical narrative for more than three millennia and that its significance for Israel's actual history as a nation is indisputable, irrespective of whether it can be corroborated by other ancient sources. In other words, the existence of the narrative is itself an indisputable fact that has shaped Israel's history over the millennia. In the words of W.D. Davies:

> For the understanding of our task in this volume, what is important is not the rediscovery of the origins of the promise to Abraham, but the recognition that that promise was so interpreted from age to age that it became a living power in the life of the people of Israel. Not the mode of its origin matters, but its operation as a formative, dynamic, seminal force in the history of Israel. The legend of the promise entered so deeply into the experience of the Jews that it acquired its own reality. What Jews believe to have happened in the Middle East has been no less formative in world history than that which is known to have occurred.[3]

The central thesis underlying this book is that a dispassionate reading of the Pentateuch, the Five Books of Moses or the Torah, will lead to the conclusion that it is first and foremost a library of essentially political teachings and documents. This is not to suggest that the Torah does not contain a great deal of guidance concerning human behavior outside the political sphere. It is my contention, however, that the biblical author's overriding concern is with the shaping of a unique civilization, within which the guidance provided in the Torah will serve to bring that civilization to its highest potential for achieving the mission believed to be divinely assigned to it. Accordingly, the primary interest of the biblical author is the promulgation of an ideological framework within which a unique society and civilization might emerge and flourish.

It may be useful to recall at this point that the notion of civilization is itself a political idea. A civilization is the morally authoritative institutional infrastructure that facilitates the flowering of society and culture, by establishing and enforcing patterns of civil relationships, in effect, by civilizing human behavior. Accordingly, it is the assigned mission of Abraham within the biblical scheme to become the founding patriarch of a nation specifically brought into being for the exclusive purpose of constituting the political and social basis for the institutional infrastructure deemed necessary to facilitate the emergence of an ideal civilization, as such is conceived and portrayed by the biblical author in the remaining volumes of the Pentateuch.

Because of its essentially political orientation, it should come as no surprise that there is very little doctrinal theology to be found in the Torah. The primary subject of the work is man rather than God; its principal concern is man in his relation to God, his fellow man, and society, and the biblical author, in dealing with this subject matter, draws no clear distinction between the sacral and the secular, a differentiation that would have been alien to the biblical worldview. The Torah generally and the Book of Genesis in particular presupposes the existence of God, who is described as the creator of the universe, but tells us virtually nothing further about the divine. Although theologians have been reading their beliefs and predilections into the biblical texts for some two millennia, sometimes rather ingeniously, the simple fact is that there is little in the Mosaic canon that reasonably lends itself to such theological interpretations. This is not to suggest that the biblical text cannot be read from a variety of perspectives, as has traditionally been the case in the long history of biblical interpretation. Ambiguities in the text certainly do encourage speculative readings of its content, ranging from the rational to the mystical and esoteric. Nonetheless, the primary focus of the Mosaic canon remains on the desiderata for the ideal society and civilization it envisages.

This study represents, in essence, a continuation of my earlier work on reading Genesis politically and is devoted to a consideration of how the biblical author sought to explain through narrative rather than analysis why Abraham was chosen to be the founding patriarch of a new nation and civilization whose mission was to achieve that which earlier civilizations had failed to do to divine satisfaction. The biblical author had previously shown that the fundamental principle of patriarchalism, the transfer of authoritative teaching and responsibility from one generation to another, which is inherent in the biblical worldview, was to be the basis of Mosaic civilization. In the process, he also illustrated in the first eleven chapters of the Book of Genesis why the creation of a new nation that was to embody that civilization was necessary in light of the failures of all earlier attempts to produce the truly moral and just society. He now turns his attention to the saga of Abraham and the founding of that nation and to the subsequent articulation of the divine principles and precepts with which it was expected to create a model civilization for eventual emulation by all the peoples of the earth.

Some of the basic principles of the biblical author's political and social philosophy that are reflected in his work continue to underpin much of responsible modern moral and political thought. First and foremost, man is held to be endowed by his creator with morally free will, however constrained by circumstances it may be, and is also endowed with the faculty of reason with which to govern and direct that will in appropriate paths. Accordingly, all men and women deemed mentally competent must be held morally responsible and accountable for their actions. Second, as creator of the universe, God is concerned and engaged with His creation, thereby establishing a necessarily interactive relationship between man and God, whether man wishes it or not. Given that involuntary relationship, prudence alone will therefore dictate that voluntary compliance with the precepts articulated and intimated in the divine guidance contained in the biblical writings is in man's best interest. Third, the idea that man can create and sustain a moral society without reference to divine authority is a delusion. Man's ability to rationalize even his most outrageous behavior clearly indicates the need for an unimpeachable source and standard of moral authority, and only divine authority can satisfy that criterion. Fourth, until all men accept the preceding principles, the idea of a universal society or state is both dangerous and counterproductive, as made clear in the biblical story of the Tower of Babel and its consequences.[4] In the twentieth century we witnessed two different attempts to create such a world state, both of which produced totalitarian monstrosities. Fifth, individualism as a social philosophy tends to be destructive of traditional values and must be tempered by the idea of communal responsibility.

These fundamental ideas underlie the elaboration of the political philosophy and the normative political theory that is reflected in the Mosaic legislation that comprises the main body of the Pentateuch, Israel's constitutional legacy. As indicated, in the view of the biblical author, the key to giving life to these fundamental principles is the creation of a uniquely constituted nation whose national mission, whose very reason for being, is to embody them in a functioning civilization. The first step toward that goal is the selection of an extraordinary but at the same time quite human being who will prove himself worthy of becoming the progenitor of that new nation. In a sense then, the story of Abraham is the saga of the making of a national patriarch, the founding father of a nation.

The Abraham saga as presented in the biblical narrative has raised many significant questions about its intent and meaning in the minds of readers ever since the Pentateuch texts were fixed, at the latest about two and a half millennia ago. Viewed superficially, the narrative appears to be made up of a series of seemingly independent incidents, the linkage between them uncertain and unclear in more than just a few instances. Nonetheless, many commentators, traditional interpreters as well as critical scholars, have been reluctant simply to accept the Abraham narratives as a series of loosely if at all connected incidents arbitrarily selected from surviving ancient lore, and insist that, contrary to possible first superficial impressions, there is a definite scheme to the organization of the narratives that clearly serves the biblical author's purpose, which is not to provide a biography of Abraham in the usual modern sense of the term but to place him in the broader context and literary scheme of the Book of Genesis.

Viewed from this perspective, to understand Abraham and his role in the biblical project, one must pay close attention to the conception and structure of the entire work. Martin Buber provides a particularly cogent insight in this regard. "The Book of Genesis intends to relate *toledot*, generations. It is concerned with deriving the *toledot* of the nation Israel from the *toledot* of the human race; and these, from the generations of the heavens and the earth. The cosmogony, the origin of the world, is related for the sake of ethnogony, the origin of the people. We are to trace the meaning of the people's origin back to the meaning of the origin of the world, and back to the intention of the Creator for His creation." It would of course ease our task considerably as modern readers of the texts if the biblical author had told us explicitly what his meaning and intention were. Alas, for reasons about which we can only speculate but not draw any firm conclusions, such is not the case. The Pentateuch obviously is not nor was it ever intended to serve as a systematic work of theology that, like most such works, is truly accessible only to a relatively few scholars who are prepared to deal with what would be excessively arcane for most people. Instead, as Buber put it, "it presents us with a story only, but this story is theology; biblical theology is narrated theology. The Bible cannot be really comprehended if it is not comprehended in this way: as a doctrine that is nothing but history, and as a history that is nothing but doctrine."[5]

Within the framework of that perhaps unique literary scheme, the saga of Abraham is presented in a series of stories, selected out of the many episodes that surely took place during his ostensibly long life, that are intended to illustrate why he was chosen to be the founding forefather of the nation of Israel, the name first applied in a national context to his grandson Jacob, the third patriarch. In recounting these stories, it would appear that the biblical writer's principal concern was to describe the discrete steps by which Abraham underwent transformation from a natural philosopher to a religious sage, from being a consummate rationalist to becoming a man of faith capable of suppressing in its favor even the most pressing demands of reason. Accordingly, in the vast literature on the biblical texts that is available to us, numerous commentators from the second century B.C.E. onward viewed these stories as interconnected not so much by their temporal sequence as by the challenge and response that is reflected in each. Moreover, the challenges that confront Abraham in each of these episodes are intimately related to his personal strengths and weaknesses. Abraham is presented to us as a human being that we might recognize as a relative or neighbor; he is not portrayed as a larger than life mythological character. Although a great man, he is by no means perfect; indeed, were he perfect, the stories would lose much of their meaning and significance. As Samson R. Hirsch wrote: "The Torah never hides from us the faults, errors and weaknesses of our great men. Just by that it gives the stamp of veracity to what it relates…If they stood before us as the purest models of perfection we should attribute them as having a different nature, which has been denied us. Were they without passion without internal struggles, their virtues would seem to us the outcome of some higher nature, hardly a merit and certainly no model that we could hope to emulate."[6] In other words, the stories are understood to reflect a series of progressively more severe tests or trials to which Abraham was subjected in order to demonstrate to all, but especially to posterity, his worthiness to be the founder of a unique nation committed to God's service and its accomplishment of the mission divinely assigned to it.

The earliest version of this interpretive tradition, of which I am aware, is that found in the post-biblical Book of Jubilees, dated to the second century, B.C.E. It alludes to ten such trials as having taken place but specifically identifies only eight of them, six of which took place prior to that of the binding of Isaac as an intended sacrifice (referred to in traditional Hebrew literature and lore as the *Akedah*). The ancient author wrote:

> And the Lord was aware that Abraham was faithful in all of his afflictions because He tested him with his land, and with famine. And He tested him with the wealth of kings. And He tested him again with his wife, when she was taken (from him), and with circumcision. And He tested him with Ishmael and with Hagar, his maidservant, when he sent them away. And in everything in which He tested him, he was found faithful. And his soul was not impatient. And He was not slow to act because he was faithful and a lover of the Lord.[7]

The excruciatingly dramatic and near tragic episode of the *Akedah*, which presumably constituted the ninth test, concludes with the death of the matriarch Sarah, Abraham's beloved wife, which is identified specifically in this source as the tenth test to which the patriarch was subjected.[8] However, the Book of Jubilees does not relate or refer to either of the two additional tests that presumably took place between or before the sixth enumerated test and the *Akedah* and this tenth and final test of Abraham's constancy. Why the author of Jubilees does not enumerate them completely remains a puzzle, suggesting the possibility that either parts of his original work are missing or that he could not identify two additional tests in the biblical text that merited identification as such. In any case, it appears that he is reflecting an already longstanding tradition that the biblical saga of Abraham is in essence a recounting of the ten trials of faith to which he was subjected. Moreover, although the biblical author does not enumerate or otherwise specifically describe any of these episodes of tribulation as a trial, with the singular exception of the *Akedah*, the author of Jubilees evidently inferred from the biblical narrative itself, or from some other no longer extant source, that the nature of those episodes and their impact on Abraham in effect made them trials in every sense of the term, even though the term is not applied to them in the biblical texts.

The tradition regarding the ten trials of faith endured by Abraham that are enumerated and alluded to in part by the author of Jubilees was subsequently asserted unequivocally in a concise teaching of the early sages of the talmudic period found in the tractate of the Mishnah known as *Pirkei Avot* or Sayings of the Fathers. "With ten trials was Abraham our father tried, and he withstood them all, to make known how great was the love of Abraham our father."[9] This statement is amplified somewhat in an alternate version, a work often considered an early commentary on the classical rabbinic tractate, although the incidents depicted as trials are not listed in the order given in the biblical text. "With ten trials was Abraham our father tried before the Holy One, blessed be He, and in all of them he was found steadfast, to wit: Twice, when ordered to move on [Gen. 12:1 ff., 12:10]; Twice in connection with his two sons [Gen. 21:10, 22:1 ff.]; Twice, in connection with his two wives [Gen. 12:11 ff., 21:10]; Once, on the occasion of his war with the kings [Gen. 14:13 ff.]; Once, at the (covenant) between the pieces [Gen. 15]; Once, in Ur of the Chaldees [Gen. 15:7]; And once, at the covenant of circumcision [Gen. 17:9 ff., 17:23]."[10] In similar fashion, the modern scholar M.D. Cassutto took note of "a chiastic relationship between the ten episodes," in which, according to his enumeration of the trials, the first and last are related by involving departures, Abram from his father and Abram from his son; the second and third and the eighth and ninth are related by the dangers brought upon Sarah from the pharaoh of Egypt and the king of Gerar respectively, and the separations from Lot and from Hagar and Ishmael; the fourth and seventh are related because they both concern the rescue of Lot, the first from captivity and the second from death in the destruction of Sodom and Gomorrah; the fifth and sixth are related in that they concern the futures of Ishmael and Isaac, the sons of Abraham.[11]

The further elaboration of the specific nature of these trials, following in sequential order and building on the trials that took place prior to the *Akedah* as identified by the author of Jubilees, was a task left to later rabbinic and other writers, who put forth a number of schemes in this regard. Perhaps the first full description of the ten trials in the literature of Judaism is to be found in a work of rabbinic pseudepigrapha, *Pirke de Rabbi Eliezer*, that has been dated to the early ninth century.[12] According to this work, the first trial, which is not recorded or even alluded to in the biblical text, came about as a result of Abraham's iconoclasm, already demonstrated while he was still a child, which resulted in the need for him to be hidden below ground for thirteen years to avoid arrest and execution by the authorities. The second trial, also occasioned by his iconoclasm, was his subsequent imprisonment for ten years, after which he was cast into a furnace from which he was rescued by the divine hand. In the unique version of the legend found in another ancient work, known as *Pseudo-Philo*, generally dated to the first century C.E., Abraham, along with eleven others, was persecuted because of his refusal to participate in the firing of bricks for the construction of the Tower of Babel (Gen. 11:3), which he considered an affront to God. The eleven subsequently recanted, leaving only Abraham who steadfastly held on to his convictions and was thrown into the furnace for his recalcitrance.[13]

The latter trial is assumed to be implicit in the biblical text that states: *I am the Lord that brought thee out of Ur of the Chaldees* (Gen. 15:7). The author of *Pirke de Rabbi Eliezer* interprets the name of the city of Abram's birth, Ur, as though it were a Hebrew word that may be used to indicate a source of heat or "furnace." The biblical verse would then read: "I am the Lord that brought thee out of the furnace of the Chaldees." That is, according to the legend, Nimrod, the ruler of southern Mesopotamia, had Abram cast into a furnace because of his iconoclastic beliefs and behavior. It is noteworthy that because these legendary incidents are not recorded in the biblical text, some later rabbinic commentators rejected their inclusion among the ten trials, as did the author of Jubilees, who either ignored or was unaware of them.[14]

The third trial, the first according to Jubilees and many if not most later commentators, involves Abraham's voluntary dislocation from his father's house and homeland in response to the divine demand: *Get thee out of thy country, and from thy kindred, and from thy father's house, unto the land that I will show thee* (Gen. 12:1).[15]

The fourth trial was the need for Abraham to leave the land of Canaan (Cisjordan), which had been promised to him (Gen. 12:7), because of a famine, which the midrashic author suggests was created for the specific purpose of testing his resolve.[16] Although he felt compelled by circumstances to leave his new homeland for Egypt (Gen. 12:10), he continued to maintain his unwavering faith in the divine promise. The fifth trial of his faith in divine benevolence occurred when his wife Sarah was taken from him and brought to the house of the pharaoh to become the latter's consort (Gen. 12:11-20).[17]

The sixth trial of faith took place when Abraham took up arms against the overwhelming might of the armies of the coalition of four kings who had defeated and sacked the city-states of Sodom and Gomorrah, taking his nephew Lot captive (Gen. 14:11-12).[18] According to the midrashic author, it was Abraham himself who was the ultimate target of the onslaught. "They [the kings] said:

Let us first begin with the house of his brother, and afterwards let us begin with him." The implication is that Abraham had sufficient faith in God's promise that he readily took the offensive against far superior forces to rescue his nephew, rather than seek refuge for his own safety (Gen. 14:14-15).

The seventh trial took place in connection with the covenant "between the pieces" (Gen. 15:1-16).[19] However, the midrashic author does not indicate the nature of the trial, leaving it to others to fill the gap. It is assumed by many that it was a test of faith in the divine promise that Abraham's descendants would inherit the land, after he was informed that they were to be subjugated to others for four centuries before the promise would be fulfilled. However, it has also been suggested that the test of faith here referred to something beyond what is explicitly stated in the biblical text. In this regard, a clue to what the midrashic writer may have had in mind is reflected in an ancient homiletic interpretation of the use of the term *also* in the biblical phrase, *and also that nation, whom they shall serve* (Gen. 15:14), which takes it as referring to additional subjugations following that of the one that is to last for four centuries.[20] This suggests that the test of Abraham consisted in his maintaining his faith after being told that, after their first protracted experience of exile and subjugation, his descendants would also subsequently be subjugated to other nations and therefore undergo additional periods of great distress in the course of their history.

The eighth trial concerned the divine instruction that Abraham undergo circumcision at the advanced age of ninety-nine (Gen. 17:1 ff.).[21] The ninth trial concerned the inter-familial conflict between Sarah and Hagar, which culminated in Sarah's demand that Abraham evict Hagar and her son Ishmael, Abraham's first-born, from his household.[22] Abraham was very troubled by her demand and, presumably, would not have acceded to it if God had not intervened in the matter and instructed him to comply with Sarah's wish in this regard (Gen. 21:12). The tenth and final test, in the opinion of the overwhelming majority of commentators, concerns the *Akedah*.[23]

Of particular importance to understanding the emphasis given in the literature to the ten trials that Abraham underwent is the assertion, cited earlier, that the purpose of these trials was "to make known how great was the love of Abraham our father," as evidenced in the biblical texts affirming Abraham's love of God, *Abraham that loved Me* (Isa. 41:8) and *Abraham that loved Thee* (2 Chron. 20:7). The implication here is that the trials to which Abraham was subjected were not intended to ascertain whether he would withstand them, something that was taken for granted, but rather to demonstrate to the world his love of God. But why was it necessary to have ten trials for that purpose?[24] Would it not have sufficed to have just two or three trials to illustrate Abraham's love of God? It has been suggested in this regard that the focus on the large number of trials is not so much to emphasize Abraham's essential love of the divine as to indicate the extent to which he was prepared to demonstrate it even in times of adversity. One may be able to undergo two or three difficult trials in the expectation of an appropriate reward—to undergo ten such ordeals demands total unflinching and selfless commitment.[25]

Another related scheme for understanding the choice of incidents in Abraham's life to report in the biblical account, as suggested by Buber, is to include those related to the seven revelations experienced by the patriarch, which are "precisely and significantly related both to one another and to the stories with which they are interspersed. Each one of the revelations and each one of the other stories has its particular place in the pattern and…appear as stations in a progress from trial to trial and from blessing to blessing; not one of them can be transposed without disrupting the whole. No theory of sources can explain this structure, which is so manifold in character and style and yet held together by a uniformly great vision."[26]

As is the case with many biblical texts, it is not always clear what the author is attempting to convey or why certain bits of information are provided and others omitted. The challenge for the sympathetic reader is to attempt to fill in the seemingly obvious gaps in the narrative and to make sense of that which is or is not said. The biblical text virtually demands the full engagement of the reader, making its study a vicarious experience; a passive reading will almost guarantee incomprehension or misunderstanding. Moreover, one must wrestle with the nuances of the Hebrew text itself if one truly wants to understand what the narrative is relating. As one ancient sage put it: "A man does not fully understand the words of the Torah until he has been tripped up over them."[27]

How does this approach fit in with the mainstream of contemporary biblical studies that are focused so intensely on critical theory, especially source criticism and the documentary hypothesis? I must admit that it does not fit well at all, which is not to negate the intrinsic validity of striving to identify the author or authors of the early biblical writings. Such knowledge would surely enable us to better understand why the narrative is presented in its current form, and might provide some answers to the many questions about the apparent anomalies to be found in the texts that have been identified and questioned for more than two millennia. Unfortunately, there is little if any prospect of unraveling these mysteries in the foreseeable future, if ever. Thus, while critical biblical scholarship has provided some useful insights into understanding some biblical texts, its obsession with identifying the probable, possible, or even remotely likely sources of the passages in the biblical narrative has made such studies primarily matters of antiquarian interest and therefore of little relevance to the approach to the biblical texts taken in this book. This is so because, in my view, the challenge of understanding the biblical narrative, in this case that concerning Abraham, requires that we strive to comprehend what the text as we have it is telling us, explicitly as well as implicitly. It makes little difference for that purpose whether or not the author or authors of the text before us drew on earlier narrative traditions. Thus, whether one accepts the view of unabashed traditionalists that Moses authored the passages before us as directly and divinely revealed to him, or the nontraditional perspective that the biblical texts represent the personal creative work of Moses regarding the origins of his people, conceived by him in accordance with his own insights or by divine inspiration, or if one prefers the modern critical theory of authorship by a variety of hands over an extended period of time, in accordance with the documentary hypotheses of higher biblical criticism, makes little difference in terms of our concerns in this book, which are with the meaning of the final product, as it has been known for some two and a half millennia.

Accepting that there appear to be some significant anomalies in the biblical text, anomalies that are by means modern discoveries but have been known and identified since early antiquity, attributing such anomalies to the anthologizing of different sources explains very little. Indeed, it merely raises the question of why the final redactor, or redactors, permitted such anomalies to remain in the final product. There are numerous biblical texts that even the most traditional commentators will agree contain modifications from the original, what are termed *tikkunei soferim* or "scribal emendations," referring to changes that were introduced well over two thousand years ago for any of several reasons, clearly indicating that there was no reluctance to make such editorial decisions when deemed necessary and appropriate. Given such leeway, why would the redactor take passages containing different names for God and conflate them into a single pericope of text, without explanation? Surely not just to provide grist for the mill of critical scholars, who have used such divergent names as a basis for postulating a continually fluctuating number of original source documents from which the biblical text supposedly was constructed. After all, why may one not assume that the biblical text employs different names for God because each one conveys a special significance, well understood by the audience to which the biblical texts were originally presented in their final form, with regard to the context of the particular narrative element in which it appears? If we were able to grasp that subtlety of composition, what may appear as an anomaly might well become transformed into a brilliant stroke of the pen, providing unsuspected insights into the biblical text.

This raises the additional problem of rendering the Hebrew original in another language, and then drawing meaning and implications from the translation rather than from the original. Nowhere is this problem more acute than in translations of the Hebrew Scriptures, which liberally employs poetic language as well as idiomatic expressions to convey mood and intent in addition to information. Thus, referring to the translations and paraphrases, principally in Aramaic, that accompanied the public reading of the biblical texts in antiquity, one of the sages of the Talmud stated, "If one translates a verse literally, he is a liar; if he adds thereto, he is a blasphemer and a libeler."[28] This adage, perhaps shorn of its stridency, remains quite applicable to most English translations. As Robert Alter put it, "The unacknowledged heresy underlying most modern English versions of the Bible is the use of translation as a vehicle for *explaining* the Bible instead of representing it in another language, and in the most egregious instances this amounts to explaining away the Bible."[29] After reviewing the available English translations of the Pentateuch, for purposes of this study I have employed the version first published by the Jewish Publication Society in 1917 as being closest to the original Hebrew, except that I have substituted the Hebrew transliterations for the names of God because the generally accepted English translations of these names are arbitrary and sometimes misleading.

Another issue concerns the approach one takes to understanding the text, and this, of course, is directly related to what one wants to read out of the text or wants to read into the text, exegesis or eisegesis. This is not to argue against homiletic interpretations of the biblical texts, which have served as a rich source for theological and moral teachings over the course of some two millennia for both Judaism and Christianity. However, it is important to bear in mind, when considering such interpretations, the adjuration of the sages of the Talmud that "a verse cannot depart from its plain meaning."[30] That is, a homiletic interpretation cannot substitute for the plain meaning of the text, although it might represent a possible sub-text. Treating a biblical text as an allegory is logically acceptable as long as one does not thereby discard what the text actually says, even if it is something difficult to comprehend.

The story of Abraham will be found to reflect a number of social relationships, evidently taken for granted by the biblical writer, which may strike the modern reader as strange, if not bizarre. Many competent scholars have argued that these social customs may be seen reflected in a variety of ancient Mesopotamian documents, especially those recovered from Nuzu. As one pair of distinguished scholars put it: "The analogies...between the society of Nuzu and of the Hebrew Patriarchs are so numerous and striking that many scholars agree that the patriarchal narratives in Genesis portray a genuine social picture. Because some of the phenomena are known from other cuneiform records, some scholars[31] have denied any relevance of the Nuzi tablets for the study of the Bible. But the fact remains that no set of known texts offers as many parallels to the patriarchal narratives as do the Nuzi tablets."[32] Although the parallels are often inexact, I have referred to these as well as other Mesopotamian documents primarily in the notes although also occasionally in the text to help explain what the biblical narrator seems to be telling us. However, the reader should remain aware that all such references by analogy are subject to challenge and in fact have been disputed.

In researching this work I have consulted a wide variety of interpretive sources, some reflecting profound scholarship and others of a more general character that, surprisingly at times, offer occasionally intuitively brilliant insights into the biblical text, many but not all of which are cited or referred to in the notes. Unfortunately, many of these sources are in Hebrew and have not been translated into English, making them directly inaccessible to those without a reading knowledge of the original language. My understanding of the Abraham saga has been enriched from a variety of perspectives by these writers, even though only a few of them have contributed directly to my thinking, and none of them are in any way responsible for the political interpretation of the biblical texts that is reflected in what I have written here.

1

The Early Life and Career of Abram

The biblical saga of Abram-Abraham, the narration of which begins with the twelfth chapter of the Book of Genesis, which will be examined closely in the subsequent chapters of this study, starts at a point where the future patriarch reportedly is already seventy-five years old. This consideration alone causes us to wonder about what took place during the preceding three quarters of a century that led, according to the biblical text, to his divine selection to become the founding ancestor of the future nation of Israel, a question that the biblical writer passes over in silence. As noted in the introduction, the absence of what would seem to be important if not critical information in this regard has left the question open to unbridled speculation and legendary treatment. Moreover, according to the biblical text, for the first ninety-nine years of his life the person named Abraham was known as Abram, the change in name being made at divine direction at a particular point in his moral and spiritual development. This seems to suggest that there was a substantial continuity of development from his earlier years through the twenty-four year period between the time that he was first given notice of his selection and the time he had reached the point where the change of name marked a major turning point in his life.

What was the course of continuous development that Abram underwent for nearly a century before he became, so to speak, a new person with a new identity—Abraham? Once again, the absence of explicatory information in this regard has contributed to sometimes rather farfetched speculation and mythological treatment because, without some grasp of the personality and life experience of Abram before his selection, significant parts of the biblical narrative before us become quite incomprehensible, unless one makes the tendentious assumption that coherence in the final product was not a criterion for bringing together the disparate elements of the saga into the amalgam that ultimately became the biblical text. The problem also appears to be further compounded rather than unraveled by a variety of attempts to identify the historical Abram, that is, the person known to historians from sources other than the biblical texts. Thus, one writer, whose work I am not in a position to evaluate properly, makes the radical and perhaps unique claim that Abram is to be identified with the famous Babylonian king Hammurabi. He asserts, "The identification is based on such factors as chronological agreement, similarity of names, analogous personalities, and the fact that the history of Abraham shows that he observed the laws found in the Code of Hammurabi."[33] If such a claim could be substantiated, it would surely cast new light on the saga of concern to us here. However, intriguing as this suggestion is, its ultimate validity or lack thereof is nonetheless essentially irrelevant to the present project, the aim of which is to attempt to understand the patriarch as the biblical writer presents him to us in the scriptural texts. In a sense then, this book is less concerned with the real person Abram may have been than with the man the biblical author conceived him as being.

The biblical narrative of the life and career of Abram is prefaced by a general description of his lineage and close family, which provides some rather specific information that will be seen to have relevance to events that occur in later narratives, but nonetheless seems puzzling here because it also provides some details that raise more questions than they answer.

> [11.27] *Now these are the generations of Terah. Terah begot Abram, Nahor, and Haran; and Haran begot Lot.* [11.28] *And Haran died in the presence of his father Terah in the land of his nativity, in Ur of the Chaldees.* [11.29] *And Abram and Nahor took them wives: the name of Abram's wife was Sarai; and the name of Nahor's wife, Milcah, the daughter of Haran, the father of Milcah, and the father of Iscah.* [11.30] *And Sarai was barren; she had no child.*

It seems somewhat surprising that, given the exceptional importance of Abram to the biblical project, we are told nothing of his lineage on his mother's side. Presumably, such information was not considered of sufficient relevance for the narrative, even though numerous other names are included that would clearly seem to be of even lesser significance and interest. It was thus left to legend to fill the gap. According to the most ancient source dealing with the question, Abram's mother was Edna the daughter of Abram, who was also his father Terah's niece through his sister. If this claim were found to be acceptable, Abram would have been named after his maternal grandfather of the same name, who presumably had died before Abram was born.[34] In any case, it is curious that Abram who, according to the sequence in which the names of the sons of Terah are listed, would appear to be the eldest of the three, is followed by Nahor, who is named after Terah's father (Gen. 11:24), which one would expect to be the name of the first-born son. It has been suggested that this is but one of the ways in which the biblical author provides hints or clues to his audience that something extraordinary was about to take place in the tenth generation after Noah. According to one commentator, it suggests that Abram, the eldest, who should normally have been named after his paternal grandfather was actually named after his maternal grandfather to emphasize that he would *not* follow in the pagan footsteps of his paternal grandfather, as would his younger brother Nahor, who was therefore named after him.[35]

Lot, who is Abram's nephew, and who plays an important part a bit later in the narrative that is to unfold, is orphaned by the premature death of his father Haran, which took place in their ancestral homeland, Ur. We are not told anything about the circumstances of his death, nor are we informed about the significance for the biblical narrative of the identification of the location of his demise. It may be that the biblical author is hinting that his death may be connected to the upheavals that attended the dissolution of the Noahide society of the plain of Shinar described earlier in the same biblical chapter.[36] It is noteworthy that the narrator's report of Haran's death *in the land of his nativity, in Ur of the Chaldees* raises the peripheral question of whether Ur was also the birthplace of Abram, for if it was, what purpose is served by telling us that he died *in the land of his nativity*? This, in addition to other possible textual clues, has led some commentators to assume that Abram and Nahor were both born in Haran, in northern Mesopotamia, and that they had moved to Ur with their father, subsequently returning with him to Haran after the death of their youngest brother in Ur, where the latter was born.[37] Where Abram was actually born is significant only in the sense that it may clarify some textual anomalies; it does not materially impact on the essence of the narrative. In any case, the apparent purpose of the information regarding Haran's death is to establish the reason why Abraham appears to "adopt" his deceased brother's son and then assumes a parent's concern and responsibility for Lot's spiritual as well as material welfare.

We are informed further that the remaining sons of Terah, Abram and Nahor, both take wives. Abram marries Sarai, who is later identified as his paternal half-sister (Gen. 20:12), and Nahor marries Milcah, who is the daughter, along with her sister Iscah, of Haran. It remains unclear why the biblical author supplies us with most of this information, which effectively generates a good deal of uncertainty if not confusion about the relationships between these various members of the family. The text thus refers to Haran twice, but it is not clear whether both references are to the same person. That is, is Haran the brother of Abram and father of Lot the same Haran that is the father of Milcah and Iscah? Although it is generally assumed that they are one and the same, and this is the supposition I make here, there are some textual problems raised by this identification that I will not pursue in this study.[38] Furthermore, who is Iscah,[39] whose name is never mentioned again, and why are we not told anything of the parentage of Sarai?[40]

These are but a few of the questions that have puzzled and troubled commentators from antiquity to the present day, but need not detain us for the purposes of this study. However, it has been suggested that at least some of these bits of seemingly unimportant information do indeed provide valuable clues to the essential character of Abram, which will be elaborated on in the following chapter. For the moment, it is of interest to note that Abram's brother Nahor married his niece Milcah, the daughter of his dead brother Haran, in accordance with ancient Hurrian practice, as reflected in the findings from Nuzu.[41] It seems likely that this practice was initiated to deal with the problems of arranging marriages for orphan daughters in the absence of a father to provide a dowry. However, it is especially noteworthy that Abram did not likewise marry Iscah, the other orphaned daughter of his brother Haran. Not only would it have been socially correct to do so, in Abram's case it was doubly so because of the fact that *Sarai was barren; she had no child.* After a wife failed to provide offspring for a substantial period of time, it was appropriate for a man to take a second wife to bear him children. Despite this, it would appear that Abram, in violation of the social norms of the society in which he lived and oblivious to the impact on his dead brother's family, declined to take Iscah as a second wife.[42]

Although there is an old interpretive tradition that Iscah and Sarai are actually names for the same person,[43] it does not address the question of why, indeed, did Abram not take another wife? The silence of the biblical writer on this issue invites the reader to surmise the reason—a reason that must be of great significance—perhaps providing an important clue to the mystery of Abram's personality and his consequent divine selection for the patriarchal role assigned to him.

The narrator informs us that *Sarai was barren.* That item of information may provide the key to the answer to our question. *We* know that Sarai was barren, but perhaps Abram did not! Surely the normal masculine ego would have suggested to him that the fault for failing to produce a child lay with his wife and not with himself. To demonstrate his virility, he would have to take another woman to bear him a child. But, for Abram to do so would have placed Sarai in social jeopardy. Proof of his virility would also demonstrate her incapacity to serve as the mistress of a new branch of the Terahide clan.

We may therefore infer that Abram's devotion to Sarai evidently was so profound that, rather then subject her to the possibility of social ignominy, he preferred to accept the burden of doubt upon himself and to absolve Sarai from all trace of suspicion with regard to her matriarchal worthiness. He accomplished this by not taking another wife or even a concubine. This abstention surely suggested to all that the problem lay not with Sarai's infertility but with Abram's impotence. Accordingly, Abram preferred that he, rather than his beloved wife, become the butt of rumor and suffer any loss of societal esteem. Abram's capacity for self-effacement and sacrifice would be put to the test repeatedly throughout his life and career. For the moment, it provides some initial insight into his towering personality and capacity for selfless commitment that helps explain why he was chosen for his patriarchal vocation.

As a result, and in stark contrast to the earlier story of Noah and his sons, who were assigned their civilizing mission as a family unit, Abram is to begin his alone, just as Adam did at the very beginning of the human enterprise. Abram is not to sire any children until he has satisfied the basic requirements of the patriarchal role for which he would be selected. To ensure this, the biblical author tells us, Abram took a single wife and she was not only childless, but was barren, or at least ostensibly incapable of conception by natural means.[44] Indeed, his wife's barrenness would constitute a test of Abram's character and his complete trust and faith in the subsequent divine promises to him that he would be the progenitor of a distinct nation with a unique divinely ordained mission.

The saga of Abram may thus be seen as essentially one describing his repudiation of the past and the future to which it would have committed him, and his striving to create a new reality, and so, most appropriately, it begins with a migration, an act of disassociation:

> [11.31] *And Terah took Abram his son, and Lot the son of Haran, his son's son, and Sarai his daughter-in-law, his son Abram's wife; and they went forth with them from Ur of the Chaldees, to go into the land of Canaan; and they came unto Haran, and dwelt there.* [11.32] *And the days of Terah were two hundred and five years; and Terah died in Haran.*

As patriarch of an extended family, Terah took Abram and his wife Sarai, and his orphaned grandson Lot, along with him en route to Cisjordan.[45] However, the text is not at all clear about who is being referred to by the word *them* in the assertion, *and they went forth with them from Ur.* It therefore seems reasonable to assume that the reference is to Nahor and his family who went along as well, and that the reason the biblical author does not mention him here specifically is probably because of his concern to focus attention exclusively on Abram, the principal actor in the events that ensue. It has been suggested that Nahor and his family may have already gone on ahead of the main body of the Terahide clan as an advance party, or, alternatively, that they may followed the main body of the clan some time later.

The migration, viewed in the context of the biblical narrative, presumably took place during the period of the migratory waves set in motion by the great dispersion that followed in the wake of the attempted apotheosis of the state by Nimrod in southern Mesopotamia,[46] and may have coincided, historically, with the westward expansion of the Amorites toward Egypt. Some have speculated that Terah may have left Ur as a result of its conquest by Hammurabi of Babylonia, its economic life having been severely damaged by the military forays that seriously disrupted trade along the caravan routes to the city. In either case, it is clear that Terah was emigrating from Ur for evidently compelling albeit unstated reasons. However, it is less clear as to where he was immigrating. It would seem that Terah intended to lead his family to Cisjordan, even though he did not actually ever go there, and the language of the text, *and they went forth with them from Ur of the Chaldees, to go into the land of Canaan; and they came unto Haran, and dwelt there*, also raises some questions. For one, as already suggested, it is not clear who, *they* or *them*, was planning *to go into the land of Canaan*.

Why would Terah wish to relocate to Canaan, which as already indicated is the name the biblical writer assigns to the geographic area of Cisjordan? Probably because it was still a sparsely settled frontier region in the land bridge connecting Africa and Asia, through which at least one major international trade route between Egypt and Mesopotamia passed, and as such offered significant commercial opportunities for those prepared to undertake a certain amount of risk. The journey from southern Mesopotamia to Cisjordan was surely long, circuitous, and arduous. However, somewhere along the line Terah evidently decided to make a detour that led his entourage northward until he reached Haran, in present-day southeastern Turkey, an important ancient crossroads city for the caravan trade between Mesopotamia and the Mediterranean and Black Sea regions.[47]

It is noteworthy that the route followed by Terah generally reflects the topographical disposition of the region. Although Cisjordan is due west of southern Mesopotamia, before domestication of the camel and its extensive use for commercial purposes, the caravan route between the two areas necessarily followed a course skirting the curvature of the Arabian Desert that separated them, along the so-called Fertile Crescent that stretches in a northerly arc from the Persian Gulf to Egypt. However, the most efficient route to Cisjordan from southern Mesopotamia would have been to proceed northward along the Euphrates to Mari, and then west to Aleppo, some distance south of Haran, at which point the road would turn south to Damascus and then Hazor, the ancient gateway to Cisjordan. For reasons that are not provided in the biblical account, Terah elected to proceed farther north to Haran, possibly because of its economic importance, but also perhaps because of its religious significance. Most scholars agree that Ur was a holy city and the center of worship of the moon, with Haran serving as the second most important center of that worship in northern Mesopotamia, the moon god being "the god of the nomads and the travelers, the god of the caravans…the god whom Abraham renounces when he entrusts himself to the guidance of YHVH."[48]

Alternatively, some scholars argue that this geographical anomaly is easily resolved if one accepts that Ur of the Chaldees was not located in southern Mesopotamia as commonly assumed, but northeast of Haran in northern Mesopotamia, perhaps in southern Armenia. According to this view, the term *Kasdim*, rendered in our verse as Chaldees, does not refer to the Chaldeans of southern Mesopotamia, but to a warlike people of the north that bore that name.[49] It is to be noted in this regard that the biblical Book of Joshua later states: *Your fathers dwelt of old time beyond the River…and I took your father Abraham from beyond the River* (Josh. 24:2-3), the river in this passage being held by all to refer to the Euphrates. However, ancient Ur in southern Mesopotamia has been located about six miles south of the Euphrates, on its west bank, that is, on the same side of the river as Cisjordan, therefore making it improbable as Abram's point of origin if the statement in the Book of Joshua is correct, a description that better suits Haran, which is east of the Euphrates.[50] If one assumes a northern location for Ur, then it becomes reasonable that the road to Cisjordan would pass through the caravan stop at Haran.

In any case, once there, Terah evidently decided to abandon his earlier plans to continue on to Cisjordan, possibly out of concern for the growing instability of the territory as competing waves of diverse peoples began flowing into the area seeking to establish footholds there. It may also have been because Terah began to have second thoughts about leaving the lands in which the Mesopotamian cultures with which he was familiar were to be found. Cisjordan was a strange land with a proliferation of alien cultures, the residue of the many and diverse armies that passed through the landbridge region in the course of the innumerable wars between Egypt and the powers that dominated Mesopotamia as well as with those whose center was in Anatolia to the north. Moreover, Egypt had long sought to keep the unstable territory within its sphere of influence, and this too may have been a consideration that troubled Terah. For whatever reason, Terah would remain in Haran for the rest of his life, as did Abram's mother, according to one legendary source.[51]

We do not have any indication of how old Abram was at the time of his family's departure from Ur or how long he remained in Haran.[52] In any case, the break with the society of his birth and upbringing undoubtedly gave Abram occasion to reflect deeply on all that he had experienced and witnessed during his already long life. The shattering of social ties provided an opportunity to begin anew, to cast off the mold of the past. His time in Haran with his father thus served as a period of transition for Abram. Having severed his linkages to the society in which he was reared, he became equally prepared to break his newly developing connections to his present circumstances and to commit all his moral strength and capacity for faith to an undreamed of future. The moment for his divine selection, to become the founder and patriarch of a distinctive nation, one intended to be the embodiment of the divine aspiration for mankind, was at hand.

The social dislocations that attended the great population movements surely had significant consequences for the religious beliefs and moral state of the various peoples affected. The accompanying confusion and despair undoubtedly led to the growth of superstition and the proliferation of animist beliefs and practices, as well as attempts to appease and placate a host of deities that were identified with the forces of nature. There is no evident reason to believe that the descendants of Eber, of the Noahide line of Shem, remained immune to the corrupting influences of the pervasively idolatrous social environment. Presumably, this also included the family of Terah, with the singular exception of Abram who, we may infer, had long demonstrated opposition to the essential irrationality of the pagan beliefs and idolatrous practices common to his society. Indeed, what seems to be implicit in the Genesis narrative is stated explicitly by the biblical author of the Book of Joshua: *And Joshua said unto all the people; Thus saith the Lord, the God of Israel: Your fathers dwelt of old time beyond the River, even Terah, the father of Abraham, and the father of Nahor; and they served other gods* (Josh. 24:2). The message is clear. They, that is, Terah and Nahor, were polytheists, but not Abram.

Abram's presumed iconoclasm, self-generated and possibly unique within his milieu, surely would have caused him to be viewed as a rebel and blasphemer against the dominant religious beliefs, something that was clearly unacceptable to the entrenched religious establishment. Indeed, it may even be conjectured that it was Abram's rebelliousness that instigated the desire if not the need of Terah to relocate his household to a distant and possibly more tolerant cultural and religious setting.[53] We may therefore assume that the characteristics which most differentiated Abram from others in his society also intimated the moral fiber and strength of will that he possessed, attributes that would be essential for the divinely appointed mission that awaited him, a mission for which he was directly being divinely recruited.

2

The Odyssey Begins

^{12.1} *Now YHVH*[54] *said unto Abram: Get thee out of thy country, and from thy kindred, and from thy father's house, unto the land that I will show thee.* ^{12.2} *And I will make of thee a great nation, and I will bless you, and make thy name great; and be thou a blessing.*

The biblical author seems to begin his narrative concerning the divine selection of Abram with a conspicuous silence and then abruptly continues with what appears to be the response to something that occurred or was said earlier. His employment of such a literary device may be construed as an invitation to the sympathetic reader to engage his intellect and imagination in surmising the character and content of that which remains unarticulated in the biblical text, as discussed briefly earlier, especially in regard to that which led to Abram being singled out for the role he is now assigned to play in history.[55]

The manner in which the divine communication to Abram is presented in the biblical narrative clearly suggests an unstated assumption of momentous significance. It is evidently taken for granted that Abram knows and understands whose commanding voice it is that he hears speaking to him. And, if this is the case, it seems reasonable to assume further that this is not the first time that Abram hears this voice, each such occasion offering new insight into the essential truth of his deepening monotheistic belief. These assumptions are of crucial importance to comprehending the seemingly abrupt character of this opening passage, which does not give any indication of Abram's being awestruck or even surprised at being addressed by what he took to be a divine voice. Earlier, in the story of Noah, the biblical author set the stage for a divine communication by first stating that *Noah found grace in the eyes of YHVH* (Gen. 6:8). Here we have no such assertion to lay the basis for this sudden intrusion of the divine into the mind of Abram. Moreover, there is no visual aid here, no burning bush such as that which engaged the imagination of Moses before God spoke to him. We are also not informed of a vision that came to him or of a dream that he had. There is no hint whatever of Abram being in some ecstatic state which made him receptive to a divine communication. The very absence of any preconditioning event itself suggests that the biblical author intends that we infer that Abram is already intimately familiar with the monotheistic idea of a one and only God who can and does communicate with man whenever He deems it appropriate. It also suggests that Abram's familiarity with God is not the result of a previous theophany or revelatory experience but rather the outcome of a long and intense intellectual voyage of rediscovery.

It should be noted that I have suggested implicitly that Abram was not the originator of the monotheistic idea of God, but rather that he reaffirmed the idea. Indeed, as the biblical writer already suggested earlier, the monotheistic idea had been embraced by at least one of the Noahides, Shem, of whom Abram was a direct descendant. This is made evident in the blessing that Noah bestowed upon this son, which he prefaced with *Blessed be YHVH, the Elohim of Shem* (Gen. 9:26), an assertion that clearly indicates that the seed of the monotheistic idea of God was implanted among the Shemites and, although long submerged over the generations, was resurrected in effect by Abram in the tenth generation after Noah.[56] As readily becomes clear from even a cursory reading of Genesis, in the biblical view polytheism emerged from monotheism and not the reverse, as many modern students of religion claim. At first, all acknowledged that there was a single supreme being that governed the world, and that concept never disappeared from human consciousness. However, it became increasingly difficult for many to find a way of interacting with such a universal but necessarily abstract God, and people began to search for intermediaries that they believed would be more personally accessible, a process that ultimately resulted in the worship of those intermediaries, and later their visible representations. In other words, polytheism began as a rational project and became transformed into irrational idolatry.[57]

Assuming that this correctly reflects the biblical author's perspective, we can begin to surmise just what it was about Abram that made him alone of his entire generation fit for the role for which he was being cast. His resurrection of the idea of the existence of a one and only God would have had to be an autonomous act of reason, an extraordinary intellectual achievement, especially in the polytheistic milieu in which he grew to maturity, which was a sophisticated world of great cities and bustling commerce that boasted great achievements, both in the intellectual and material realms. In a universe believed to be governed by the stars, the sun, the moon, and the forces of nature, Abram would have had to assess the natural limitations of each and ultimately conclude that there had to be a single force superior to all, a true master of the universe. The logical consequence of such a conclusion would be a categorical rejection of any adoration or worship of such natural phenomena as deities, as well as of the priesthoods associated with such worship; he thus became an iconoclast in both thought and deed that might eventually be perceived as a threat to the established power structure in a polytheistic society such as existed in Ur or Haran, in which there was no clear demarcation between politics and religion.

With characteristic subtlety in the use of a pregnant silence, the biblical writer thus allows the perceptive reader to grasp that the one chosen to be the founding patriarch of the line of descendants that is to play a crucial role in the divine scheme for man, is in essence a philosopher whose initial encounter with the divine is achieved through the force of his unaided reason and a person capable by force of intellect and personality to influence others. Clearly reflecting such a perception of the patriarch, the first century historian Josephus described him as,

> a person of great sagacity, both for understanding all things and persuading his hearers, and not mistaken in his opinions; for which reason he began to have higher notions of virtue than others had, and he determined to renew and change the opinion all men happened then to have concerning God; for he was the first that ventured to publish this notion, that there was but one God, the Creator of the universe; and that, as to other [gods,] if they contributed anything to the happiness of men, that each of them afforded it only according to his appointment, and not by their own power.[58]

Abram is not simply to become the founder of yet another mystery religion, but rather the progenitor of a new civilization built on the rational ordering of a moral and just society designed to fulfill the intent of God in granting to man the divine-like capacity for creativity. If Abram is to persevere where his ancestors failed, failures described clearly by the biblical author in the first eleven chapters of the Book of Genesis, his induction into his ultimate civilization-building role must proceed along different lines. Abram is to undertake his vocation in the full light of critical reason. Subsequently, step-by-step, he will come to recognize and accept that which in its essence transcends reason. And only then will he be ready to carry out the task of initiating the moral redemption of mankind. Abram thus begins with an unaided and purely intellectual conception of God, arrived at in reaction to the intrinsic irrationality of the idolatry and polytheistic beliefs that were pervasive in the world in which he lived. It was to be but the first stage in the moral education of the future patriarch.

The biblical author thus begins the narrative with what seems to be the conclusion of an antecedent interaction between God and Abram, about which the text is silent. The reader is at once confronted by the need to choose between one of two basic approaches to understanding the nature of that divine-human encounter. One may assume that there simply is something missing in the biblical text, a passage that was lost in transmission or omitted for some unfathomable reason. In this case, the divine communication may be understood as the conclusion of that mysterious passage which, if it existed, may have also answered some of the issues raised earlier. The other approach, and in my view the more fruitful option, is that the text is complete as it stands and that the biblical author has chosen to begin the saga in this abrupt manner to permit a surprisingly counterintuitive understanding of the narrative. That is, the antecedent colloquy between God and Abram may be conceived, in essence, as an exercise in abstract reasoning that is taking place entirely in Abram's mind, with Abram himself as one protagonist, and God speaking through Abram's intellectual or perhaps imaginative faculty as the other. Interpreted in this manner, the biblical author's citation of the divine communication to Abram may implicitly be understood to suggest that Abram's imagining of what the divine response to his arguments might be was in fact the divine response, even though Abram may not have been aware of it at the time. Indeed, given his circumstances, the substance of God's call to him to sever all his existing ties was not so farfetched that he would not likely have come to a similar conclusion by himself.

Abram must have found himself in an increasingly untenable social situation in Haran. A known iconoclast, he of necessity stood in opposition to the mainstream of his society, including the members of his very own family. A man of great intellect and exceptional will power, he could hardly have regarded with equanimity the moral lassitude and degradation that pervaded his social environment. He would, of course, actively oppose the superstition and non-rationally grounded religious beliefs that he encountered at every turn. Surprisingly, he evidently was able to do this and get away with it, at least to some extent, notwithstanding the legends regarding his youthful incarcerations in Ur for iconoclasm. Presumably, as subsequent events related in the narrative will corroborate, he must have possessed sufficient wealth and status to be able to pursue his calling without serious reprisals from the vested interests associated with the existing religious establishments in Haran.

Nonetheless, and notwithstanding his presumed ability to expound his ideas publicly with relative impunity, as well as to serve as a rallying point for others of similar inclinations who became his disciples, as a practical matter Abram hardly represented a significant threat to the cultural underpinnings of the society in which he lived. His sophisticated arguments, reflecting the intellectuality of his approach, could be but of little interest to the vast majority of the people he might encounter. He offered no mysterious ritual with which to entice the superstitious by appealing to their deepest fears. He provided no emotional outlet for those who went about in constant awe of nature and its hidden powers, which could be unleashed at any moment if not properly propitiated. He could not even describe in readily comprehensible terms that which he urged people to recognize as the only true God. As a result, barring some truly radical steps on his part, all he could really look forward to was to live the rest of his life content with the knowledge that he and a few followers had a truer understanding of the universe than his neighbors. He certainly could not expect to bring about any widespread cultural change in his society unless he raised the personal stakes for himself significantly, and even then the prospects of significant success were not very attractive. Being a prudent man, he surely understood that the cost versus benefit probability was not at all favorable and had desisted from advancing his convictions in a manner that might place him and others who adopted his views in serious physical jeopardy.

Abram's sense of frustration must have been compounded by his personal circumstances. His public activity could not but have been a constant source of embarrassment to his family. The very radicality of his views undoubtedly caused severe strains in a family that was surely part of the mainstream of the society. Moreover, although monogamous for many years, he had sired no children. As discussed earlier, he evidently abstained from taking another wife in addition to Sarai, if not in her stead, even though it was perfectly acceptable in his milieu for a man to have more than one wife under the circumstances. Here again, the biblical author is silent with regard to what is obviously an important consideration, especially in a society in which great store is set by having a large number of sons, both to provide a natural labor force and to enhance the collective strength of the extended family.

To add to Abram's concerns, the devaluation of the human spirit inherent in animism and idolatry had its repercussions on the moral stature of his society. Abram increasingly found himself repelled by the prevailing social mores and could not but feel an incrementally growing estrangement from his surroundings. He was ultimately confronted by the necessity to choose a course of action that would irreversibly establish his lifelong vocation. On the one hand, he could continue in the direction he had already set out upon, devoting himself to the reform of his society. To accomplish this, he would first have to succeed in a program of conversion to his views of sufficiently large numbers of people to be able to withstand the inevitable attempts at suppression of his reform movement by the entrenched societal power structure. Only then, as already suggested, through a protracted active and possibly violent struggle, would he be able to shatter and remove the pagan underpinnings of the prevailing culture and replace them with the monotheistic ideology he came to believe in.

Despite the ardor of his convictions, Abram surely understood the improbability of his succeeding in such an endeavor. He also had to take into consideration the potential risks of retaliation to which he might be subjecting the members of his extended family, most of whom did not share his beliefs, as well as the dangers it posed to his disciples who did. Moreover, the very intellectuality of his approach, unadorned by the aura of cultic mysteries, could have little attraction to the vast majority of the populace, thereby precluding the possibility of his initiating a significant popular movement for religious reform. Finally, the awkward personal situation in which he had consciously placed himself on account of his devotion to Sarai, made it even more difficult for him to capitalize effectively on his evidently considerable personal charisma.

The other basic alternative open to him was to put aside his attempts to reform the society of which he was a part, and to undertake a far more ambitious and radical approach, that of attempting to found a new civilization, one predicated on the fundamental concepts of human equality, individual responsibility, and social justice. Pursuing this course meant abandoning his society, leaving behind its every cultural vestige, and wandering in search of an appropriate place in which to found a new moral society, a place where entrenched interests would not stymie his efforts. But this option was also fraught with great risks. It would be unlikely that all of those who had accepted discipleship in Haran would be willing to uproot themselves totally from their families and surroundings to follow Abram into the unknown. Moreover, since he had no children of his own to succeed him, he could not even assure the continuation of what he might start once he himself succumbed to the ravages of time. Finally, such a move would also involve a radical change to his life and lifestyle. He would have to assume new roles in addition to that of savant and social critic. He would have to become the leader of a non-family based clan which had no foundation or support in a larger tribal confederation, something unheard of in the agricultural-pastoral societies of the Mesopotamia of his day. He and his band of followers would have to be completely self-reliant, both in peace and in the event of conflict in a strange land.

As Abram pondered his dilemma and deliberated the alternatives open to him, we may imagine him framing the issue in his mind as a question in a dialogue with God that took place entirely in his imagination.[59] Which course of action, weighing all the respective risks and possible achievements, would best serve the ends of his enlightenment? The divine response was unequivocal: "*Get thee out,*" or more literally, "*Go for yourself,*" that is, do it for your own sake if you want to preserve your intellectual and spiritual integrity! Abram was being urged to select the more radical alternative, which demanded a great deal of courage. It was one thing to take a radical stance from a position of relative ease, to conduct a spiritual and intellectual campaign from the comfort of one's home. It was quite another matter to give tangible expression to one's ideals; to do this would constitute the first real test of Abram's commitment to his professed beliefs.[60] He would need to turn his back on the civilization and culture within which he had been nurtured. He would also have to surrender his identity as a scion of one of the prominent families of Haran. Indeed, Abram would even need to sever his ties with his immediate family.[61] It would be necessary for him to completely uproot himself so that he could begin wholly anew, without the inhibiting residue of familial ties and loyalties.[62] He would have to transform himself utterly so that he could become the creator of a new society, a model of rationality, morality, and humaneness, predicated on the acknowledgment of a one and only God who had given man the faculties and abilities with which to create and sustain such a society.

Breaking all ties to the past, however, was a necessary but by no means a sufficient step. Abram's task would be to create a new civilization, and to do so he would have to establish conditions of social stability that would allow a society predicated on such a civilization to flourish. Moreover, a functioning society in the real and not in a theoretical world must be rooted in the soil, and if he was going to sever the roots with his homeland, it would be necessary to sprout new roots elsewhere.[63] There was little question in his mind regarding where the appropriate soil might be found. It clearly would be in Cisjordan, in the land later to be known as Canaan, the destination for which the Terahides had long ago set out when they emigrated from Ur, long before they decided to settle in Haran instead.

The choice of Cisjordan seemed propitious. To some extent, the territory served as a no-man's land between the pales of settlement of the Semites in Mesopotamia and the Hamites in Egypt and northeastern Africa. It was the land bridge between the centers of the two great civilizations of the ancient world that dominated the region. Traversed by important trade routes and flecked by a relatively small number of strongholds held by various migrant groups, it offered ample opportunities for settlement. It still constituted a fringe region whose political destiny had not yet been settled. Moreover, even though polytheism surely was rampant there as well, it was not of any one particular system but varied in accordance with the ethnic origins of the diverse peoples to be found in the land. In other words, the existing religious diversity there would facilitate the introduction of new ideas and forms of religious worship. Accordingly, this relatively sparsely settled land, sitting astride the lines of communication between Africa and Asia, could be the place from which the new civilization would spread its influence to the more populated centers of the wider region.

Given that all this may have seemed self-evident to him, why did the voice he heard not simply tell him to go to Cisjordan, which originally had been the destination for which the Terahides set out when they migrated from southern Mesopotamia? Why the vague instruction to go *unto the land that I will show thee*? It has been suggested, in this regard, that the biblical writer may be telling us that, at the time Abram heard this voice, the land to which he was being directed was not yet named Canaan, presumably because the Canaanites had not yet achieved a dominating presence in the territory,[64] and perhaps hinting in this manner that the Canaanites were not the indigenous population of the land and therefore had no historically unassailable claim to it.

Given its evident ambiguity, what was Abram to understand by the advice to go *to the land that I will show you*? It surely did not mean to go to "the place to which I will direct you," because if that were its intent, at the least Abram would have had to have specific instructions regarding which direction he should travel before he even departed Haran.[65] Perhaps the direction in which he would go really made little difference, at least at the outset. The first and most important thing was for Abram to make a decisive break with the past. Although it seemed eminently reasonable to set out for Cisjordan initially, and to Abram that was the most logical choice for the reasons already discussed, perhaps Cisjordan was not intended to be his final destination, in which case he was being asked to set out blindly on a voyage to some indeterminate location where he and his small band of followers might settle. The voice might thus be telling Abram in effect that it wasn't essential that he know in advance precisely what his ultimate destination was to be. Moreover, even if he were certain that he was being urged to go to Cisjordan, the question remained as to where he was to go in that geographical area, leading to the conjecture that the meaning of the instruction might be that he would recognize where he was to settle once he arrived there.[66] Setting out on a trek on this vague basis would demand a far greater amount of faith in the commanding voice directing him than would be the case if he knew in advance the specific locale in Cisjordan or elsewhere that was to be his final destination.[67] It would thus be the first of a series of trials of faith, of increasing severity, to which Abram would be subjected.[68]

As a practical matter, the uncertainty about exactly where he was going probably helped him with the difficult task of breaking his ties to his father and his family. The ambiguity about his final destination would act as a deterrent to a decision by his aging father to emigrate with him rather than shatter the cohesiveness of the Terahide clan. A voyage into the unknown from a life of relative affluence and comfort would have little appeal to Terah and the members of his extended family.

But what of the risks that were inherent in such an enterprise? Would a microcosmic civilization founded by Abram in an as yet relatively unsettled territory be able to have any significant impact on the surrounding societies? Would it be viable, socially, politically, and economically? What would happen to it after Abram was no longer there to inspire and lead it? Was there among his followers one upon whom he could rely to carry on the enterprise he had started, one upon whom he could place his mantle of leadership? In answer to these soul-searing queries, he heard the enigmatic divine response: *"And I will make of thee a great nation, and I will bless you, and make thy name great; and be thou a blessing."*

Abram heard himself being assured that his concerns were groundless and that they would be accommodated to an extent beyond his most reasonable expectations. He, being without children of his own and therefore unable to be the progenitor of his own family line, would somehow become the progenitor of not merely a people but a great nation. This must have struck Abram as a particularly strange notion. After all, what is a nation? In antiquity, a nation surely meant a people of common ancestry bound together as a body, and connected to a specific land.[69] Indeed the ancient Hebrew term for nation, *goy*, used in the biblical text under discussion, derives from the same root as the word for a physical body, even a corpse. This, of course, did not mean that no outsider could become part of the nation; it did not imply opposition to exogenous marriage. It simply meant that outsiders could only become part of the nation by marrying into it, and not merely by residing among its members. The notion of a polyethnic nation, one that was not based on some degree of common ancestry was a contradiction in terms.[70] Yet, in his mind's ear, he heard the divine voice assuring him that, despite his childlessness, he was to be the father of a nation. This could only mean that he would found a *new* and unprecedented kind of nation, one presumably based on common beliefs, interests, and purposes rather than merely common ancestry and a shared land. This was surely a revolutionary concept, one that was millennia ahead of its time, and one that the realization of which in antiquity seemed quite unrealistic. On a personal level, it clearly implied that, although Abram was to turn his back on his patrimony, he would not thereby become a man without a country. His very departure from the old would herald the founding of a new national identity.

Moreover, he was assured that his endeavors would be blessed with success, albeit as determined by some as yet undefined measure. In addition, instead of being viewed as an aberration of Mesopotamian civilization, he would be accorded wide recognition of his greatness, a stature not easily achieved by mere mortals. Finally, he and the byproducts of his civilization-building efforts would serve as blessings to humanity by showing the way to the reconstitution of a moral social order that comported with the divine plan for mankind.[71]

The promise to *make thy name great*, it has been argued, is an allusion by the biblical writer to the idea that, by undertaking this mission, Abram would in effect begin the process of undoing the errors of the past committed by the society out of which he emerged. In this regard, we need but recall that the great event recorded by the biblical author prior to the call of Abram was the attempt by the people of Mesopotamia to defy the will of God that they spread out and populate the earth. In their defiance, they argued: *Come let us build us a city, and a tower, with its top in heaven, and let us make us a name; lest we be scattered upon the face of the whole earth* (Gen. 11:4). Their plot was foiled and the great dispersion took place through compulsion. Now Abram is being urged not to repeat the experience of the past but to be fearless and leave the security of his city to go to an as yet unspecified place on earth and to begin building a new nation and civilization there.[72] It should be noted, however, that the notion of achieving a "great name" has also been understood as simply advising Abram that he will be acknowledged as a great man because of the favor shown to him by God, as will be manifested in his worldly successes.[73] Although the latter reading is certainly plausible, it tends to trivialize the import of what Abram is being told by reducing it to an ego-bolstering assertion, making the subtlety of the former reading seem to fit better with the tenor of the narrative taken as a whole.

Perhaps to assuage Abram's reasonable concern about the gross disparity between the divine promise and the reality of his present circumstances, perhaps to strengthen Abram's resolve to undertake the seemingly impossible task, he heard the divine voice within him elaborate how he would realize fulfillment of the particularly puzzling assertion, *be thou a blessing*, which has been understood by some to mean simply that once Abram receives the blessings promised him, he will be perceived as exemplifying one who has been blessed.[74] Others, however, have taken the assertion as though it were intended as an imperative. That is to say, if Abram is to merit the promised reward, he must live and act in such a manner as to be perceived as a blessing by others.[75] What he is to strive after is to be a blessing rather than merely to be blessed, a distinction which will make him unique among the men of his time, and probably of later times as well. Moreover, he is told:

> [12.3] *And I will bless them that bless thee, and him who curseth thee will I curse; and in thee shall all the families of the earth be blessed.*

From the perspective of Abram as an individual, he is being told that the long period of his moral apprenticeship would soon be over; the years of being ridiculed and even persecuted for his beliefs were coming to an end. Henceforth he would be perceived as a force to be reckoned with by those with whom he came into contact. His influence will therefore become widespread. Abram is also to rest assured that God will become actively involved in his evolving career, and will intervene as necessary to facilitate his success. Accordingly, those persons who are brought to recognition of the validity and value of Abram's ideas and who acknowledge their debt to him, blessing Abram for their enlightenment, will also be recipients of divine blessing. On the other hand, any who actively seek to thwart Abram and all that he stands for, who curse his every effort to construct a new moral order, will in turn be cursed, not by Abram but by God in whose service Abram is acting. In other words, Abram is being assured that the way peoples and nations relate to him and his descendants will determine how God deals with them; the enemies of Abraham will also be the enemies of God.[76]

This biblical assertion also has far-reaching theological implications. Abram, and all of us as well, is being given to understand that God is the master of history and that there may be divine intervention in the course of human events whenever there is a divine determination that such intervention is appropriate. For Abram, this idea adds a new insight in his quest for knowledge about the divine and its relation to man; God is not only transcendent but also immanent, in a more interventionist sense than he had previously imagined, a concept that Abram will soon come to appreciate more fully as he undergoes additional trials during the spiritual odyssey he is about to undertake.

It has also been pointed out that the divine assertion explicitly indicates that God is not promising an idyllic existence for Abram and his descendants; the biblical writer makes it quite clear that in fact they will have enemies that will curse them and presumably seek to do them harm.[77] Nonetheless, it does promise that Abram's efforts will not be in vain, that divine intervention will assure that

Abram's teaching by example becomes known far and wide and will begin to be taken seriously by people in many different societies. Alternatively, it has been suggested that these assurances were also intended to serve as promises of compensation for the trials and tribulations Abram experienced earlier because of his open expression of his belief in the existence of a one and only God.[78] Moreover, to assuage any concern he might have about the magnitude of the task he is to undertake, Abram is assured that those who will accept his spiritual leadership will far outnumber those who will actively oppose his efforts. God tells him, *I will bless them that bless thee, and him who curseth thee will I curse*; those who will bless Abram are spoken of in the plural, while his detractors are referred to in the singular.

The implications for the nation that would emerge from Abram are even more far reaching. Nations, like individuals, tend to seek to be blessed; they are not normally characterized by any inclination to seek the well being of other nations except when it is clearly in their interest to do so. Even the compassion and humanity that may reasonably be expected of individuals as human beings are virtues that typically remain unrecognizable among nations; international morality has never been a corollary of interpersonal ethics. Nonetheless, the avowed purpose of the nation Abram is to found is to be fundamentally different in this regard from all other nations, setting itself a national mission that it would have to struggle very hard to be worthy of and to accomplish. As the prophet Isaiah would later put it with regard to that nation, *I YHVH have called thee in righteousness, and have taken hold of thy hand, and kept thee, and set thee for a covenant of the people, for a light of the nations* (Isa. 42:6). In this same sense, Abram hears the divine voice reassuring him, that because of his endeavors "*shall all the families of the earth be blessed.*"[79]

The biblical writer seems to be telling us that with Abram's enlightenment, a new era for the world had begun. Indeed, it has been suggested that, by analogy, this is signaled by use of the of word 'bless' no less than five times in the opening verses of the Abram narrative, just as the word 'light' appears five times in the story of creation. That is, Abram is being called upon to play a major role in the inauguration of a new mode of human relations, one characterized by blessings to be given to man by man.[80] And, it has been suggested further, the very name of Abram will evoke the sense of a reversal in the moral decline of mankind that necessitated the great dispersion of the peoples and the confounding of their ability to communicate in a fundamental manner with each other. Invoking Abram's name will give those who do so the inspiration to begin to reconstitute their societies along those lines that will help turn the tide of history in a positive direction.[81]

The colloquy with God that took place in the field of Abram's imagination had come to an end. Abram had now reached the point where he needed to make a choice and to pursue the course he chose in whatever direction it led him. Although possibly still intrigued and puzzled by the enigmatic promises he heard with his mind's ear, his direct experience of the divine was not as yet such that would allow him to grasp and evaluate the full import of what he had been told. Perhaps his intrinsic humility would not allow him to believe that it was anything more than wishful thinking on his part, delusions of grandeur that should be stricken from his thoughts. Nonetheless, the main thrust of the divine message, the need for him to act decisively and sever his connection to his family and society, struck a responsive chord. Abram became determined to follow the voice he heard within him.

> 12.4 *So Abram went, as YHVH had spoken unto him; and Lot went with him; and Abram was seventy and five years old when he departed out of Haran.*

Abram responded affirmatively to the divine voice urging him to uproot himself, characteristically not through words alone but by taking action. The voice he heard told him to go and he went, without procrastination and, most importantly, without having witnessed an inspiring sign or omen, without having consulted an astrologer or seer first to determine if such a move was propitious. He acted solely in response to the divine voice he heard within him.[82] Moreover, there is no suggestion here that Abram's decision was influenced in any way by the promises of future greatness that had been mentioned during the course of the divine communication. All of these probably seemed too far-fetched at the time to be taken seriously, given his immediate circumstances. We are told that he simply responded by deed *as YHVH had spoken to him*. Abram was making a choice out of deep personal conviction. He was not motivated by a vainglorious desire for power and fame, which would have been out of character for him.

The choice he made was momentous and dramatic, as well as carefully considered. His decision was not that of a brash romantic seeking fame and fortune as an adventurer. As we are informed, Abram was already a fully mature man of worldly experience, no less than seventy-five years old, when he decided to leave Haran and undertake his seemingly quixotic mission. No longer a young man with his vision clouded by naïve perceptions of his role in life, his complete break from everything he had known, including the general culture in which he had grown to maturity and probably even the language in which he communicated as well, could not but have been very painful for him. For one thing, he had to leave behind his aged father, and possibly his mother as well, which a person of Abram's sensibilities surely would not find easy to do. Undoubtedly, Abram did not see eye to eye with his father on a great many things. This would be the understandable consequence of the wide divergence in their approaches to comprehending the apparent natural order of the universe and man's place and role in it. However, such disagreements would not have affected the basic filial respect and concern that Abram would bear toward his aged father. To depart from Terah at this point in his life surely involved a serious test of Abram's resolve to pursue the extraordinary course to which he believed he was called upon to undertake.

As though to lend emphasis to this last point, the biblical author almost casually advises us that Abram's nephew Lot accompanied him. Lot, who had already lost his natural father much earlier, had attached himself to the household of Abram and Sarai, possibly because they alone among the Terahides were without heirs. We are given no indication here or later that Lot joined Abram because he shared his outlook and convictions, although it is quite possible that this was the case, at least at this stage of Lot's life.[83] Regardless of the reason, even though Abram chose to leave behind a life of material well being among the extended family of the Terahides for a possibly calamitous voyage into the unknown, Lot elected to emigrate along with his adopted parents. One can imagine how much more difficult it was for Abram, whose natural ties to his father were far stronger than that of Lot to him, to face the necessity of consciously sacrificing the loyalty that a son properly owes a parent in order to pursue an inspired but still not clearly conceived and articulated higher goal. In an essentially clan-based society and culture that set great value on filial piety, such a choice would have been difficult for a young person, stirred by a spirit of adventure; it was surely much more so for a man such as Abram, who *was seventy and five years old when he departed out of Haran*, an age at which prudence and caution are more likely to be determining factors than inspiration alone in undertaking what amounted to more of a dislocation than a relocation.[84]

At this point, the biblical writer directs our attention to some significant aspects of Abram's departure from hearth and kin. Setting out for a new life, Abram severs his ties to the past, but does not do so capriciously. He is no wild-eyed ascetic wandering off into the desert seeking solitude and anonymity. He does not steal away in the middle of the night with a pack on his back. Abram is a man with a keen sense of personal and social responsibility. He does not depart with his affairs unsettled, relying on others to deal with them on his behalf. Moreover, he is not blinded by a missionary zeal that assumes that his future needs will be taken care of by fate or divine intervention. Quite the contrary, Abram's departure from the family home in Haran is more like a carefully prepared emigration than a precipitous act triggered by a sudden inspiration. His decision to act did not come easily or abruptly, but only after the careful deliberation befitting a man of Abram's years and character.

> *12.5 And Abram took Sarai his wife, and Lot his brother's son, and all their substance that they had gathered, and the souls they had gotten in Haran; and they went forth to go into the land of Canaan; and into the land of Canaan they came. 12.6 And Abram passed through the land unto the place of Shechem,*[85] *unto the terebinth of Moreh.*[86] *And the Canaanite was then in the land.*

Abram gathers his immediate family and the other members of his household, all of which will accompany him on his journey southward to Cisjordan. In describing this process, the biblical author once again reminds us that Abram embodies a remarkable personality. Determined to go out and create a new moral order, Abram does not use the occasion to leave behind his wife, who was unable to bear him the children that might be expected to contribute significantly to the ultimate success of the enterprise. Nor does he, even at the time of departure, take another wife or even a concubine to provide him with a direct heir to whom he could entrust his grand project when the time came for him to withdraw from its active leadership. He takes as his personal companions only his wife Sarai and Lot, his heir apparent, who we are reminded is not his natural son but only his nephew.[87] His sense of personal mission does not override his solicitude for his beloved wife of many years. This strong sense of family ties suggests that, although Abram did not intend to return to Haran at some point in the future, his very personality would not permit him to leave in a manner that would generate resentment and ill will. Indeed, as will be seen later, Abram will have no compunction about renewing the family connection at the appropriate time.

To assure his economic viability in a new land, Abram also took with him all of his portable property, household effects as well as servants, monetary wealth as well as whatever livestock he may have possessed, noting that at this point it is hardly likely that Abram's principal occupation was in anything but commerce. While it has been suggested by some that all this preparation represents a certain lack of faith on the part of Abram that God, who has called him, will see to his essential needs, others, and I would include in this category the biblical writer, have perceived the steps he took as commendable acts of prudence. Man has been given the faculties of will and intellect as innate gifts, and it his responsibility to use those gifts to the limit of his ability in carrying out the charge first given to Adam, *Be fruitful, and multiply, and replenish the earth, and subdue it; and have dominion over the fish of the sea, and over the fowl of the air, and over every living thing that creepeth upon the earth* (Gen. 1:28). Accordingly, man should seek divine assistance only as a last recourse and not as a first resort. In this regard, one medieval commentator points to Abram's actions here as an exemplar of desired and appropriate behavior, teaching that prudent self-reliance is meritorious and a posture to be emulated.[88] Alternatively, another medieval commentator sees Abram's behavior here as actually exemplifying a profound trust in God. His argument is that, as a matter of prudence, when someone ventures from his home into the unknown, he would normally take only what he expects will be necessary until he has a firm understanding of his situation, and only then send for all his belongings. In this instance, however, Abram's faith in the divine voice that he hears is so profound that he throws caution to the wind and takes with him everything he owns in the firm belief that his trust in the divine is neither exaggerated nor misplaced.[89] Finally, Abram and Sarai, his loyal and unwavering partner in the enterprise, mobilized all their disciples, *the souls they had gotten in Haran*, which is best understood as referring to those who had responded to Abram's teachings and indicated a readiness to follow them in their great venture, the creation of a new civilization and society.[90] With all these in tow, *they went forth to go into the land of Canaan.*

The biblical writer omits any mention of their itinerary en route to their destination, presumably because it is incidental to the main thrust of the story. Nonetheless, we may assume that Abram followed the caravan routes from Mesopotamia to Egypt, following the Balikh River from Haran until it approached the Euphrates, which was crossed near that point, and then proceeded to the oasis of Tadmor (Palmyra), after which he passed through Damascus before turning in a southwesterly direction to Hazor, the principal northern gateway to Cisjordan, skirting the Sea of Galilee, and then entering into the heart of Cisjordan, a distance of some 600 miles.[91] As a practical matter, considering the distance involved, it is quite understandable that Abram would take everything he owned with him, since it would be no simple matter to go and scout out the land and then return to Haran, only then to gather his belongings and make the difficult trek a second time, as some have suggested. We may also assume that some of Abram's followers dropped out along the way even as others joined the group, particularly Eliezer of Damascus, who plays an important role in subsequent events as the trusted major domo of Abram, whom the biblical author will introduce into the narrative a bit later. Finally, it appeared that the long trek had come to an end, *and into the land of Canaan they came.* But, as the biblical author advises us, the necessary political conditions in the country for the successful emergence of a new civilization, the one to be founded by Abram, were not yet at hand, because the *Canaanite was then in the land.*

No sooner had Abram arrived in Cisjordan than he was once again confronted by a dilemma, one far more serious than any he had struggled with earlier. He had uprooted himself, his household, and his followers, for the purpose of founding a new moral order. However, such an order could not be established without viable social and political roots in some territory, and for that reason he had journeyed to Cisjordan. There he expected to find a lightly populated land where he could plant new roots from which his society of the future would grow and flourish. Yet, upon his arrival there, it became readily apparent that he had been cherishing an illusion. Instead of a sparsely populated and relatively untroubled land on the fringes of Semitic civilization, he found a land seething with political turmoil, the object of a struggle for control between the primarily Semitic and other peoples and tribes of the north and east and the primarily Hamitic and other peoples and tribes of the south and southwest, which included the Canaanites, after whom the land would later be named. The tribes under the leadership of the Canaanites, which was also subsequently used by the biblical author as a generic name for the mélange of peoples and tribes found in Cisjordan, had just recently obtained a strong grip on a significant part of the country and were building a power base there that they clearly would not surrender without a major struggle.[92]

Assessing the situation with which he was confronted, Abram quickly came to the conclusion that he did not have the human resources that would be required to compete effectively with the Canaanites, whose primary areas of concentration were in the arable lowlands of Cisjordan, for possession of the country. Demonstrating his adaptability, a most important quality for a leader, he perhaps reluctantly concluded that until such a time when the number of his followers increased substantially and he was in a position to take on the Canaanites in a struggle for land, the outcome of which would inevitably be determined on the battlefield, he would effectively be compelled to confine himself to the more sparsely populated and economically limited hill country, into which the Canaanites had not yet penetrated to any great extent. This in itself posed another significant dilemma for Abram. The hill country offered little opportunity for agricultural development and the social stability that it implied, a critical factor for building the kind of society he envisioned. Instead, he would have to rely almost exclusively on animal husbandry to achieve economic viability, which meant a perennial search for pastures and grazing lands and the consequent difficulty in establishing firm roots in the soil, a virtual precondition for a stable society. Abram, however, was not deterred by these considerations, and remained determined to continue on the course he had set for himself. With unwavering faith in the future that he had been assured was to be his, Abram brushed aside these problems as merely temporary impediments that he somehow would eventually overcome. In the meantime, he would do what he could to make the best of the circumstances in which he found himself. If necessary, he would become an animal breeder, a vocation for which he had little if any prior preparation, living on the fringes of Canaanite agricultural society.

There were, however, some serious political considerations that had to be taken into account as well, considerations that could put his entire enterprise and the welfare of his followers in mortal jeopardy. As long as he shied away from the major concentrations of Canaanite settlement, he and his relatively small but soon to be growing band of followers were not likely to be perceived as posing any serious threat to the emerging political order in Cisjordan and would therefore able to move through the countryside in search of open pasture and grazing lands unopposed. However, the situation might change dramatically if Abram's intent to establish a permanent base even in the hill country were to be perceived by the Canaanites as a potential threat to their hegemony in the area, in which case he might find himself struggling for survival against far more powerful foes before he was strong enough to enter into such a contest. Given these concerns, he was faced by the dilemma of what to do next? He seemed to have only two basic options, both extremely unattractive. On the one hand, he could commit himself to what seemed like a virtually hopeless struggle with the Canaanites, realizing that without some supernatural intervention on his behalf there could be very little if any prospect of his emerging victorious. On the other hand, he could simply turn back to Haran, admitting to himself, as well as to those who had joined him in his venture, that he had been pursuing an unrealizable dream. Faced with this choice, Abram placed what amounted to blind faith in the voice that he heard urging him to break with his past, even though it was for a clearly uncertain future, at least at this point.

Once again, Abram elected to pursue the original course he had set out upon, despite the significant risks that it entailed. He remained determined to begin to lay the groundwork for the new society he aspired to found in Cisjordan. Acting as prudently as possible to avoid engendering active opposition to his plans from the Canaanite populace, he would have to take the steps necessary to ensure the economic and political viability of his civilization-building enterprise. At a minimum, this would entail the establishment of a territorial base around which the envisioned nation and civilization might ultimately evolve. But where should this base be established? He had responded positively to the divine call to sever his ties with the past. He had now arrived in Cisjordan, but still had no clear sense of what his actual destination was in that troubled land. He had been told to go *unto the land that I will show thee*, but had no notion of specifically where that land was or how he would recognize it even if he stumbled upon it as he moved through the countryside.

Unsure both of what to do and of his ultimate destination, Abram continued to travel southwards through the hill country, probably experiencing a growing anxiety over the likely outcome of what was beginning to seem like a misadventure. He and his entourage proceeded, stop and go, until they found themselves in the vicinity of Shechem, a Hivite city-state in the heart of the country, the Hivites being but one of the many ethnic groups subsumed under the rubric of Canaanites.[93] Reflecting on his situation, Abram soon found himself undergoing an agonizing test of his faith, both in his ability to succeed in his mission under the prevailing circumstances and in the divine promise that he was so sure he heard earlier. His decision to turn his back on Haran and to venture forth into the unknown had represented a reasonable choice, given the circumstances in which he found himself. However, the situation had changed radically once he reached Cisjordan. He now realized that he had no reasonable way of following through successfully on the commitments he undertook when he left Haran. His initial act of rational faith had resulted in drawing him into a morass from which he was not sure he could extricate himself. It became clear to him that he needed further divine reassurance that he would somehow persevere if he persisted on the path he had chosen. He desperately needed to hear the divine voice speak to him once again. In the past, he had been the passive recipient of such divine communication. The question was how to actively initiate such a communication and evoke a divine response.

At this point, the biblical author injects a subtle detail into the narrative that is surprisingly revealing about the state of Abram's still rather rudimentary theological conception of the God he had come to believe in. Not knowing what else to do, we are told, Abram moved his camp to the outskirts of the city, to the site of the *terebinth of Moreh,* the sacred turpentine tree that served as a center of the pagan cult adhered to by most of the people of the immediate area.[94] Although Abram rejected such beliefs, he evidently still hoped that the alleged sanctity of the site would somehow make it propitious for a divine communication. There

Abram waited, hoping to hear the divine voice tell him where to settle and begin to build the new society he had dreamed of for so long.

It was at this critical point, a point at which Abram was faced by the threat of despondency and despair, that God intervened, not indirectly as at Haran but directly through a theophany. It is noteworthy that the narrator of these events subtly reminds us of the central importance of the land in Israel's national narrative—it is only after Abram enters Cisjordan that he is privileged to experience a theophany. In a manner left unstated, God now appeared to him, not within the context of an imaginary rational deliberation as before but rather through an ostensibly sensory perception that transcended all rationality.

> 12.7 *And YHVH appeared unto Abram, and said: "Unto thy seed will I give this land"; and he builded there an altar unto YHVH, who appeared unto him.*

The vision that Abram beheld conveyed a brief but critical message, one sufficient to allay his most immediate concerns and to bolster his confidence in the ultimate purpose and value of his mission, but one that must also have caused him dismay.[95] Abram is told that it is not he and his followers that are to inherit the land upon which he stands, but only his direct descendants. This assurance was double-edged. One the one hand, it dealt effectively with his immediate practical concerns about remaining viable in the prevailing political climate in Cisjordan; he was not expected to challenge the Canaanites for control of the land. He would merely lay the essential albeit still undefined groundwork for the task that would be completed by his descendants. On the other hand, it constituted yet another test of Abram's faith and commitment since he was already past his prime, was still childless, and had already probably given up hope that he would have any direct offspring to continue the task after him, let alone take control of a land that was already the subject of destabilization by diverse peoples and conflicting interests. Moreover, it also effectively precluded his nephew Lot from that role with regard to the land since he was not a direct descendant of the future patriarch. It had been made quite clear that the land was to be awarded exclusively to the new nation that would emerge from Abram's direct progeny. In effect, Abram was being asked to accept on faith alone that the work he had begun would in fact be brought to fruition by his as yet unborn descendants, a prospect that both delighted him as it strained his credulity.

Another matter that caused him serious concern was what this divine message meant for those who voluntarily had accompanied Abram and Sarai in their venture, the *souls that they had gotten in Haran*. Were they not to have any share in the inheritance of the land? And, if not, why had Abram led them away from their homes to a foreign land in which neither they nor their descendants were to have any future? Indeed, had Abram clearly understood at the outset that this was to be the ultimate disposition of his disciples, would he have found it conscionable to cause them to sever their connections to their homeland and to follow him to Cisjordan? Nonetheless, even though the content of the divine message seemed to him to defy reason, it was sufficient for Abram immediate needs. He had arrived at the point where he was prepared to suppress what seemed reasonable to him in favor of a trust in that which he could not fully comprehend. He was learning to place constraints on reason as his sole guide in life.

The biblical author tells us nothing of how Abram dealt with the very substantial problem that resulted from the fact that he had misconstrued the message of his earlier imaginative colloquy with God, that when the latter told him, *I will make of thee a great nation*, he meant *of you* literally and not figuratively. In other words, the new nation that would emerge from Abram was to have a familial foundation, constructed on the basis of kinship rather than on ideology alone. This must have struck Abram as strange if not incomprehensible, given that the belief system that Abram was evolving clearly had universal application. Nonetheless, the implication of the message was that it was not his assigned goal to attempt to proselytize all the peoples of the earth, a quite unrealistic if not impossible task. His sole mission was to lay the groundwork for the emergence of a nation dedicated to the service of God that would serve as a model for emulation by others, and, at least in its infancy, such a nation needed the internal cohesiveness and nurture that could best be assured in the context of a closely related family and clan.

Abram surely experienced some discontent as well as inner turmoil because of this aspect of the revelation and its implications for his followers. It seems reasonable to assume that Abram would not have revealed the full content and meaning of the divine message to them, a message stipulating that it would only be his descendants and not theirs that would bring the vision of a new civilization to realization in the land to which he had led them. Of course, this did not preclude them from carrying the vision of a society based on righteousness and justice to the far corners of the earth, but it clearly did preclude them from becoming an integral part of the nation that would be founded in Cisjordan by the direct descendants of Abram. Informing them of the full content of the divine message would have served merely to exacerbate their already growing concerns about the nature of the enterprise in which they were partaking, given the objective circumstances in which they found themselves. The most that Abram probably would have told them was that the goal of creating a new society and civilization could not be accomplished by them in their lifetimes, but only by future generations. Under the circumstances, we cannot but assume that all but those most devoted to Abram and his beliefs were unable to overcome the resulting disillusionment and were eventually assimilated into Canaanite society, or made their way back to Haran. If this did indeed occur, one can readily imagine the emotional torment that Abram would have suffered on their account, having uprooted them only to have them follow him in pursuit of a dream that not only did not apply to them but that would not become a reality in their lifetime or even that of their immediate descendants.

Despite his misgivings, Abram now gained renewed personal faith and confidence in the ultimate value of the mission he had undertaken, and he erected an altar on the spot to commemorate the theophany he had experienced there, a well-intentioned act that further illustrates the religious dimension of the challenges that confronted him.[96] He had received the direct divine communication at the terebinth of Moreh, the venerated tree that served as a sacred site for the worship of the local pagan deity, and had built an altar there dedicated to God.[97] Yet, although Abram's God could find acceptance as just another divine being in the pantheon of pagan deities, the reverse was inconceivable. Abram could not proclaim the exclusive divinity of God without attacking pagan beliefs and worship, and this he clearly was not in a position to do, especially not at Shechem, which was a major population center in which he would quickly become an unwelcome stranger. However, if he did not proclaim the exclusive divinity of God, the very altar that he built might be viewed as his tribute to the gods of the Canaanite pantheon. This paradoxical situation demanded that he remove himself from the environs of all large population centers. Otherwise, he would soon find himself in the same uncomfortable situation that precipitated his departure from Haran in the first place.

> 12.8 *And he removed from thence unto the mountain on the east of Beth-el, and pitched his tent, having Beth-el on the west and Ai on the east; and he builded there an altar unto YHVH, and called upon the name of YHVH.*

Abram relocated his camp from the outskirts of Shechem to a nearby and higher location in the mountains, a more sparsely populated area where he thought he might be able to establish a permanent site dedicated exclusively to the proclamation of the existence of a one and only true God, and to teaching the religious, social, and moral implications of that assertion. The site he selected was chosen because, although some distance from the more populous areas, it was still close enough to be able to exert some influence on the urban centers that flanked it on both sides. His choice fell on a point strategically located between the towns of Beth-el and Ai, perhaps at the same location where some centuries later Joshua mounted a successful ambush of the Canaanites that led to the conquest of Ai (Josh. 8:9, 12), a good example of the historiosophical perspective of the biblical authors in which the acts of the first patriarchs of the nation presage and are reflected in later historical developments.

At this mountain site, Abram built another altar from which, possibly for the first time since entering Cisjordan, he *called upon the name of YHVH*. That is, the biblical writer is telling us, Abram invoked God, using an unspecified name for the deity that corresponded in significance to the Tetragrammaton, *YHVH*, the name of God that Abram himself never came to know, as will become clear later. From this location he would once again call for moral regeneration, but this time he would predicate it on the prior acknowledgement of God as the sole master of the universe and ultimate moral authority. And, by contrast with his earlier activities in Mesopotamia, he no longer actively sought disciples; he was content merely to get his message across to those ready to listen, possibly hoping to make the social environment more conducive to the faith-driven family he now expected to rear, a family that would evolve into a distinct nation at some time in the future. His most immediate task, however, was to take measures to assure the economic, social, and political viability of the core entity from which that nation would emerge.

The biblical author does not tell us anything more about Abram's mountain settlement other than that he eventually abandoned it. It is left to the reader to surmise the reasons for this from what is already known about Abram's situation. For one thing, if he found it both necessary and desirable, in order to build the strength of his newly reconstituted group, to avoid the major centers in the land and thereby to maintain a certain social isolation, he would have to establish an economically viable community in the mountain. This was essential, because the building of a new civilization required the stability of deep roots. However, the mountain site did not really have the potential for the necessary growth and development to become the seat of a new society. Secondly, the vicinity of the mountain site did not afford sufficient grassland or forage for a significant animal husbandry operation, thus forcing Abram to seek pasturage elsewhere if he was to remain economically viable and still avoid the problems associated with being near large population centers. The only direction he could go in Cisjordan that might satisfy these requirements was southward, to the area closer to the fringe of the wilderness. Thus, we are told:

^{12.9} *And Abram journeyed, going on still toward the South.*

Abram's immediate goal had now undergone a significant revision. Although he left Haran for the purpose of founding a new civilization and society in Cisjordan, he now truly comprehended how complex and difficult a task this was going to be, and accepted that he would not see its realization in his lifetime. However, he would not allow himself to succumb to depression over this traumatic disappointment. Instead, he redefined the task before him as that of preserving and enhancing the moral and spiritual integrity of his house, in order that it serve as the reservoir from which the future generations of his descendants would draw their inspiration and example. He would have to devote the rest of his life and career to self-perfection in order to represent an exemplar to those who would follow. It was to be through his descendants that he would found a new moral order. In the meantime, he would prepare the groundwork, educating those willing to listen and teaching all by example, abstaining from zealous controversy and the active iconoclasm that had not proven very productive in the past. At this point in time, Abram could not have fully realized that his own personal odyssey toward spiritual and moral greatness had in some respects only just begun.

3

Detour to Egypt

The only incidents in the life of Abram recorded by the biblical author that took place subsequent to the theophany at the terebinth of Moreh, in keeping with the author's purpose, are those that relate directly to the patriarch's further moral and spiritual development. As discussed earlier, Abram's quintessential genius resided in his sharply honed rationality. His original conception of God was purely intellectual. However, as the narrative progresses, he will increasingly find himself challenged by experiences that will confound his rationalism. Ultimately, he will come to exhibit a reliance on faith to an extent that will transcend the bounds of reason; he will arrive at a higher level of faith that begins where man's capacity for rational understanding ends.

It was not very long after Abram received the divine assurance that his direct descendants would inherit the land in which he now found himself that it came about that the land itself seemed to reject his presence in it. Cisjordan is heavily dependent on seasonal rainfall for its life-sustaining waters and, unexpectedly, the rains failed to come in their season and the country was soon afflicted by famine. As the crops withered and pasturage became increasingly scarce, Abram was forced to rely on whatever food stores he may have been able to stockpile for the sustenance of his household. It presumably also became necessary for him to begin slaughtering some of his flocks and herds, both for food as well as because of the lack of feed and water for the animals. Eventually, under the pressure of objective circumstances and sheer physical necessity, he was compelled to choose among a set of unpalatable options. He could remain where he was, in total reliance on the idea that, because it was in accordance with the divine wish that he came to this land, God would not forsake him in his hour of need. A second option that lay open before him was to relocate to one of the main population centers and seek to ensure the survival of his household through means of commercial arrangements based on the wealth he brought with him from Haran. Finally, he could emigrate, as many others did, at least until the famine was over, to a land not so afflicted, presumably a land not subject to the same climatic conditions as Cisjordan. The only such land within Abram's reach was Egypt, where the water supply was far less dependent on rainfall than on the regular periodic overflow of the Nile.

The first option, which amounted to passive reliance on faith in the absolute necessity for God to intervene on Abram's behalf in order for him to be able to realize the divine promise, was one to which Abram could not reconcile himself.[98] He was by his very nature a man of action and could not simply abdicate direct responsibility for himself and those who followed him. To do so might even suggest a fatalism that Abraham had long since rejected on purely intellectual grounds. No! Abram believed strongly that man must assume responsibility for his own welfare and must take appropriate steps to assure his survival and viability as a precondition to pursuing a life based on higher personal and public morality.[99]

The second course open to him, although less objectionable than the first, carried great risks of another sort. Such a step could lead to cultural assimilation with the host Canaanite society, a danger Abram had specifically sought to avoid by adopting a pastoral existence that provided sufficient isolation to preclude just such an outcome. To reverse this policy now, in a time of great need, could result in nullifying the very purpose of the departure from Haran. It might undo a life's work in the struggle against moral decay. Abram dared not pursue this course.

The only reasonable alternative left to him was to temporarily relocate to Egypt, remaining there only until the worst of the famine passed and then returning to the "promised" land. Egypt, being essentially Hamitic in its ethnic composition and alien in its culture and language, would be sufficiently strange to Abram's entourage to preclude any ready assimilation, something that was far more likely to be the case in Cisjordan were he to have pursued the option of relocating to a major population center. Coincidentally, the decision to proceed to Egypt may also have had the effect of causing all but the most closely attached of his followers to defect from him, and either return to Haran or blend into the Canaanite world, in order to survive. In effect, the descent to Egypt may have had the perhaps unintended consequence of reducing to some extent Abram's earlier concerns about how to deal with his growing band of followers who, at this stage, were to be excluded from a direct or even indirect but significant role in the divine promise of the nation to be and its assigned territory, which was to be reserved for his direct descendants alone. The biblical author does not address any of these issues, which are left for us to speculate about, and simply notes:

¹²·¹⁰ *And there was a famine in the land; and Abram went down to Egypt to sojourn there; for the famine was sore in the land.*

As Abram approached the Egyptian frontier, perhaps already having passed the point of no return, he suddenly became conscious of an additional concern, one regarding a serious potential danger that simply had not occurred to him earlier. It was as though it came to illustrate to him the inherent limitations of human reason, reminding him that man is incapable of thoroughly assessing all seemingly rational courses of action, let alone those resulting from unanticipated contingencies.

What had escaped Abram's calculations was something so obvious that it should have triggered immediate concern. Abram, Sarai, and probably most if not all of their followers were Semites, and as such were fair-skinned by comparison with the much darker Hamites. As they approached closer and closer to Egypt and encountered fewer and fewer Semitic tribesmen, it occurred to Abram that he and his band might not simply be able to blend unobtrusively into the Egyptian social landscape.[100] The deeper into Egypt he penetrated, the greater would be the physical contrast with the native population, and the more attention he would draw to himself and his entourage. It further occurred to him that Sarai's presence in his company could result in great personal danger to her as well as to himself.

¹²·¹¹ *And it came to pass, when he was come near to enter into Egypt, that he said unto Sarai his wife: "Behold now, I know that thou art a fair woman to look upon.* ¹²·¹² *And it will come to pass, when the Egyptians shall see thee, they will say: This is his wife; and they will kill me, but thee they will keep alive.*

Presumably, a still very attractive albeit mature fair-skinned Semitic woman would be quite uncommon in Egypt and might therefore be particularly in demand to grace some household.[101] Her safety was completely dependent on Abram's ability to protect her, yet the fact that he was her husband exacerbated the danger. Abram would be seen as a complete alien in Egyptian society, without friends or advocates in his behalf. What could be simpler than to eliminate Abram and then do whatever anyone wished with his desirable and helpless widow? Giving a certain edge to Abram's concerns in this regard was the known fact that, as he was evidently well aware, such things did take place in the Egypt of his time.[102] Accordingly, it would be necessary to keep her effectively hidden from public view, for as long as possible. Of course, it was quite possible that nothing of the kind would transpire and their sojourn in Egypt might pass innocuously. However, he clearly needed a reasonable contingency plan in the event that her presence became exposed, at which point her attractiveness could become the security liability he so feared. Increasingly desperate for some means of assuring Sarai's safety as well as his own, Abram conceived of a ruse he hoped would achieve that goal in the event that her presence in his entourage were to be discovered.[103] In that case, he urged Sarai,

> 12.13 *Say, I pray thee,*[104] *thou art my sister, that it may be well with me for thy sake, and that my soul*[105] *may live because of thee.*

If Sarai, notwithstanding her evident maturity, were to be portrayed as an unmarried, indeed, a never married woman, their otherwise precarious situation would substantially be altered to their advantage. If Abram, rather than being perceived as Sarai's husband, were thought to be her brother, the incentive to do away with him would diminish significantly, if not vanish entirely. The procurement of an attractive Semitic woman would become a goal worth negotiating and bargaining over, a custom that Abram either knew or assumed was practiced in Egypt just as it was in Mesopotamia. As Sarai's brother, he would also be recognized as her legal guardian and surrogate father, someone with whom prospective suitors might be expected to haggle over terms and conditions for her hand.[106]

However, even with such a contingency plan in mind, it would be necessary to preempt any rash action by the Egyptians with regard to Sarai. They might not wait to discover Abram's relation to her, and simply assume that he was her husband and therefore try to do away with him. Accordingly, if the ruse were to work, and Abram was to survive any possible attempts on his life and remain in a position to protect Sarai from being subjected to any indignities, Sarai herself had to play an active part in the scheme. She could not simply await inquiries regarding her identity and status, but needed to take the initiative if she were discovered and let it be known to all that she was Abram's sister. By so doing she would in effect be proclaiming, as might be inferred by her age alone, that as a mature and attractive woman she would be prepared to consider a marital alliance, which would have to be negotiated with her brother. In this manner, if the feared contingency arose, they might both manage to procrastinate and drag out negotiations until the famine subsided and they were able to return to Cisjordan and comparative safety. However, if at any time a real danger to Sarai emerged, Abram still had the option of abandoning his possessions in Egypt and fleeing back to Cisjordan with her.

This scheme has raised many questions from commentators, some of whom have castigated Abram for engaging in such a deception, which would seem to be quite out of character for him. How, they ask, could Abram, of all people tell such a bald lie? The simple answer may be that there are many occasions on which prudence dictates that prevarication is ethically preferable to revealing the truth, especially when the consequences of the truth are likely to prove more harmful. In a case where one is confronted by and is effectively at the mercy of forces far more powerful than he, his very survival may hinge on his ability to maneuver his way out of such a situation.[107] In this instance, in Abram's best judgment, it was likely to be a case of lie or die. In other words, in the biblical writer's perspective, always telling the truth is not an absolute moral imperative and, just as there are times when it is appropriate to kill, so too are there times when it is appropriate to prevaricate.[108]

It is interesting to note that a number of commentators, some of them perhaps indulging in apologetics, have pointed out that, as will be seen later, Sarai may indeed have been Abram's half-sister by a common father but by different mothers, in which case the deception here would only have involved failing to fully disclose the marital dimension of their relationship but not any actual prevarication.[109] Moreover, since neither Abram nor Sarai were under any moral obligation to provide information that could endanger their lives, the scheme would appear to have been quite proper and prudent under the circumstances.

Abram evidently was persuasive and Sarai agreed to participate in the charade that he proposed. And, as it turned out, some time after Abram arrived in Egypt events began to take a dangerous turn, as he had anticipated. Despite their efforts to maintain a low profile among the Egyptians, at some point the presence of the fair Semitic woman in Abram's encampment became known. The biblical author does not indicate how long Abram was able to keep Sarai secluded from public view. According to one ancient legendary account of the story, Sarai had remained concealed from the public for no less than five years before she was discovered during a celebratory event at Abram's home.[110] In the biblical text, however, the period of Sarai's concealment is completely ignored, possibly because the matter was considered to be largely irrelevant to the biblical author's purpose. What was of interest was what happened when Sarai was discovered.

> [12.14] *And it came to pass, that, when Abram was come into Egypt, the Egyptians beheld the woman that she was very fair.* [12.15] *And the princes of Pharaoh saw her, and praised her to Pharaoh; and the woman was taken into Pharaoh's house.* [12.16] *And he dealt well with Abram for her sake; and he had sheep, and oxen, and he-asses, and men-servants, and maid-servants, and she-asses, and camels.*

The biblical writer simply states, without any further elaboration, that once her presence was exposed the Egyptians took note of Sarai's beauty. However, we may also assume that as they exhibited greater interest in her, the prearranged deception regarding Sarai's relationship to Abram was brought into play. It probably was not too difficult for Abram, a man of obvious substance, to fend off potential suitors with demands for compensation that exceeded their capacities. To that extent the scenario was played out as Abram had projected.

It was not long, however, before events took a turn that Abram did not anticipate. He did not expect that, as a stranger without local connections, he would come to the attention of the higher levels of Egyptian society. Once word of Sarai's beauty and general demeanor, surely enhanced with each retelling, reached the ears of the *princes of Pharaoh*, Abram began to lose control of events. Although he might still be able to fend off even these men of greater affluence with excessive demands as long as matters were kept on a personal transaction basis, there was little he could do once the question of Sarai was transformed into a political matter. And it was the latter that occurred.

If Abram's asking price for Sarai was equivalent to a king's ransom, then perhaps the king might be interested in acquiring and installing such an extraordinary female personality in his palace. Accordingly, the officials *praised her to Pharaoh* as a woman worthy of his personal attention. As one commentator observed, "Something about her state and dignity and her general magnificence attracted the notice of the king, and he thought it would be an addition to have her attached to his own court. At her age it would be that rather than her physical beauty that would be attractive in her."[111] Once the king's interest in her was kindled, there was nothing that Abram could do to protect her any further, flight no longer being a realistic option. He could neither refuse her to the king nor make excessive demands on her behalf. Either course would have constituted an unacceptable affront, which could easily prove fatal. At this point, he could not even tell the truth, that Sarai, although she was his half-sister, was also his wife. He had consistently denied the latter, and to reverse that claim now might well be interpreted as an attempt to deny her to the king on the basis of a feeble lie, an act that could not but have deadly consequences. Abram was therefore compelled to stand by helplessly as his wife was taken to the palace of the pharaoh, the king of Egypt whom the biblical writer evidently does not deem worthy of being specifically named, presumably to become a member of his household.

It is noteworthy, as the text puts it, *the woman was taken into Pharaoh's house*; the implication of this statement being that she did not go voluntarily—she was *taken*. Moreover, she was not taken to the king personally, presumably for his immediate amusement, but *into Pharaoh's house*. This in itself must have drawn special attention to her, namely that she was being treated as a person of importance, to be presented to the king at an appropriate time.[112] Ostensibly, the opportunity to become a consort of the Egyptian king was an honor that unmarried Egyptian women dreamed of, and this was a foreign woman who displayed no interest in such an opportunity and had to be taken to the court against her will.[113]

Although the biblical author, consistent with his approach to the narrative, skimps on the details that are not essential to his purpose, the context of the story suggests that the king intended to marry Sarai, it being unlikely that he would expend a small fortune in gifts to her brother if she were to become a mere concubine. Accordingly, Sarai most likely had to undergo a course of preparation for a royal wedding, a process that took some time. According to one ancient account, it took two years.[114] During this period, the king *dealt well with Abram for her sake*. It is clear from Abram's earlier discussion with Sarai that his sole purpose in proposing the deception was to enable him to protect her to the greatest extent possible, certainly not to profit from it in any way. Nonetheless, he now found himself in the doubly awkward position of being unable to protect her at all, and at the same time seeming to benefit handsomely from Sarai's discomfiture through the receipt of lavish gifts from the king, which he could hardly refuse without arousing suspicion. Sensitive to this consideration, the biblical writer evidently attempts to direct the attention of the reader to the recognition that Abram had no need or desire for the royal gifts. Thus, he does not say that the king bestowed wealth on Abram, but rather that *he had* a variety of servants and domestic animals. The implication being that though the king did indeed present gifts to Abram, as Sarai's brother and guardian, such gifts merely augmented the wealth he already possessed, and that such benefits as he received were really of relatively minor significance to him.[115] Abram's main concern had been for Sarai's welfare and now he was helpless in that regard, the gifts he received from the king being like salt poured into an open wound.

The episode made clear to Abram the frailty and tentativeness of man's plans and ability to control events. His carefully conceived deception produced consequences that were diametrically opposed to those he originally intended. Had the king known that Sarai was Abram's wife there was a good chance that he might have left her alone, it possibly being beneath the royal dignity to coerce into marriage a woman who had been the wife of a minor and ostensibly Canaanite sheik. However, given what had actually transpired, if Sarai were now to be saved from being forced into an adulterous relationship, it would require the intervention of a higher power than man.

Sarai, no less than Abram, was also well aware of the precariousness of her situation. She too was confronted by the need to do something to regain control of events. The options open to her, however, were painfully limited. Moreover, overhanging anything she might have elected to do was the deep concern that, in her efforts to protect herself, she not inadvertently be the cause of grave harm to Abram. There were only two seemingly viable courses open to her. One was to confess the truth to the king and hope that he would be understanding and forgiving. If he were not, it would probably result in the execution of both Sarai and Abram. The other option simply required passive acceptance of whatever might happen to her at the hands of the king, without her making any overt attempt to influence the outcome. Notwithstanding the severely constrained range of possibilities open to her, Sarai had to choose, to act or to do nothing. It is not clear which option she chose, the narrative being susceptible to an interpretation that would support either.

On the one hand, it seems reasonable to assume, from the general context of what follows in the biblical narrative, that Sarai chose to confess the truth about the deception. She surely would have explained to the king that when they had concocted the scheme, it was only intended to afford a modicum of protection for them from the common people, and that they never imagined that the king would somehow become aware of her existence and show an avid interest in bringing her into his household. Once that happened, they were afraid to tell the truth and thereby be found guilty of perjury. But now, as the king seemed determined to take Sarai as a wife, she had no acceptable alternative but to tell him the truth in order that he not be misled into committing an act beneath the dignity of a great ruler, that of taking for himself the wife of many years of another man.

Assuming that this was the nature of Sarai's appeal to the king, it does not appear to have had a deterrent effect on him. It may be that he simply didn't believe her, possibly attributing her tale to a pre-marital hysteria. On the other hand, he may have believed her but had become so enamored that he didn't care, attributing the entire affair to a destiny over which he had no control.[116] In any case, it became increasingly evident that if Sarai's honor were to be preserved, given the king's intentions, divine intervention would be necessary. Accordingly, the biblical author tells us that once Sarai's effort at explanation failed to achieve the desired end, if this is what she actually did, God intervened on her behalf. Alternatively, as will be seen, it is quite possible that she had no confidence in the efficacy of a confession that she was already married. Indeed, she may have been concerned that it might not have any effect other than to enrage the king, thereby assuredly precipitating disaster. If this truly reflected her perception of the situation, she may have elected to do nothing and simply place her and Abram's safety and welfare in God's hands. In either scenario, only a divine intervention could save her from being forced into an adulterous relationship, something that God clearly did not want to happen.

> [12.17] *And YHVH plagued Pharaoh and his house with great plagues because of Sarai, Abram's wife.* [12.18] *And Pharaoh called Abram, and said: 'What is this that thou hast done unto me? why didst thou not tell me that she was thy wife?* [12.19] *Why saidest thou: She is my sister? so that I took her to be my wife; Now therefore, behold thy wife, take her, and go thy way.'* [12.20] *And Pharaoh gave men charge concerning him; and they brought him on the way, and his wife, and all that he had.*

To satisfactorily unscramble this complicated situation, the divine intervention had to be of such a nature that the king would immediately associate it with the matter of his impending marriage to Sarai. If Sarai had confessed to him that she was already married, it seems likely that his perception of such a cause and effect relationship might have been spurred in part by Sarai, who may have said something to him to the effect that she would pray for divine help in her hour of need, once the king rejected her pleas to desist from compromising her virtue. Presumably, it would have been immediately following Sarai's confession and plea that, God *plagued Pharaoh and his house with great plagues.*

The biblical writer does not inform us of the precise character of the malady that struck the king, but we may certainly assume that its nature was such as to prevent the marriage from being consummated. Moreover, to preclude him from concluding that his sudden affliction was a mere coincidence, his entire household was similarly afflicted, another coincidence that he could not simply shrug off. The Egyptian ruler would surely have interpreted such a calamity as a warning by the gods of Egypt not to proceed with his plans concerning Sarai. The intervention thus had the intended effect, even though the king probably misperceived the source of his affliction. In any case, he desisted from any further attempts to compromise her.

The king was now confronted by the need to repair the loss of self-esteem that he suffered as a result of the incident, and therefore summoned Abram to an audience for the purpose of justifying his conduct in the affair. Though the king may have entertained initial thoughts of wreaking some sort of vengeance on Abram for causing him such discomfit and embarrassment, he soon dismissed all such notions. He would not tempt the fates and risk the further displeasure of the gods who apparently were somehow involved with Sarai and Abram. He needed no further involvement with them, only an expedient means of terminating the affair.

Assuming a pose of innocence in the matter, the king took care to obscure the fact that it was probably Sarai herself who had confessed to him that she was a married woman, and suggested by implication that he discovered this on his own and was therefore outraged over the fact that they, Abram and Sarai, had deliberately involved him in an immoral triangle, something he would never have engaged in knowingly. Alternatively, Sarai may have remained silent until after the affliction struck, at which time the king may have demanded that Sarai reveal her knowledge of anything that might have caused it to occur. In either case, he was outraged at the effrontery of Abram in allowing the deception to go on until it compromised the king's moral integrity. *What is this that thou hast done unto me? why didst thou not tell me that she was thy wife?* How dare Abram ensnare the pharaoh of Egypt in such an abhorrent scheme? Moreover, he complained, *Why saidest thou: She is my sister? so that I took her to be my wife.* At the least, Abram should have said nothing, in which case the king would have had her identity investigated further. But once Abram declared her to be his sister, no further inquiry was necessary.[117] Was it Abram's intention, by claiming Sarai was his sister and thereby in effect contriving that she be taken to the king, to extort gifts to enrich himself at the expense of the king as well as his own wife? Even if Abram had legitimate concerns about their safety among the common people, surely he knew that he could have told the king the truth. After all, it was the king's intention to treat Sarai with the greatest honor he could bestow on her, making her his wife and a queen of Egypt. Abram's scheme was therefore both senseless and an act of *lèse-majesté* that resulted in the very threat to the honor of Sarai that he sought to preclude. Indeed, if it were not for the king's concern about maintaining the dignity and moral integrity of his house, Abram's ploy might not have been discovered before it was too late. Still enraged, he told Abram, *behold thy wife; take her, and go thy way.*

Abram stood speechless before the king, not knowing how or what to respond. Much of what the king said to him was true. What he thought was a clever scheme backfired in a manner that he never suspected could happen. Yet, miraculously, he and Sarai were both coming out of the incident chastened but unscathed. Somehow everything was working itself out regardless of his own feeble attempt to exercise control of events. Abram had no way of knowing in what way God had intervened; he only understood from the king's demeanor that something extraordinary had taken place to prevent the consummation of an adulterous marriage.

The entire episode was a powerful lesson in humility for Abram, even though he had nothing to regret over having tried to do whatever he could to maintain control over and responsibility for his and Sarai's welfare. But his experience in Egypt served as a poignant lesson to him about the limits of man's ability to control his destiny. He had now come to the unequivocal realization that while man may take actions which appear most appropriate in a given set of circumstances, the success of such endeavors rested with a higher power, that of the omnipresent God whose intervention in Sarai's behalf was beyond question, and without whose beneficence both he and his wife would never have left Egypt alive. Nonetheless, man cannot sit back and wait for God to tend to his needs; he himself must first do whatever he can in such regard and hope that it will succeed. What happens beyond that is out of his control. Did Abram, in taking the steps described in the narrative, consciously place Sarai's moral welfare in jeopardy? The answer must be in the affirmative. But, as a pair of modern commentators put it, "When faced with famine, we must first find food, then question its cost. If like Abraham and Sarah, we are forced to choose between the chastity of our marriage and survival, we must choose survival."[118] Although the course Abram and Sarai chose entailed great risks, some of which came so close to being realized that divine intervention became necessary, the narrator has nothing negative to say about what took place. They did what they could. Had there not been divine intervention, it would have ended badly but they nonetheless might have survived, and as long as they lived there was hope for the future, no matter how bleak the present. Humbled and awed by the experience, Abram gladly took his nearly lost wife and departed in silence from the presence of the pharaoh, a silence more expressive than a torrent of words.

For his part, the king was determined to close the matter without further incident. He wanted Abram and Sarai safely out of Egypt, and provided them with a royal escort to make sure that nothing happened to them or their household until they crossed the frontier. The king, who might have had Abram killed had he not been afraid to antagonize the gods, also permitted Abram to retain all the gifts that had been lavished upon him on account of Sarai, probably including the young female attendant Hagar whom, it is assumed by some commentators, he had given Sarai. He also made sure that Abram left nothing of his own behind so that there might be no excuse for him either to delay his departure or for him to return later.[119] The king himself surely felt that he too was playing a part in some cosmic drama that he neither understood nor liked. He was anxious for the whole affair to come to a definitive end with the safe departure of Abram and Sarai from his territory.

> 13.1 *And Abram went up out of Egypt, he, and his wife, and all that he had, and Lot with him, into the South.* 13.2 *And Abram was very rich in cattle, in silver, and in gold.* 13.3 *And he went on his journeys from the South even to Beth-el, unto the place where his tent had been at the beginning, between Beth-el and Ai;* 13.4 *unto the place of the altar, which he had made there at first; and Abram called there on the name of YHVH.*

It is not clear just how long Abram's stay in Egypt endured, and a wide range of conjecture in this regard is to be found in a variety of ancient literary sources.[120] However, since there is no further biblical reference to the famine in Cisjordan, it would appear that it had run its course, or at least had been mitigated to the extent that Abram was able to return without being subjected to the same conditions that caused him to go to Egypt in the first place. In any case, Abram, along with his entire entourage and possessions, left Egypt to return to the land of the divine promise.

The biblical author notes specifically, albeit almost as an afterthought, that Abram's nephew Lot also went up from Egypt with him. This is somewhat surprising since we were not previously informed that Lot had accompanied Abram to Egypt. Presumably this was to be taken for granted because Lot had attached himself to Abram since their original departure from Haran. Now, by explicitly advising us that Lot also went up from Egypt, the biblical writer appears to be subtly suggesting to the reader that Lot, as will be seen shortly, emerged from Egypt no longer simply as the heir apparent of Abram and a member of his household, but rather as an autonomous figure in his own right, one no longer subservient to Abram in any significant manner.[121]

Abram had gone down to Egypt as a man of considerable material substance. As an unforeseen and unintended outcome of the episode with the Egyptian ruler, he emerged from the country with significantly enhanced wealth. The very size of his herds and the need for forage made relocation cumbersome and difficult. Still, Abram pressed onward, slowly retracing his steps back to the mountain site between Beth-el and Ai where he had previously established his base. There he had built a permanent altar to God and had begun to preach about the fundamental truths of monotheism after the theophany that took place at the terebinth of Moreh on the outskirts of Shechem. Now he was returning to the place from which his Egyptian misadventure began. The biblical author is silent with regard to why Abram chose to return to that mountain site, and his very silence would seem to suggest that the answer to this question is so self-evident as not to require any explication.

The misadventure of Abram and Sarai in Egypt almost resulted in disaster despite Abram's plans, which only proved adequate for the problems he could foresee. He and Sarai had escaped unscathed from their mishap, not as a result of their own efforts but rather because of the providential divine intervention into their affairs. To Abram this was a clear sign of divine favor, evidence of the immutability of the divine promise to him. Once delivered from a situation of utter helplessness and anguish, Abram decided to work his way back to the place where he had basked in the exhilaration of the theophany he had been privileged to experience. As suggested earlier, although that astounding event took place at the terebinth of Moreh, near Shechem, where he erected an altar as a memorial, it was only outside the corrupting influences of the nearby city that he could with untrammeled fervor once more proclaim the sovereignty of God over the universe, and for this reason he chose to return to the site near Beth-el. Perhaps it also reflected Abram's wish to efface the memory of all that happened to him since he first worshipped at that site, and in a sense to begin afresh with renewed faith in God and confidence in his mission.

Another obstacle, but only one of many that still lay ahead, had been surmounted in Abram's preparation for his role as progenitor and patriarch of the new civilization that was to derive from him.

4

Abram and Lot: Irreconcilable Differences

As suggested earlier, childless and without any realistic prospect of having children of their own, Abram and Sarai had most likely adopted Lot as their son and Abram's presumptive heir. True, Abram had been promised that he would be the progenitor of a great nation, but it was never made explicit that he was to fulfill this role in a physical as well as in a spiritual sense. It would not be surprising then if Abram had assumed, quite naturally, that his descendants were to be his spiritual offspring, perhaps physically originating from his familial bloodline through his adopted nephew Lot. However, it had subsequently been made clear to Abram that Lot would in fact not be his heir with respect to the divine promise concerning the land that was to be given to his descendants, but Abram may still have harbored hopes that Lot might nonetheless serve as his spiritual successor. Now, even in the latter regard Abram was about to be put to another test of his resolve to follow the path set for him by God notwithstanding the seemingly overwhelming obstacles to be placed in his way. Lot, through whom Abram probably expected his civilization building goals to be pursued and ultimately fulfilled, had become alienated from him, at least in Abram's perception of the situation. In effect, Lot rejected the role of spiritual heir for which Abram had earmarked him.

It would appear that Lot was able to reap substantial benefit from his sojourn in Egypt, probably as a direct result of the favor shown to Abram by the king on account of Sarai. As a member of Abram's immediate family and his heir, Lot somehow managed to accumulate a significant amount of wealth in his own right. Although the biblical writer does not provide any clues as to how this came about, legend sought to fill the gap with suggestions that Lot contrived to capitalize on the fact that the Egyptian king had shown favor to his uncle, perhaps by casting himself in the role of an agent of influence with access to the royal palace, that is, through what has become known as influence peddling. Regardless of the dubious provenance of such speculation, the point it seems to be making is that there is reason to believe that Lot may have preferred to remain in Egypt, where he was prospering, rather than return to the uncertainties of a Cisjordan undergoing the throes of political struggle and disruptive population movements. We may assume, however, that this option was foreclosed by the king's desire that no vestige of Abram's presence remain in his country after the incident with Sarai. Accordingly, Lot, whom the Egyptians may have viewed as an appendage to Abram, likely had no choice but to return to Cisjordan with his uncle.

> [13.5] *And Lot also, who went with Abram, had flocks, and herds, and tents.* [13.6] *And the land was not able to bear them, that they might dwell together; for their substance was great, so that they could not dwell together.* [13.7] *And there was a strife between the herdmen of Abram's cattle and the herdmen of Lot's cattle. And the Canaanite and the Perizzite dwelt then in the land.*

As suggested, perhaps compelled by circumstances to leave Egypt with Abram, Lot emerged from there a man of substantial means and, apparently, no longer economically dependent on his uncle. As time passed, he became increasingly less concerned about his status as Abram's legal heir, an attitude perhaps conditioned to some extent by his uncle's evidently robust health. And, as will become evident from subsequent events, he was by no means deeply committed to Abram's beliefs and ideals. Lot's developing estrangement from Abram would seem to have grown in step with his increasing economic independence.

Barely recovered from the anguish and trauma of his misadventure in Egypt, Abram now found himself challenged from within his camp in a manner that might negate everything he had worked for since leaving Haran. Lot, his spiritual heir presumptive, was turning away from him. The objective circumstances with which Abram had to cope merely provided a convenient rationale for finalizing the rupture with Lot that had begun earlier, perhaps while they were still in Egypt. But, if now left without an heir, how would God's promises to him be fulfilled? Abram could not but have felt that he was again undergoing some sort of trial, the purpose of which was not at all clear to him at the time, but which obviously constituted a new test of his faith and resolve. Consistent with his strength of both character and commitment, Abram's faith did not falter even for a moment. Despite considerable cause for doubt, he evidently remained convinced that God's promises would somehow be carried out.

As time passed, the relationship between Abram and Lot deteriorated to the point where any further procrastination in dealing with what was rapidly becoming an untenable situation would clearly be counterproductive. It was essential that some accommodation between them be reached, and, if this were not possible, then a definitive parting of their ways would be required. In describing the problem that precipitated the break between Abram and Lot, the biblical author adds the seemingly enigmatic comment that *the Canaanite and the Perizzite dwelt then in the land*, the significance of which requires some analysis.

Presumably, it was during the period of Abram's stay in Egypt that the Canaanites and the Perizzites began to extend their control from the low-lying areas of the countryside to the foothills of the central range, impinging on the area where Abram originally had established his base. The mutual competition between these conquering peoples had the net effect of further diminishing the pasturage available to small unaligned groups such as those headed by Abram and Lot, who needed to expand beyond the confines of their common center in the hill country. Clearly, as the Canaanite-Perizzite struggle for dominance intensified, each group would attempt to define its boundaries or areas of control as broadly as possible to allow for continued growth. As this process took place, the presence in the area of the combined herds and flocks of Abram and Lot and their households represented a third force that might ultimately be capable of upsetting whatever delicate political balance the Canaanites and Perizzites achieved. The problem was further exacerbated by the continuing influx of other groups that also were land hungry. The growing need to partition the land between these competitors for pasturage left fewer and fewer open areas to meet the needs of Abram and Lot. If they were to maintain the economic viability of their households they would either have to act in concert, confronting their new neighbors as a force to be reckoned with, or diminish their presence in the area.

Notwithstanding these considerations, some viable arrangements might yet have been worked out between Abram and Lot had there been a basic mutual desire to do so. However, a concomitant of Lot's financial independence was his rejection of Abram's spiritual leadership and the latter's insistence that it was necessary for them to maintain a significant degree of cultural alienation from the surrounding peoples. The tension between Abram and Lot began to spread beyond them to their households as well. This resulted in *"strife between the herdmen of Abram's cattle and the herdmen of Lot's cattle,"* each rallying behind their respective masters. The mutual accommodations that are natural to members of a common group were no longer feasible as their mutual antagonisms intensified. Reconciliation soon seemed beyond their reach, and it became obvious to all that a separation was essential if each were to continue to thrive.

Objective circumstances were such as to favor a break between Abram and Lot. For one thing, they could not avoid being eyed with concern by the surrounding peoples. Cisjordan, as indicated, was still in a state of seemingly endless political turmoil and the presence of a clan with the combined wealth of Abram and Lot represented a force with which the region's power brokers had to reckon. For this reason, *"the land was not able to bear them, that they might dwell together."* The *land*, in this instance, may be understood not only as a reference to the actual ground that could not support the volume of sheep and cattle they may have possessed but also as a reference to the leaders of the people of the land, who viewed their combined wealth and the strength it gave them as a threat to the existing political order. This in turn posed a serious challenge to Abram's desire to remain dissociated from the general social environment in order that he might be able to pursue his inspired mission without having to deal with external societal constraints. It has also been suggested that Abram feared that if word got out about the emerging conflict between him and Lot it might be perceived as a sign of weakness and possibly precipitate adventurism on the part of the Canaanite and Perizzite leaders.[122]

Despite these weighty considerations, Abram was evidently more concerned about the potential damage from the mounting dissension within the camp he now shared with Lot than from the external forces that might be brought to bear on him. He therefore deemed it prudent to separate his and Lot's holdings to reduce the unintended effects of the disputes between them on the morale of their respective followers, notwithstanding the risks this entailed of becoming directly involved in regional politics and the power struggles that were taking place in the area.[123] At the same time, although Abram may have preferred to continue to use the site between Beth-el and Ai as his home base, it soon became apparent that the available pasturage in the area was insufficient for their combined flocks and herds. As a practical matter, *their substance was great, so that they could not dwell together.* Moreover, once they separated and effectively split their forces, it seemed likely that the Canaanites and Perizzites would attempt to encroach on their grazing areas and water sources, making it difficult if not impossible to remain where they were without constant struggle with their neighbors.[124] Since Abram and Lot were moving apart rather than coming together, the only practical option before them became self-evident—they would have to separate as well as to relocate.

It would seem that since it was Lot who had initiated the change in his relationship with Abram, it would also be up to him to initiate the break that now appeared necessary. However, Lot actually had little incentive to do so. Despite the growing incompatibility with his uncle, he was still heir to Abram's estate. Although he had become independently wealthy and was therefore not dependent on any forthcoming legacy for his economic security, Lot showed little inclination to sever his ties to Abram. For one thing, living with Abram afforded him greater physical security than he could have mustered on his own, and in the highly turbulent political environment of a country in turmoil, such additional security could not be discounted lightly.

Abram certainly understood from Lot's demeanor that the hopes he had placed in his nephew as his spiritual heir were vain. It was not Lot who would continue the work that Abram began. Still, even if Abram could no longer view Lot as his son, he nonetheless remained a close relative, a nephew, and as such Abram continued to harbor warm feelings toward him. As a result, it fell to Abram, as painful as it undoubtedly must have been for him, to make the first move.

> 13.8 *And Abram said unto Lot: 'Let there be no strife, I pray thee, between me and thee, and between my herdmen and thy herdmen; for we are brethren.*

Abram confronted Lot about the ill feelings that pervaded the atmosphere, which he fervently wished to eliminate. He urged, *Let there be no strife between me and thee*, effectively addressing Lot as an equal, a clear sign that he wished to reach an accommodation with him. As a practical matter, eliminating the contention between them meant the acknowledgement by Abram that Lot was free to pursue his own lights and was no longer bound by the constraints that were imposed on him as Abram's heir. However, it soon became evident that even though Abram and Lot might have been able to reach an accommodation on a personal level, it seemed unlikely that it would eliminate the tensions that existed and were building among their respective households and retinues, which were only being exacerbated further by the increasingly obvious change of Lot's status relative to Abram. It ultimately became clear to Abram that there was little prospect that the budding strife between their respective households could be resolved or even severely constrained, and allowing such a volatile situation to fester served neither Abram's or Lot's interests, either on the personal level or because of the appearance of weakness it might suggest to the surrounding peoples. It has been suggested that Abram may have been concerned that the growing disputes between his men and those of Lot might be perceived as an irreparable breach between them that meant that one would not support the other in a time of crisis, as was expected, *for we are brethren*, who may quarrel but will nonetheless support each other against third parties.[125] It was thus important for both to maintain a public face of unity, even if the only practical solution of the problem between them were to be a complete physical separation between their respective households and animal stock. Again taking the initiative, Abram suggested to Lot that, despite the increasing colonization of the region by the Canaanites, there still remained substantial stretches of pastureland that were as yet unsettled. He therefore invited Lot to separate from him, and as a further inducement to do so Abram tells him that he, Lot, may have first choice with regard to the area where he may elect to resettle.

> [13.9] *Is not the whole land before thee? separate thyself, I pray thee, from me; if thou wilt take the left hand, then I will go to the right; or if thou take the right hand, then I will go to the left.*

Abram assured him that he would respect Lot's choice and would in no way encroach on him. Regardless of the direction Lot chose to go, Abram would remain at some distance from him. However, separation did not mean that Abram intended to completely sever their personal relationship. Although no longer his heir, Lot nonetheless remained a member of his extended family, and as such Abram was committed to come to his defense or aid should the need arise.

Once Abram had taken the initiative by asking Lot to leave him, the latter no longer had any realistic option other than to comply with his uncle's wish, particularly since Abram's additional assurances probably assuaged his primary concerns about security. Moreover, as already indicated, it was also evident to both that a separation would in any case become necessary sooner or later because the available grazing and pasture in the area where they now found themselves, the hill country between Beth-el and Ai, was no longer adequate for their combined needs. Despite Abram's wish to remain in close proximity to the site of the altar he had reestablished there after his return from Egypt, he would soon be forced by objective circumstances to abandon the area. By asking Lot to leave first, and allowing him to choose to settle in whatever lands most appealed to him, Abram effectively granted his nephew a bonus which could be viewed as compensation for the inheritance Lot might now have to forego. The proposal was acceptable to Lot and he agreed to the separation.

The only question that remained was the direction in which Lot would relocate. As Abram put it, *if thou wilt take the left hand, then I will go to the right; or if thou take the right hand, then I will go to the left.* The options Abram proposed require some analysis. Which direction is represented by the left hand, and which direction by the right? The answer, of course depends on one's point of reference. What was Abram's point of reference? Today, we would normally assume that the point of reference is north, because that is the point of reference for the magnetic compass. But what was it in antiquity, before such an instrument was conceived and developed? It seems most likely that geographical orientation in antiquity was in the direction of the rising of the sun—to the east. Accordingly, what Abram is telling Lot is that he can choose to move northward, that is, to the left, or he may move southward, to the right. Abram is therefore assuming that Lot, after spending such a long time under his wing, shared his concern about remaining in the less populated hill country, a geographical preference that reflected Abram's commitment to isolate himself as much as possible from centers of paganism, as discussed earlier, rather than establishing his domicile in the more populated lowlands to the west and east.[126]

It has been suggested that there is an element of disingenuousness in Abram's approach to dealing with Lot. After all, Abram had already received the divine promise that the land of Cisjordan was to become the patrimony of his descendants (Gen. 12:7), so that allowing Lot to settle where he chose in it would be of little consequence in the long run because, no matter what he chose, it would have no effect on the ultimate disposition of the land.[127] Nonetheless, it was still a magnanimous gesture on the part of Abram to permit Lot to choose first the area to which he would relocate, since doing so could result in considerable hardship for Abram in the short run.

To his chagrin, Abram soon learned that he was mistaken about his nephew, that in fact Lot did not share a common perspective with him. Instead of moving either north or south, Lot would chose to move to the east, an option that Abram never seriously considered.[128]

> [13.10] *And Lot lifted up his eyes, and beheld all the plain of the Jordan, that it was well watered every where, before the Lord destroyed Sodom and Gomorrah, like the garden of the Lord, like the land of Egypt, as thou goest unto Zoar.* [13.11] *So Lot chose him all the plain of the Jordan; and Lot journeyed east; and they separated themselves the one from the other.* [13.12] *Abram dwelt in the land of Canaan, and Lot dwelt in the cities of the Plain, and moved his tent as far as Sodom.*

It has been pointed out that the biblical writer has very subtly been signaling all along that, despite Abram's hopes and expectations, Lot was never destined to be his spiritual heir.[129] This may be seen in a number of earlier passages in the narrative, in which the biblical author portrays the relationship between Abram and his nephew as becoming increasingly distant over time, changes that are subtly reflected in the context and word order in which the two are mentioned together. Thus, at the outset we are told, *And Terah took Abram his son, and Lot the son of Haran, his son's son, and Sarai his daughter-in-law, his son Abram's wife* (Gen. 11:31). Terah is the principal actor here, and the order of those he took with them reflects their relative standing in his view. The order given is Abram, Lot, and Sarah. A few verses later, we are told, *Abram went, as YHVH had spoken unto him, and Lot went with him* (Gen. 12:4). Here, both Abraham and Lot are equally the actors, joining in a common enterprise. But in the very next verse, a significant change takes place. *And Abram took Sarai his wife, and Lot his brother's son* (Gen. 12:5). Now it is Abram alone who is the actor, taking Sarai and Lot along with him, in that order of significance. After their subsequent sojourn in Egypt, a most dramatic change in their relationship is indicated. *And Abram went up out of Egypt, he, and his wife, and all that he had, and Lot with him* (Gen. 13:1). Here the order is Abram, Sarai, their possessions, and Lot. Lot is placed in a position of less significance than Abram's baggage. The distance that has emerged between the two men is now patent and comes to its logical conclusion in Abram's effective albeit reluctant severance of their now almost completely estranged relationship. Freed from further consideration of Abram's preferences, Lot clearly pursues a course that Abram could hardly approve of.

From the vantage point of one of the hills in the area, Lot surveyed the land about him as far as the horizon. Off to the east he spotted the verdant plain of the Jordan which was well watered by offshoots and feeders of the river, which the biblical author notes, parenthetically, is the way it was as far south as the ancient Egyptian frontier fortress of Zoar, at the edge of the desert, in the period prior to the destruction of Sodom and Gomorrah.[130] The plain was considered to have been lush and fertile as the Garden of Eden, which was also watered by the rivers that traversed it. But perhaps most important for Lot, it resembled the rich alluvial plain of the Nile that had so impressed him during his stay in Egypt.[131] *So Lot chose him all the plain of the Jordan*, as the region in which he would pitch his camp and pasture his herds and flocks.

It is noteworthy that Abram and Lot would appear to have very different perspectives on the significance and function of the land, and this helps us understand why Abram seemed so unconcerned about what area Lot might choose for his settlement. As one writer put it: "Where Lot sees land as pastures, more or less fit for grazing, Abraham sees the Land as a marker of his spiritual and intellectual life...Abraham sees the Land as whole and as representational. For him, geography is symbolic, intellectual, sublime."[132] His mission is to build a new nation and civilization, and Cisjordan as a whole, despite the various peoples that were presently in control of segments of it, was to be its provenance. It probably never occurred to Abram that Lot might seek to relocate to the very frontiers of Cisjordan, the territory generally held to be bounded by the Mediterranean in the west and the Jordan River and the Dead Sea to the east.

Lot moved eastward from their common site in the hill country, *and they separated themselves the one from the other.* For the time being, Abram remained in place, even though his place of domicile was rapidly coming within the Canaanite sphere of influence. The biblical writer points out that Lot initially relocated to vicinity of the cities of the plain, thus drawing a sharp contrast to Abram who continued to avoid unnecessary contact with any of the nearby population centers. In this subtle manner the reader is advised that Lot clearly did not fully share Abram's perspective on questions of public and private morality or social purpose, which argued for a degree of isolation from pagan cultures. By contrast, Lot seemed rather eager to assimilate into the general culture of the area. As a result, it was not long before we find Lot moving farther south towards the metropolis of the Jordan plain, the sister cities of Sodom and Gomorrah.[133] Interestingly, Lot did not immediately settle in Sodom itself. He remained on its outskirts, continuing to use his tent as his residence. As far as the Sodomites were concerned, Lot was an alien. It would take some time before he was able to gain their acceptance and eventually move into the city itself.

At this point, the biblical writer offers some further vindication of Abram's decision to disinherit Lot, who would no longer be heir to his property once he effectively disqualified himself from serving as Abram's spiritual heir. He does this by a terse evaluation of the people of Sodom, with whom Lot voluntarily chose to associate himself.

[12.13] *Now the men of Sodom were wicked and sinners against YHVH exceedingly.*

This characterization of the Sodomites allows us to sketch out a rough picture of their society, which was the very antithesis of the society Abram sought to establish. The term, "wicked," relates to a moral stance, especially with regard to human relations. Wickedness is a conscious acting out of the will, the deliberate choice of harmful behavior toward another fellow human.[134] The most telling indication of this in the text before us is that Lot initially remained outside the city, living in his tent instead of a house within its walls. There is no reason to assume that Lot had any compunction about residing in Sodom. After all, we have been told explicitly that Lot had been a resident of the cities of the plain, of which Sodom was but one. Yet Lot remained outside. Why? Presumably, it was because he had no choice in the matter. The implication of this is that what was at work there was a basic antipathy to strangers, a negativity that will be described in greater detail later on in the story. Lot does not move into the city because he is not welcome there; he may conduct business there but is unable to reside there until much later. Although we may reasonably assume that Sodom, located in the rich Jordan plain, was a wealthy city, it was unwilling to offer its hospitality to the stranger who appeared at its gates.

Furthermore, the biblical author characterizes the Sodomites as sinful. The implication of this is that they forgot the fundamental truth that man, though part of nature, transcends nature in his spiritual aspect, which is constituted to reflect the image of his divine creator. To the extent that man is able to exercise effective control of the natural animal aspect of his being, he remains human, a true reflection of the divine image. However, when man allows himself to surrender to the animal within him, succumbing to the dominance of natural drives which, when indulged in without conscious control by man's rational faculty result in vice, he becomes a sinner. And the Sodomites were *were wicked and sinners against the Lord exceedingly.* They were morally bankrupt, voluptuaries who chose to thrive on vice. They perverted the divine image in man, leaving him without a trace of humanity, which, we are being told, is also an offense against God.

Nonetheless, it was to such a society that Lot, since youth a valued member of Abram's household and presumably nurtured and educated to be his spiritual heir, chose to become affiliated. Clearly, the gulf between Abram and Lot was becoming ever wider. However, as will be seen shortly, Lot nonetheless retained some of that which he had imbibed from Abram. Thus, by comparison with the Sodomites among whom he elected to live, Lot may have stood out as a paragon of virtue.

How did all this affect Abram? After the rupture between him and Lot, Abram was in desperate need of further reassurance that he still found favor with God, and that nothing had changed with regard to his mission, even though he was now without an obvious heir. Lot represented the only direct physical link between the childless Abram and those descendants who were to inherit the land allocated to him in the divine promise. Lot's departure could not but have been a severe blow to him, one that put his faith in God to a new test. Although Abram never wavered in this regard, he was clearly distressed over the rational impossibility of the promise being realized without some sort of further divine intervention. To relieve his distress, God once again spoke to him:

> 13.14 *And YHVH said unto Abram, after that Lot was separated from him: 'Lift up now thine eyes, and look from the place where thou art, northward and southward and eastward and westward;* 13.15 *for all the land which thou seest, to thee will I give it, and to thy seed for ever.*

In his mind's ear, Abram now heard the familiar voice that he now was convinced was not simply his imagination. It was God speaking to him through the medium of his imagination. It was a voice that gave him the reassurance he so wanted, and advised him implicitly that his hopes in Lot were misplaced from the very outset. His nephew was never intended to be the vehicle by which Abram's great enterprise would come to fruition in the generations to come. The very fact that the voice had not spoken to Abram since his return from Egypt until after the departure of Lot seemed to be an indication that his break with his nephew was essential to creating the appropriate psychological environment for the divine communication. The prospect of Lot's presumed status as Abram's spiritual heir had placed the entire plan in jeopardy. Now that he was gone, the immediate danger had passed, but Abram was once again anxious about how his line would be continued without a direct heir.

It was at this point that he received the reassuring but simultaneously perplexing message. From where Abram stood, near Beth-el some 900 meters above sea level, one can see vast areas of the country, including those parts of the Jordan Valley that Lot had selected as his homestead, and it was from that vantage point that he was told that, for as far as his eye could see in all directions, *all the land which thou seest, to thee will I give it, and to thy seed for ever*. That is, figuratively speaking, all the land as far the horizon in all directions was to be his patrimony, which also presumably included some of the land east of the Jordan. The divine communication not only confirmed that which was promised earlier, it went farther. It asserted that not only would Abram's descendants inherit the land, but also that it would remain their inheritance forever, implicitly asserting that they were to be granted an eternally valid claim to the land whether they actually occupied it or not. Furthermore, it stated that the land that Abram's descendants would inherit in the future, that is the land they would at some point take physical possession of, had already been designated as their patrimony through the divine gift of it to Abram. In other words, whereas Abram had earlier been promised that the land would be given to his direct descendants, but not to him, he is now told that the land is to be given to him, as well as to his descendants after him as their eternal patrimony. But why is there this change in the language of the divine commitment? It has been suggested that as long as Lot was perceived as Abram's spiritual heir, there was a danger that he might be commonly viewed as

Abram's legal heir as well, and this was not the divine intent. However, once Lot had effectively disqualified himself from being Abram's heir in any respect, there was no longer any danger in awarding title to the land to Abram during his lifetime since there were none yet alive that could claim it as their inheritance, because if Lot, who was in fact a blood relative of Abram, could not make such a claim neither could any of the completely unrelated people who had become followers of Abram's teachings.[135]

The divine message also presented Abram with a subtle but crucial distinction, that between ownership and actual possession at any point in time, a distinction of enormous importance to the biblical author. Abram is to be given ownership of a land that he not only does not possess, but one that he will not possess during his lifetime. Nonetheless, he is instructed to go out and take a good look at it, walk through it and get the feel of it. He is told that it is his even though it is currently occupied by the Canaanites. They may have temporary possession of it, but the ownership is Abram's to pass on to his descendants.

Then, in carefully constructed phrases that bear several layers of meaning, Abram is told that he, who as yet does not have a single son to serve as his heir, will be the progenitor of innumerable descendants.

> 13.16 *And I will make thy seed as the dust of the earth; so that if a man can number the dust of the earth, then shall thy seed also be numbered.*

One cannot but wonder what Abram made out of this strangely worded simile. Does it mean that Abram's seed are literally to be as numerous as the dust of the earth? Or, is it to be understood as indicating that their number will be so great throughout the course of history that Abram's line will never cease, just as one cannot envision an end to the dust of the earth? In either case, the simile is problematic, its implications quite unclear.

However, the simile may also be understood as conveying a much more profound message than merely assuring Abram that he will have a lot of descendants. When the Creator made man, He first gathered the dust of the earth and formed him, and then blew the breath of life into man transforming him from an inert mass into a living being (Gen. 2:7). It may be that Abram is now being told in this oblique manner that it is the mission of his descendants to serve as the life-giving counterpart to the dust of the earth, which is mankind without the divine spirit. It will be the responsibility of Abram's seed to serve as the divine surrogate, to infuse material man with the spirit of the "image." And, in order to accomplish this task, his progeny will be as numerous, in the language of the simile, as the dust of the earth. The additional implication of this understanding of the text is that Abram is also being assured that the mission of his descendants will continue throughout the entire course of human history, requiring that their aggregate number will ultimately be innumerable if not infinite. In other words, the biblical statement may be understood as asserting that the line of Abram's descendants will continue for as long as humankind continues to exist. After being given this assurance regarding the future of his enterprise, he is given an additional instruction regarding the land he is to inherit.

> 13.17 *Arise, walk through the land, in the length of it and in the breadth of it; for unto thee will I give it.*

Abram is told, in effect, to move about the land and familiarize himself with every corner of what is to be his territorial patrimony. However, there is another more dramatic implication of the divine instruction that Abram clearly seems to have taken as his guidance for the foreseeable future; one that would cause him renewed anguish. He was not merely to make a general survey of the land before settling in some part of it. As Abram evidently understood it, judging from what he subsequently did, he was to live as a sojourner in the land; he was not to establish permanent roots in any one place, despite the fact that he had just been told that the land was to be his, and not only to be later given to his descendants.[136] He would have to continue to live and prosper at the sufferance of others, knowing that what they permitted him to do with the usufruct of the land as a privilege he had already been granted as a right. Once again, Abram accepted this new disconcerting revelation with continued trust in the God who spoke to him.

On the positive side, the revelation also had an immediately beneficial implication. Having now been given assurance that all the land that he could see in every direction was to be his legacy, Abram no longer felt a compelling need to remain in the vicinity of the site between Beth-el and Ai, and was now free to relocate to other parts of the land that were better able to meet his practical needs for space and pasturage for his flocks and herds.

> 13.18 *And Abram moved his tent, and came and dwelt by the terebinths of Mamre, which are in Hebron, and built there an altar unto YHVH.*

Abram soon relocated some distance away from the central hill country of Cisjordan to a point in the southern hill country, in the vicinity of the town that would later be called Hebron, setting up his camp at the nearby terebinths of

Mamre.[137] There are two noteworthy points that are being made in this statement. First, *Abram moved his tent* to this new location. As will be pointed out again later, Abram, presumably following the guidance he had just received, did not take up permanent residence there but continued to live in a tent, as a semi-nomad. Second, when he earlier first arrived at the terebinth of Moreh near Shechem, where, as the biblical author tells us, he first experienced a theophany, he subsequently felt compelled to remove himself to a site more distant from any large population center. There he could declaim in the name of the Lord without concern about being viewed as the priest of just another pagan sect. Now, armed with renewed confidence in himself and in his capacity to assert the truth of his belief in God and the implications of monotheism, he was no longer concerned about proclaiming his beliefs in close proximity to a site of pagan worship, such as the sacred grove of the terebinths of Mamre, *and built there an altar unto YHVH*.

Although Abram would not settle even temporarily in Hebron itself for the same reasons that he would not settle in Shechem, he no longer felt the need for the more extreme isolation that he sought when he expected Lot to be his heir, when he was concerned about the possible corrupting influences that the Canaanite practices might exercise on his nephew. In a sense, Abram may now have felt that since the land had been promised to him personally, those who practiced paganism there were the intruders and that as a consequence the best place for him to proclaim his beliefs was at the very site that they considered sacred. However, chastened by his earlier experiences in such regard, we must assume that Abram now approached his advocacy of monotheism in a positive and not a negative manner. That is, to maintain civil relations with the surrounding society, he surely avoided any overt criticism of their prevailing religious beliefs and practices while affirming his own. He thus approached his mission with renewed confidence and zeal, but tempered by prudence. It was surely such an approach that enabled him, wisely, to establish more than just cordial relations with the political leaders of the area; he was also able to form strong bonds with them that would serve him well in the years to come.

5

Abram the Warrior

It was not long after Abram had established his new base at Hebron that he was to be tested once again, this time in a manner far different from the trials he had previously undergone. The land his descendants were to inherit and upon which their new civilization and society were to be built would make great demands on its possessors. Both from the standpoint of its physical and its sociological environments great fortitude and resolve would be required of its masters. Abram had already tasted the bitterness of famine, which had forced him temporarily to abandon the country for Egypt. He was now to experience the vicissitudes of a land that served as the land bridge between Mesopotamia and Egypt, a land plagued with endemic political instability. To survive and prosper here would require determination and boldness; qualities without which the new society for which Abram strove to lay the groundwork would remain but a vain dream.

In an unusual digression from his very focused approach to the narrative, the biblical author describes very tersely the complex political environment into which Abram was to be drawn unwittingly as a consequence of his lingering attachment to and concern for the welfare of his nephew Lot, with whom he presumably maintained sporadic contact.

> 14.1 *And it came to pass in the days of Amraphel king of Shinar, Arioch king of Ellasar, Chederlaomer king of Elam, and Tidal king of Goiim,* 14.2 *that they made war with Bera king of Sodom, and with Birsha king of Gomorrah,*[138] *Shinab king of Admah, and Shemeber king of Zeboiim, and the king of Bela—the same is Zoar.* 14.3 *All these came as allies unto the vale of Siddim—the same is the Salt Sea.* 14.4 *Twelve years they served Chederlaomer, and in the thirteenth year they rebelled.*

It appears that some fourteen years earlier, probably even before Abram left Haran for Cisjordan, an expeditionary force dispatched by an alliance of Mesopotamian kings had attempted an invasion of Egypt that evidently was repulsed, reflecting but another of a long series of conflicts between Egypt and the ruling powers in Mesopotamia that took place throughout the ancient history of the region. In the course of their march on Egypt, the expeditionary force probably came down the King's Highway[139] in Transjordan and then crossed the Jordan valley, where they subjugated the Sodom-dominated confederation of five city-states located at its southern end.[140] The biblical writer appears to be informing us that the rulers of this confederation of city-states had convened in *the vale of Siddim*, where they concluded a peace treaty with the leaders of the Mesopotamian alliance, under which they agreed to acknowledge the suzerainty of the king of Elam, to whom they were required to pay an annual tribute. For a period of twelve years, during which time Abram had immigrated to Cisjordan and sojourned in Egypt, the confederated city-states observed their obligations under the treaty and paid the required annual tribute. However, during that same period they also proceeded to reconstitute their military capabilities in anticipation of the day when they would be able to throw off the foreign yoke. Finally, in the thirteenth year of their vassalage, they concluded that they were sufficiently strong to repudiate their subservience to Elam, which they clearly signaled by a refusal to continue to pay the annual tribute, an act that constituted open rebellion against their previously acknowledged suzerain. This, of course, was a frontal challenge that the Mesopotamian alliance could not permit to go unanswered.

> [14.5] *And in the fourteenth year came Chederlaomer and the kings that were with him, and smote the Rephaim in Ashteroth-karnaim, and the Zuzim in Ham, and the Emim in Shaveh-kiriathaim,* [14.6] *and the Horites in their mount Seir, unto El-paran, which is by the wilderness.* [14.7] *And they turned back, and came to En-mishpat—the same is Kadesh—and smote all the country of the Amalekites, and also the Amorites, that dwelt in Hazazon-tamar.*

Once it became clear that the Sodomite-led confederation was in open rebellion, the Mesopotamian alliance mobilized a new army to mount a punitive expedition against the confederation and to re-impose Elamite suzerainty in the Jordan valley. It evidently took some time to organize and outfit such an expeditionary force, and, in the fourteenth year, that is, at about the same time that Abram had reluctantly become directly involved in the political dynamics of the region, the king of Elam, together with his allies mounted the anticipated punitive expedition against the city-states of the Jordan plain, in an effort to restore the political *status quo ante*.

With the reasonable expectation that the Mesopotamian alliance to which they had been subjugated for so long would not allow them to alter their status as vassals unilaterally, the rulers of the city-states needed to take steps in their defense against the anticipated assault. For this purpose, it would appear that they entered into alliances with the semi-nomadic hordes that virtually surrounded the plain, purchasing their services and thereby effectively creating a series of buffer zones through which the armies of the Mesopotamian alliance would have to fight their way before reaching the Jordan plain. As a result, Chederlaomer, the Elamite leader of the alliance, and his allies had to dispose of these buffer forces before being able to compel the city-states of the plain to submit to them once again and renew the presumably substantial tribute that they had previously paid.

The biblical author tells us very briefly that the Mesopotamian forces swept down the eastern flank of the Jordan once again, defeating in succession the Rephaim, Zuzim, Emim, and Horites, then turned westward skirting the wilderness of Paran and continued in a northwesterly direction until they encountered and defeated the Amalekites at Kadesh. They then swung in a northeasterly direction and overran the Amorite enclave at Hazazon-tamar (Ein Gedi) in the hills west of the Dead Sea. Having thus eliminated the protective ring around the city-states of the Jordan plain, the Mesopotamian forces were now poised for a direct assault on the home territory of the Sodomite-led confederation. Abram's large encampment, located in the hill country farther to the west, remained effectively isolated and untouched by the turmoil that engulfed the southern and eastern parts of the country. It would also appear from the narrative, that the Mesopotamian forces stopped to rest and recuperate from the arduous battles against the various hostile tribes of the region before mounting what would be the final stage of the entire campaign. This, in effect, gave the Sodomite-led confederation the opportunity to seize the initiative with harassing attacks on the encamped Mesopotamian forces, further sapping their strength and hoping to draw the weakened invading army onto a battlefield of their choosing.

> 14.8 *And there went out the king of Sodom, and the king of Gomorrah, and the king of Admah, and the king of Zeboiim, and the king of Bela—the same is Zoar; and the set the battle in array against them in the vale of Siddim;* 14.9 *against Chederlaomer king of Elam, and Tidal king of Goiim, and Amraphel king of Shinar, and Arioch king of Ellasar; four kings against the five.* 14.10 *Now the vale of Siddim was full of slime pits; and the kings of Sodom and Gomorrah fled, and they fell there, and they that remained fled to the mountain.* 14.11 *And they took all the goods of Sodom and Gomorrah, and all their victuals, and went their way.*

Adding what may be seen as a touch of historical irony to the situation, the Sodomite-led confederation chose to set the decisive battle with the Mesopotamians in the *vale of Siddim*, the same site where they had acknowledged Elamite suzerainty fourteen years earlier.[141] As a practical matter, the site of the final battle was evidently chosen by the Sodomite-led confederation in the expectation that the terrain there, which contained large numbers of bitumen pits that would limit the mass movement of the attacking forces, could be exploited effectively for defensive purposes. However, it proved of little avail with regard to the ultimate outcome of the battle, and the Sodomite-led confederation was decisively defeated, the kings of Sodom and Gomorrah themselves being subjected to the indignity of having to hide in those same bitumen pits to avoid capture while the remnants of their forces fled for safety to the nearby hills.

Having vanquished all effective opposition, the Elamite-led alliance displayed no interest in destroying the rebellious city-states and thereby losing them as a lucrative source of annual revenue. Instead, they seized all the readily portable wealth of Sodom and Gomorrah, and presumably also that of the other members of the confederation of city-states, as well as all the available food supplies, presumably to limit the need to forage for food on the long march back to Mesopotamia. In effect, they took booty in lieu of the tribute payments that were now two years in arrears, left the cities intact, and began the trek home.

Although the purpose of relating this entire episode relates to what happened next, commentators have been hard pressed to come up with a reasonable explanation of why it is presented in such detail, since it is only of peripheral interest to the story of Abram. However, one medieval commentator provides a perspective on the matter that does neatly tie the episode to subsequent events that are of direct relevance to the spiritual and intellectual odyssey of Abram. What is being described here, according to this view, is the failure of Sodom and its sister cities of the Jordan plain to observe the basic rules of civic behavior, even in matters of state. The Sodomite-led confederation, after having been defeated in battle, and in order to avoid destruction of their cities, had agreed to acknowledge Elamite suzerainty. This allowed them to continue to grow and prosper, their primary obligation to the victors who permitted this to happen being an annual payment of tribute, something quite common and a generally accepted outcome of interstate conflict in antiquity. However, the Sodomite-led confederation of city-states chose to violate their solemn undertaking as soon as they felt they could do so with impunity, and the biblical writer, it is suggested, deems this sort of breach of trust unacceptable.[142] We are not told what the war was about initially, and therefore cannot draw any conclusions about whether it was or was not justified. All we are told is that the Sodomite-led confederation unilaterally abrogated the suzerainty treaty they had previously agreed to, presumably as soon as it became practicable for them to do so; that is, they sacrificed principle to expediency when they found it in their interest to do so, and this clearly illustrated the corrupt nature of their regimes. In other words, one may see in this an early intimation of what would much later become a basic principle for the conduct of all subsequent human relations, whether of individuals and societies or between states, namely, the principle that solemnly undertaken agreements must be honored. Were this principle to be routinely ignored, all international conflicts, whatever their original cause, would eventually become wars of annihilation.

It also appears that by the time the Mesopotamian invasion took place, Lot had already become a resident of Sodom, either because he was finally accepted as worthy of citizenship there, or that he was permitted to move into the city because of the impending war in which his resources could be used to bolster the defense of the city-state. In either case, when the invading forces entered the city and found him, he was taken captive and held for ransom.

> 14.12 *And they took Lot, Abram's brother's son, who dwelt in Sodom, and his goods, and departed.*

Presumably, the Mesopotamian forces, making use of local informants, determined which local residents were likely to command a handsome ransom to be paid by persons whose wealth had escaped confiscation or who resided outside the conquered city-states, and they evidently included Lot among those they considered likely candidates for such redemption from captivity. Since the entire expedition seems to have had a primarily financial purpose, it seemed most appropriate to hold Lot against a high ransom that might be extracted from his by now evidently well-known and rather wealthy uncle, who was reportedly still devoted to him despite their differences and separation. In this regard, it is by no means certain that they planned to take these captives with them back to Mesopotamia, which would have made ransoming the prisoners rather difficult. It seems more likely that they were planning to bring them to a rear staging area somewhere in southern Syria, where communications between them and their ransoming benefactors might be facilitated. In light of what took place subsequently, the location of the staging area was probably in the vicinity of Damascus.

For the ransom scheme to work with regard to Lot, however, it was necessary for his capture to be made known to Abram, and this was evidently soon arranged.

> ^{14.13} *And there came one that had escaped, and told Abram the Hebrew—now he dwelt by the terebinths of Mamre the Amorite, brother of Eshcol, and brother of Aner; and these were confederate with Abram.*

Thus the web was spun that would draw Abram deeply into an affair that was in all essential aspects of little direct interest to him, except that by chance his estranged nephew now desperately needed his help. For Abram, the problem of retrieving his nephew from captivity was complex and posed great dangers for him. Any misstep could render stillborn his dreams of creating a new society.

Abram had established his headquarters near the religious site at the terebinths of Mamre on the outskirts of Hebron, some distance to the west from the Jordan valley. There he prospered and substantially expanded the size of his retinue. To maintain his independence of the neighboring tribes and peoples, it had become necessary for him to be perceived not only as the advocate of a new creed but also as a military power that had to be taken into account by the local political leaders. It may have been to emphasize this latter point that the narrator identifies Abram here as an *Ivri* or Hebrew, a name of uncertain origin but bearing strong similarity to the *Hapiru*, who were known throughout the region in part as a class of mercenaries, thus implying that Abram was himself a man of significant martial experience.[143] This was important because the ongoing political turbulence in the region demanded that any assertion of cultural autonomy had to be supported by sufficient armed force to deter any casual aggression. Similarly, as indicated in the preceding chapter, it was prudent for Abram not only to be a good neighbor to the Amorite lords of the Hebron area, but also to enter into a mutual security alliance with them directed against external aggression.

Although Abram undoubtedly was aware of the war between the Mesopotamian alliance and the city-states of the Jordan plain, and was probably deeply concerned about the welfare of Lot, it was out of the question for him to align himself with likes of the kings of Sodom and Gomorrah, who represented the very antithesis of everything Abram stood for. He surely would not jeopardize the great enterprise he had undertaken to help defend a place like Sodom, even if his nephew lived there. At best, Abram watched what was happening in the Jordan plain with something more than detached interest because of Lot.

As suggested, it was necessary for Abram to be made aware that Lot had been taken captive by the Mesopotamians for the purpose of being ransomed, if that intent was to be carried through effectively. Accordingly, and conveniently, *one who had escaped* from his Mesopotamian captors, or was allowed to escape, as the case may be, headed directly for Abram to inform him of the predicament of his nephew Lot. The escapee himself presumably was a member of the household of Lot, who knew where to find Abram and deliver the disturbing news.

Notwithstanding their differences, Lot had long been treated as an intimate part of Abram's immediate family, and Abram may even have felt a bit guilty over his failure to win Lot over to share his beliefs. Now that Lot had desperate need of him, Abram simply could not ignore his nephew's plight and turn his back on him. What should he do? Abram was confronted by a choice of one of only two reasonable courses of action, both of which left much to be desired. He could send a messenger to the king of Elam, who was already on the march homeward, indicating his readiness to negotiate an appropriate ransom. However, Abram evidently was concerned that this choice could leave him open to continuing similar attempts at extortion in the future, since Lot was not living under his protective wing, a common dilemma that has persisted to the present day for wealthy individuals as well as governments. The other highly problematic approach would be to attempt to rescue Lot before his captors left the country with him. To do so, however, meant attempting to take him out of the hands of a far superior force, a risky enterprise at best and one that might well end in disaster for Abram as well as Lot.

The only consideration that made the second, more dangerous, option the more attractive of the two was the fact that Abram could count on his Amorite allies for direct support. In their sweep of the region surrounding the Jordan plain, the invading armies inflicted defeats on the Amorite clans living in the not very distant area of Hazazon-tamar. The idea of a launching an attack on the slow moving rearguard of the withdrawing forces, which contained the baggage and supply trains as well as the prisoners, as they made their way up the Jordan valley toward their rear staging area in southern Syria, had a certain appeal for Abram's Amorite allies. Such a joint raid with Abram on the Mesopotamian rearguard would allow his Amorite confederates a measure of revenge, as well as the restoration of some of the booty taken from their fellow Amorites earlier. After quickly deliberating the matter, timing being critical, and perhaps bolstered by the repeated divine assurances that his descendants would inherit the land that may have allayed any fears that he might not survive to have or see any such progeny, Abram felt sufficiently confident of his ability to succeed regardless of the odds against it, and elected the bolder but riskier course of military action.

> 14.14 *And when Abram heard that his brother was taken captive, he led forth his trained men, born in his house, three hundred and eighteen, and pursued as far as Dan.* 14.15 *And he divided himself against them by night, he and his servants, and*

smote them, and pursued them unto Hobah, which is on the left hand of Damascus. ¹⁴·¹⁶ *And he brought back all the goods, and also brought back his brother Lot, and his goods, and the women also, and the people.*

This passage reveals a side of Abram upon which the biblical author does not choose to elaborate, except in this one instance. However, the text raises several considerations that should not be ignored if we are to have a clearer picture of who and what Abram is. It seems clear that, although the narrative makes no direct reference to it, the political and security environment of Cisjordan, as indicated earlier, was far from idyllic. It was not a peaceful land. On the contrary, it was a land seething with conflict between numerous city-states and peoples of different ethnic backgrounds and with marauders coming in from the desert to the east and the wilderness to the south. For Abram to survive and thrive in this volatile and violent environment he had to be capable of defending his encampments and his animal stock, and to do this he must have had a small army of trained men at his ready disposal. Thus, when the text refers to his *hanikhov*, his *trained men*, it most likely is talking about his militarily trained and battle-experienced men.[144] Moreover, if he mobilized 318 of such men, born and raised in his household and therefore presumably highly motivated to take risks at his command, for the expedition he was about to undertake, it also seems reasonable to assume that he must have left behind a force sufficiently large to assure the security of his encampment and his pasturing and grazing livestock in his absence.[145] Also implied by all this is the consideration that Abram must have had extraordinary personal charisma to be able to maintain intact such a large organization of tribal size that was made up for the most part of ethnically unrelated individuals or small families that joined him over the years. In other words, we are being told, albeit indirectly, that Abram has in fact developed into a powerful sheik, with a relatively small battle-hardened force at his disposal, who clearly was a person not to be trifled with. Moreover, he had entered into mutual security alliances with the Amorite chieftains of the region in which he had set up his camp, and it surely was in concert with the forces of his local Amorite allies that he went in pursuit of the rearguard and baggage train of the withdrawing armies of the Mesopotamian alliance.

Taking the watershed route through the hill country to the north on the west bank of the Jordan, and moving far more rapidly than the Mesopotamian rearguard and baggage train that were proceeding up the Jordan valley, which we may reasonably assume were slowed by the large numbers of captives and booty they were transporting, Abram and his allies were able to intercept them at the point that would later be called Dan, at the very northern frontier of Cisjordan, before they turned east to rejoin the King's Highway near Damascus. Being outnumbered, Abram and his allies eschewed a frontal attack and opted for a multidirectional assault on the enemy camp late at night, when it was most vulnerable, a tactic designed to maximize confusion and create a good deal of panic among the defending forces which had no idea as to who or how big the attacking force was. The biblical author omits the details of the remarkable encounter as irrelevant to his purpose, telling us only that the ploy was successful.[146] At least that part of the Mesopotamian expeditionary force that constituted the rearguard was defeated and put to flight, leaving behind the baggage train that included all the booty they had taken from the cities of the plain as well as the captives they had brought with them. To forestall the possibility of their regrouping and counterattacking, Abram's forces pursued them into Syria as far as the area west of Damascus before turning back.

The exploit had met with success beyond anyone's expectations. They brought back the spoil that had been taken, which was the main objective of the Amorite chieftains, as well as Lot and his household, which was Abram's primary concern. In the process, they also liberated the women and other captives that had been taken as the spoils of war. The news of Abram's victory spread rapidly in advance of his necessarily slow return to the south, with the recaptured baggage train in tow.

> 14.17 *And the king of Sodom went out to meet him, after his return from the slaughter of Chederlaomer and the kings that were with him, at the vale of Shaveh—the same is the King's Vale.*

The king of Sodom, alone among the rulers of the city-states of the Jordan plain, felt able to make a plausible claim upon Abram to restore some of the booty that he had retaken from the invaders. After all, had not Sodom provided shelter to Abram's nephew and allowed him to benefit from the amenities of the city? If Abram's concern for his kinsman were such that he was moved to undertake such a risky exploit against far superior forces, surely he would look with favor upon the ruler of his nephew's home city. Accordingly, the king of Sodom, in a conspicuous display of deference, went north to meet Abram on his return march, intercepting him near the mountain town of Salem, later to be called Jerusalem. He may have felt that joining in the triumphal march back to Hebron would somehow cast him as an ally of Abram and thus entitle him to a share of the spoils in the captured Mesopotamian baggage train. In the meantime, as

Abram's column passed in the vicinity of Jerusalem, the news of his success thrilled its priest-king, Melchizedek.

> 14.18 *And Melchizedek king of Salem brought forth bread and wine; and he was priest of El Elyon [God the Most High].* 14.19 *And he blessed him, and said: 'Blessed be Abram of El Elyon, Maker of heaven and earth;* 14.20 *and blessed be El Elyon, who hath delivered thine enemies into thy hand.' And he gave him a tenth of all.*

Despite the predominance of the Canaanite religion in the area, which was based primarily on the worship of Baal and Astarte, Melchizedek worshipped *El Elyon* [God the Most High or Supreme God], a vestige of the ancient belief in God the creator, although his understanding of God as the supreme deity differed significantly in some respects from the conception which Abram had been propagating. It could be argued that the principal distinction between them was that Melchizedek advocated henotheism, the belief that *El Elyon* was the supreme deity in the divine pantheon, whereas Abram argued for monotheism, the belief that *El Elyon* was but another name for the one and only true deity. In any case, their ideas were sufficiently compatible for Melchizedek to relish Abram's feat of arms as a vindication of the truth and power of *El Elyon*.[147] Accordingly, once Abram came within the vicinity of Jerusalem, Melchizedek came out to greet him with a traditional offering of bread and wine accompanied by lavish praise and blessings.

For Abram, his successful military exploit seemed to be a mixed blessing. On the one hand, it provided visible evidence to the general populace of the favor of the gods and would therefore significantly enhance Abram's already considerable stature. On the other hand, the success itself obscured Abram's true motives for undertaking such a dangerous venture. His intent was only to rescue his nephew, for whom he still felt responsible, and not to profit in any other way from the conflict. In other words, it seems reasonable to assume that Abram believed that non-defensive armed struggle should be undertaken only for moral purposes and never just for plunder or self-aggrandizement. Nonetheless, in the process of rescuing Lot he also recaptured the booty, both human and material, that the invading armies had accumulated in the course of their sweep through the Jordan plain and its outlying areas. This created a problem for Abram who did not want to be identified primarily as a successful military leader or warlord. His aim was to be the progenitor of a new civilization, one based on the concepts of justice and righteousness and not on the notion that might makes right.

Of course, there would be occasions when force and violence might become necessary, as had been the case with the rescue of Lot, but such instances must never be construed as mere opportunities for lust and profit. Abram therefore concluded that it was essential quickly to divest himself of any material benefit from his exploit. It was simply unacceptable to him that his welfare should be enhanced through violence perpetrated by him, even when done in a just cause. Accordingly, the unanticipated appearance on the scene by Melchizedek provided a chance opportunity for Abram to make visibly clear his motives for undertaking the campaign. He presented Melchizedek, as priest of *El Elyon*, with a tithe offering from the booty taken from the vanquished forces, an offering which represented a significant portion of the share of the spoils that Abram, as commander of the victorious troops was probably entitled to in accordance with ancient custom and traditional rules of war.[148] However, misinterpreting Abram's offering of a tithe to Melchizedek as an indication of his intent to avail himself of the remainder of the spoils to which he was entitled by custom, the king of Sodom hastened disingenuously to offer Abram that which was already in his hands in the hope that he, the king of Sodom, might yet recoup some of the losses he incurred as a consequence of his ignominious defeat in the recent conflict.

> 14.21 *And the king of Sodom said unto Abram: 'Give me the persons, and take the goods to thyself.'*

Arrogantly presenting himself as an ally who was equally responsible for the defeat of a common enemy, he suggests that he and Abram divide the spoil between them. Abram, who has already made use of some of the material goods in his gift to Melchizedek, should take possession of the remainder of the goods while he, the king of Sodom, would take as his share all the captives, presumably both those previously taken by the defeated enemy as well as any additional captives taken subsequently by Abram's forces. Abram, probably taken aback by his effrontery, refused to provide a direct response to the king's proposal, or even to consider or discuss it. He was unwilling to be drawn into haggling about how to divide the spoil and who should get what share.

> 14.22 *And Abram said to the king of Sodom: 'I have lifted up my hand unto YHVH, El Elyon, Maker of heaven and earth,* 14.23 *that I will not take a thread nor a shoe-latchet nor aught that is thine, lest thou shouldest say: I have made Abram rich;* 14.24 *save only that which the young men have eaten, and the portion*

of the men which went with me, Aner, Eshcol, and Mamre, let them take their portion.'

To the surprise of all, Abram declares unequivocally that he has no intention of benefiting personally from so much as an iota of the spoils. In this regard, he tells the king that he has sworn an oath to such effect to *YHVH, El Elyon, Maker of heaven and earth*, so that there should never be any doubt as to the source of Abram's wealth. His riches will derive from the beneficence of God and not from the machinations of scheming men. His entry into the conflict was not precipitated on the basis of what he might gain from it; it was a war of duty and not one of aggrandizement. Indeed, to profit from it would have denigrated his true intentions and would have changed his engagement in violence from an act of virtue to one of sheer opportunism, an inclination that was quite alien to him. Abram thus implicitly rejected the proposal of the king of Sodom, disavowing any further interest in the matter beyond indicating that, of course, the foodstuffs and other supplies consumed by his forces in the course of the campaign would not be restored to the king, nor would Abram offer any compensation to him for them. In other words, these constituted legitimate expenses that the king of Sodom would have to absorb. Although the biblical author makes no mention of it, it would appear that Abram also included in this category the tithe of the spoils that he gave to Melchizedek, which some suggest might have represented part of the spoils to which he was entitled as compensation for their recovery. Accordingly, to demonstrate the purity of his motive for the campaign, he gave away part of the share that would normally have been his. However, with regard to those from outside his immediate household who took part in the campaign, such as the forces of his Amorite allies, he made it clear that they were fully entitled to their shares of the spoil in accordance with prevailing law and custom, and that any agreements the king of Sodom wished to make regarding the disposition of the spoil would have to be negotiated with them and not with Abram.

It is noteworthy, with regard to the spiritual aspect of the episode, that Abram employs the same designation for God, *El Elyon, Maker of heaven and earth*, as does the priest king Melchizedek, which attests to both divine transcendence and immanence. The implication of this is that Abram, continually wrestling intellectually with the consequences of a monotheistic belief in a one and only God, found the theological synthesis contained in Melchizedek's formula, although related to the idea of a henotheistic Supreme God, particularly meaningful and helpful, and so adopted it, thus indicating that he had passed another milestone in his spiritual odyssey.[149] However, Abram took the idea one step farther and linked it directly to *YHVH*, the one and *only* deity, whose designation as *Maker of heaven and earth* is to be understood as a declaration of divine sovereignty, a theological concept with far reaching political implications.[150] If God as Maker is sovereign over His creation, then a claim by one of His creatures to sovereignty is both pretentious and arrogant, because sovereignty is essentially indivisible, and this raises the issue of the source of legitimate authority for states and rulers, an issue of utmost importance in the history of the world and an issue that Abram's descendants would deal with extensively in their cultural tradition. Viewed from a theopolitical perspective, this episode provides a significant indication that, although Abram is already a man in his eighties, he is still moving upward along a learning curve toward an ever-deepening comprehension of God and His role in the universe, and the concomitant understanding of man's relation to God.

Having fulfilled what he considered to be his responsibility to his nephew and former adopted son and heir, it could not but have been a great disappointment to see Lot once again return to Sodom and away from any part in the realization of Abram's dreams. It may well have been his secret wish that Lot would have derived some moral lesson from his near disastrous experience, and return to Abram's household. However, it soon became unequivocally clear to him that Lot, who upon his rescue chose to return to live in the corrupt society of Sodom, would never play the role that Abram fervently hoped he would accept. Abram's initial euphoria at having rescued Lot, with no little risk to himself, must have dissipated quickly, to be replaced by a profound dejection, as he once again pondered his future and the lack of an heir to carry on his great task.

6

The Covenant Between the Pieces

Reflecting upon the events surrounding the rescue of Lot that had just concluded, Abram could not but feel a growing sense of frustration. In some respects it might have appeared to him that his personal situation had actually deteriorated subsequent to the episode and that his capacity to carry on with his mission successfully had diminished. Despite his exertions on Lot's behalf, he had failed to bring him back into his fold to be his successor, and without an heir to carry on in his place he could not rationally conceive how the task he had undertaken would be fulfilled, even though as a matter of faith he remained convinced that it would somehow be accomplished.

On another score, he had refused to reach an accommodation with the king of Sodom that would have made them allies, but nonetheless restored to him most of the spoil taken in the war. This had the effect of strengthening Sodom, lending support to the very model of a corrupt society that he so detested, without extracting any concessions in return. This surely did nothing to enhance his stature among the peoples of the area with whom he had to contend on a regular basis over water and grazing rights, who would have seen it as irrational and possibly evidence of growing weakness, a perception that could lead to dangerous consequences for him. Moreover, he may have been concerned that he had presumed too much to reject the spoils of war that were already in his hand in anticipation of continued divine beneficence in the future, while simultaneously lending support to a corrupt society that could not but be an offense to God. Had he, in the final analysis, acted properly or merely arrogantly?

It has also been suggested that Abram may have been undergoing a period of soul-searching because of the blood he had spilled, not only of some of his own men who may have been killed or wounded in the campaign, but possibly also those enemy soldiers who may have been personally righteous men.[151] Another consideration, perhaps the most pragmatic, concerned the potential consequences of his defeat of the rearguard of the invading alliance. Although a stunning victory, it was in the final analysis far from being a crippling blow against the Mesopotamian powers. What would be his chances of surviving a confrontation with their main forces should they decide to retaliate against him?[152]

It surely occurred to Abram that, notwithstanding the clarity of his initial intention to simply rescue his nephew, his actions in the episode produced a complex of results, not all of which he anticipated and some of which had possibly serious future ramifications. Although there is no hint in the narrative that Abram had any regrets about his part in the recent events, he certainly had grounds for deep concern over what was to happen next in light of all these considerations. He was indeed being rigorously tested and honed and, understandably, he was sorely in need of further reassurance that he was comporting himself in a manner consonant with the larger mission he had undertaken. And, once again, at a moment of deep anxiety, God intervened to give Abram the reassurance he needed so much.

> [15.1] *After these things the word of YHVH came unto Abram in a vision, saying: 'Fear not, Abram, I am thy shield, thy reward shall be exceeding great.'*

In his mind's eye, Abram beheld a vision in which the divine word was communicated to him in some unspecified manner. The message he received dealt with the two concerns that most troubled him following the immediately preceding events. With regard to Abram's well grounded concern about renewed belligerency by the kings of Mesopotamia, the divine word to him was: "*Fear not, Abram, I am thy shield.*" He had been placed under divine protection and would not be permitted to succumb to them should they seek to retaliate against him. We are not told what form such divine intervention might take. But, since there is also no mention that Abram was subjected to an attack from outside the country at any later time, perhaps the promised intervention may be assumed to have taken the form of redirecting the attention of the Mesopotamian rulers to regional affairs that were of greater importance to them than a punitive expedition against Abram who, in the larger scheme of things, was nothing more in their eyes than a petty sheik who had been lucky.

This visionary communication produced a profound change in Abram's understanding of both God and himself. The expression of providential concern infused him with a new sense of connection to the divine, the immediate feeling of intimacy between Abram and his "shield." If God was prepared to intervene in human affairs to the extent necessary to preclude a retaliatory attack against Abram from the Mesopotamian kings, there was every reason for him to believe that his mission and role must indeed be of cosmic significance. Accordingly, although he had undertaken his burden and life task voluntarily, he now began to recognize that he was also serving as an instrument of the divine in a manner he could sense but not yet fully comprehend. It now seemed clear to him that his relationship with God was analogous to that of a servant to his master, who had now once again promised his retainer that for his exemplary fealty his *reward shall be exceedingly great*. It has also been suggested that this promise is given at this point in specific reference to his having placed himself and his household at risk solely in order to rescue his estranged nephew from captivity, without consideration of any other benefit that might accrue as a result of his actions, a selfless act deemed especially meritorious from the biblical perspective.[153]

As Abram reflected on the reality of his situation in the light of the divine promise, the distance to be bridged seemed beyond his ability. Now, perhaps for the first time, Abram felt impelled to give voice to his frustrations within the context of his perception of the new intimacy he had achieved with God, whom he addresses as his personal lord and master. God had assured him that his *reward shall be exceedingly great*. Certainly Abram is appreciative of the God's favor, but questions the ultimate value such reward will be to him if he has no heir to carry on his work after he is gone.

> 15.2 *And Abram said: 'O Adonai YHVH, what will Thou give me, seeing I go hence childless, and he that shall be possessor of my house is Eliezer*[154] *of Damascus?'*

In his despair, Abram laments, *I go hence childless*; that is, he expects to die without any children of his own.[155] Moreover, even Lot, who as his adopted son could have been Abram's heir, had returned to Sodom, which alone disqualified him for the role of moral and religious leader to continue what Abram had begun. Abram personally had need of little additional material wealth, and without a direct heir the promised reward would ultimately become the possession of his steward Eliezer who would be recognized by the traditional Hurrian family law, which Abram and Sarah brought with them as a guide to practice in their household, as an appropriate albeit indirect heir to Abram's estate.[156] However, although Eliezer was unquestionably a faithful and trusted retainer, in Abram's judgment he was already too old, that is, perhaps too set in his ideas, to be capable of succeeding to Abram's spiritual mantle. The clear implication of Abram's remark is that he would gladly forego any reward for a son to be his heir, not knowing that having a son of his own, albeit not necessarily one that would be his heir, might actually be the unspecified reward promised to him.

Although the text is silent with regard to the matter, it is also possible that, with Lot being estranged from him, Abram may have adopted Eliezer, perhaps not initially for purposes of being his heir but only to make it easier for him, in accordance with business practice at the time, to obtain a wider range of credit with the merchants of Damascus, which was Eliezer's home.[157] Accordingly, Abram's lament is not that the *"possessor of my house is Eliezer of Damascus,"* as the translation has it, but rather as the Hebrew text literally suggests, the *"Damascus of Eliezer."* That is, should Abram's legacy pass to Eliezer, it will by default end up in the hands of Eliezer's Damascene family, thereby subverting its value as providing the material means for carrying on Abram's mission. The grand endeavor would thus come to naught.

Abram's outburst met with an awesome silence. Had he spoken improperly? God had promised him earlier that his seed would grow to become a vast multitude. Was Abram expressing doubt that the divine word would be fulfilled? Abram quickly concluded that his outburst was intemperate, and he once again prepared to address God in a more carefully thought through manner. He would point out that he was as yet without a direct heir, and with Lot's defection he feared that he might be too old, when he would eventually have a son of his own, to ensure that the child would actually succeed him. Consequently, it seemed probable, as a practical matter, that Eliezer, who was his chief steward, would become his heir instead of his as yet to be born progeny.[158]

> 15.3 *And Abram said: 'Behold, to me Thou hast given no seed, and lo, one born in my house is to be mine heir.'* 15.4 *And, behold, the word of YHVH came unto him, saying: 'This man shall not be thine heir; but he that shall come forth out of thine own bowels shall be thine heir.'*

Abram began to set out his argument that, as yet, *to me Thou hast given no seed,* and implicitly suggested that unless this happened immediately, he could not see how *one borne in my house is to be mine heir;* that is, that his heir would actually be someone of his bloodline. However, the biblical author indicates that it was not necessary for Abram to conclude his plea. As if to spare him the anguish of further detailing his concerns, God immediately interjected, in a manner that clearly negated the essence of what troubled him, *This man,* that is, Eliezer, *shall not be thine heir.* Abram is again assured that he has no reason for concern. His very own as yet unborn son will be his heir.

Then, as though to put to rest any vestige of doubt in Abram's mind, within the context of the vision, Abram is led outside of his abode where the vision came to him and is bidden to look up and count the stars, if he could. For, just as the stars seem to be without number, so too, he is assured, will be the aggregate number of his descendants throughout the ages.

> 15.5 *And He brought him forth abroad, and said: 'Look now toward heaven, and count the stars, if thou be able to count them'; and He said unto him: 'So shall thy seed be.'* 15.6 *And he believed in YHVH; and He counted it to him for righteousness.*

Abram, thus reassured, *believed in YHVH*, that is, he reaffirmed his trusting belief in the word of God that he was privileged to hear.[159] And, reflecting on the content of this most recent vision and the intimations of doubt that he betrayed, Abram considered himself unworthy of the divine trust being placed in him. He therefore accounted the solicitous and compassionate treatment he had received, despite his lapse of steadfastness, as a manifestation of divine righteousness, an attribute to be emulated by all truly human beings in the civilization he was charged to create.

It should be noted that in Hebrew the phrase translated here as *and He counted it to him for righteousness*, is actually ambiguous with regard to whom the pronoun "he" is referring. By capitalizing the pronoun, as the translator and numerous commentators do, the phrase is understood to indicate divine appreciation of Abraham's righteousness in reaffirming his firm faith in God and His promises.[160] However, the connection, in the present context, between faith, which is a psychological or emotional factor, and righteousness,[161] which is a matter of behavior, is not at all clear and, therefore, many commentators think that the pronoun in this biblical text refers to Abraham rather than God, which seems to me to better fit the overall context of the narrative.

At this point in his saga, Abram had already traveled a considerable distance on the road from being a rational philosopher to becoming a man of faith. Though he would yet have to pass through severer tests of his mettle as a man of faith, he was now at the threshold of a new and momentous relationship to God. It was now essential for him to gain a clearer understanding of his role and place in the divine scheme of history, to strengthen his resolve in preparation for the trials that still lay ahead. At this critical juncture, he once again sensed the word of God entering and engulfing his mind.

15.7 And He said unto him: 'I am YHVH that brought thee out of Ur of the Chaldees, to give thee this land and to inherit it.' 15.8 And he said: 'O Adonai YHVH, whereby shall I know that I shall inherit it?'

Now, for the first time, it became clear to Abram that his mission did not begin in Haran, where he first decided to set out on his civilization-building venture. It began much earlier while the Terahide family was still in Ur, where he first began to question the basic premises of the society and its culture and found them wanting. Abram is being told that it was not mere chance that led his father to emigrate along with his family from Ur; it was God who caused this to happen in order to remove him from the growing danger he was facing there and to preserve him for the mission he was now in the process of undertaking. The voice that spoke to him was indeed that of the divine sovereign, the lord of history who could intervene at will in the course of events of both men and nations. It was God who had precipitated the migration of the Terahides from Ur as a preliminary step to the later migration of Abram himself from the Terahides in Haran. His personal destiny was bound up in a divine plan of which he was only now beginning to see a vague outline.

He had been promised once again that his direct descendants would be his heirs and inherit the land upon which he stood, and that they were destined to become a great nation. But now, for the first time, Abram began to understand the process by which his legacy would be established. The land had indeed been promised to his progeny, for without a definite territory within which to erect a new moral society it would remain without roots and a foundation in the world of history. However, being given a divine deed to the land was a necessary but not sufficient condition for the fulfillment of the divine commitments made to him in Haran. Abram would be obliged, through his descendants and heirs, to participate actively in creating the reality of the spiritual heritage they would pass on to his successors, before they became the great nation he was promised, greatness now being understood by him in a spiritual and cultural rather than only in a political sense.

In carrying out the divine commitment regarding the land as the national patrimony, God would award Abram's descendants, through him, title to the real estate that would serve as the nurturing ground for the new society and civilization they were to constitute. However, that title would have to be given practical effect by Abram and his descendants. Others currently occupied the land and, though Abram might lay claim to it on the basis of the divine grant, he would have to establish his authority over the land through his own efforts. It would be necessary to conquer the land and dislodge or assimilate the existing inhabitants who would quite understandably reject and resist any attempt to put into effect the divine transfer of title. In light of this realization, Abram might well question if his recent experience in the struggle against superior forces had been precipitated to test his resolve and ability to undertake the necessary struggle to gain acceptance of the political authority awarded to him and his descendants by the divine grant. Was he to now mobilize his household and allies for an immediate war of conquest for the territory that had been allocated to him? Was he, a man presumably already well past the prime of life, to spend his remaining years in a long and unrelenting series of wars against the numerically far superior peoples, tribes, and cities of the Canaanites? Such a prospect surely was disturbing for a man of Abram's disposition and years. Yet, he had not been told explicitly that he was to undertake such a struggle now.

Abram sought clarification, but did not have the temerity to ask for a timetable. What he sought was some indication of the objective circumstances that would have to prevail before the promise would be fulfilled. Accordingly, he asked, "*Whereby shall I know that I shall inherit it*," that is, how, not when, will I know that the time is ripe to begin to attempt to impose my authority over the land?[162] It has been suggested that there is also a profounder implication to Abram's question. The divine promise that *he that shall come forth out of thine own bowels shall be thine heir* (Gen. 15:4), was a promise to Abram as an individual that he could immediately take steps to realize. However, the latest divine commitment, *to give thee this land and to inherit it*, went beyond a promise to Abram as an individual; it was a commitment to his descendants as well; it was a commitment to a people and nation. He understood that this was not something that he could accomplish single-handedly, but had no indication of what circumstances had to prevail before his as yet non-existent descendants would be able to bring the promise to realization.[163]

The answer to this query was to be one that would shake him in the very core of his being. Abram would need to be bolstered to withstand the shock of what was about to be revealed to him. Since he had already reached the stage of accepting the ultimate reality of the lord-servant relationship with God, that relationship would now be solemnized by an explicit unilateral covenant to be concluded with him.

> [15.9] *And He said unto him: 'Take Me a heifer of three years old [meshuleshet], and a she-goat of three years old, and a ram of three years old, and a turtle-dove, and a young pigeon.'* [15.10] *And he took him all these, and divided them in the midst, and*

laid each half over against the other; but the birds divided he not. [15.11] *And the birds of prey came down upon the carcasses, and Abram drove them away.* [15.12] *And it came to pass, that, when the sun was going down, a deep sleep fell upon Abram, and, lo, a dread, even a great darkness, fell upon him.*

Instead of an immediate response to Abram's request for clarification, he was instructed to prepare for the enactment of a covenant through a long-established traditional symbolic ritual. This involved cleaving an animal in two and having the parties to the covenant pass through the opposite parts, figuratively reuniting that which had been separated through the sealing of the covenant.[164] However, for the covenant to be concluded between God and Abram, the traditional rite would be modified to enhance its symbolic significance for Abram. The elements to be used in the rite would in themselves symbolically reflect the answer that Abram now awaited with great anticipation and anxiety.

For purposes of the ritual, Abram is told to gather three different domestic animals, each of which was to be a *meshuleshet*, translated here as "three years old," but also perhaps better rendered by some commentators as "third-born" and therefore considered to be in prime state.[165] In addition, he was to provide two birds to complete the ritual ensemble. These requirements could not but place an onerous burden on Abram who would have to sort and scour through his livestock to locate the required animals, a process that would consume a good part of the day. We may assume that Abram went about this task in a state of high anxiety, having received no response to his innocent question and completely unsure regarding what was about to take place in this extraordinary enactment of a covenant between him and the unseen God.

He carried out the instructions to the letter, gathering the specified animals. In accordance with the common tradition, he slaughtered the animals and then cleaved them in two, placing the parts so that if the space between them were to be removed the animals would again form a whole. However, he did not cut the birds in two. Presumably, the birds played no part in the traditional ritual and Abram was unsure of how to deal with them since they evidently had some symbolic significance that he could not grasp as yet. It has been suggested in this regard that the symbolism of the ritual may actually have been quite evident to Abram, who would surely have questioned, in his own mind at least, what the significance was of sacrificing three animals instead of one, which would normally have been sufficient for purposes of concluding a covenant. According to this view, the three animals represented the covenant that would be concluded with each of the three generations of Abram's descendants that would experience exile and servitude before the fourth generation, would return to the promised land as free men in fulfillment of the covenant. It is the fourth generation that is represented by the birds, which as symbols of complete freedom were to be left intact.[166]

Suddenly, birds of prey appeared and swooped down on the freshly killed carcasses. Were these birds of prey sent by God as messengers to conclude the covenant? Abram could not accept the notion of such scavengers feeding on carrion as divine representatives, and almost without hesitation drove them off. Only after he had done so could he begin to recognize the symbolic significance of the matter. Was he being told in this way of the eternal vigilance that would be required of himself and his descendants to protect the testimony of the covenant from depredations?[167] This incident surely served to heighten Abram's sense of anticipation to a new peak as the day wore on without further communication from God.

Then as evening approached, Abram's swelling tension dissolved into a deep sleep born of his emotional exhaustion.[168] As he began to dream, he sensed a foreboding darkness descending upon him, setting the stage for the profoundly disturbing prophetic message he was about to receive as the eagerly awaited response to his query. He had asked, *whereby shall I know,* and now the dreaded response came:

> [15.13] *And He said unto Abram: "Know of a surety that thy seed shall be a stranger in a land that is not theirs, and shall serve them; and they shall afflict them four hundred years;* [15.14] *and also that nation, whom they shall serve, will I judge; and afterward shall they come out with great substance.* [15.15] *But thou shalt go to thy fathers in peace; thou shalt be buried in a good old age.* [15.16] *And in the fourth generation they shall come back hither; for the iniquity of the Amorite is not yet full."*

Abram was not to undertake the conquest and subjugation of Cisjordan himself. That task would fall to his descendants at the proper time. He himself would not have to fight any more serious battles and would live to a ripe old age, eventually joining his ancestors "in peace." However, his descendants would not all be so fortunate. They would have a long and troubled road to follow until they were fully prepared to undertake the challenge of Abram's legacy, his mission of civilization building.

The establishment and further development of a new moral society would require a people inured to hard and sustained labor. It would demand a people capable of subduing and cultivating the environment so as to prepare the material basis for a civilization that would exemplify higher morality. Unfortunately, Abram and his men are pastoralists, living in tents as semi-nomads and moving from place to place as required to meet the need for fresh pasturage for their herds, a mode of existence unsuited to the task of civilization-building. Were Abram to undertake the immediate conquest of the land promised to him, he might well ultimately succeed in transferring control of the land to his successors. However, although they might prove capable of exercising political control of the country, they would more than likely forfeit the very ends for which the land had been granted to Abram in the first place. His descendants would likely continue to live as semi-nomads like their ancestor, and as such prove themselves inherently incapable of building the firmly rooted institutions necessary to the society Abram had set out to found.

Before his descendants would be prepared appropriately for their ordained role in the divine scheme, they would have to undergo a radical transformation. They would have to make the transition from shepherds to farmers and from wanderers into a people that would cherish the very plot of land on which they settled. They would have to abandon the life of the tent and turn instead to the building of houses and cities, rejecting the relatively responsibility free life of the semi-nomad for the burdens of civilization building. Such a transformation would not simply take place voluntarily on the basis of some inner compulsion, nor could it be commanded.[169] Nor would it be likely to happen at all if his descendants were to remain in the land, where they might eventually abandon the enterprise entirely and become assimilated to the very nations they were destined to replace. It would require the acquisition of a habit of long duration, formed of necessity in deference to externally imposed pressures and compelling forces. Accordingly, Abram's descendants will need to serve a long apprenticeship under alien rule in alien lands before they will be ready to fully appreciate the significance of the land promised to them and the covenantal obligations it would in turn impose on them. Through oppression they will discover the true meaning of freedom, and from compulsory labor for others they will learn the virtue and value of labor in their own behalf.[170] This period of tutelage is destined to last four hundred years.[171] Upon its conclusion, they will return to conquer the land promised to them, giving force to the title to that land which God had transferred to Abram as his homestead in perpetuity. At that time, they will undertake the subjugation of the Canaanite nations which were in effective possession of the land, nations collectively also referred to as Amorites.

Abram had asked for an indication, a sign, of the prerequisite conditions for his descendants to take control of the land as a nation, and he received a very clear answer; *thy seed shall be a stranger in a land that is not theirs, and shall serve them; and they shall afflict them four hundred years.* It has been observed that this prophecy contains three distinct elements, alienation, servitude, and affliction, which may reflect three distinct aspects of the historical process that will consume four centuries. The period of alienation, which clearly began during Abram's early years, will continue throughout the period, all three patriarchs living as alien sojourners, even when in their home territory of Cisjordan. The period of servitude will begin about 120 years before the Exodus, following the death of the last of the children of Jacob. The period of affliction, which will have begun some 80 years before the Exodus, about the time of the birth of Moses, will signal the final stage of the historical process and will culminate in the Exodus and national redemption.[172]

Finally, in this profoundly prophetic communication, Abram is given insight into the true nature of human history as it evolves within the divine scheme of things. He is told that there is indeed a divine plan governing the universe, but that man cannot have full knowledge of it other than through the extraordinary insights granted to the rare individual, a grant of prophecy such as that which Abram had now been privileged to receive. For the purpose of ultimately being ready to carry out their mission, his descendants would serve and be afflicted by the people of an alien land. However, the nation that oppresses them will be held to account before the God of history for its actions—*that nation, whom they shall serve, will I judge.* A nation bears a collective responsibility for the behavior of its people. Thus, while it may be historically necessary for Abram's descendants to undergo a period of purgation to satisfy the divine purpose, the oppressors are not compelled to act as they do—they are not unwilling accomplices. They oppress others in their own perceived interests and must render account for their transgressions. Abram is therefore not told which alien people will oppress his descendants, because it is as yet uncertain. Each nation is free to choose its own course. It need not have been the Egyptians who undertook the role of being the oppressors of Abram's progeny. That they later did so was entirely their own choice.

Abram is also told that the reason why the period of preparation shall last for four hundred years is because, *the iniquity of the Amorite is not yet full.* With this he is given further insight into the unfolding of human history. Given that God is sovereign of the universe, the tenancy of nations in a territory is a privilege granted to them, contingent on behavior deemed acceptable to Him. That is, no nation has an inherent right to the territory it occupies—it does so only by divine forbearance for as long as the public manifestations of its national ethos are within acceptable limits. Once those limits are breached, the nation may lose its privilege of tenancy, to be replaced by another.

Accordingly, Abram is informed prophetically that the iniquity of the Amorite will be "full" in four centuries. It would seem that, in contrast to the nation that will oppress his descendants and which will be judged at the end of that period, the Amorite is being pre-judged. Yet, in the distinction drawn between the oppressor nation and the Amorite, the biblical writer directs our attention to an essential truth. Man, individually and collectively, is fully capable of moral choice. However, where a society fails to build those moral structures that will encourage and reward moral choice, it will inevitably decline. Where the seed itself is rotten, its fruit will not be otherwise. Consequently, although it may take four hundred years for the corruption to reach the point where God is no longer willing to tolerate it, in a very real sense its historic mission has already been fulfilled. The subsequent four hundred years are simply the result of the inertia inherent in the dynamics of human events.

Presumably, although the Amorites theoretically could change the course of their moral history and thereby avert their eventual destruction, the ingredients essential to precipitating such change were absent from the outset in the society. Indeed, it would seem that, as time went by, the moral climate in Amorite society was such as to inhibit the emergence and development of a countervailing trend. It will therefore be at that juncture in time when the readiness of Abram's descendants to undertake the conquest and settlement of the land coincides with the moral decline of the Canaanite nations, making the latter ripe for defeat, that the divine promise to Abram will be redeemed.[173]

Now, at the end of Abram's prophetic dream, the clue to the symbolism of the elements of the rite associated with the covenant is given to him as well. In this way, the memory of what he himself had helped prepare would stay with him throughout the rest of his life as a constant reminder of the prophecy he had been granted. He is told that *in the fourth generation, they shall come back hither.* It seems evident, as pointed out by numerous commentators, that there is no correlation between the four generations and the 400 years of alienation, servitude, and affliction, which would make each generation equal more than a century. It is therefore presumed by some that the four generations are understood to refer to those who would go into exile in Egypt during the life of Abram's grandson Jacob and remain there until the Exodus.[174] Three of those generations would suffer rending anguish, as symbolized by the three animals that were rent apart. But the fourth generation will earn its freedom and will emerge intact, as did the birds which Abram was instructed to add to the ritual, but which he did not cleave in two.

> [15.17] *And it came to pass, that, when the sun went down, and there was thick darkness, behold a smoking furnace, and a flaming torch that passed between these pieces.* [15.18] *In that day YHVH made a covenant with Abram, saying: 'Unto thy seed have I given this land, from the river of Egypt unto the great river, the river Euphrates;* [15.19] *the Kenite, and the Kenizzite, and the Kadmonite,* [15.20] *and the Hittite, and the Perizzite, and the Rephaim,* [15.21] *and the Amorite, and the Canaanite, and the Girgashite, and the Jebusite.'*

It was already completely dark when Abram roused from his deep prophetic sleep. And then, in a vision he could not distinguish from reality, he witnessed *a smoking furnace, and a flaming torch that passed between these pieces,* sealing the covenant on the part of God, a unilateral covenant in which no further explicit demands were made on Abram.[175] All that was required of him was the strengthening and deepening of his faith in God and in the truth and ultimate fulfillment of the mission for which he had self-selected himself to become the divine choice. That is, his faith would still have to be further steeled and tested if it were to retain its potency in its transmission to and inculcation of the generations that were to follow.

Now also, for the first time, Abram is given a general geographical indication of the scope of the territory his descendants are to inherit, *from the river of Egypt unto the great river, the river Euphrates,* that is, the coastal strip along the Mediterranean littoral from *the river of Egypt,* subsequently identified by some scholars as the Nile, and by others as the present-day Wadi el-Arish in the Sinai, to as far north as the Euphrates in northwestern Syria.[176]

7

The Birth of Ishmael

The word that Abram received in these latest visions served both to reaffirm his faith in the ultimate fulfillment of his mission and to bring him to a new threshold of anguish. Twice before he had been promised that his descendants would become a great nation and inherit the land of Cisjordan. Being childless, and uncertain whether the problem lay with him or Sarai, he had expected his nephew and adopted son to be his heir and the progenitor of the descendants that would constitute his posterity. But, as discussed earlier, Lot had demurred from this role and had in effect severed the tie of familial intimacy that Abram had so desired, leaving him nonplussed as to who might become his heir and assume leadership of the civilization building enterprise.

Now he had just been told that his heir was to *come forth out of thine own bowels* (Gen. 15:4). He was to be the biological father of his heir rather than merely a legal and spiritual sire. This tiding of good news carried with it very troubling implications. The climatic and environmental change from Mesopotamia to the hill country of Cisjordan had not brought about any apparent change in his or Sarai's capacity for bearing a child. Ten years had passed since they left their family in Haran, and Abram was now eighty-five years of age and Sarai was already well past her prime years for childbirth. It seemed reasonable that if he were still to father a son, it would have to be soon and apparently through someone other than Sarai.

Out of his deep devotion to Sarai, Abram had never seriously considered taking another wife, even though that would have been acceptable under the traditional Hurrian family law in an instance where one's wife failed to produce children. He clearly preferred leaving a reasonable doubt in his and everyone else's mind as to which of the couple was responsible for their failure to produce any offspring. In this way he spared his beloved Sarai the opprobrium of barrenness. By declining to demonstrate his virility through another woman he had covered their relationship with a canopy of deliberately formulated doubt. Now,

God had made it clear that it was Sarai and not Abram who was infertile, dispelling unequivocally any uncertainty Abram may have harbored about his capacity to sire a child. But, unhappily, if he were to become the biological father of his heir, their present childlessness would have to be attributed to Sarai, bringing their longstanding charade to an end and making it clear to all that it was she who was incapable of conceiving and delivering an heir to him. Given the divine assurance regarding his virility, was he now compelled to take a second wife in order to bring the divine promise to realization? Was Sarai, who shared with him the exigencies of his spiritual odyssey all these many years, now in her maturity to be set aside in favor of a new and younger woman who would displace her as mistress of the household upon giving birth to his heir? Was the actualization of the divine covenant with him to be contingent on the destruction of his domestic tranquility, with his beloved Sarai bearing the brunt of the damage? Yet, what alternative did he have? There seemed to be no change in Sarai's physical state subsequent to the vision granted him. How much longer, given their ages, could they go on hoping that somehow Sarai who had been barren all these many years would suddenly become capable of conceiving and bearing an heir?

The text is silent on the matter, but it would seem reasonable to assume that Abram revealed the contents of his vision to Sarai. Surely he would do nothing to alter their relationship after so many years without first confiding in her and sharing with her the terrible dilemma with which he was now confronted. Abram's vision had revealed that he was to be the biological father of his heir, but was silent with regard to who would be the biological mother. Evidently it was not to be Sarai. Once having overcome the initial shock that not she but another was to be the mother of Abram's child, Sarai regained her composure and responded to Abram's depiction of his dilemma with realism and astuteness. Clearly, she did not wish in any way to become an impediment to the fulfillment of the covenant and its promise for the future, a future she desired and had worked for no less than her husband. Since it was now evident that it was she who was incapable of producing an heir, she concluded that Abram must indeed take another woman to bear him a son.

Under normal circumstances this would present no serious problem. It was accepted practice, under the customary law that they continued to consider authoritative, for a wife who proved unable to bear offspring to provide her husband with another woman to bear him children in her stead.[177] However, Abram needed more than just a physical heir. He required that his heir be nurtured intellectually and spiritually in a manner that would both ensure and inspire him to the extent that he might willingly assume the burden of Abram's civilization building mission. Such nurturing required the sort of home environment that Sarai and Abram had created together. The problem was how to maintain that environment intact if an alien element in the form of a wife nurtured in a pagan culture were to be introduced into it in a position of direct influence, such as would most likely be the case if such a woman, without undergoing a process of acculturation to the beliefs held by Abram and Sarai that could take years, suddenly were to become Abram's wife and mother of his son and heir.

While Abram equivocated, Sarai was resolute and decided to take a personally painful but not unprecedented approach to resolving these concerns. She would not simply find Abram another woman to bear him a son; she would formally present one of her servants to Abram as her surrogate. The child that would be born would therefore be considered hers and not that of the biological mother; Sarai would thus be able to give Abram a child, albeit through a surrogate mother. Once the child was born, the surrogate would revert to her original status as Sarai's servant without any legal standing as biological mother of the child, and would not be entitled to any formal change of status in Abram's household. Sarai chose for this purpose her personal slave, Hagar, over whom Abram had no proprietary rights. Hagar was an Egyptian who presumably was acquired by Sarai as a gift from Pharaoh during her stay at the palace, and was acknowledged by Abram as her personal chattel.[178] With typical economy of expression, the biblical author simply states:

> [16.1] *Now Sarai Abram's wife bore him no children; and she had a handmaid,[179] an Egyptian,[180] whose name was Hagar.* [16.2] *And Sarai said unto Abram: 'Behold now, YHVH hath restrained me from bearing; go in, I pray thee, unto my handmaid; it may be that I shall be builded up through her.' And Abram hearkened to the voice of Sarai.* [16.3] *And Sarai Abram's wife took Hagar the Egyptian, her handmaid, after Abram had dwelt ten years in the land of Canaan, and gave her to Abram her husband to be his wife.*

Sarai broached the idea to Abram, and he found it an optimum solution since it provided a means for obtaining a direct heir without destroying or radically altering the domestic environment that he and Sarai had developed and nurtured with such care over so many years. At Sarai's suggestion and insistence, he agreed to take Hagar to be his consort, either as a wife or more likely as a concubine,[181] something he was clearly disinclined to do on his own initiative, as it turned out, for good reason.[182] It has been suggested that Sarai's insistence on this matter was not entirely selfless since, as she herself indicated, *it may be that I shall be builded up through her*. In the culture in which Sarai matured, the line of descent was matrilineal, and she undoubtedly was concerned that Abram's heir should be acknowledged as her son.[183] That she would not be the actual biological mother was evidently not very important. Neither was the fact that the biological mother did not even have any blood relationship to Sarai a deterrent.[184] By thus assuring that the nominal line of descent was through her, Sarai assured the continuity of her status of female primacy in Abram's household. It also seems clear that Abram may have acceded to Sarai's proposal for this very reason. Thus the narrator does not tell us simply that Abram accepted the proposal, but that *Abram hearkened to the voice of Sarai*. That is, as one medieval commentator put it, as much as he wanted a son and heir, he deferred entirely to Sarai in this matter, leaving it completely in her hands to arrange for him to have an heir as she saw fit.[185]

Taking a second wife carried far-reaching social implications of which Abram probably, and the biblical writer certainly, was well aware. Earlier in the Book of Genesis it was related that Lamech, the patriarch of the fifth generation in the line of Cain adopted a new approach to human relations and the organization of society that set it on its course of moral decay and social decline. He introduced the concept of social inequality by taking two wives (Gen. 4:19). Previously, it had been divinely determined that it was not good for man to be alone. Adam, the archetypal man, had need of a female counterpart to complement him and to share with him the moral burden of humanity. Their relationship was to be one of complete equality. His son Cain also recognized the need for a female counterpart to collaborate with him in the task of civilization building he was compelled to undertake. Moreover, it would not be sufficient merely to have a female companion with whom he might cohabit for the purpose of rearing children, it was necessary for him to take a wife as a coequal, someone to share in the task of civilization building as well as to place constraints on man's otherwise unfettered egoism. After the passage of the generations, however, the essential reason for taking a wife appears to have been forgotten, and dramatic consequences ensued. Lamech deviated from the norm established by his ancestors and took two wives, thereby critically undermining the concept of social equality that was the very foundation of his civilization. A wife could be man's counterpart and therefore his equal. But two wives could not each individually be an equal counterpart to their common husband. Each, of necessity, became something less than an equivalent person unless the husband came to be considered as more than a mere person. Lamech is thus clearly identified by the biblical author as the first to violate the fundamental moral principle of human equality, always to treat persons as ends in themselves and not as means to one's own ends. His wives were compelled, by the very fact of their having a common husband, to compete with one another in an effort to displace the other in his eyes and attentions.

Presumably well aware of the potential moral implications of polygamy, Abram nonetheless found himself in a situation in which he was trapped, on the one hand by the divine promise that he would sire the son he so desperately wanted and needed, and on the other hand by Sarai's physical inability to mother that son. Effectively immobilized by this dilemma, it took Sarai's initiative to break the deadlock by urging him to make use of Hagar as a surrogate for Sarai in bearing his son and heir. It seems reasonable to assume that Hagar, although perhaps unhappy about having herself used in this way was nonetheless agreeable to the arrangement if for no other reason than that it would surely elevate her personal status within the household; although the arrangement did not affect Hagar's legal status relative to Sarai. As the narrator indicates, Sarai *gave her to Abram her husband to be his wife*, or, as already suggested, more likely his concubine. In any case, for all practical purposes, Hagar became a second wife to Abram, and was presumably treated as such.

16.4 *And he went in unto Hagar, and she conceived; and when she saw that she had conceived, her mistress was despised in her eyes.*

In accordance with the understanding reached with Sarai, Abram cohabited with Hagar, who soon became pregnant, all according to plan. What was not according to plan was the fact that almost immediately Hagar's demeanor toward Sarai underwent a radical change. Hagar's pregnancy seemed to stand as incontrovertible evidence of Sarai's barrenness, and it was not long before Hagar began to hold Sarai in open disdain, the very thing that Sarai feared might happen once Abram had to have recourse to another woman to fulfill his desperate yearning for a direct heir.

When Sarai, deeply offended by the insolence of her handmaid, reflected on what had brought about this change of attitude and demeanor in Hagar, she attributed the root cause to Abram. But why blame Abram? Wasn't the whole scheme Sarai's in the first place? Indeed it was, but what seemed to upset Sarai was Abram's apparent indifference to her sacrifice in sharing his bed with her servant. She evidently felt that her loyalty to him was not reciprocated with respect to his treatment of Hagar.[186] In Sarai's view, it must have been Abram who had given Hagar the impression that, now that she was about to bear his child, she was under his direct protection as part of his household and no longer the exclusive property of Sarai. Perhaps Hagar had come to believe that Abram even intended to set her free. If this were not the case, how would a chattel servant such as Hagar dare to affront her mistress? When it reached the point that she could tolerate it no longer, Sarai resolved to confront Abram over the matter, before the peace and tranquility of Abram's household were irreparably shattered.

> [16.5] *And Sarai said unto Abram: 'My wrong be upon thee: I gave my handmaid into thy bosom; and when she saw that she had conceived, I was despised in her eyes: YHVH judge between me and thee.'* [16.6] *But Abram said unto Sarai: 'Behold, thy maid is in thy hand; do to her that which is good in thine eyes.' And Sarai dealt harshly with her, and she fled from her face.*

Sarai reproached Abram for having violated their understanding and improperly taking unwarranted liberties with what was, after all, her personal property.[187] In so doing she declared, *hamasi alekha*, translated here as *my wrong be upon thee*, but which literally means, "my violence on you." Scholars have generally understood this as meaning "the wrong done to me is your responsibility." However, it can also be read as meaning, "the violence I am about to perpetrate is your responsibility," it being unclear whether such violence was to be directed at Abram or Hagar.[188] If this latter interpretation is what the narrator intended, Sarai's remark would have served Abram with notice that this was not a mere household squabble among its female members that he could overlook in the expectation that whatever it was that precipitated it would soon be set aside and matters would return to normal, without any intervention on his part. Sarai was warning him that unless he took some remedial action, he could not hold her responsible for what she might do to deal with what she considered a completely unacceptable situation.

Abram immediately recognized that his natural expressions of solicitude and consideration toward the biological bearer of his future heir had unintended consequences. He realized that he had inadvertently conferred on Sarai's chattel servant an apparent elevation of legal status that he was not entitled to do. His conduct toward Hagar had indeed led her to expect a formal and permanent change in her personal status once the child was born. It was unlikely that Hagar fully understood the merely surrogate mother role she had been asked to perform on behalf of her mistress. Out of solicitude for Sarai, Abram had assented to her evidently unrealistic plan for using Hagar as a surrogate mother of an heir rather than contract a legitimate second marriage with someone outside his household, and now the whole scheme seemed to be unraveling into an unwholesome situation that benefited no one.

Once again Abram was confronted by a painful decision. On the one hand, he clearly placed the highest immediate value on the restoration of his harmonious relationship with Sarai, which was now in serious jeopardy because of his relationship with Hagar. On the other hand, it probably seemed unnatural, and certainly not in accord with his own nature, not to exhibit caring behavior toward the woman who was carrying his child. Given these irreconcilables, Abram evidently felt that justice as well as prudence demanded that he respond affirmatively to Sarai's complaint and challenge. However, he apparently did not feel it proper for him to personally take any punitive action against Hagar. Accordingly, he effectively washed his hands of the affair and returned Hagar completely to Sarai's charge, even though she was carrying his as yet unborn child, telling his wife to do what she willed with what was after all her personal property.[189] He may have believed that once he demonstrated his priority commitment to Sarai in this way some of her concerns would be allayed, and that she would regain her composure and continue to treat Hagar as decently as she had in the past.

Sarai, however, feeling great need to reassert her dominant position in Abram's household, undertook to discipline Hagar in a manner designed to emphasize that her actions as Sarai's surrogate with respect to bearing Abram's child entailed no change whatever in her status. Hagar was to be made to understand that, even though it was she that had conceived while Sarai remained barren, she would never be acknowledged by Abram as his legitimate wife. Consequently, Hagar had no choice but reconcile herself to her appointed role as nothing more than Sarai's servant. As far as her motherhood was concerned, she had to be brought to understand that she was nothing other than a vessel carrying Abram's seed on behalf of Sarai. Her child when born would be Sarai's, not hers. In conveying this message to her, Sarai indeed *dealt harshly with her*. Nonetheless, it would seem to be out of character for Sarai to have caused Hagar deliberate suffering out of personal pique. It therefore seems reasonable to assume that Sarai, except perhaps for some strident speech, probably acted towards her no differently than before.

But, from the standpoint of Hagar's own perception of her new more elevated status Sarai's treatment of her surely seemed unduly harsh. Once she had tasted and savored the status of a free woman in the household of Abram, Hagar found it difficult to accept the reality of her situation. She was unwilling to turn back the clock, to return to her state of subjugation, even to a relatively benign mistress such as Sarai. Instead, she ran away taking with her Abram's as yet unborn heir. The silence of the biblical writer on the matter does not deter the sympathetic reader from imagining the anguish experienced by Abram as a result of the incident. When at long last it finally seemed that the divine promise of an heir to carry on after him was about to be realized, the unborn child is whisked away by its mother, possibly to succumb to the elements or to any number of other potential mishaps.

While the biblical author is again silent with regard to the matter, it seems reasonable to assume that Abram, upon learning that Hagar had fled, went in anguished search after her. True, he had turned her over to Sarai, but she nonetheless was carrying his child. Given that it was not Abram who finds her, we must assume that he looked for her in the wrong direction, most probably to the west or north. In both these directions she might have sought shelter among the relatively nearby Canaanite settlements. He probably would not have expected her to have headed southward into the wilderness in a vain attempt to reach her homeland, Egypt, an impossible journey for a pregnant woman traveling alone. One can imagine further Abram's sense of forlornness in not being able to find her and his unborn child. To make matters worse, Abram's vain search of the inhabited areas in the vicinity of his base gave Hagar the opportunity to cover substantial additional ground in her flight southward.

Hagar, exhausted and distraught, perhaps fearing that the rigors of the trip thus far had caused her to miscarry, arrived at an oasis on the road to the south and collapsed beside the running waters of the fountain. It is at this point that the biblical author continues with the narrative, and by repeating and thereby emphasizing that she was at the named fountain, in his own subtle way informs us that there is an intimate connection between the fountain and what takes place thereafter.

> 16.7 *And the angel of YHVH found her by a fountain of water in the wilderness, by the fountain in the way to Shur.* 16.8 *And he said: 'Hagar, Sarai's handmaid, whence camest thou? And wither goest thou?' And she said: I flee from the face of my mistress Sarai.'* 16.9 *And the angel of YHVH said unto her: 'Return to thy mistress, and submit thyself under her hands.'*

It is easy to visualize an exhausted Hagar gazing intently into the running water and thereby inducing a reverie that provided the provenance for divine intervention in Abram's behalf.[190] The divine scheme evidently required that Abram have a son by Hagar that he will believe to be the long-awaited heir promised to him for many years to come. It was therefore essential that Hagar be convinced to return voluntarily to Abram's household, there to give birth to his son. Since control of the situation appears to have slipped out of Abram's grasp, divine intervention again became necessary. Thus, within the context of the reverie induced by her exhaustion and the hypnotic effect of the running water which transfixed her attention, Hagar perceived a divine communication, which the text informs us was delivered to her through an intermediary, a *malakh*, translated as either an angel or as a messenger.[191]

The intervening voice that she heard in her imagination urged her to consider fully her situation. Despite everything, the voice made clear, by addressing her as *Hagar, Sarai's handmaid*, that Sarai had a legitimate claim to her as a slave, which meant that she was now a fugitive. In this regard, it also was made clear to Hagar by the essentially rhetorical questions posed to her regarding where she had come from and to where was she going that she needed to carefully consider the implications of what she was doing. Would she indeed be better off if she succeeded in reaching Egypt as a runaway slave, one presumably given to Sarai as a gift by none other than the pharaoh himself, than she was in the humane and tolerant household of Abram and Sarai?

Hagar's hurt did not permit her to make such an objective assessment at once. Consequently, her response to the questioning voice reflected only her lingering sense of disaffection from Sarai, *I flee from the face of my mistress Sarai*. There is no consideration of past or future here; it is simply a spontaneous reaction to her perceived deliberate persecution by Sarai, whom she continued to acknowledge as her mistress. The voice then urged her to overcome her feelings and to do that which was surely in her better interest, saying, *Return to thy mistress, and submit thyself under her hands*. But it was to no avail. Nothing yet said could assuage Hagar's resentment of her treatment at the hands of Sarai. Effectively rebuffed, the voice then appealed to her vanity. If Hagar returned and her son became Abram's heir she would be the mother of a new and great people.

> 16.10 *And the angel of YHVH said unto her: 'I will greatly multiply thy seed, that it shall not be numbered for multitude.'*

Once again the voice failed to touch Hagar. After all, if she did return and bear a son to Abram, he would be considered as Sarai's child, not hers, and Sarai would be known as the mother of that numerous people. The voice then spoke to her a third time, this time in terms that touched her maternal instinct, terms that she ultimately found irresistible.

> 16.11 *And the angel of YHVH said unto her: 'Behold, thou art with child, and shalt bear a son; and thou shalt call his name Ishmael, because YHVH hath heard thy affliction.*[192]

The fact is, the voice told her in effect, you are about to give birth to a son.[193] What would you wish for him, regardless of who is identified as his mother? Would you rather he grew up as the son of a runaway slave or as the prince of the house of Abram? Think of it! You are and will remain a slave. But you have the capacity to give your son freedom, if you but will it. Moreover, she was told:

> 16.12 *And he shall be a wild ass of a man: his hand shall be against every man, and every man's hand against him; and he shall dwell in the face of all his brethren.*

Her son will have the freedom of the Bedouin, living in highly mobile groups, like the wild asses of the desert, and able to roam at will. His very existence will reflect the ongoing tension between the men of the open spaces, such as the Bedouin, and the sedentary population, which will result in an ongoing conflict between the two.[194] Moreover, he will not be bound by externally imposed commitments or constraints, but *he shall dwell in the face of all his brethren*. That is, he will live as he wishes regardless of the desires of others, including any other future siblings.[195] This notion was bound to find favor with Hagar, who was not only angry with Sarai for mistreating her, but also with Abram for not doing anything to protect her. Now she hears herself being told that although Abram might expect her son to follow in his footsteps, he will choose his own course and pursue it regardless of Abram's wishes. Giving birth to a son such as that would serve as sweet vengeance for her; it only required that she return and deliver Abram's child.

The latter argument hit the mark. Hagar snapped out of her reverie, intuitively recognizing that something extraordinary had occurred to her. Indeed, she had heard a voice telling her that the God in whom Abram had invested his faith was responding to her despondency by assuring her that she had it within her power to bequeath the gift of freedom to the unborn child she carried within her, and that to commemorate that realization she should name the child Ishmael. Now, in wonder she called out to the voice that gave new purpose to her life:

> 16.13 *And she called the name of YHVH that spoke unto her, Thou art an El of seeing; for she said: Have I even here seen Him that seeth me?* 16.14 *Wherefore the well was called Beer-lahai-roi; behold it is between Kadesh and Bered.*

Hagar then returned of her own free will to her mistress Sarai to bear Abram' child on Sarai's behalf. In concluding this aspect of the episode, the biblical writer notes that the very location where a mother's self-sacrifice for her children was so exemplified by Hagar was subsequently named as a memorial for all future generations.

> 16.15 *And Hagar bore Abram a son; and Abram called the name of his son, whom Hagar bore, Ishmael.* 16.16 *And Abram was four score and six years old, when Hagar bore Ishmael to Abram.*

Hagar's return to was to prove a mixed blessing to the house of Abram. On the one hand, he was certainly delighted to have her back given that she carried his long awaited son and heir. On the other hand, her relations with Sarai must have become increasingly strained as her pregnancy advanced and of necessity she had to be treated with greater consideration by her mistress. Furthermore, she had surely related with some relish her experience at the fountain in the wilderness. Sarai could not but have been struck by Hagar's claim to have heard directly a divine communication, while Sarai herself had never been so privileged. Hagar's claim, however, effectively received substantiation from Abram himself upon the birth of the child. Abram named the child Ishmael, as Hagar told him that she had been instructed to do by the divine voice. Under normal circumstances, in biblical tradition, the mother names the child. However, in this instance, because Hagar is both a slave and a surrogate, Abram does so for her, using the name she gives him. It also seems quite likely that Hagar never revealed the promise she had received that her son would *be a wild ass of a man: his hand shall be against every man, and every man's hand against him; and he shall dwell in the face of all his brethren*, a potential that Abram and Sarai would have found quite disturbing and inconsistent with their own expectations for his son and heir.[196]

Following Ishmael's birth, even though Abram never formally acknowledged Hagar as his spouse in the same sense that Sarai was his wife, her status within the household must have changed for the better, to the chagrin of Sarai. This in turn probably led to a certain sense of tension in the air that disturbed the usual tranquility of Abram's household. It seemed quite unlikely that Sarai's scheme for using Hagar merely as a surrogate mother would be realized as she had intended, a situation that is hinted at in the textual reference to Ishmael as the son *whom Hagar bore*. He is not identified as the son whom Hagar bore to Abram on behalf of Sarai.[197] Hagar, not Sarai, was perceived as Ishmael's mother, even though she remained, nominally at least, the servant of Sarai.[198] Nevertheless, Abram, now eighty-six years old, finally had an heir—the first crucial step in bringing about the fulfillment of the covenant, even though it was not the child of his beloved Sarai.

8

Abram Becomes Abraham

Thirteen years had passed since the birth of Ishmael, but the biblical text is silent with regard to what transpired during that period of time. However, from what follows it would appear that the years passed in relative tranquility for Abram, although it would be unrealistic to assume that he did not have to deal on a continuing basis with the endemic instability of the region in which he lived. The absence of any information about that more than decade-long period should be understood only as an implicit indication that Abram was not confronted by any crisis that seriously challenged his faith, and not that it was an idyllic time for him.

Approaching the natural limits of life expectancy, Abram would have devoted much of his time to the education and moral preparation of his son Ishmael who would succeed him as his material and spiritual heir. Abram would likely also have spent a good deal of time reflecting on the spiritual odyssey he had undertaken beginning in his youth in Mesopotamia and continued throughout his subsequent years, presumably resting content with the knowledge that he had sown the seeds of a new moral society and civilization to be fully realized by his descendants in accordance with the divine covenant. Little could he have suspected that his trials of faith were not only unfinished but in some respects had hardly begun. Thus, it must have come as a shock to him at the venerable age of ninety-nine, some fourteen years since his last vision of the divine, that Abram was suddenly made aware that he had hardly completed his life's task as he once again underwent the awesome experience of a theophany.

> [17.1] *And when Abram was ninety years old and nine, YHVH appeared to Abram, and said unto him: 'I am El Shaddai; walk before Me, and be thou wholehearted.*[199] [17.2] *And I will make My covenant between Me and thee, and will multiply thee exceedingly.'* [17.3] *And Abram fell on his face.*

Until now, the divine communications to Abram were confined to the sphere of his personal disposition, his mission as he perceived it and his capability for assuring its continuing pursuit through his descendants, and culminated in the "covenant of the pieces," which assured him that the land of Cisjordan was to be his national patrimony. This latest revelation to Abram added a new theological dimension that transcended anything that Abram had previously grasped. This time the revelation began with the awe-inspiring proclamation, *I am El Shaddai*.[200] For the first time, God explicitly reveals one of His names to Abram, the particular significance of which is neither explained nor elaborated by the biblical writer. The biblical author would later indicate that this was indeed the only name of God that was revealed to Abram and the other patriarchs. *And I appeared unto Abraham, unto Isaac, and unto Jacob, as El Shaddai, but by My name YHVH I made Me not known to them* (Ex. 6:3). In other words, when Abram earlier referred to *YHVH* (Gen. 14:22), we must assume that the biblical author had substituted the Tetragrammaton for the equivalent descriptor actually used by Abram. We cannot be certain about the content of the theological vocabulary employed by Abram, the only clear indication we have in this regard being his recorded use of such designators as *El Elyon* and *Maker of heaven and earth*, which he appears to have adopted from Melchizedek (Gen. 14:19). This newly revealed name, if it means Almighty God as long generally understood,[201] was an unequivocal declaration of divine omnipotence that conveyed to Abram the realization that despite the occasions of divine expression of concern for him in the past, he was but a small element in the divine scheme of the universe. *YHVH* was now addressing him in His more readily comprehensible aspect of being *Shaddai*, the sovereign and omnipotent master of the universe. In effect, Abram is being told that it is *Shaddai* who brought him out of Haran and who, as omnipotent sovereign of the universe, promised that his descendants would ultimately become a great nation and who gave him an heir to begin the process of building that nation through natural means. The further implication of this is that Abram, and the nation that will emerge from him, has a designated role in the future order of the universe, a role that will be revealed progressively and more clearly later when the nation is constituted and is in a position to assume it.

This revelation also made it clear to Abram that he had reached a new stage in his spiritual odyssey and was now ready to ascend to a qualitatively higher level in his evolving relationship to the divine. *Walk before Me, and be thou whole-hearted*, he is told. The biblical writer is making a momentous point here. Prior to Abram, as he had previously told us, only two men "walked" with God: Enoch (Gen. 5:22) and Noah, who was also *whole-hearted* (Gen. 6:9). The first simply disappeared without leaving any mark on mankind, and the second, who started off so brilliantly wound up as a drunk and an object of ridicule by his own son. Noah, in the final analysis, contributed little of lasting spiritual or moral substance to mankind, other than the memory of his unquestioning faith in God. Although both surely served God faithfully, neither transmitted a moral heritage to subsequent generations to ennoble human existence. To their eternal credit, they both "walked with God" at their own initiative and not in response to any higher calling and were thus unique in their respective periods. However, the situation with regard to Abram was radically different. Although raised in a very different social, political, and moral environment than his two spiritual predecessors, he rediscovered God by his unaided reason but he did not simply "walk" with God of his own volition; Abram is now commanded by God to do so, in contrast to the case with Enoch and Noah.[202] Moreover, Abram is not commanded to *walk with* but to *walk before* God, that is, to assume a leadership role in following divine guidance.[203] Abram's self-motivated proactive approach to dealing with the declining moral state of mankind, deriving primarily from the polytheistic beliefs they embraced and the resulting distorted perceptions of justice and morality thus produced, had demonstrated his capacity for taking on the mission of founding and becoming the role model for a holy nation that will be dedicated to the improvement of mankind.

Abram is thus offered the opportunity to assume a role in the divine scheme that far exceeded anything he had ever imagined, to become a human representative of the omnipotent will of *Shaddai*. Such a role would be the logical extension of Abram's mission of founding a civilization based on a higher morality. It would allow him to be whole-hearted in his endeavors. He would thus become, so to speak, a partner with God in the moral renaissance of the universe. The society that Abram wished to see emerge under his descendants would therefore not be an end in itself, but would serve a larger purpose as well. Were Abram to be prepared to undertake the rigors of this elevated role, rigors that would bring him to the pinnacle of whole-heartedness, of moral perfection, then God would assign him the responsibility for serving as the covenanting partner in a renewal of the ancient divine covenant originally made with the Noahides ten generations earlier.

Following the great Deluge, which radically altered the environmental conditions under which man would have to struggle to maintain his essential humanity, the God undertook unilaterally never again to *curse the ground any more for man's sake* (Gen. 8:21). Man's moral career would subsequently be whatever he made of it. However, the ten generations from Adam to Noah proved incapable of arresting the moral decline of man. Now, another ten generations later, there was new hope for the moral ascendancy of man through the intervention of Abram and his descendants. Abram would assume the role of trustee of the divine covenant with mankind. He would assume the burden of moral leadership of mankind as a whole, and in so doing restore man's shattered providential relationship with God to once again reflect the true *image of Elohim* (Gen. 1:27) in which he was originally created.

Accordingly, God now informs Abram, in effect, that a new covenant is required to govern the future relations between man and God, superseding that originally concluded with Noah. This time, the divine voice tells him, *I will make My covenant*, not unilaterally as was the case with the ancient covenant, but *between Me and thee*. This new covenant will be bilateral in nature, with the parties to it having reciprocal obligations. God will continue to observe the unilateral commitment made to Noah not to *curse the ground any more for man's sake*, that is, not to intervene in history in a manner designed to radically alter the human environment, and Abram will assume formal responsibility for initiating a movement for the moral improvement of mankind, to obviate the conditions that caused the covenant to be undertaken in the first instance. The ancient covenant with Noah reflected unilateral divine restraint, and in itself did not contribute to mankind's self-improvement. Through Abram's efforts a new positive partnership between God and man will be established; the new reciprocal covenant with Abram will effectively supersede the unilateral one made with Noah.

If Abram has reached the point of moral perfection and consequently that of moral responsibility to mankind, and agrees to accept this great burden, he will be given the capability to fulfill the role for which he is being chosen. He is assured that the Creator *will multiply thee exceedingly*. Despite the fact that he and his household, as would be the case with his descendants after him, may never be more than a small fraction of mankind, their abiding influence will be grossly disproportionate to their numbers. Indeed, the role he and his descendants and spiritual heirs will perform will be central to the moral development and moral history of mankind, as though it were being carried out by the most multitudinous and powerful of nations.

Abram makes no articulated response to the momentous challenge being urged on him. Instead, *he fell on his face*. His response was a simple act of total acceptance, the traditional ritual act of obeisance demonstrating unquestioning obedience to a commanding authority. With his unequivocal acceptance of his expanded mission, Abram enters into a new realm of moral preparation. He had now committed himself to a new and exceedingly difficult series of intellectual and emotional ordeals designed to steel his resolve, and through him the generations of his descendants to come, to carry out the terms of the covenant he had freely and willingly entered. Following Abram's acceptance of the role cast for him, the biblical author sets forth the additional divine commitments under the covenant:

> 17.3 *And Elohim[204] talked with him, saying:* 17.4 *'As for Me, behold, My covenant is with thee, and thou shalt be the father of a multitude of nations.* 17.5 *Neither shall thy name any more be called Abram, but thy name shall be Abraham; for the father of a multitude of nations have I made thee.* 17.6 *And I will make thee exceedingly fruitful, and I will make nations of thee, and kings shall come out of thee.* 17.7 *And I will establish My covenant between Me and thee and thy seed after thee throughout their generations for an everlasting covenant, to be Elohim unto thee and to thy seed after thee.* 17.8 *And I will give unto thee, and to thy seed after thee, the land of thy sojournings, all the land of Canaan, for an everlasting possession; and I will be their Elohim.*

Abram's principal concern for more than a decade had been the lack of an heir to continue after him the slow and arduous process of securing a monotheistic base in a polytheistic world, from which a distinctive society and civilization ultimately would emerge. One can imagine both his shock and exhilaration on learning that, at his already advanced age, he was not only reassured about the continuity of his mission and the nation that would emerge directly from him to carry out that mission throughout history, but that he was also to become the progenitor of a *multitude of nations*, which presumably would be domiciled beyond the frontiers of Cisjordan, and that some of his descendants were to become the rulers of those nations.[205] By making the assertion, *kings shall come out of thee*, the biblical writer seems to be implying that kingship represents the "climax of national development," a view that will be disputed by the later prophet-judge Samuel.[206] However, it has also been understood as an additional assurance to Abram that the nations that derive from him will have kings of their own, and therefore be independent and not subordinate to the rulers of other nations or empires.[207]

To signify the expanded vision of Abram's historical role, he is to assume a new name, Abraham. A name is normally given to a person at the outset of life; Abram receiving a new name at his already advanced age may thus be taken as indicating that he is to be as one reborn, as beginning a new and especially significant stage in his already long life. The name Abram, or *Av-ram*, which literally means "exalted father," is assumed by some to be a contraction of *Av Aram*, "father" (most likely in the sense of "teacher") of Aram or Syria.[208] That name is now to be expanded to Abraham or *Av-raham*, meaning "*father of a multitude*" of peoples and nations.[209] That is, Abraham will serve as the center of gravity for an international movement to reject polytheism and to accept the monotheistic conception of God, and most importantly, the moral and social implications of that idea. The instrumentality for achieving this is to be the nation that emerges directly from him, which will inherit *the land of thy sojournings, all the land of Canaan, for an everlasting possession*. That is, the divine grant of Cisjordan to Abraham and his descendants will make that land forever inalienable to others, even when Abraham's descendants do not actually control or even live in it.

It is especially noteworthy that nowhere in these passages concerned with the covenant is there any mention of what Abraham is supposed to do specifically to merit the stipulated rewards. Presumably, the course upon which Abraham had already set himself since his youth was the one that he was to continue to pursue, namely, to struggle against polytheism and its moral consequences. What is specifically required of Abraham at this juncture is to take upon himself a ritual commitment that will forever bind him and his descendants, natural as well as spiritual, to the covenant. It will keep them continuously aware of their obligations to follow the path set by Abraham, which earned him entry into the divine covenant. For Abraham, the requirement to carry out that ritual signified that, for the first time, he was actually made an active party to the covenant, which is no longer unilateral as before. However, all this is contingent on fulfillment, by both him and his descendants after him, of this basic obligation under the covenant, which is an essential prerequisite to the reciprocal divine fulfillment of the remainder of its terms.

> [17.9] *And Elohim said unto Abraham: 'And as for thee, thou shalt keep My covenant, thou and thy seed after thee throughout their generations.* [17.10] *This is My covenant, which ye shall keep, between Me and you and thy seed after thee: every male among you shall be circumcised.* [17.11] *And ye shall be circumcised in the flesh of your foreskin; and it shall be a token of a covenant betwixt Me and you.* [17.12] *And he that is eight days old shall be circumcised among you, every male throughout your generations, he that is born in the house, or bought with money of any foreigner, that is not of thy seed.* [17.13] *He that is born in thy house, and he that is bought with thy money, must needs be circumcised; and My covenant shall be in your flesh for an everlasting covenant.* [17.14] *And the uncircumcised male who is not circumcised in the flesh of his foreskin, that soul shall be cut off from his people; he hath broken My covenant.'*

Abraham is told in unambiguous terms that he and his descendants must forever bear witness to their participation in the covenant by effectively incising it into their flesh as a visible sign of their membership in the covenantal community. However, the repeated assertion that it is every *male* that must be circumcised clearly indicates that the rite of *female* circumcision practiced in some societies is specifically precluded.[210] Although no specific rationale is given for employing circumcision as a sign of the covenant, at least two explanations may reasonably be surmised. By making circumcision of the reproductive organ a sign of the covenant, it not only sanctifies procreation but is also a visible reminder that the nation Abraham is founding will be realized through the procreation of his own seed, in accordance with the divine commitment.[211] Moreover, bearing in mind that circumcision was believed to have been practiced by the priests of ancient Egypt,[212] and that the further unfolding of the covenant following the Exodus from that land includes the statement, *and ye shall be unto Me a kingdom of priests, and a holy nation* (Ex. 19:6), another reason for circumcision as the sign of the covenant becomes abundantly clear.[213] Circumcision itself was already a widely acknowledged sign of priesthood, as presumably known by Abraham from his stay in Egypt, even though it was not a sacral practice in Mesopotamia, and Abraham and all of his progeny are to serve as ministering priests to mankind in the service of God.[214] The symbolic significance of the act itself is also indicated by the Hebrew term for that which is to be circumcised, the *orlah*, referring in this case to the foreskin but which also has a more general meaning as an obstruction or barrier impeding a beneficial result.[215]

Moreover, because diverse peoples normally used circumcision as a rite signifying puberty, admitting a young male into manhood as part of a fertility cult, its special importance for Abram and his descendants is set forth by giving the rite a new covenantal significance. Requiring circumcision when the infant is but eight days old clearly severs any connection between the covenantal rite and any traditional fertility rite.[216] It also emphasizes that the entry of Abraham's descendants into the covenant is not dependent on individual choice, as it will be for others; through circumcision, they are bound by it from infancy, a consideration that places the burden of responsibility on the parents to make sure it is carried out. But what if the parents fail in this duty and do not circumcise their newborn sons? With regard to this contingency, they are forewarned, *the uncircumcised male who is not circumcised in the flesh of his foreskin, that soul shall be cut off from his people; he hath broken My covenant.*

This assertion carries far reaching social and political implications. It makes it quite clear that the covenantal bond supersedes the familial and must be treated as inviolate. Even if a parent fails to circumcise his son as required, that child must, when he reaches the age at which he is considered to have the relevant degree of autonomy, undertake to have himself circumcised in order to remain part of the people. Moreover, even if no others know that he is not circumcised, God surely does know and will presumably take appropriate action to deal with him if he fails to comply with this demand. Because this demand is set forth as inviolable, nonconformity represents an evidently unpardonable breach of the covenant, effectively making the violator the equivalent of an outlaw, not because of anything he did but because of that which he failed to do, creating an anomalous situation in which the punishment for the son failing to correct this particular breach of the covenant is more severe than that for his parent breaching it in the first place. In other words, Abraham is being told that although ethnicity, for the reasons discussed earlier, may be a necessary initial condition for bringing a new nation into being, it is not in itself sufficient. Commitment to the covenant, symbolized by circumcision, is the critical and irreducible minimum criterion for male membership in the nation that is to emerge from Abraham, and anyone who does not satisfy that criterion is to be excluded.

Although Abraham may have immediately surmised the reason for his own circumcision and that of his descendants in connection with the covenant, the stipulation that it also was to apply to those *bought with money of any foreigner, that is not of thy seed* must have come as a surprise. This new revelation had two unanticipated implications. With regard to the latter stipulation, it meant that persons not of Abram's seed and regardless of personal status could become participants in the covenant, something that Abraham had perhaps earlier been led to believe was not the case. We may postulate that this was demanded to assure that there would be no conflicting belief systems within Abraham's household, something that could preclude its religious harmony. Presumably, anyone who would not abide by Abraham's belief system and its behavioral implications would no longer have a place within his household and, if a slave, would have to be sold or set free.[217] And, with regard to the general requirement for male circumcision, as a practical matter, the provision effectively undermined the Mesopotamian tradition of matrilineal descent, setting the stage for the emergence of Israel as a patriarchal society based on patrilineal descent, which would exclude anyone who failed to be circumcised regardless of bloodline.[218]

Perhaps to ensure that the shift from matrilineal to patrilineal descent not be perceived as a downgrading of Sarai's status in the patriarchal society to come, her position in the new order was to be elevated from mistress of Abraham's household to that of matriarch of the society and nation to come. She too would be renamed to signify a new beginning for her as well.

> 17.15 *And Elohim said unto Abraham: 'As for Sarai thy wife, thou shalt not call her name Sarai, but Sarah shall her name be.* 17.16 *And I will bless her, and moreover I will give thee a son of her; yea, I will bless her, and she shall be a mother of nations; kings of peoples shall be of her.*

Reflecting her new role as *a mother of nations*, Abraham is to change her name from Sarai to Sarah.[219] Sarah is no longer to play a secondary role to Abraham in terms of her historical importance; the nations that emerge from the seed of Abraham in fulfillment of the divine promise will be rooted in both Abraham and Sarah, who will be the first matriarch of the people of Israel. She is no longer to be considered merely the biological vessel through which Abraham's mission is to be fulfilled; she is in her own right to be seen as co-founder of the nation.[220] The significance of the name change is not immediately apparent since the former name is but an archaic form of the latter, having the same meaning, and either is a name befitting the matriarch whose direct descendants will include future royalty. There is, however, an interpretive tradition that suggests that, despite the fact that the meaning of the two names is identical, the change itself signifies a major development. In this case it clearly marks the end of the period of the barrenness of Sarai and the beginning of one of fecundity for Sarah, notwithstanding her advanced age.[221]

Abraham was clearly stunned by this divine instruction, not knowing whether he had actually heard this in his mind's ear or whether he was delusional.

> 17.17 *Then Abraham fell upon his face, and laughed, and said in his heart: 'Shall a child be born unto him that is a hundred years old? and shall Sarah, that is ninety years old, bear?* 17.18 *And Abraham said unto Elohim: 'Oh that Ishmael might live before Thee!'* 17.19 *And Elohim said: 'Nay, but Sarah thy wife shall bear thee a son; and thou shalt call his name Isaac; and I will establish My covenant with him for an everlasting covenant for his seed after him.*

Abraham did not know whether to cry or laugh, and probably did both. For one thing, what he had been told seemed to defy reason. But, he had already learned from his own experience that reason alone was not always an unerring guide, and taking what he had heard on faith, he *fell upon his face* in gratitude for this extraordinary promise of divine grace. At the same time, he could not but laugh inwardly at the seeming absurdity of the proposition that he, at age one hundred was still capable of siring a child and that Sarah, who had not been able to conceive before, would suddenly be able to do so at age ninety, an age well past the normal for childbirth.

In reflecting on the implications of this new revelation, Abraham soon evidenced concern about what all this meant for his son Ishmael. Indeed, it may be because Ishmael was now entering puberty that it was deemed important for Abraham to understand that Ishmael was not intended to be his successor with regard to the divine promises to him, and that he therefore should avoid saying or doing anything that might further complicate the situation.[222] For the past thirteen years Abraham had pursued his enterprise under the assumption that Ishmael was to be his heir and would carry on his work after him. Now he was told in effect that Sarah was to be the biological matriarch of the society and nation of which he was to be the progenitor, and that Ishmael, the son of Hagar, would therefore be displaced as his heir. Could it be that this was happening because God had actually disapproved of the steps he and Sarah had taken on their own initiative to ensure an heir? Sarah had offered her handmaid to him to serve as a surrogate mother out of concern for what she perceived as his desperation over not having an heir, a noble and unselfish act on her part. But why had he gone along with the idea? Was it because he was concerned that the divine promise would not be fulfilled unless he took extraordinary steps to ensure an heir himself? And, was this not a clear demonstration of his insufficient faith in God? Was the divine solicitude shown to Hagar and the naming of her son Ishmael intended to delude Abraham into believing that he had acted appropriately, only to have that illusion shattered now by the revelation that the son he and Sarah had long hoped to have together would soon become a reality? Did this new revelation mean that his beloved son Ishmael had no further role in the divine scheme? Concerned about the possible implications of this thought, Abraham pleaded, *Oh that Ishmael might live before Thee*, that is, please let nothing befall him. Abraham may be understood as suggesting that he would rest content if Ishmael were to continue as his sole heir, barring the necessity for some divine intervention to overcome Sarah's barrenness at her already advanced age.

However, the option proposed by Abraham was unacceptable, perhaps because it would have denied Sarah her destined role as matriarch of the future nation. Accordingly, Abraham is told that the divine promise is irrevocable; Sarah will give birth to an heir, who is to be named Isaac (*Yitzhak*, meaning one who will laugh) as a reflection and reminder of Abraham's incredulity. He will be Abraham's heir, and it is with him that God will renew the covenant He made with Abraham, and through him that covenant will be transmitted to subsequent generations throughout history. It has been suggested that there is also an implicit subtext to all this, namely, that primogeniture is not to be the decisive factor in leadership, spiritual or political.[223] One of the lessons to be learned by Abraham and transmitted by example to his descendants is that other considerations than date of birth are to determine who shall wear Abraham's mantle of national leadership in the future. The firstborn will receive a double share of material inheritance, but no special preference in any other regard. In the case at hand, for reasons that are not given, Ishmael is not to be Abraham's heir with regard to the covenant. Nonetheless, Abraham is assured that he need have no concerns about the fate of his beloved son Ishmael; he too will be blessed as well, albeit not in the same manner as the child of Sarah.

> [17.20] *'And as for Ishmael, I have heard thee; behold, I have blessed him, and will make him fruitful, and will multiply him exceedingly; twelve princes shall he beget, and I will make him a great nation.* [17.21] *But My covenant will I establish with Isaac, whom Sarah shall bear unto thee at this set time in the next year.'* [17.22] *And He left off talking with him, and Elohim went up from Abraham.*

Ishmael would become the progenitor of a great nation and of a dozen princes, but the covenant will remain in the hands of Isaac, who will represent the confluence of the patrilineal and matrilineal natural and spiritual heritages of Abraham and Sarah. At this point the dialogue with the divine is brought to an end and *Elohim went up from Abraham*. Now it was time for Abraham to commit himself to the covenant in accordance with the instructions given to him and, in effect, to prepare the home environment for the anticipated arrival of Isaac a year later.

> [17.23] *And Abraham took Ishmael his son, and all that were born in his house, and all that were bought with his money, every male among the men of Abraham's house, and circumcised the flesh of their foreskin in the selfsame day, as Elohim had said unto him.* [17.24] *And Abraham was ninety years old and nine, when he was circumcised in the flesh of his foreskin.* [17.25] *And Ishmael his son was thirteen years old, when he was circumcised in the flesh of his foreskin.* [17.26] *In the selfsame day was Abraham circumcised, and Ishmael his son.* [17.27] *And all the men of his house, those born in the house, and those bought with money of a foreigner, were circumcised with him.*

Abraham did not hesitate to carry out what God had demanded of him to seal the covenant, notwithstanding the trauma it would inflict on a man of his age. That very day, he and Ishmael were circumcised. At the same time he began to psychologically prepare the others who were to be circumcised as well, explaining the significance of the ritual circumcision to *all the men of his house, those born in the house, and those bought with money of a foreigner.* Once undertaken, given the size of Abraham's household, the process probably took more than one day to complete.[224] By so doing, Abraham had, through this singular act transformed his entire encampment into a covenantal community in which every male had a direct but unspecified share. At least in this one respect all were equal, even though the reason for making them all parties to the covenant that was to be the exclusive heritage of his as yet unborn son Isaac and his line of descendants was not at all clear. Perhaps, as suggested, it was to assure that the environment in which his son and heir would mature was sufficiently conducive to imbuing him with the values professed by Abraham and Sarah, bearing in mind that Abraham had formulated his belief system after many years of contemplation and argument within a non-supportive social environment, something that it would be desirable to make unnecessary for his heir. Perhaps it was to establish the principle that participation in the covenant was open to anyone, even if it was not realistic at the time that these events, preliminary to the founding of a nation dedicated to the covenant, were taking place.[225] At this early stage in the history of the nation to be built out of Abraham and Sarah, connection by blood was clearly necessary to ensure its future.[226] It is therefore noteworthy that *"the souls that they [Abram and Sarai] had gotten in Haran"* (Gen. 12:5), as well as those circumcised along with Abraham are never mentioned again in the narrative, suggesting that once Abraham passed from the scene, the non-ethnic covenantal community that he created soon dissolved. It was effectively replaced by a family-based association, in which the descendants of the earlier covenantal community who were not of the line of Abraham and Sarah no longer found their place as full participants.[227] It was of necessity to become a patriarchal tribal community in which unrelated males (but not exogenous females) could not have equal status as members.

Recuperating from the physical trauma of the crude surgical procedure, and perhaps reflecting on the import of recent events, Abraham experienced yet another theophany, the purpose of which remains unclear, that involved the sudden appearance of three messengers who came as wayfarers that he welcomed most hospitably.

> [18.1] *And YHVH appeared unto him by the terebinths of Mamre, as he sat in the tent door in the heat of the day;* [18.2] *and he lifted up his eyes and looked, and, lo, three men stood over against him; and when he saw them, he ran to meet them*

from the tent door and bowed down to the earth, ^{18.3} *and said: "Adonai, if now I have found favour in thy sight, pass not away, I pray thee, from thy servant.* ^{18.4} *Let now a little water be fetched, and wash your feet, and recline yourselves under the tree.* ^{18.5} *And I will fetch a morsel of bread, and stay ye your heart; after that ye shall pass on; forasmuch as ye are come to your servant." And they said: "So do, as thou hast said."* ^{18.6} *And Abraham hastened into the tent unto Sarah, and said: "Make ready quickly three measures of fine meal, knead it, and make cakes."* ^{18.7} *And Abraham ran unto the herd, and fetched a calf tender and good, and gave it unto the servant; and he hastened to dress it.* ^{18.8} *And he took curd, and milk, and the calf which he had dressed, and set it before them; and he stood by them under the tree, and they did eat.* ^{18.9} *And they said to him: "Where is Sarah thy wife?" And he said: "Behold, in the tent."*

One cannot but wonder why the biblical author provides so much detail about the staging of the theophany this time, given that in previous instances it was reported in a much more direct and less elaborate manner. Upon reflection, it becomes increasingly clear that the purpose of this seemingly irrelevant scene in the larger drama is to emphasize to the reader (or listener) that Abraham had now reached a new and notably significant stage in his personal odyssey of the spirit. Let us take a moment and unpack the story told in these nine verses.

Abraham, age ninety-nine, is sitting at the entrance to his tent during the heat of the day, recuperating from his recent circumcision and evidently hoping to catch whatever breeze there might be to help alleviate his discomfort.[228] It is noteworthy that Abraham is still living as a semi-nomad; he has not built a house, but resides, presumably as does his entire entourage, in a tent or other form of portable housing. This suggests that Abraham still views himself as a wanderer, without a permanent home, notwithstanding the divine promises regarding possession of the land upon which his tent is pitched. Nonetheless, it would appear that Abraham fully accepted the idea that although God had given title to the land to him, neither he nor his descendants would be in a position to give effect to that title until some time in the still distant future. Accordingly, he continued to live as a man without a home in a place where anyone else who had resided there for as long as he had would have asserted squatter's rights and built a permanent structure as evidence of his assertion of those rights. Since it was clear to Abraham that it was not his role to struggle for the land, a task assigned to his future descendants after their subjugation in an alien land, why build a permanent residence when you are confident that neither you nor your family will be able to live in it for very long? What is of particular interest is that Abraham has apparently reconciled himself to this essentially rootless existence without demurer or complaint—he is fully prepared to mortgage the present for a future in which he will have a decisive influence but no direct part.

We are told that Abraham experienced this latest theophany at the terebinths of Mamre, the same site near Hebron where he established his base following the split between him and Lot more than a dozen years earlier, and from where he departed to engage the forces of the Mesopotamian alliance to rescue his nephew. It was at that location that he subsequently experienced the earlier theophany through which his role in history had been redefined. However, it is not clear as to where he spent the intervening years. Even if he remained in the general area, engaged as he was primarily in animal husbandry, he would have been on the move periodically to satisfy the grazing needs of his flocks and herds. Now, the text makes clear that he is to be found at the terebinths of Mamre once again. Is this a mere coincidence? It has been suggested that the reason the precise location at which the new theophany took place is specified in the text is to inform us implicitly of the grave risk that Abraham took in circumcising his entire camp as well as himself at virtually the same time. By thus effectively incapacitating his entire force of persons capable of defending his encampment, Abraham placed them all in danger of attack by marauders or even by former enemies such as those from Mesopotamia who still harbored a grudge against him for their earlier defeat at his hands. Possibly to diminish this danger, Abraham may have decided to move his tents back to the terebinths of Mamre for the circumcisions and recuperation period to follow. Presumably, at that location, his longstanding Amorite allies, Mamre and his brothers, would protect him and his encampment until they were sufficiently healed to be able to take care of themselves.[229]

The next consideration that engages our attention is that for the first time in the saga a theophany experienced by Abraham is indirect, taking place in the guise of the visit of three "men" who appear in every visible way to be normal living human beings. This change in procedure seems both strange and untimely. After all, it is precisely at this point in the story that Abraham, who has just committed himself unreservedly to the divine covenant and undergone circumcision at a very advanced age to demonstrate that commitment, that God appears to choose to distance himself from Abraham, communicating with him, for the first time, through an intermediary. The only explanation that readily comes to mind is that this in itself constitutes a further test of Abram's faith—will his ego permit him to accept what can only reasonably be construed as a reduction in his status relative to the God into whose covenant he had entered so wholeheartedly?

Moreover, why three visitors and not merely one, given that only one appears to actually communicate with Abraham? Speculation on this question has given rise to the midrashic assertion that a divine messenger or angel is only capable of carrying out a single mission at a time.[230] From this perspective, it may be conjectured that the three "men" were needed because three separate albeit somewhat interrelated missions were to be undertaken virtually simultaneously. One was to reaffirm to Abraham that Sarah would become pregnant and give birth to a son at the same time in the following year, or, alternatively according to some, to help heal him quickly so that he might resume his educational activity. A second mission was to rescue Lot from the impending destruction of his home, and the third to bring about the destruction of the cities and societies of Sodom and Gomorrah.[231] Presumably, it was to make Abraham aware of all these impending events, for reasons discussed below, that the three "men" were sent to him at the same time. Although this solution of the problem raises many other issues, it has the distinct merit of giving some coherence to the story, at least from the perspective of the biblical author.

Another issue of interest in this narrative segment is the behavior of Abraham, which may strike one as somewhat exaggerated. Seeing the three men approach, Abraham *ran to meet them from the tent door and bowed down to the earth*. Abraham, almost a centenarian, ailing and still recuperating from his recent surgery, does not send an attendant to greet the approaching strangers but chooses to do so personally. The norms of even the most gracious hospitality do not require that a host run the risk of causing himself harm by personally engaging in tasks that others might do for him as easily, yet Abraham elects to do just that. But would it not have reflected the same merit if he had told others in his household to do this for him? Of course, it would! But, Abraham knows that the other men in his household are also all recovering from their circumcisions, and it would be unseemly to expose the women of his household to strangers. It would thus appear to be out of solicitude for the welfare of the men of his household that Abraham chooses to do whatever he can personally to avoid burdening them with it unnecessarily as they recuperate from their surgical ordeal. The narrator thus describes Abraham as an essentially action-oriented man, free from the snares of self-importance and arrogance. He sees no shame in menial work and is prepared to do it whenever necessary, and in this instance he deemed it to be such.

Moreover, uncertain that they are even coming to visit him, Abraham nonetheless displays what appears to be an exaggerated graciousness toward these strangers, bowing down to the ground and pleading with them not to bypass him and his home, but to accept his hospitality and have a refreshing respite from their travel. Once they agree to do so, he again involves himself personally to an extraordinary extent in hosting them. He does not turn to Sarah, the mistress of his household, and ask her to see to the preparation of an appropriate meal for his uninvited guests; he personally decides the menu, instructs Sarah as to what baked goods to prepare, selects the livestock to be slaughtered and prepared for the occasion, and serves it to them along with some side dishes.

What are we to make of such a story? For one thing, it strains the imagination to visualize the still ailing ninety-nine year old Abraham scurrying around his encampment, frenetically whipping up a meal while his male and female servants, of which he had no shortage, stand around watching him, bewildered by his seemingly bizarre behavior. Can it be that Abraham somehow knows that the three men are in fact not really men at all but divine messengers in the form of men? If not, why does he address them as *Adonai* (my lord), a form of address he never uses even when addressing kings? But how could he know this, unless the entire incident took place within a vision?[232] In this regard, it has been argued that the biblical text intimates as much in its description of the situation in which all this takes place. Abraham is pictured as sitting in the opening of his tent *in the heat of the day*, probably still recovering from his recent operation, and most likely dozing off or entering into a reverie because of the heat, as one is wont to do in such a circumstance, an ideal condition for having a vision.[233] But, even if it all took place in a vision, what is the significance of Abraham's peculiar conduct in it? What is it that the biblical narrator is trying to convey to us through this strange story? To resolve this question, many traditional commentators point to Abraham's behavior as exemplifying the overwhelming importance of the idea of man's concern for his fellow human beings, manifested here through the imperative of hospitality to strangers, an explanation that seems wanting and somewhat out of context here.

There is, however, another way to read this entire story that will resolve some although perhaps not all of the difficulties already suggested. The key to this approach is the fact that in addressing the visitors and in their responses, both singular and plural pronouns are used, suggesting the possibility that the narrative intertwines two distinct but related stories. The first begins with the theophany: *And YHVH appeared unto him by the terebinths of Mamre, as he sat in the tent door in the heat of the day*. In the course of this vision, Abraham *lifted up his eyes and looked, and, lo, three men stood over against him; and when he saw them, he ran to meet them from the tent door*. While entranced by the vision he was having, Abraham noticed something that disrupted his train of thought. He saw three men approaching during a time of the day when the heat was at its peak and only persons lost or in a desperate hurry would be traveling at such a time. His concern for their welfare caused him to interrupt the vision he was experiencing in order to deal with what he perceived as a problem that had to be dealt with immediately. Accordingly, he *bowed down to the earth, and said: "Adonai, if now I have found favor in Thy sight, pass not away, I pray Thee, from Thy servant."*[234] He begged God's indulgence, pleading that He not terminate the vision but merely allow Abraham to deal with the immediate human crisis that he saw unfolding before his eyes.[235] Abraham then proceeded to attend to the needs of the strangers, who surely needed both shade and refreshment, and did so with the alacrity described in the verses that follow, such that he amazed and overwhelmed his guests with his personal attention to their needs, causing them to wonder why he was doing all this personally. *And they said to him: "Where is Sarah thy wife?"* They evidently knew who Abraham was and wondered why he and not his wife Sarah was engaged in overseeing the preparation and serving of the food and drink presented to them, perhaps thinking that she was away for some reason. No, Abraham told them, she was at home, but *in the tent.* That is, she was in seclusion for personal reasons and was therefore not available to play hostess to them.[236] Abraham was therefore overseeing everything personally because of his concern over their welfare—it was dangerous to be up and about during the intense heat and he wanted to be sure that they were properly taken care of. In other words, he felt a personal responsibility for their welfare, and therefore exhibited such extraordinary behavior in caring for them.

It seems, clear, however, that the visitors are aware of what is really troubling Sarah, as well as Abraham, information they could have garnered from neighbors, if a prosaic solution is preferred to a supernatural one. After all, Abraham is not living in the wilderness, but in close proximity to the traditional religious site, at the sacred grove of the terebinths of Mamre, near Hebron. With a large household, including many servants as well as shepherds and field hands, it would be surprising if what went on in Abraham's camp were not a topic of local gossip.[237] Perhaps out of solicitude for Sarah's plight, which caused Abraham to undertake personally the exceptional hospitality shown them despite his extreme discomfit, one of the guests, either through prophetic inspiration or simple gratitude, sought to assure Abraham that virtue would indeed be rewarded, knowingly or unknowingly reiterating the promise of a son by Sarah given to Abraham only a few days earlier in a previous theophany (Gen. 17:19, 21).

> 18.10 *And He said: "I will certainly return unto thee when the season cometh round: and, lo, Sarah thy wife shall have a son."*

Although the translation, by capitalizing the pronoun for the speaker, indicates that it is God or, as many traditionalist commentators claim, an angel representing the deity that is speaking, this understanding of the verse is problematic to say the least, and has been the subject of controversy for nearly a millennium if not longer because of its evident redundancy with the identical statement in Gen. 17:21. However, the original Hebrew is less clear about whether the statement is a divine communication. As already suggested, it may merely have been an inspired assertion by a thankful guest. In any case, it appears that Sarah, although not appearing, was nonetheless curious about what Abraham and the guests were talking about and was quietly eavesdropping on the conversation.

> 18.10 *And Sarah heard in the tent door, which was behind him—*18.11 *Now Abraham and Sarah were old, and well stricken in age; it had ceased to be with Sarah after the manner of women—*18.12 *And Sarah laughed within herself, saying: "After I am waxed old shall I have pleasure, my lord being old also?"*

Sarah was both incredulous and amused by the reassertion by a total stranger of the message that Abraham had surely told her about after receiving a promise to that effect from God. More down to earth than her husband, perhaps more grounded in reality than in hope, Sarah evidently did not take Abraham's revelatory experiences too seriously, especially with regard to her. After all, she was, as the narrator interjects, fully aware that she was long in a post-menopausal state and well past the age of childbearing. At the same time, she also entertained some doubt about Abraham's continuing virility, as evidenced by her own words. But, one may ask, if Sarah were in fact so certain that she was past childbearing, what difference would the extent of Abraham's virility or lack thereof make, and why even raise it? Pondering this question has led one modern commenter on the text to suggest that the physical changes that giving birth requires may have already begun to manifest themselves in Sarah's body, at the same time that there were no perceptible changes taking place in Abraham's deportment.[238] After all, he had not had any additional children with Hagar during the past thirteen years, and there was no reason why he would not have tried to have more, if he could. Her presumption, then, would be that even though it might be possible for her to bear a child at her advanced age, it did not seem likely that Abraham could father one at his. In any case, Sarah's bemusement and evident skepticism about the possibility of something she thought highly improbable to come about, although unheard by human ears, did not go unnoticed.

> ¹⁸·¹³ *And YHVH said unto Abraham: "Wherefore did Sarah laugh, saying: Shall I of a surety bear a child, whom am old?* ¹⁸·¹⁴ *Is any thing too hard for YHVH? At the time set I will return unto thee, when the season cometh round, and Sarah shall have a son."*

Abraham was made aware of Sarah's lack of faith in the possibility of childbirth at her age and physical situation, without also being informed about her doubts about his virility. Why? Presumably because if she did not have any confidence in the possibility, and at the same time was uncertain that Abraham was even capable of siring another child, she might lose interest in any further attempts to conceive, a concern that God does not mention to Abraham, thus saving him personal embarrassment. God thus affirms to Abraham that He is in fact the omnipotent deity who can intervene in the course of nature, if He but chooses to do so. However, the divine intent is that Abraham's true heir and successor be born naturally and not miraculously, and for this to happen, there must be a proper understanding of the situation by both Abraham and Sarah. At this point, the theophany is brought to a close, and it is left to Abraham to deal assertively with the situation.

Accordingly, Abraham confronted Sarah over her having laughed to herself about the prospect of becoming pregnant at her age. Sarah must have been taken aback and concerned at being challenged by Abraham in this regard—how could he possibly know that she had laughed to herself in silence? Her first instinct was to reject his criticism outright.

> ¹⁸·¹⁵ *Then Sarah denied, saying: "I laughed not" for she was afraid.*

But Abraham brushed off her denial dismissively.

> *And He said: "Nay; but thou didst laugh."*

Once again the translator capitalizes the pronoun, assuming that it is God that is speaking, but it seems far more likely that it is Abraham's voice that she hears, there being no indication of Sarah herself experiencing a theophany. The biblical author drops the matter at this point, leaving us to speculate about what took place between Abraham and Sarah subsequent to this exchange. In this regard, it seems reasonable to assume that Sarah was somewhat bewildered by Abraham's evident faith that they would indeed have a child together at their advanced age and, perhaps, she too began to believe it as well, in effect making it possible.

9

A Question of Justice

The visit of the three strangers who seemed to have appeared from nowhere had come to an end, and the time had arrived for them to leave Abraham and continue on their journey.

> 18.16 *And the men rose up from thence, and looked out toward Sodom; and Abraham went with them to bring them on the way.*

Although the narrator never indicates the place from which the men had come, or how they were traveling, by donkey or by foot, he does make it clear where they were heading—Sodom. Abraham, evidently feeling stronger after their visit, lending support to the traditional theory that the mission of at least one of the men, serving as a divine messenger, was to help speed Abraham's recovery, decided to extend his hospitality even farther by accompanying them part of the way, at least to the crossroads at which they would turn onto the road leading to their destination.

The narrator does not tell us what Abraham and his visitors spoke about during their stay with him, which must have lasted for at least several hours. During that time, it seems reasonable to assume that he inquired about their destination, which they surely told him was Sodom. However, they evidently did not volunteer to discuss what their business was in Sodom, and Abraham would not be so impolite as to ask them such a question directly. Nonetheless, he must have wondered about what these wayfarers sought in Sodom, a city notorious for its lack of hospitality toward strangers. At the least, Abraham would have informed them that his nephew Lot lived in Sodom, and that he was sure that they would be welcomed as guests in Lot's home if they chose to visit him.

As Abram was accompanying his visitors toward the point where they would proceed onward and he would turn homeward, the biblical writer interjects an extraordinary simultaneous development into the narrative, a depiction of God engaging in a deliberative thought process of utmost importance to the entire biblical project.

> ^{18.17} *And YHVH said: "Shall I hide from Abraham that which I am doing;* ^{18.18} *seeing that Abraham shall surely become a great and mighty nation, and all the nations of the earth shall be blessed in him?* ^{18.19} *For I have known him, to the end that he may command his children and his household after him, that they may keep the way of YHVH, to do righteousness and justice; to the end that YHVH may bring upon Abraham that which He hath spoken of him."* ^{18.20} *And YHVH said: "Verily, the cry of Sodom and Gomorrah is great, and, verily, their sin is exceeding grievous."*

The issue that the biblical writer conceives God as debating with himself concerns the purpose for which Abraham was selected, namely, *that he may command his children and his household after him, that they may keep the way of the Lord, to do righteousness and justice* (Gen. 18:19). What comes through to the reader in these passages is the biblical notion of a sort of partnership between God and Abraham, predicated on the covenant, in which both parties will work in tandem to transform the world of man from its present state to one characterized by righteousness and justice. The ideal society to be created by Abraham and his descendants is intended to be the institutional embodiment of the principles of righteousness and justice. But, righteousness and justice may not always seem compatible, and this is a problem which will likely trouble Abraham. How will Abraham, who repeatedly shows intense concern for the welfare of others and already exemplifies the later biblical injunction, *thou shalt love thy neighbor as thyself* (Lev. 19:18), reconcile this adjuration with the destruction of an entire society in the name of justice? Abraham is surely aware of the reprehensible conduct of the Sodomites, but undoubtedly believes that the Sodomites are ultimately redeemable through moral suasion, a notion that divine judgment had already rejected in favor of the justice of meting out collective punishment for their transgressions. The critical question is whether Abraham will comprehend the necessity for setting aside righteousness, as manifested in active compassion for one's fellow man, to satisfy the need for justice as determined in accordance with divine judgment.

Accordingly, it is crucial that Abraham come to understand and appreciate the overriding importance of justice as a social value when it appears to conflict with the principle of righteousness. The pursuit of justice is demanded of Abraham's covenantal heirs, the children of Israel, as the very justification for their collective existence as a distinct nation. The biblical imperative in this regard is explicit and unequivocal: *Justice, justice shalt thou follow, that thou mayest live, and inherit the land which YHVH thy Elohim giveth thee* (Deut. 16:20). Possession of the national patrimony is thus made contingent on the collective pursuit of justice.

But, and herein lies the nub of the problem, how does one know what is just? Is justice presumed to be self-evident, or is man to guide his conduct in accordance with the principle of *imitatio Dei*, the emulation of God, which would seem to be the essence of the notion of what it means to *keep the way of YHVH?* Is it intended that we define and apply our concepts of justice by reference to how the manifestations of divine justice are presented in Scripture? But, as one ponders the idea of justice it readily becomes apparent that certain fundamental and possibly unbridgeable distinctions must be drawn between the concepts of divine and human justice. That the two are not necessarily commensurate or even compatible becomes rather evident as one considers the implications of the biblical narratives about the Deluge and about the impending destruction of the societies of Sodom and Gomorrah.

In the story of the Deluge, we were told that *the earth was corrupt before Elohim, and the earth was filled with violence…And Elohim said unto Noah: The end of all flesh is come before Me; for the earth is filled with violence through them; and, behold, I will destroy them with the earth* (Gen. 6:11, 13). Only Noah and his family were to survive along with representatives of the diverse animal species, presumably those required to reestablish the environmental conditions necessary for human survival and development. Here we have an extreme example of divine justice at work. The societies of the earth are depicted as corrupt and violent and are therefore to be destroyed, because, it would seem, they had become dysfunctional within the context of the divine plan.

Let us attempt to understand the underlying reason for the harshness of the divine decree by considering the story of the tower of Babel, and the rather different outcome in that case. There, although the building of the tower was seen as a direct affront to God, the society that perpetrated it was not annihilated. The society was disintegrated and the peoples dispersed, but not destroyed. From this one may conclude that whereas God might forgive a violation of the norms that govern the relations between man and God, no such latitude would be granted to gross transgressions against the norms governing the relations between man and man.[239]

But, we may ask, is the biblical author to be understood as suggesting that *all* the people of the earth, with the exception of Noah and his family, were corrupt and violent and therefore deserving of the collective fate that awaited them? Were there no gradations of culpability? Might there not be a milder punishment for the less corrupt than for the more corrupt? In this regard, is it just to punish unequals equally? Moreover, can we even conceive of a violent and corrupt society in which there are no victims? And, if there are victims, can we conceive of a concept of justice that will condemn the victims of oppression to the same fate as their victimizers? From the standpoint of any rational conception of justice, the biblical story of the Deluge cannot but leave us bewildered. The intrinsic problem with the biblical portrayal of divine justice at work is brought into even sharper relief by the story of the impending destruction of Sodom and Gomorrah.

Although the biblical narrator does not make clear the precise nature of the transgressions of which the two ill-fated societies were guilty, we are told that *the cry of Sodom and Gomorrah is great, and, verily, their sin is exceeding grievous.* Presumably, the level of corruption and violence in the cities had reached the point where their continued existence could no longer be justified as acceptable within the divine plan for the universe. In other words, the biblical writer is implicitly asserting that there has always existed a universal moral law that all men are obligated to obey, irrespective of their religious beliefs, a "natural" law intended to assure the viability and stability of human society. When that law is violated consistently, creating an outcry that is heard in heaven, the offending society will ultimately be held accountable for its offenses. What this suggests is that from the standpoint of divine justice, the people are to be held collectively accountable for character of the society in which they live. Corrupt leaders can exist only with the complicity of public passivity. Unless there is clear evidence of attempts to reform society, or to take even stronger action to eliminate corruption, even the victims become culpable for the sins of their society. This was the case in the time of Noah and it was the case now with Sodom and Gomorrah, which were therefore marked for total obliteration; a punishment that evidently was considered appropriate retribution for their crimes in accordance with the requirements of divine justice.

However, before this sentence could be carried out, there was another problem that had to be dealt with first. God had entered into a covenant with Abraham, in accordance with which he was to become the progenitor of a new nation committed to the creation and upholding of a truly just and moral society. It was therefore imperative that Abraham should fully comprehend and appreciate the justice of the impending destruction of the offending societies. It simply would not do to leave Abraham wondering why such a punishment was being inflicted on Sodom and Gomorrah, to have him undertake his civilization-building mission burdened with unanswered questions regarding the nature of divine justice.

This concern over how Abraham would perceive the workings of divine justice was fully justified. Because in the case of the two cities the *way of YHVH* clearly included the collective punishment of their inhabitants, an approach to the rendition of justice that is inherently repugnant to human reason.

The biblical author thus describes how, for this very reason, God decides to revisit the issue one more time, to determine if any mitigation of the collective punishment to be inflicted on the populations of Sodom and Gomorrah merits consideration. Accordingly, God informs Abraham of His intention, adding,

> 18.21 *"I will go down now, and see whether they have done altogether according to the cry of it, which is come unto Me; and if not, I will know."*

Whatever he may have thought earlier, Abraham now understood clearly why he had been graced with the three visitors. Two of them were to go to Sodom in the form in which they had come to Abraham to determine empirically whether there were any exculpatory reasons for revoking the punishment ordained for that center of iniquity and moral corruption. But why, we may ask, was it necessary to go through this process? God surely had certain knowledge of the sins of Sodom, in which case is not this whole business of the angels in the form of men visiting the city nothing more than some cosmic charade? One poignant answer given to these questions suggests that there was never any question, from the perspective of the divine, that Sodom and its sister cities merited obliteration. However, it was deemed equally important that there be a story told illustrating the depravity of Sodomite society as a lesson to the world about the consequences that ultimately would befall other morally dysfunctional societies, and that the episode took place in the manner described for that very purpose.[240]

According to some ancient commentators, the notion of a divine "descent" is to be understood as providing a last opportunity for the condemned to repent of their ways and thereby gain a reprieve from their sentence.[241] The realization that divine justice was principled and not arbitrary must have been very reassuring to Abraham. That God was prepared to reconsider His decision if conditions warranted it clearly also provided an opening for Abraham to attempt to intercede on behalf of his fellow men, as individuals even if not as a society, further suggesting that true justice required that someone serve as advocate on behalf of the indicted, no matter how grave the offenses with which they are charged. As matters stood, Sodom and Gomorrah were to be obliterated along with their populations, knowledge of which was revealed to Abraham as he accompanied his visitors, leading them to the intersection with the road to Sodom. Once having reached the crossroad, they parted company.

> 18.22 *And the men turned from thence, and went toward Sodom; but Abraham stood yet before YHVH.*[242]

No sooner was Abraham freed of the obligations of courtesy to his departing guests than he assumed the role of advocate for the condemned and directly and pointedly challenged the justice of the divine decision. He simply could not accept the idea that *all* the people of the condemned cities were so irredeemably evil as to merit annihilation. In sharp contrast to Noah, who apparently received the divine decision to totally eradicate his society with equanimity and without murmur, Abraham was deeply troubled by the news of the impending disaster. One might have expected that Abraham would be delighted by the news that God intended to destroy Sodom and Gomorra, cities that exemplified the baseness and depravity to which corrupt societies can descend, cities that represented the very antithesis of the ideals to which Abraham had committed his life. But Abraham was fully committed to the pursuit of justice.[243] And so Abraham, the prince of faith, challenges the justice of God, essentially demanding that divine justice reflect standards acceptable to human reason. He simply was unable to reconcile the idea of collective punishment with the most elementary concepts of justice, and did not hesitate to voice his concerns to God.

> 18.23 *And Abraham drew near, and said: "Wilt Thou indeed sweep away the righteous with the wicked?* 18.24 *Peradventure there are fifty righteous within the city; wilt Thou indeed sweep away and not forgive the place for the fifty righteous that are therein?* 18.25 *That be far from Thee to do after this manner, to slay the righteous with the wicked, that so the righteous should be as the wicked; that be far from Thee; shall not the Judge of all the earth do justly?*

Abraham evidently could not conceive of how the indiscriminate collective punishment of an entire population could be justified, nor could he understand how a just God could entertain imposing and executing such a sentence. Collective punishment causes the righteous to suffer along with the wicked, and therefore seems self-evidently incompatible with the most basic notion of justice as equitable treatment. Moreover, as one ancient sage put it, Abraham argued, in effect, that if the world is to survive there can be no absolute justice, that is, justice that is not tempered by mercy, and it would seem that if God does in fact deal with Sodom from the standpoint of absolute justice, it will prove counterproductive to the divine purpose.[244] It has also been suggested that Abraham is also making a somewhat more sophisticated argument here, with his reference to the possibility of there being fifty righteous people *within the city*. This has been interpreted as a plea by Abraham that God not judge the city by a universal standard of justice but take into consideration that, in a society as corrupt as Sodom, there probably will not be found fifty people who would be considered righteous by any universal standard but should nonetheless be considered relatively righteous when compared with others *within the city,* and that they should be spared for that reason.[245] But Abraham also goes farther, asking that the entire city be spared for the sake of the righteous people who reside in it. After all, to allow the righteous to survive but to destroy everything around them is still to punish them by forcing them into exile from their homes and homeland, for some a fate equivalent to death. This is no longer merely a matter of an argument for justice but a plea for divine compassion and mercy, even if it required continued tolerance for those meriting punishment.

Abraham's argument implies that there is greater injustice in the death or punishment of the righteous than in allowing the wicked, even if they constitute the majority of the society, to go unpunished. What he proposed, in effect, was to supplant the idea of collective responsibility with that of collective merit. That is, contrary to the idea that the righteous as well as the wicked members of a community might be punished for the sins of the wicked, he suggested that the wicked as well as the righteous members of a community might be saved on account of the merit of the righteous.[246] For Abraham, it has been argued, the moral objective is not primarily the suppression and punishment of the wicked, but the eradication of the evil that makes them perverse.[247] According to this view, all men are redeemable, even the most wicked, and that even they, as a group although not necessarily as individuals, should therefore be spared for the sake of the righteous, since at some point they too might be brought to repent and change their ways.

Contemporary readers may also see in this a discussion over the legitimacy of inflicting collateral damage while attacking a villainous individual, group, or government. Abraham, an idealistic lover of his fellow man, is prepared to tolerate a corrupt society in order to avoid wreaking collateral damage on its righteous members. However, according to the biblical author, God, in His infinite divine wisdom, is unwilling to accept this constraint on the workings of divine justice, a constraint which, in the long run, will prove both unwise and counterproductive, and His decision regarding Sodom and its sister cities remained irreversible.

Perhaps somewhat surprisingly, by the nature of the divine response to Abraham, the narrator implicitly suggests that God was quite pleased with Abraham's righteous indignation and irrepressible sense of justice, one that drove him to challenge perceived injustice regardless of source, even when it had explicit divine sanction. Thus, an ancient sage applied to Abraham the words of a later biblical writer, *Thou hast loved righteousness and hated wickedness; therefore God, thy God, hath anointed thee with the oil of gladness above thy fellows* (Ps. 45:8).[248] We may assume that it was for this reason that Abraham was permitted, in effect, to negotiate with God regarding the threshold at which the collective punishment of Sodom and Gomorrah would take effect; that is, the number of righteous people that had to be present in order for the destruction order to be rescinded. Indeed, as we shall see, it is God that opens the bidding, so to speak, in this most extraordinary life and death negotiation, a clear indication of divine willingness to participate in such a deliberative process, possibly as a test of the limits of human reason and judgment, notwithstanding that the outcome will not deviate from the decision already made.

Thus, for reasons that remain unarticulated by the biblical author, but about which we are free to speculate, divine justice demanded the collective punishment that was about to be inflicted on the condemned cities. How can we account for the fate of those innocent of any wrongdoing? It is important to note that Abraham, notwithstanding his love for his fellow man and his readiness to allow the wicked to survive in order not to make the righteous suffer on their account, does not ask if God will spare the city if there are fifty innocent people in it, but only if there are fifty *tzaddikim* or righteous people there.

It is noteworthy, in this regard, that the new JPS translation renders the Hebrew, *ha'af tispeh tzaddik im rasha* as *Will You sweep away the innocent along with the guilty?* in contrast to the old JPS translation used in this book, which renders the statement as *Wilt Thou indeed sweep away the righteous with the wicked?* In explanation of why such a change was made in the translation, it was asserted, "the Hebrew words *saddik* and *rasha* are legal rather than moral-ethical terms," in the context in which they appear.[249] This, however, is a dubious proposition, and in my view, an arbitrary and incorrect one. It should be noted in this regard that all eight major English translations of the Bible from the Tyndale (1530) to the Revised Standard Version (1960) also render the Hebrew phrase as "the righteous with the wicked," and I take this translation to be the more accurate one in this case.[250] The divine judgment of Sodom and Gomorrah is not presented to us by the biblical author as a legal proceeding concerning application of the law, but as a political one concerning the broader concept of justice; whether a society merits destruction is not a legal question, and the attempt to force a legal interpretation of the biblical terms seems to miss the point of the whole passage. The biblical writer is dealing with the matter of righteousness and wickedness as it applies to an entire society and not to the innocence or guilt of individuals within it.[251]

Abraham is not raising the issue of individual as opposed to collective responsibility; that only those guilty of wrongdoing should be punished and the innocent left untouched. What is at issue here is not the guilt or innocence of individuals but the broader question of whether a society that has become so dysfunctional as to be irredeemable should be permitted to continue to exist, and at what degree of dysfunction a negative response is appropriate.[252] Innocence and righteousness are not synonymous. Innocence is passive, whereas righteousness is active. Abraham evidently understands that there will always be innocent people in even the most corrupt society, and that in the course of historical events the innocent often get caught up in a web of circumstances that leads to their unwarranted suffering and death. But he also understands that the suffering of the innocent is not what is at issue in determining whether a society has become dysfunctional to the extent that its continued survival cannot be justified. The mere presence of even large numbers of innocent people does not in itself contribute to reforming a corrupt society. To do that requires righteous people who are prepared to act to improve their society. It requires that righteous people *within the city* be actively engaged in attempting to bring about the necessary change, if there is to be any hope for redeeming the society.[253]

> [18.26] *And YHVH said: "If I find in Sodom fifty righteous within the city, then I will forgive all the place for their sake."* [18.27] *And Abraham answered and said: "Behold now, I have taken upon me to speak unto YHVH, who am but dust and ashes.* [18.28] *Peradventure there shall lack five of the fifty righteous; wilt Thou destroy all the city for the lack of five?" And He said: "I will not destroy it, if I find there forty and five."* [18.29] *And he spoke unto Him yet again, and said: "Peradventure there shall be forty found there." And He said: "I will not do it for the forty's sake."* [18.30] *And he said: "Oh, let not YHVH be angry, and I will speak. Peradventure there shall be thirty found there." And He said: "I will not do it if I find thirty there."* [18.31] *And he said: "Behold now, I have taken upon me to speak unto YHVH. Peradventure there shall be twenty found there." And He said: "I will not destroy it for the twenty's sake."* [18.32] *And he said: "Oh, let not YHVH be angry, and I will speak yet but this once. Peradventure ten shall be found there." And He said: "I will not destroy it for the ten's sake."* [18.33] *And YHVH went His way, as soon as He had left off speaking to Abraham; and Abraham returned unto his place.*

God patiently permitted Abraham to negotiate with Him, and Abraham does so in as respectfully and self-demeaning a manner as possible. He realizes that he is participating in an extraordinary and unprecedented negotiation with the master of the universe, and he must be careful not to overstep his bounds into the vast chasm separating them. Accordingly, he proceeded with great caution and circumspection from one stage of the negotiation to the next, progressively getting his divine interlocutor to reduce the threshold at which the collective punishment would take effect from fifty righteous persons to ten, but no lower. It has been suggested that the biblical author sought to indicate in the divine responses that God had already taken into account Abraham's plea that the righteousness of those who might so be characterized in Sodom not be assessed against a universal standard but relative to the society in which they attempted to act righteously. He did this, it is argued, by deliberately writing the Hebrew word *tzaddikim* (righteous persons) in the biblical text defectively, omitting one of its letters, and thereby indicating that it was understood and accepted that their righteousness was similarly defective in some significant respects from what a universal standard would require, a deficiency that would not affect the outcome here.[254] Nonetheless, even with a relaxed standard, at best there were fewer than ten, and ten was evidently the critical minimum that would be acceptable as a threshold for purposes of saving the city from destruction.[255] That is, God agreed that if there were to be found at least ten righteous people in the cities, He would forego the collective punishment of their entire populations. But, as He surely knew beforehand, not even that small number of righteous persons were to be found there, and the cities were subsequently destroyed along with their inhabitants, except for Abraham's nephew Lot and his immediate family, who were permitted to survive. It may be that they were the only righteous persons in the city, and were therefore permitted to flee in time to avoid being caught up in its destruction. It may also be that they were merely innocent but not righteous, and that their survival was a divine gift to Abraham and not something they actually merited. In any case, the biblical text does not even suggest implicitly that their survival was the result of an act of divine justice. Indeed, as will soon become increasingly clear, it was more than likely an unmerited act of divine grace, an act of beneficence that superseded the requirements of divine justice.

It is noteworthy that the biblical author did not have Abraham argue that collective punishment is unjust even if there were only a single righteous person who would unjustifiably be affected by it. Presumably, Abraham agreed, at least from the standpoint of divine but not necessarily human justice, that if a community did not have a critical mass of righteous people it might be considered irredeemable. Without at least a given minimum of active virtuous people upon which to build, the essential basis for progressive improvement of the society simply would not exist. Under such circumstances divine collective punishment of the offending societies could conceivably be justified, even though it might involve what we in modern times have come to call "collateral damage," that is, inadvertently subjecting some innocent persons to unwarranted suffering. In effect, divine justice overrode divine compassion, for to spare the city even if it did not contain a saving minority would be tantamount to condoning the outrages that led to the original determination that the city had become irredeemably dysfunctional. Abraham has to learn that evil cannot be condoned before he can teach others *the way of the Lord, to do righteousness and justice*.[256] Compassion may, under certain circumstances take precedence over law, but not over justice, indeed, never over divine justice which is absolute.

The point of the exercise had been realized. Abraham had come to understand that divine justice and human justice are not always fully compatible because they reflect different imperatives. Man and God are not equals even though man is urged to follow in God's ways to the extent possible, but this must be understood to apply to positive actions such as those that enhance humanity and not to negative ones that are destructive of it. Although Abraham might have been prepared to spare a corrupt society as long as there was a single decent human being in it, he now understood that divine justice was more demanding and, as a result, Sodom and Gomorrah would be subjected to cataclysmic destruction.

At this point in the narrative, attention is diverted temporarily from Abraham to Sodom and the fate of his nephew Lot, a digression that is important in that it has significant consequences for the descendants of Abraham later on in their history. Although Abraham had three visitors, one of them simply disappears from the scene, presumably having fulfilled his mission during the visit, the remaining two arriving at Sodom. And now, for the first time, the biblical writer describes the men as angels, raising the inevitable question of why they were not so identified by him earlier.

Putting aside fanciful notions about the earlier and later materials deriving from different sources, which the final editor was for some reason unable to modify in any way even for consistency, I would suggest that a simpler resolution of the problem lies in the matter of function. Although the three "men" of the visit to Abraham were indeed angels according to the biblical author, they were not identified as such because only one of them, the one whose function was to speed Abraham's recovery, in line with traditional interpretations, was functioning in such a capacity. The two remaining "men," as they approach Sodom, only now begin to take on their angelic roles, and are therefore identified as such. Their initial aim would then be, as a sort of divine scouting party, to assess whether there was a basis for any mitigation of the decision to obliterate Sodom and Gomorrah for their crimes against humanity. This understanding of the narrative also lends some additional credence to the alternate interpretation of the events of the visit to Abraham discussed above.

> [19.1] *And the two angels came to Sodom at even; and Lot sat in the gate of Sodom; and Lot saw them, and rose up to meet them; and he fell down on his face to the earth;* [19.2] *and he said: "Behold, now my lords, turn aside, I pray you, into your servant's house, and tarry all night, and wash your feet, and ye shall rise up early, and go on your way." And they said: "Nay, but we will abide in the broad place all night."* [19.3] *And he urged them greatly; and they turned into him, and entered into his house; and he made them a feast, and did bake unleavened bread, and they did eat.*

In a place known to be especially inhospitable to strangers, Lot clearly represents a person not completely attuned to the society of which he had sought to be a part. Nonetheless, his behavior seems quite exaggerated even for a cultural maverick. Let us therefore assume that Lot is sitting *in the gate of Sodom*, the area of the entrance to the city where merchants and traders greet caravan traffic for the purpose of conducting business, just before evening set in and the gates closed for the night.[257] Seeing two strangers approach, presumably unaccompanied by a string of pack animals hauling merchandise, Lot is curious and goes to greet them. Let us further assume that in the process of exchanging greetings, the strangers ask for directions to the house of Lot to whom they have been requested to bring greetings from his uncle Abraham. Upon hearing that, Lot, estranged but nonetheless owing his life to Abraham, *fell down on his face to the earth*, emulating the approach to hospitality that he had learned in the house of his uncle. Although the men, having fulfilled their obligation to Abraham by extending the latter's greeting, indicate their readiness to spend the night outdoors, Lot successfully insists that they have dinner and then spend the night at his home, taking charge of preparations as did Abraham the previous day, *and he made them a feast, and did bake unleavened bread.*[258] That is, although he superficially seemed to be emulating his uncle's famous hospitality, there was in fact very little similarity between them even in this regard. Whereas Abraham asked his traveling guests to stop for a little bread and water, and then prepared a sumptuous meal, promising little but doing a lot, his nephew behave quite differently. Lot prepared a feast for his guests, which the biblical writer tells us consisted essentially of some unleavened bread. This helps explain why when these same men came to Abraham they unhesitatingly accepted his offer of hospitality (Gen. 18:5), their initial reaction here was to indicate that they preferred to sleep in the street. In any case, having accepted his hospitality, they washed themselves, and after eating the meager fare prepared for them by Lot, the men prepared to go to bed for the night.

> [19.4] *But before they lay down, the men of the city, even the men of Sodom, compassed the house round, both young and old, all the people from every quarter.* [19.5] *And they called unto Lot, and said unto him:* "*Where are the men that came in to thee this night? Bring them out unto us, that we may know them.*" [19.6] *And Lot went out unto them to the door, and shut the door after him.* [19.7] *And he said:* "*I pray you, my brethren, do not so wickedly.* [19.8] *Behold now, I have two daughters that have not known man; let me, I pray you, bring them out unto you, and do ye to them as is good in your eyes; only unto these men do nothing; forasmuch as they are come under the shadow of my roof.*"

It is difficult for a modern reader to imagine the degree of depravity depicted in this narrative, notwithstanding the not inconsiderable depravity so rampant in our own age. The picture the narrator sets before us is that of a society in which hospitality is a crime and pederasty a popular sport, much as is the case with the latter in some contemporary prisons. Learning that Lot had the temerity to offer hospitality to two strangers, the whole town, figuratively speaking, became aroused at this violation of its social norms and demanded that the men be handed over to the assembled crowd to dispose of according to their pleasure. In Sodom, this meant male rape, and the name of the city in which such maltreatment of strangers was acceptable public behavior subsequently became immortalized in the widely considered perverse sexual practice known as sodomy. It is noteworthy, bearing in mind Abraham's earlier confrontation with God over the proposed destruction of Sodom, in which Abraham was told that the place would be permitted to survive if ten righteous men were found in the city, that, *the men of the city, even the men of Sodom, compassed the house round, both young and old, all the people from every quarter*. What is conspicuous by its absence in the narrative is even a single voice among the Sodomites protesting against what the townspeople were planning to do.[259] The sins of Sodom thus consisted not only in what the people did, but also in what they failed to do—passivity in the face of evil is a sin of omission that makes one complicit in that evil.[260] This also provides an answer to one of the most troubling questions about the entire affair, namely, if Sodom and Gomorrah are to be destroyed because *the cry of Sodom and Gomorrah is great*, are there not among the oppressed in the city more than ten who merit being saved from the destruction? What we are being told is that Sodom typifies a society that has become so corrupt that the oppressed are no less evil than their oppressors, and that although there may be many innocent among them, there are very few if any righteous.

Having offered his hospitality to the two strangers, Lot also assumed responsibility for their protection and stepped out of the house to meet the ringleaders of the mob that had assembled and surrounded his home. Closing the door behind him, he stood facing the crowd alone and pleaded with them desperately not to carry out their vile intentions. As an alternative, he offered to turn over his two virgin daughters for their pleasure, a proposal that strikes the modern reader as being as depraved as the demand of the Sodomites.[261] What are we to make of this? Is Lot really proposing to throw his daughters to the mob in place of surrendering the strangers? Does it represent a deliberate choice based on considerations of political expediency, since safeguarding guests incurs reciprocal obligations whereas protecting his daughters neither adds nor subtracts from his position in Sodomite society?[262] Or, is it simply a ploy to shock the people surrounding him into backing off from their demand?

The answer may lie in a proper understanding of the political culture of Sodomite society. First, it is inconceivable that Sodom could have survived until this point as a prosperous city if it was characterized by continuous random violence; pervasive chaos would make commerce impossible. Accordingly, it seems reasonable to assume that it was in fact a city in which law and order prevailed. The problem therefore lay in the nature of its laws and social and political order. Second, the violation of social norms that Lot appears to have committed, according to the narrator, is that of extending hospitality to strangers. It is noteworthy in this regard that when the two strangers indicated to Lot that they were planning to spend the night outdoors while in the city, Lot did not tell them that they should come to his house because it would be unsafe for them to sleep outside. Since it is most unlikely that Sodom could be autarkic, the presence of alien merchants and caravan drivers was probably a common sight in the city; there may have even been hostels or inns to accommodate them for brief stays during inclement weather. At other times of the year, particularly during the dry season, such wayfarers probably slept outdoors, along with their animals, in some designated public areas such as "the broad place" spoken of by the two strangers.

Why then was hospitality shown to strangers in one's home considered so offensive? It would seem that Sodom's very security and prosperity had led its leaders to cultivate a culture of narcissism that became pervasive in the society, even among the disadvantaged. This suggests not only that the Sodomites were xenophobic; they also exhibited an extreme self-centeredness that bred apathy and insensitivity to the needs of others, which led to active abuse of the helpless. As later explained by Ezekiel, one of several prophets that drew analogies to Sodom and Gomorrah, *Behold, this was the iniquity of...Sodom: pride, fullness of bread, and careless ease was in her and her daughters; neither did she strengthen the hand of the poor and needy. And they were haughty, and committed abomination before Me; therefore I removed them when I saw it* (Ezek. 16:49-50).[263] This suggests a significant class division in the society, with those at the bottom of the social and economic ladder left bitter, neglected, abused, and, probably as prone to employ violence in search of relief, as were their oppressors in denying it to them. This in turn led to a fear by those higher up on the ladder that others both at home and abroad were envious of their good fortune, and raised concern about a possible joining of those elements against them, a fear which caused them to guard it ever more zealously. This xenophobia made hospitality a crime against the society; welcoming a stranger in to one's home was seen as equivalent to allowing a foreigner to establish a foothold in the city, and this was not to be tolerated. The societal elite would not tolerate any association of strangers with the lower classes, and the latter would similarly be opposed to any strangers in the city who were perceived as strengthening the hand of the ruling class. As a result, hospitality to strangers was frowned upon by all segments of the society and was acceptable only under the most restrictive conditions; above all, strangers were not to be encouraged to remain in the city any longer than absolutely necessary for conducting their legitimate business there. By violating this societal norm, Lot, who was surely considered a member of the upper class of Sodom, given his wealth, would be seen as treasonous by the lower class. The implication of all this is that the problem with Sodom was not its endemic lawlessness but the dysfunctional character of its laws, which promoted social unrest. As one modern writer put it: "Sodom represented a philosophy which was translated into practice. It placed law above justice, order above compassion, self-interest above sharing. Giving charity was a punishable offence; welcoming a stranger was a crime."[264]

It would not have been difficult for the leaders of Sodom, once learning of what Lot had done, to quickly organize a rabble to demand that the strangers, perceived as a danger to them, be turned over to the mob to be abused and humiliated, probably as a warning to other strangers not to attempt in any way to make an inroad into Sodomite society. Lot's vain effort to get them to back off by offering them his daughters instead of the strangers missed the mark; the authorities would hardly condone the mass rape of citizens of Sodom, and Lot as well as the people who confronted him surely was aware of that. The issue was not satisfying some perverse lust for a few people who would take advantage of the opportunity; it was making an example of anyone who violated the prevailing culture of narcissism and its strictures. Accordingly, Lot's appeal was rejected out of hand.

> [19.9]{.sup} *And they said: "Stand back." And they said: "This one fellow came in to sojourn, and he will needs play the judge; now we will deal worse with thee, than with them." And they pressed sore upon the man, even Lot, and drew near to break the door.* [19.10]{.sup} *But the men put forth their hand, and brought Lot into the house to them, and the door they shut.*

What took place should dispel any notion that it was a spontaneous mob action that was taking place. It will be recalled that when Lot first separated from Abraham and chose to live in the Jordan valley, he initially lived in a tent near the entrance to Sodom instead of in a house within its walls. Lot remained outside the city because he presumably was not welcome as a resident. He might conduct business there but was unable to reside there until much later, possibly not before Abraham succeeded in recapturing the wealth of Sodom that was seized by the invaders from Mesopotamia, whom Abraham boldly attacked. It is conceivable that it was only because of this act of his kinsman that the Sodomites, probably most reluctantly, agreed to allow Lot to become resident in the city, presumably permitting him to assume the status of a citizen.

Although many years had passed since then, Lot evidently was never seen as a true Sodomite, which indeed he was not, and this is made very clear in the manner in which he was addressed by the assembled crowd. He was and remained a stranger, one who merely *came in to sojourn* in the city, a temporary resident at best. Here he is, a tolerated stranger, fortunate above other men in a similar situation, and he presumes not only to violate the established norms of the society that has graciously allowed him to participate in its benefits, but also to dare to *play the judge*, in effect demanding that the rules be set aside because he elected to do what they forbade. To a disinterested observer, this would appear to be an opportunity for which some Sodomite leaders had long waited to deal with the alien element among them that Lot may have been perceived to represent. Not only would they ignore his pleas but would take reprisals against him as well as against the strangers he was trying to protect. However, the men they sought within the house were not going to permit anything of the kind to happen. They seized Lot and brought him back into the house, bolting the door, and took steps to prevent the mob from breaking into the house.

> ¹⁹·¹¹ *And they smote the men that were at the door of the house with blindness, both small and great; so that they wearied themselves to find the door.* ¹⁹·¹² *And the men said to Lot: "Hast thou here any besides? son-in-law, and thy sons, and thy daughters, and whomsoever thou hast in the city; bring them out of the place;* ¹⁹·¹³ *for we will destroy this place, because the cry of them is waxed great before YHVH; and YHVH hath sent us to destroy it."*

The narrator tells that, in some unspecified manner, the Lot's visitors managed to cause the men at the door of the house to be struck with a temporary blindness.²⁶⁵ Nonetheless, we are told, they were so determined to carry out their nefarious purpose that, even though temporarily blinded, they did not cease to attempt to find the door to the house. It was only after groping for it unsuccessfully for some time that they gave up trying, disbanded, and returned to their homes. However, the danger was far from past, and there was every expectation that they would return in daylight to carry out their threats, possibly with even greater determination. The time had come for Lot's visitors to reveal who they were and why they had come to Sodom. They had reassessed the conditions in Sodom and had concluded that the initial divine judgment for its destruction was fully justified, and that they would now carry it out. However, Lot, his household, *and whomsoever thou hast in the city*, that is, whether they live with him or not, are to be spared, but for this to happen they must leave the city before it is too late.

It is interesting to note that Lot and his entire household are to be spared, even though it seems that the angels are unaware of how many people may be included in that category, since they asked about sons, which Lot evidently did not have, although they may have been referring to grandsons by his married daughters. Moreover, even if we assume that Lot is indeed a righteous person, deserving to be saved because of his own merits and not merely on account of Abraham, can we say the same about his entire family? Based on what occurs subsequently, we must assume that not all of Lot's family might be characterized as among the righteous, and that they were to be saved only because of the merit of Lot, if they so chose.

Lot, evidently still bearing the marks of his upbringing in the household of Abraham, takes the words of his visitors to heart and proceeds to organize the exodus of his family from Sodom.

> ¹⁹·¹⁴ *And Lot went out, and spoke unto his sons-in-law, who married his daughters, and said: "Up, get you out of this place; for YHVH will destroy the city." But he seemed unto his sons-in-law as one that jested.*

Lot was faced by a difficult task: he had to convince his sons-in-law, whom we may assume were native Sodomites, to leave their homes immediately because the city was about to be destroyed by a god in whom they did not believe, and about whom Lot himself may have had some doubt, notwithstanding his earlier long association with Abraham. Nonetheless, the fact that his visitors were able to save him and themselves from the crowd that threatened them by miraculously blinding those who attempted to break into his house was sufficient for him to take their warning seriously. Predictably, his sons-in-law would not take him seriously; they were not about to abandon their homes and positions in a prosperous city on the fantastic whim of their father-in-law. For Lot, this meant, of course, that he would also lose his two married daughters, as well as their children if they had any, in the impending disaster.[266]

> 19.15 *And when the morning arose, then the angels hastened Lot, saying: "Arise, take thy wife, and thy two daughters that are here; lest thou be swept away in the iniquity of the city."* 19.16 *But he lingered; and the men laid hold upon his hand, and upon the hand of his wife, and upon the hand of his two daughters; YHVH being merciful unto him. And they brought him forth, and set him without the city.* 19.17 *And it came to pass, when they had brought them forth abroad, that he said: "Escape for thy life; look not behind thee, neither stay thou in the Plain; escape to the mountain, lest thou be swept away."*

As dawn approached, Lot was told that he could delay no longer; he had to give up any hope that his sons-in-law might have a change of heart and still save his married daughters. Nonetheless, he still lingered, perhaps out of a sudden fear that he was casting away everything he had built for himself over many years on the basis of something he was not entirely sure was real, perhaps out of a desire to take as much of his wealth and property with him as possible,[267] perhaps simply because Lot was inherently indecisive.[268] Unable to wait until Lot made up his mind, the two angels forcibly took him and his wife and remaining daughters out of the city, where they were instructed, *Escape for thy life; look not behind thee*, that is, get moving and do not even take the time to look back; every moment will count until they reach safety because, once the cataclysm begins, nature will not distinguish between those who are intended to suffer and those who might merit salvation. In this regard, the adjuration, *Escape for thy life*, has been understood by some to relate to Lot's hesitancy about leaving his property behind. He is being told, in effect, to forget about such concerns and concentrate on saving his life and that of his family.[269]

What is the significance of the instruction that they should not look back at the destruction that was taking place behind them? One school of thought suggests that, because they were not being saved because of their own merit but only because of the merit of Abraham,[270] it was inappropriate for them to put themselves in a position to gloat over the fact that they were surviving while the others were being destroyed.[271] The implication of this being that if Lot and his family had merited salvation on their own account, their looking back on the suffering of others would have been acceptable, presumably because punishment of the wicked may be seen as evidence of divine justice and should be welcomed by the righteous.[272] Others, however, maintain that gleefully contemplating the suffering of others under any circumstances is unacceptable, because even if God causes it to take place, He takes no pleasure in it.[273]

To avoid getting caught in the destruction that was to sweep the entire Jordan plain, Lot was told to get to higher ground on one of the nearby mountains of Moab, but he objected on the grounds that he could not make it there in time, either because of age or infirmity, if the destruction was about to ensue.[274]

> [19.18] *And Lot said to them: "Oh, not so, my lord;* [19.19] *behold now, thy servant hath found grace in thy sight, and thou hast magnified thy mercy, which thou hast shown unto me in saving my life; and I cannot escape to the mountain, lest the evil overtake me, and I die.* [19.20] *Behold now, this city is near to flee unto, and it is a little one; oh, let me escape thither—is it not a little one?—and my soul shall live."* [19.21] *And he said unto him: "See, I have accepted thee concerning this thing also, that I will not overthrow the city of which thou hast spoken.* [19.22] *Hasten thou, escape thither; for I cannot do anything till thou be come thither."—Therefore the name of the city was called Zoar.—*[19.23] *The sun was risen upon the earth when Lot came to Zoar.*

Instead of attempting to make his way to the mountain, Lot proposed that he be permitted to flee to a small town not very far away in the Jordan plain, one he characterized as inconsequential when compared with Sodom and Gomorrah, which if it were allowed to escape the destruction was a destination he could reach in time. Conspicuous by its absence in this part of the narrative is any attempt whatsoever by Lot to intervene in the impending destruction of Sodom—he is no Abraham. Indeed, the only thing he appears to be concerned about is his personal safety. He pleads with the angel, *thou hast magnified thy mercy, which thou hast shown unto me in saving my life; and I cannot escape to the mountain, lest the evil overtake me, and I die.* Everything he says is couched in the first person singular, as though no one else was any longer of any consequence to him, including his surviving family members.

Lot's discussion evidently took place, according to the biblical writer, with only one of the angels, presumably the one dedicated to Lot's rescue, the other being concerned primarily with confirming the appropriateness of the mandated destruction. His guardian angel, perhaps exhibiting a bit of frustration with Lot's last minute demands, but pressed by time, agreed to his request so that they could get on with their mission and allowed the town spoken of by Lot to remain untouched. Lot managed to reach his haven by the time that the dawn had passed and it was morning. The biblical writer adds the interesting touch, for the benefit of the curious, that because the town was so small it was called Zoar.[275]

> [19.24] *Then YHVH caused to rain upon Sodom and upon Gomorrah brimstone and fire from YHVH out of heaven;*[276] [19.25] *and He overthrew those cities, and all the Plain, and all the inhabitants of the cities, and that which grew upon the ground.* [19.26] *But his wife looked back from behind him, and she became a pillar of salt.*

With Lot safely out of the way, the destruction of Sodom and Gomorrah, as well as the other cities of the Jordan plain, began. Lot's wife, however, evidently trailing behind Lot and their daughters, began to linger, looking backward despite the specific instructions she had been given not to do so, perhaps searching for a sign that her other daughters were somehow making their way out of the condemned city. As a result, she was overtaken by the *brimstone and fire* that the others managed to avoid and was transformed into what the narrator describes as *a pillar of salt*;[277] that is, as one commentator describes it, "Her body became encrusted and saturated with a nitrous and saline substance, that very likely preserved it for some time from decay."[278]

It seems reasonable at this point to ask, what is the significance of this episode—why are we being told about what happened to Lot's wife? One commentator suggests that its importance lies in what happened later with respect to Lot and his incestuous relations with his daughters, the children to which they gave birth, and their subsequent impact on the history of the descendants of Abraham. Had Lot's wife survived, it is argued, she would never have permitted those improper developments to take place.[279]

> [19.27] *And Abraham got up early in the morning to the place where he had stood before YHVH.* [19.28] *And he looked out toward Sodom and Gomorrah, and toward all the land of the Plain, and beheld, and, lo, the smoke of the land went up as the smoke of a furnace.* [19.29] *And it came to pass, when Elohim destroyed the cities of*

the Plain, that Elohim remembered Abraham, and sent Lot out of the midst of the overthrow, when He overthrew the cities in which Lot dwelt.

At the same time that the cataclysm was taking place in the Jordan plain, Abraham evidently had spent a restless night, probably in anticipation of the impending destruction about which he had been foretold. He arose early in the morning and went to the crossroads at which his angelic guests departed from him to go to Sodom, and at which location he experienced his colloquy with God regarding the fate of Sodom and Gomorrah and their people. From there he could see the billowing smoke arising from the plain, probably transfixed by the sight and the thought of the suffering that was being inflicted on a society that had permitted itself to become so totally and irredeemably corrupted that it no longer served any purpose in the divine scheme for the universe; he could not but marvel at the awesomeness of divine justice applied to an entire civilization. It was, however, as the biblical author reminds us, Abraham's sense of justice that so endeared him to God that, before destroying the cities of the Sodomite alliance, *that Elohim remembered Abraham, and sent Lot out of the midst of the overthrow*, affirming that it was not Lot's righteousness but Abraham's that saved him and his daughters from destruction along with the Sodomites.

At this point, the biblical author deviates once again from his central theme to describe the somewhat bizarre series of events that followed Lot's escape from the destruction that engulfed the region of Sodom and Gomorrah; events the outcome of which had significant effects on the subsequent history of the nation that Abraham was founding. As already indicated, the small nearby town that was renamed Zoar was spared at Lot's request so that he might find shelter there. But for reasons that are not clear, Lot decided to abandon Zoar and relocate to the mountain to which he was told to flee for safety in the first place.

19.30 *And Lot went up out of Zoar, and dwelt in the mountain, and his two daughters with him; for he feared to dwell in Zoar; and he dwelt in a cave, he and his two daughters.*

What was it that made Lot afraid to remain in Zoar? Could it have been that he saw no essential difference in the culture of its society than of the larger metropolises of Sodom and Gomorrah, and that he feared that, notwithstanding the assurance he was given that he would be safe there, it too might eventually face the same fate as its sister cities, something that does not appear to have occurred?[280] Perhaps he encountered the same sort of hostility to strangers in

Zoar that he had originally met in Sodom and could not bear the thought of willingly subjecting himself and his daughters to such a humiliating experience again. In any case, it must have been something rather extreme that made him prefer to live as a virtual hermit outside the framework of the society so close at hand.

We have no indication of how long Lot remained in Zoar before deciding to relocate to a cave in a not too distant mountain. Given what took place next, we may assume that his break with Zoar and its people was total. But if this was the case, we cannot but wonder how he managed to survive, along with his daughters, living in isolation in a mountain cave. Where and how did he obtain the food necessary for their survival? The biblical writer is not forthcoming on such questions, presumably because they are incidental to the main point of the narrative, and we are left to the use of our imaginations to fill in these not really insignificant difficulties in comprehending the story being related.

It has been suggested that one factor that contributed to Lot's viability in his mountain cave retreat was a direct consequence of the environmental conditions in the Jordan plain. Because of the intense heat in the southern part of the plain, well below sea level, the Sodomites used to store their wine, and possibly other of their more perishable foodstuffs in the cool caves of the nearby mountains.[281] Since the peoples of the several cities of the plain were annihilated, whatever was to be found there was now ownerless and available for the taking. There might conceivably have been a sufficient abundance of such food and drink to permit Lot and his two daughters to survive on it for some time, if this presumption is at all valid. In any case, the cave dwelling hermit-like lifestyle of Lot and his daughters eventually, although we have no indication of how long it took to reach that point, came into conflict with the normal feminine instincts of his daughters.

> [19.31] *And the first-born said unto the younger: "Our father is old, and there is not a man in the earth to come in unto us after the manner of all the earth.* [19.32] *Come, let us make our father drink wine, and we will lie with him, that we may preserve seed of our father."*

As the months and possibly years passed by, the daughters of Lot became fearful that, cut off from Zoar, and with the rest of the people of the region annihilated, it would take a miracle for men to come to their mountain caves in search of wives. Moreover, as Lot was already well advanced in years, he was increasingly unlikely to be willing or even able to relocate to another more distant place untouched by the destruction. Accordingly, unless they took drastic measures, they would remain spinsters and die childless, effectively lopping off their father's branch of the tree of humanity. Those who are inclined toward adopting this understanding of their motive, tend to see the actions of the daughters as reasonable and appropriate under the circumstances.

An alternative explanation reflects a rather different perspective with regard to the episode. The key to this view of the matter is the statement, *and there is not a man in the earth to come in unto us after the manner of all the earth.* First of all, we must ask on what basis the older daughter asserted, and the younger evidently concurred, that *there is not a man in the earth to come in unto us.* There surely were men in Zoar to whom they could be married, as undesirable as such a prospect may have been. Moreover, as one commentator suggests, there was no reason for them to believe that Abraham and his encampment had been destroyed as had Sodom and the other cities of the plain; from their mountain location they could surely have observed that there were no clouds of smoke arising in the west, where their grand uncle lived. This suggests further that the only way they could have reached such a conclusion is that Lot himself convinced them of it. But why would he do such a thing? One possible answer is that his pride would not permit him to go to Abraham with empty hands, pleading for assistance, given everything that had passed between them earlier. He would rather live as a hermit, even at the expense of his daughters, than submit himself to such an indignity and blow to his self-esteem.[282] An alternate approach reads the statement, *there is not a man in the earth to come into us,* as asserting that, following their narrow escape from Sodom, no decent person would have anything to do with them; they would be viewed as lucky pariahs that had somehow managed to escape the destruction.[283]

A second question concerns what the biblical author meant by the phrase, *after the manner of all the earth.* It has been suggested that this phrase refers to the usual practice in arranged marriages, whereby couples are appropriately matched in accordance with their social status. If this were the case here, then what Lot's older daughter appears to be saying is that after the destruction in Sodom, there are no longer any "suitable" men in the region, especially in Zoar, for them to marry, and that it would be demeaning for them to marry below their station in life. Accordingly, they preferred an incestuous relationship with their father to marrying suitors they considered to be beneath them.[284] Those who might be inclined to accept this explanation are apt to view Lot's daughters as true daughters of Sodom, preferring incest to a reduction in their social status.

However, there may also have been more pragmatic reasons for their readiness to enter into incestuous relations with their father. First, it seems obvious that they could not have had much regard for their father after he was ready to throw them to the mob in order to save perfect strangers from indignity. Second, if the legend that Lot once had another daughter whom he allowed to be burned to death by the Sodomites for showing compassion to a beggar were true,[285] the same Sodomites to whom their father was prepared to give them, they might be concerned that he would trade them off again if required to assure his own security. However, by having sons of their own to care for them as they aged they would be taking steps to assure their own welfare and long-term viability.[286]

In either case, it must have been clear to them that Lot would not agree voluntarily to sire their children, which they may have proposed to him and which he presumably had rejected, and that they therefore needed to employ a stratagem to achieve their goal. They would, in effect, have a drinking party on some pretext and make sure that Lot was so inebriated that he would unconsciously respond to sexual stimulation without being consciously aware of what he was doing or with whom he was doing it.

> [19.33] *And they made their father drink wine that night. And the first-born went in, and lay with her father; and he knew not when she lay down, nor when she arose.* [19.34] *And it came to pass on the morrow, that the first-born said to the younger: "Behold, I lay yesternight with my father. Let us make drink wine this night also; and go thou in, and lie with him, that we may preserve seed of our father."* [19.35] *And they made their father drink wine that night also. And the younger arose, and lay with him; and he knew not when she lay down, nor when she arose.* [19.36] *Thus were both the daughters of Lot with child by their father.* [19.37] *And the first-born bore a son, and called his name Moab—the same is the father of the Moabites unto this day.* [19.38] *And the younger, she also bore a son, and called his name Ben-ammi—the same is the father of the children of Ammon unto this day.*

Lot was evidently prone to drinking to excess and it was not difficult for his daughters to put their plan into action. He did become intoxicated, as they wished, and was easily manipulated and seduced. Once the incestuous act was consummated, the eldest daughter arose from his bed while he was still in a drunken stupor, leaving him blissfully unaware of what had happened. What worked the first time was tried again the following night, and it again succeeded, both daughters now becoming pregnant by their father.

The troubling question, however, is whether Lot was as drunk as he seemed or was he simply pretending to be so in order not to interfere with his daughters titillating albeit highly questionable plans. One ancient commentator observed that the early scribes interposed a superfluous diacritical mark above the Hebrew term for *when she arose* with regard to the older daughter but not when the same word is used in connection with the younger. The implication drawn from this was that the anomaly in the written text was placed there deliberately to draw a significant distinction between the two events. It is suggested that Lot was indeed so inebriated when he went to bed with his older daughter that he was unaware of what he was doing. However, when she arose from his bed, he awoke and became fully aware of what they had done. But this did not dissuade him from getting drunk again the following night, and that second time he was fully aware of what was about to transpire.[287]

Needless to point out, the narrator tells us nothing of what happened when Lot discovered that both his daughters were pregnant and that he was the only male there, or whether Lot and his daughters spent the rest of their lives in the cave. As suggested earlier, such details were irrelevant to the biblical writer's concerns, which in this instance was to set forth the origin of the Moabites and Ammonites, whose eponymous ancestors were bastard sons of Abraham's nephew Lot, whose descendants would play significant roles later in the history of Abraham's descendants.

10

The Birth of Isaac

Although the next significant stage in Abraham's odyssey begins with the birth of Isaac, for reasons that are not at all clear, the biblical writer interjects a curious incident into the narrative. Following the destruction of Sodom and Gomorrah, Abraham decides to pull up stakes and relocate out of the Hebron area. No reason is given, but several can be surmised. For one thing, the destruction of the cities of the Jordan plain may have had serious economic repercussions in the broader area, Hebron being a mere forty miles distant, disrupting trade and commerce generally. From this standpoint, moving out of the area, at least temporarily, may have been a strictly pragmatic business decision.[288] A second possibility is that Abraham may have been concerned about the environmental effects of the massive fires burning only a relatively short distance away and the resultant air pollution, especially the danger it might pose to an aging Sarah who, according to the divine promise, was soon to conceive and give birth to a child of her own. In any case, Abraham decided to move southward toward the southwestern fringe of the Negev region.

> [20.1] *And Abraham journeyed from thence toward the land of the South, and dwelt between Kadesh and Shur; and he sojourned in Gerar.* [20.2] *And Abraham said of Sarah his wife: "She is my sister." And Abimelech king of Gerar sent, and took Sarah.*

Abraham pitched his tents in the territory of the city-state of Gerar, grazing his flocks and herds in the general area between the major oasis of Kadesh-barnea in the northwestern Sinai and Shur, the "wall," probably referring to the Egyptian defensive wall guarding the frontier in the eastern Nile Delta, a line that generally represents the southernmost limit of Abraham's movements in the country. Leaving his encampment behind, as well as his men, it would appear that Abraham traveled a bit farther northward on occasion, from Kadesh to the city of Gerar itself, presumably for purposes of negotiating contracts for his pastoral products as well as the purchase of supplies. Being a newcomer to the region and essentially unknown there, especially while visiting Gerar, which had long been within the Egyptian sphere of political as well as cultural influence, Abraham felt it necessary to resort to the same sort of deception he had engaged in during his sojourn in Egypt many years earlier. Now as then, he was concerned about the safety of Sarah as well as himself and decided to try once again the same ruse that ultimately failed in Egypt, creating a situation in which divine intervention became necessary to extricate them from the dangerous clutches of the pharaoh.

What, it seams reasonable to inquire, was Abraham so worried about? Sarah was now almost ninety years old and, even if still an essentially beautiful woman, especially to him, it hardly seems likely that her identification as Abraham's wife would automatically place them both in danger; Abraham of losing his life and Sarah her virtue. As indicated shortly by the text, Abraham claimed that asserting she was his sister was a standard device employed by him whenever they traveled alone into strange territories, and he therefore simply went ahead and once again identified Sarah as his sister, merely as an extra precaution against what he did not expect to occur, but unfortunately did take place. But why, we cannot help wondering, would Abraham, at his advanced age, place Sarah and himself in such a vulnerable position in the first place? Did he not have trusted aides and servants that could handle for him whatever transactions brought him to Gerar? He would later trust his loyal major domo Eliezer with a most delicate and vitally important mission; why did he not do so now? The only solution, if we are not to succumb to the issue-begging temptation to simply characterize this episode merely as an alternate version of that which took place earlier in Egypt but now transposed to a Cisjordan locale, is to assume that Abraham, and perhaps Sarah with him, took a certain delight in living dangerously. After all, he was now almost a centenarian, and Sarah not far behind. But who, as a practical matter, would want to take this kind of advantage of such a venerable elderly couple visiting the big city from the rough countryside? Indeed, Abraham is well aware that Sarah is no longer quite the beauty she once was, and does not even suggest, as he did earlier, that her beauty could cause their downfall. But it probably does feel good for both to pretend that this might be the case, and they therefore do identify themselves as brother and sister. What harm can it cause? And now, for a second time, Abraham's scheme, seemingly entirely reasonable if not innocent in its conception and purpose, takes an unexpected turn and develops into a crisis that would once again require divine intervention to save Sarah from the ignominy of adultery. It turns out that the king of Gerar is anxious to add Sarah to his palace.

Why did Abimelech, the king of Gerar, send men to bring Abraham's "sister" to his harem? Indeed, the text even goes farther and indicates that he sent men who "took" Sarah, presumably against her will, an act that raises questions about the civic culture of a society where the ruler treats people within his domain as subject to his whim. The text does not provide a single clue as to why this occurred, leaving us free to speculate about various possibilities, three of which come readily to mind. One is predicated on the assumption that Abimelech had no prior knowledge of Abraham. In this case, someone who had seen and then inquired about Sarah must have reported to the king that a highly attractive and unattached albeit older woman had arrived in his realm and was residing in the camp of her brother. In a society where women were normally married off when they were quite young, it was exceptional to find a still attractive older woman who was unmarried, either because of spinsterhood or widowhood, or perhaps even divorce. Accordingly, Sarah was taken, perhaps simply to add a fresh albeit mature face to the king's harem, presumably without Abraham even being consulted about it. A second possibility is that there may have been a shortage of women in Gerar, in which case the arrival of an attractive unattached albeit older woman would have aroused immediate interest, and if what happened earlier in Egypt had reoccurred, Abraham could hardly reject the king's assertion of interest in Sarah, and was in no position to do anything about it once Abimelech sent men to take her.

The third possibility, and to my mind the most likely, is that Abimelech was fully aware of who Abraham was, either because his reputation had preceded him or because the king inquired about the apparently wealthy sheikh who had moved into his territory and was now visiting his capital. When his inquiries revealed that Abraham had an unmarried albeit aging sister in his household, Abimelech may have considered that a marital alliance with the house of Abraham might well serve his interests and therefore made Abraham an offer for her that the latter could not refuse without offending the king, who was after all his host. In other words, it made little practical difference whether Sarah was young or old, beautiful or homely. Indeed, the fact that she was an older woman made it appear that the king was actually doing Abraham a favor by relieving him of responsibility for a sister already well past the normal age for marriage. If this was what occurred, it would imply that, although Abraham believed the situation to be too fraught with danger to attempt to thwart the direction of events, Sarah balked at going voluntarily and was therefore taken to the king against her will.

In any case, Abraham again discovered the limits of reason, and once more could do little but pray for a miracle to save the honor of his beloved Sarah, a prayer that was to be answered promptly.

> 20.3 *But Elohim came to Abimelech in a dream of the night, and said to him: "Behold, thou shalt die, because of the woman thou hast taken; for she is a man's wife."* 20.4 *Now Abimelech had not come near her; and he said: "Adonai, wilt Thou slay even a righteous nation?* 20.5 *Said he not himself unto me: she is my sister? And she, even she herself said: He is my brother. In the simplicity of my heart and the innocency of my hands have I done this."* 20.6 *And Elohim said unto him in the dream: "Yea, I know that in the simplicity of thy heart thou hast done this, and I also withheld thee from sinning against Me. Therefore suffered I thee not to touch her.* 20.7 *Now therefore restore the man's wife; for he is a prophet, and he shall pray for thee, and thou shalt live; and if thou restore her not, know thou that thou shalt surely die, thou, and all that are thine."*

One is immediately struck by the similarities and differences between this episode and the earlier one concerning Abraham and Sarah in Egypt. In the latter, the Egyptian king was adjudged guilty of a serious transgression against morals and punished with an affliction that prevented him from carrying out his immoral design. In the present instance, Abimelech, as will be seen below, is also afflicted in a manner that prevents him from consummating an intimate relationship with Sarah. However, Abimelech is treated as innocent of intentional wrongdoing, and is graced with a divine warning that cautioned him against compromising Sarah, an act that would prove to be a fatal error, not only for him personally but for all his household as well. In other words, not only he but also his entire family and dynasty would be held culpable for his dishonoring Sarah and would suffer for it with the ultimate punishment. He is therefore urged to make his peace with Abraham by promptly restoring his wife to him, in return for which Abraham, who is a *prophet*, and therefore has a special relationship with God, will pray for the continued well being of the king and his house. It is especially noteworthy that it is only after Abraham's confronting God over Sodom and Gomorrah, and thus revealing the depth of his compassion for his fellow men, that Abraham is spoken of as a prophet, thus casually indicating to the reader that he had passed another major milestone on his spiritual odyssey.

Abimelech was clearly taken aback by the message from a God he did not know but from whom he received a communication in his dream, one that contained an explicit threat. As the narrator tells us, in a manner reminiscent of Abraham's colloquy with God about the fate of Sodom and Gomorrah, in his dream Abimelech challenged the concept of the collective punishment with which he was threatened: *Adonai, wilt Thou slay even a righteous nation?* Even if he were guilty, which he insisted he was not, why threaten to punish the entire nation for his transgression by decapitating its ruling dynasty and thereby reducing the kingdom to chaos? It is noteworthy, that the content of Abimelech's plea reflects the longstanding influence of Egyptian political culture in Gerar. As in Egypt, the nation is wholly identified with the ruler, both people and territory belong to him and their fortunes are contingent on his personal welfare.

However, a careful reading of the biblical text discloses a subtlety that adds a new dimension to the imaginary colloquy. Abimelech protests, *In the simplicity of my heart and the innocency of my hands have I done this.* But the divine response, in his dream is, *Yea, I know that in the simplicity of thy heart thou hast done this, and I also withheld thee from sinning against Me.* God acknowledges the simplicity of Abimelech's heart, but not the innocency of his hands. That is, although Abimelech did not intend to commit adultery, he was only prevented from violating Sarah by divine intervention, and that does not attest to his proclaimed innocence. After all, he did have a woman taken to his harem against her will, and the biblical writer may be hinting here that such behavior, while common in antiquity, is essentially unacceptable to God.[289] This appears to be the implication of the assertion that, *I also withheld thee from sinning against Me.* That is, although Abimelech might be considered innocent of any crime in the eyes of society, because he was unaware that Sarah was a married woman, he was not considered innocent in the divine view, since he would have violated Sarah had he not been prevented from so doing by divine intervention.[290] Once again, the biblical writer implicitly seems to be cautioning against making the assumption that divine justice must be modeled after the accepted norms of human justice; God's reasons are His alone, and this is a reality that man must learn to accept. Put another way, God is sovereign, and as such is not answerable to man.

> [20.8] *And Abimelech rose early in the morning, and called all his servants, and told all these things in their ears; and the men were sore afraid.* [20.9] *Then Abimelech called Abraham, and said unto him: "What hast thou done unto us? and wherein have I sinned against thee, that thou hast brought on me and on my kingdom a great sin? thou hast done deeds unto me that ought not to be done."* [20.10] *And Abimelech said unto Abraham: "What sawest thou, that thou has done this thing?"* [20.11] *And Abraham said: "Because I thought: Surely the fear of Elohim is not in this place: and they will slay me for my wife's sake.* [20.12] *And, moreover, she is indeed my sister, the daughter of my father, but not the daughter of my mother; and so she became my wife.* [20.13] *And it came to pass, when Elohim*[291] *caused me to wander from my father's house, that I said unto her: This is thy kindness which*

thou shalt show unto me; at every place whither we shall come, say of me: He is my brother."

Thoroughly disconcerted, Abimelech awoke immediately after the dream had concluded and roused his advisors to seek some possible insights into the meaning and significance of his bizarre dream. However, none could explain or interpret it, and Abimelech's concerns soon turned into a fear that gripped all of them. He then concluded that it would be best to confront Abraham regarding the violation of norms that he was about to commit, that he was informed about in his dream. Assuming a posture of innocence, he berated Abraham for having deliberately created such a mess and demanded to know why he had done it. What, he wanted to know, made Abraham conclude that identifying Sarah as his wife would be tantamount to signing his own death warrant? What did Abraham witness or experience in the society of Gerar that could possibly have led him to such an outrageous perception?

To our surprise, Abraham's response, at first glance, hardly seems an exemplar of sound rational thought. Because the people of Gerar were polytheists, he asserts, it was natural to assume that they would kill him in order to seize his enticingly beautiful ninety-year old bride. Needless to point out, this response does not appear to make much sense, since there were very few places in the world where there was *fear of Elohim*, but that did not mean that murder of husbands was acceptable as a social norm in all places where there was no such fear. All societies have rules that would prohibit such behavior, even though enforcement of such rules with regard to strangers might be lax in some.

However, on further reflection, the words that the narrator reports to have come from Abraham may be seen to have very significant implications. When Abraham said that he thought, *Surely the fear of Elohim is not in this place*, he was not suggesting that Gerar was therefore uncivilized, a city-state without laws designed to ensure the security and welfare of its citizens. What he was asserting was that where there was no fear of a one and only God, the sole source and authority of law is man's reason and, because man is not only a rational being but also a rationalizing being, the law will tend to be subverted when it is considered in one's interest to do so. And so, even if there were laws against adultery, there was still high risk that *they will slay me for my wife's sake*. That is, even if murder as such may be prohibited by law, if someone so chose, Abraham could secretly be done away with in a variety of ways and thereby make Sarah publicly available. In other words, where there is no fear of God, where man is not guided by a higher authoritative ethic, law in itself is an insufficient safeguard for the prudent person.

Moreover, this was especially so in the case of the king, who in practice even if not in theory was effectively above the law because he was the law. Killing Abraham, who was an alien without any legal status or right to protection in Gerar, was therefore a distinct possibility in order to avoid the even graver universally recognized offense of adultery, which was to be eschewed because it was so destructive of family life. In other words, perhaps reflecting on his earlier experience in Egypt where the king was above the law, Abraham's comment was actually, albeit unintentionally, directed against Abimelech himself, who had no *fear of Elohim*, and without such fear could do as he pleased with impunity.[292]

It would seem that, as the words came out of his mouth, Abraham himself suddenly understood the implications of what he was saying insofar as they related to the king whom he was addressing, and he quickly redirected his remarks to an equally contentious proposition, namely, that he had not really lied about Sarah's status. She was indeed his paternal although not his maternal sister. In the society of Mesopotamia from which he came, it was permissible for paternally related siblings to marry, and so Sarah could actually be both his wife and sister.[293] However, all that this explanation managed to accomplish was to self-describe Abraham as only partially untruthful, but deliberately deceptive in not revealing the more morally important aspect of the truth, namely, that Sarah was a married woman.

One cannot but wonder about what was happening to Abraham. Given the near disaster that took place years earlier in Egypt as a result of the deception regarding the personal status of Sarah, why did he not learn from that experience instead of continuing to pursue what was clearly a dangerous practice that surely was not generally adopted by all or even most persons traveling abroad with their wives, at least some of whom were probably also beautiful. But, one might object, surely the biblical writer does not intend to portray Abraham, who is to be the father of a nation committed to God, in such a flawed manner? However, I think the biblical narrative does intend to portray Abraham as an exceptional, indeed extraordinary, personality who is nonetheless flawed, as are all human beings, in one way or another. Abraham, as will become increasingly evident throughout the remainder of the narrative, is very much a human being who must continually confront the problems of reason versus faith, a person whose conscious choices do not always evoke praise from us. Abraham is thus presented to us as a real human, and to be human is to be flawed, as are all of his descendants along with the rest of humankind. The point is that Abraham remains a great man and founder of a special nation, not because he is perfect but in spite of his imperfections.

The biblical author clearly did not choose to deal explicitly with this issue, and so the text does not discuss Abimelech's reaction to Abraham's awkward apology. Nonetheless, it seems reasonable to assume that he may have evaluated Abraham as perhaps suffering from one of the not uncommon ravages of aging, assessing him as a person well intentioned but prone to occasionally bizarre behavior.

> 20.14 *And Abimelech took sheep and oxen, and men-servants and women-servants, and gave them unto Abraham, and restored him Sarah his wife.* 20.15 *And Abimelech said: "Behold, my land is before thee: dwell where it pleaseth thee."* 20.16 *And unto Sarah he said: "Behold, I have given thy brother a thousand pieces of silver; behold, it is for thee a covering of the eyes to all that are with thee; and before all men thou art righted."* 20.17 *And Abraham prayed unto Elohim; and Elohim healed Abimelech, and his wife, and his maid-servants; and they bore children.* 20.18 *For YHVH had fast closed up all the wombs of the house of Abimelech, because of Sarah Abraham's wife.*

The similarities and differences between the reactions of the Egyptian pharaoh and Abimelech to the episodes with Abraham and Sarah in which they were involved are also notable. The pharaoh permitted Abraham to retain the lavish gifts he had received *before* the deception was revealed. Abimelech provided Abraham with lavish gifts *after* the deception was revealed. The pharaoh effectively told Abraham to leave Egypt immediately and not return, and had him escorted to the frontier. Abimelech told Abraham that he was not only welcome to remain in his territory but to *dwell where it pleaseth thee*, that is, he was invited to become a permanent resident and pitch his tents anywhere he chose. Moreover, Abimelech also gave a very large monetary gift to Abraham specifically as *a covering of the eyes to all that are with thee*, a metaphor for compensation for any possible damage done to Sarah's reputation. That is, the lavish gift was to serve as a means of making those who were aware of the incident blind to the wrong she had almost suffered at Abimelech's hands, a way of indirectly declaring that both he and Sarah were completely innocent in the affair. It is noteworthy that in doing this, Abimelech told her, *Behold, I have given thy brother a thousand pieces of silver*, referring to Abraham, perhaps sarcastically, as Sarah's brother rather than as her husband, thus again dismissing any suggestion of intended marital impropriety.

For his part in resolving the crisis that had largely arisen as a result of his dissimulation, Abraham prayed for relief to be granted to Abimelech, his wife and his maidservants, presumably his concubines, whose reproductive organs and processes had ceased to function normally for as long as Sarah was in danger. This is the first time mention is made in Scripture of a man's prayer to God and, most remarkably, this is the prayer of a husband, whose wife was almost assaulted by another man, for the well being of that other person; it surely was not something that Abraham could do lightly. Although the text does not say so, we may assume that Abraham's prayer was duly answered positively, and normalcy returned to the king's household.

One cannot but wonder not so much why this incident occurred as to why it is related at this point in the narrative. Upon reflection, however, it may be construed as being intimately connected to the events that follow immediately thereafter, namely the fulfillment of the divine promise that Sarah would give birth to the son who will be Abraham's true heir. A clue to this may be seen in the emphatic assertion that *Abimelech had not come near her*, and the further statement that divine intervention assured that Abimelech was not able *to touch her*. It may be that the purpose of these statements was to forestall any malicious implications that may have been construed from the fact that, shortly after being taken to Abimelech's harem, Sarah finally became pregnant, even though the biblical text does not provide a specific timeline for these events. The consideration that some question might arise as to whether Abraham, a centenarian, was actually the father of the child she would carry, would surely be sufficient to depress even the most patient and forgiving person. How Abram would deal with such seemingly plausible innuendos would be yet another test of his character and faith. Indeed, it is possible that this was the very reason for incorporating this strange story into the narrative at this particular juncture.

> [21.1] *And YHVH remembered Sarah as He had said, and YHVH did unto Sarah as He had spoken.* [21.2] *And Sarah conceived, and bore Abraham a son in his old age, at the set time, of which Elohim had spoken to him.* [21.3] *And Abraham called the name of his son that was born unto him, whom Sarah bore to him, Isaac.* [21.4] *And Abraham circumcised his son when he was eight days old, as Elohim had commanded him.* [21.5] *And Abraham was a hundred years old, when his son Isaac was born unto him.* [21.6] *And Sarah said: "Elohim hath made laughter for me; every one that heareth will laugh on account of me."* [21.7] *And she said: "Who would have said unto Abraham, that Sarah should give children suck? for I have borne him a son in his old age."*

It is interesting to note the number of times, in this passage, that the fatherhood of Abraham is emphasized, which as indicated above may have come into question because of the proximity in time between Sarah's brief confinement by Abimelech and her subsequent pregnancy. Sarah was obviously overwhelmed with joy at what happened, which surely struck everyone as nothing short of miraculous that a woman of her age could not only conceive but actually give birth to a healthy child. Indeed, Sarah was convinced that everyone who heard of what occurred would chuckle at the idea of a ninety-year old giving birth, and there was no doubt in anyone's mind that she was the child's natural mother. However, there was also a bittersweet element in her laughter, because she was also concerned that the paternity of the child might be in doubt.[294] After all, it was fourteen years since Abraham had last sired a son through Hagar, and he may already have become the subject of malicious gossip during Sarah's pregnancy suggesting that not he but Abimelech was the father, thereby casting doubts on Isaac's legitimacy. Understandably, this would become a source of consternation to Sarah who, as will be seen shortly, would react very strongly to any such implication, no matter how indirect.

The one person who clearly did not share Sarah's joy at the birth of a child was her handmaid Hagar, who surely viewed this development as detrimental to her interests. Whatever special consideration Abraham had accorded to her as the mother of his previously only son Ishmael was now in serious jeopardy. It is not difficult to imagine that relations between the two women began to deteriorate once again, this time with more far-reaching consequences.

> 21.8 *And the child grew, and was weaned. And Abraham made a great feast on the day that Isaac was weaned.* 21.9 *And Sarah saw the son of Hagar the Egyptian, whom she had borne unto Abraham making sport.* 21.10 *Wherefore she said unto Abraham: "Cast out this bondwoman and her son; for the son of this bondwoman shall not be heir with my son, even with Isaac."*

It seems clear that relations between Sarah and Hagar had deteriorated even further after Isaac's birth than before. The fact that Sarah had given birth made Hagar's presence a visible reminder that the entire episode of giving her to Abraham as a surrogate for the purpose of allowing him to sire a son was a great mistake on her part, as well as on the part of Abraham. After all, if he had only had more faith in the divine promise, it would have been fulfilled through Sarah in the first place, albeit some fourteen years later. Now that Sarah had given Abraham a son, her maternal instinct came into play and she became determined to assure that Isaac alone would be Abraham's heir. But what was going to happen to Abraham's older son Ishmael? Did he not have a legitimate right to be Abraham's heir along with Isaac? As far as Sarah was concerned, this was out of the question. In her own mind, Ishmael had automatically been disowned the moment Isaac was born, a notion reflected in the narrator's remark that *Sarah saw the son of Hagar the Egyptian*; not Ishmael, Abraham's son, but the anonymous son of the alien Hagar. Sarah knew that Abraham had been promised that God would extend His covenant to Isaac, and that in that sense he alone would be Abraham's spiritual heir. However, she was equally concerned about assuring that Isaac would also be Abraham's sole material heir, and about this she was uncertain. Abraham certainly loved his older son and would find himself in a quandary over how to deal with the problem of arranging the inheritance after his passing. Sarah evidently intended to make sure that she had the decisive word on that subject, regardless of Abraham's paternal inclinations, and she came up with a plan to deal with the problem at an appropriate time.

The opportune moment to set her plan in motion seems to have come with the customary celebration in honor of Isaac's completion of his period of weaning, probably at age two or three.[295] At that affair she saw Ishmael, now sixteen or seventeen years old, *making sport*. It is not clear as to what Sarah saw him do that she took to be the last straw, so to speak, as far as she was concerned. It has been suggested that what upset Sarah so much was that Ishmael was *making sport* of the fuss being made over Isaac, since it was he, Ishmael, that had long been acknowledged by Abraham as his firstborn son.[296] As such, it was he who was Abraham's principal heir, and he would therefore be entitled to the traditional double share of Abraham's estate.[297] Some modern commentators take this interpretation a step farther and argue that the Hebrew term *metzahek,* translated as *making sport*, should be understood as implying that Ishmael "was playing the role of Isaac," that is, he was pretending as though he and not Isaac was to be the successor to Abraham in all respects, spiritual as well as political and economic.[298] Alternatively, Sarah's chagrin may have been aroused because Ishmael was joking about the possibility that Isaac was not really the son of Abraham but rather of Abimelech, as rumor had it. This would have cast doubt on Isaac's right to any part of Abraham's estate.[299]

In any case, it must have been something that Sarah found abhorrent and intolerable, and something she could use to press Abraham to take a step that he probably would never do on his own initiative, namely to get rid of Sarah's nemesis Hagar, and along with her Ishmael, who would be a serious rival to Isaac. On the basis of a list of grievances, on which this latest affront was presumably the seal, Sarah demanded of Abraham, *"Cast out this bondwoman and her son; for the son of this bondwoman shall not be heir with my son, even with Isaac."* As far as she was concerned, she and Hagar could no longer live in the same household. As for

Ishmael, regardless of Abraham's affection for him, he too had to go. She implicitly argued that one could not draw a practicable distinction between the spiritual and material heritage, both of which were bound up together in the covenant that God had made with Abraham. His heir had to be either Ishmael or Isaac; the inheritance could not be shared, and it was clear that God had designated Isaac to be its recipient. Sarah thus implicitly recognized that under established Mesopotamian law and custom, Ishmael would have a legitimate claim to a substantial share of Abraham's estate. But, since Hagar, and therefore Ishmael, was her property, why did she not simply banish them? Perhaps because that would not solve the inheritance problem, Ishmael could return after Abraham's death and make a legitimate claim for his share of the inheritance. Sarah needed Abraham to repudiate Ishmael as his son, and thereby impugn the legitimacy of any claim he might later make. To achieve that effect, she must have indicated her readiness to transfer Hagar, who was legally her property, to Abraham so that he would take the necessary steps to disown Ishmael.

It has been pointed out that there was a stipulation in ancient Mesopotamian law that if a father granted freedom to a slave woman and the children she bore him, they would forfeit their share of his estate, and, according to some, it evidently was this sort of loophole that Sarah demanded Abraham use to assure an unchallenged inheritance for Isaac.[300] Perhaps needless to point out, Abraham and Sarah no longer lived in Mesopotamia and could not therefore be bound by such law, even if they accepted it as a normal guide to practice in the absence of another system of customary laws in accordance with which they might feel obligated to live. Accordingly, overemphasis on what was or was not permitted under Mesopotamian law may be misleading, if not irrelevant, in terms of the biblical narrative.

> [21.11] *And the thing was very grievous in Abraham's sight on account of his son.* [21.12] *And Elohim said unto Abraham: "Let it not be grievous in thy sight because of the lad, and because of thy bondwoman; in all that Sarah saith unto thee, hearken unto her voice; for in Isaac shall seed be called to thee.* [21.13] *And also of the son of the bondwoman will I make a nation, because he is thy seed."*

Abraham was deeply troubled by Sarah's demand and unsure of how to respond to it. Although Hagar was legally Sarah's personal property and she could do with her as she chose, as a practical matter Hagar was also mother of his eldest son and therefore had attained, *de facto* if not *de jure*, a somewhat different status than that of a chattel servant of Sarah's. He was surely disturbed by the idea that Sarah might simply free her from her servitude and then throw her out of the house after these many years, something that Sarah surely understood she could no longer do, as a practical matter, without Abraham's consent. Where would Hagar go, and who would care for her? And Ishmael, whose exile Sarah was also demanding, how could he justify sending his son off into exile for some reason that he could not fully fathom? Despite Sarah's misgivings, Ishmael was still his son, a son he had longed for most of his life and one he finally was given only a few short years ago. He was distraught over the matter and was effectively immobilized, not knowing how to deal with the family crisis that had erupted with full force and did not seem susceptible to being contained.

It was at that point that God intervened once again, presumably appearing to Abraham in a dream and telling him that he should put aside his misgivings and follow Sarah's wishes in this regard. As cruel as it might appear to him, he was told, Sarah's judgment in this matter was more prescient than his.[301] She understood, better than he did, that Ishmael, by his natural disposition and nurturing, was unsuited to the covenantal role reserved for Isaac. Moreover, Ishmael's continued presence and influence on Isaac could prove detrimental to Isaac's fitness for the spiritual trials that lay ahead for both Abraham and his heir. It was therefore necessary that Hagar and Ishmael be sent away to ensure the future integrity of the covenant. The nation that was promised to Abraham would come into being through Isaac and not Ishmael, *for in Isaac shall seed be called to thee*.[302] At the same time, Abraham was reassured that he need not be overly concerned about the fate of Ishmael, because he too would be permitted to found a nation because of the merit of his father Abraham, but it would not be the nation of the covenant. And, indeed, we are told later that Ishmael sired twelve princes, who became founders of a dozen specifically named nations (Gen. 25:12-16).

Upon reflection we might ask, as Abraham may well have asked himself, what was the purpose of the entire affair with Hagar and Ishmael, which endured for more than a decade and a half, if it was to simply end by his sending them both away? If it was the divine wish that he should not have another son beside Isaac, why did divine intervention bring Hagar back to him after she had run away so that she would give birth to that very son? It would seem that the only purpose served was to put Abraham to another test of his faith in God, a faith that transcended the logic of familial attachment, a faith that demanded that Abraham give up his son for which he had yearned for so many years, and only after having doted on him as his heir for the last decade and a half. Surely traumatized by what was being demanded of him, yet mollified by the assurance that Ishmael, and presumably Hagar as well, would be taken care of by God, Abraham again yielded to the demands of faith and carried out the extremely distasteful task of disinheriting his son Ishmael and evicting him and his mother Hagar from his household.

> 21.14 *And Abraham rose up early in the morning, and took bread and a bottle of water, and gave it unto Hagar, putting it on her shoulder, and the child, and sent her away; and she departed, and strayed in the wilderness of Beer-sheba.* 21.15 *And the water in the bottle was spent, and she cast the child under one of the shrubs.* 21.16 *And she went, and sat down over against him a good way off, as it were a bowshot; for she said: "Let me not look upon the death of the child." And she sat over against him, and lifted up her voice, and wept.*

At the conclusion of his prophetic dream, Abraham awoke and proceeded to carry out the extremely distasteful task of effectively disowning his son Ishmael and sending him away together with his mother Hagar, whom he now divorced, so to speak. Sarah evidently had already transferred her chattel slave to Abraham so that he could grant her freedom from her bondage, thereby terminating their long relationship. Surprisingly, Abraham provided them with only a minimum amount of supplies, some bread and a bottle of water, to take on their journey, the destination of which we are left uninformed, but which we may presume was Egypt where Hagar may have had family or other connections. However, if they were proceeding on foot, as would appear to have been the case, it would have been counterproductive to burden them with more than they could reasonably carry until they reached their first rest stop, where they presumably could obtain whatever supplies they needed. It is also quite possible that he sent them away with empty hands at the insistence of Sarah, who may have insisted that he do so in order to make it clear to Ishmael that he was being disinherited, which might perhaps explain why he did not provide them with at least an ass. In any case, it seems quite unlikely that Abraham simply threw them out without making sure that they had a clear travel plan and adequate means of getting where they were going. It has also been suggested that Abraham probably did not intend that they go very far, so that he would be able to continue to provide for them, presumably without Sarah's knowledge.[303]

Unfortunately, it appears that Hagar somewhere took a wrong turn and got lost in the wilderness in the vicinity of the place that would later become known as Beersheba. Once the water ran out, their situation soon became desperate, Ishmael being the first to succumb to dehydration. Unable to proceed farther, and not knowing where to go even if they could, Hagar placed Ishmael under a shrub, where he would have a bit of shade, while she moved away some distance so as not to witness his suffering which she could do nothing to alleviate. All she could do was cry out in anguish and burst into tears. It is noteworthy that in relating this part of the story the biblical author three times describes Ishmael as a child, even though we know that he is at least sixteen or seventeen years old, an age at which one is already long considered a young man in the cultures of the region.[304] However, it would appear that the biblical author may be telling us by means of this subtle use of language that the experience of being sent away had a dramatic effect on Ishmael, who suddenly lost the cockiness of a teenager and took on the aspect of a pitiable child. It also has been suggested, in explanation of how it came about that Ishmael, a strapping lad of sixteen or seventeen, succumbed to the rigors of the desert before his mother, that whereas Hagar had previously been exposed to the problem of survival in the desert, both on her own and traveling with Abraham and Sarah, Ishmael had not been so exposed previously, having spent most of his life in the shelter of Abraham's encampments. It would still take some time before he became inured to the rigors of desert life.[305] Alternatively, an early commentator suggested that Ishmael may have felt ill at the time and consumed the available water more quickly than might have been anticipated.[306]

Probably because Hagar's problems were seen as the result of her own making, the biblical writer expresses little sympathy for her plight. Thus, when relief is to come as a result of divine concern, it is concern for Ishmael and not for Hagar that triggers subsequent events.

> [21.17] *And Elohim heard the voice of the lad; and the angel of Elohim called to Hagar out of heaven, and said unto her: "What aileth thee, Hagar? fear not; for Elohim hath heard the voice of the lad where he is.* [21.18] *Arise, lift up the lad, and hold him fast by thy hand; for I will make him a great nation."* [21.19] *And Elohim opened her eyes, and she saw a well of water; and she went, and filled the bottle with water, and gave the lad to drink.* [21.20] *And Elohim was with the lad, and he grew; and he dwelt in the wilderness, and became an archer.* [21.21] *And he dwelt in the wilderness of Paran; and his mother took him a wife out of the land of Egypt.*

God *heard the voice of the lad*, not that of his mother. Now, as the text subtly suggests, Ishmael is no longer considered as the pitiable child that his mother sees in him but as the lad in trouble that he really is, and the son of Abraham that God had promised to look after. It is interesting to note in this regard that Ishmael is henceforth referred to as a lad five times in the remainder of the biblical passage.

Hagar nonetheless has an important role to play in securing the well being of Ishmael, and for this purpose is contacted by a divine messenger, who reassures her concerning the fate of her son, *where he is.* That is, his physical salvation is at hand. However, it is she who must take the necessary step to actually save his life. She must find the well of water, which in fact exists in the place where she is, but she is so overwrought that she does not see it. It takes an act of God to *open her eyes* to what exists in plain sight, and she soon sees the well, goes to it and fills her water bottle, and gives Ishmael the fluids he needs to survive and recover.

The episode concludes with the assertion that, as promised to Abraham, God was with the lad. Hagar evidently decided not to continue on to Egypt and remained in the wilderness, where Ishmael grew and thrived, becoming an archer, a skill that enabled him from his youth to hunt successfully as well as to defend himself and his mother against enemies, both man and beast. Here in the wilderness he grew to become the *wild ass of a man* promised to Hagar many years earlier, his mother finding a wife for him from Egypt to share his nomadic existence.

The fact that Hagar obtains a wife for Ishmael is noteworthy on two counts. In the world of the ancient societies of the region, it was the responsibility of the father to obtain a wife for his son; because Ishmael is now fatherless as a practical matter, his mother assumes that responsibility. However, the responsibility of obtaining a wife for a son also meant incurring all the costs involved, such as the bride price. Thus, if we imagine Hagar being cast out with only some food and a bottle of water, from where did she obtain the wherewithal to obtain a bride for Ishmael from Egypt? The most plausible answer to this question is, from Abraham. It seems inconceivable that Abraham actually would send them away penniless. This suggests that Abraham must have made some financial arrangements for Hagar and Ishmael, perhaps a letter of credit to someone with whom Abraham did business in the area, which would permit them to thrive once they arrived at their destination.

The biblical writer tells us nothing of how Abraham dealt with the sudden loss of the son he had loved and nurtured for so many years, leaving that gap to be filled by imaginative speculation,[307] and concludes the story of the birth of Isaac and the subsequent disavowal and disenfranchisement of Ishmael with a historical note about how the well at Beersheba that served to save the lives of Hagar and Ishmael came to be dug and named. It would therefore seem that the events described in this historical note took place prior to the incident concerning Hagar and Ishmael at the site of the well, and explain why, although they had to be made aware of it by divine intervention, their means of their salvation had already been established in fact by Abraham.

21.22 And it came to pass at that time, that Abimelech and Phicol the captain of his host spoke unto Abraham, saying: "Elohim is with thee in all that thou doest. 21.23 Now therefore swear unto me here by Elohim that thou wilt not deal falsely with me, nor with my son, nor with my son's son; but according to the kindness that I have done unto thee, thou shalt do unto me, and to the land wherein thou hast sojourned." 21.24 And Abraham said: I will swear." 21.25 And Abraham reproved Abimelech because of the well of water, which Abimelech's servants had violently taken away. 21.26 And Abimelech said: I know not who hath done this thing; neither didst thou tell me, neither yet heard I of it, but today." 21.27 And Abraham took sheep and oxen, and gave them to Abimelech; and they two made a covenant. 21.28 And Abraham set seven ewe-lambs of the flock by themselves. 21.29 And Abimelech said unto Abraham: "What mean these seven ewe-lambs, which thou hast set by themselves?" 21.30 And he said: "Verily, these seven ewe-lambs shalt thou take of my hand, that it may be a witness unto me that I have digged this well." 21.31 Wherefore that place was called Beer-sheba; because there they swore both of them. 21.32 So they made a covenant at Beer-sheba; and Abimelech rose up, and Phicol the captain of his host, and they returned into the land of the Philistines. 21.33 And Abraham planted a tamarisk-tree in Beer-sheba, and called there on the name of YHVH, the El Olam.[308] 21.34 And Abraham sojourned in the land of the Philistines many days.

    The interchange described above seems to have taken place at the site of the well at Beersheba, to which Abraham evidently relocated after his sojourn in the region between Kadesh and Shur. But why, we may ask, is the king of Gerar, accompanied by the commander of his armed forces, visiting Abraham in the desert instead of sending a messenger to summon him to the city for an interview? Moreover, why is the king appealing to Abraham for a treaty of fealty that should last for at least for three generations? What could have precipitated the king's overture to him in this regard?

    It would appear that following their earlier encounter Abraham had relocated to the then neglected oasis of Beersheba, which was several miles from Gerar. At the same time, Abimelech had been attempting to expand his jurisdiction in that direction. What had emerged, as a matter of serious concern, was a dangerously escalating conflict between them over water rights. Survival in the region during the long dry season was dependent on ground water resources, access to which was problematic. Accordingly, ownership of wells and privileges of access to their contents were matters over which men were prepared to wage battle, and it seems that Abraham was incensed over the fact that someone claiming royal authority seized a well to which Abraham had a prior claim. Although Abraham evidently did not act to forcibly prevent the seizure, it is quite likely that he took steps to prevent it from happening again, even if it meant fighting for his rights. We may also reasonably assume that Abimelech and his advisors knew the tale of Abraham's earlier successful battle with the forces of the kings of Mesopotamia, and were aware that he had had Amorite allies that assisted him. Accordingly, it seems reasonable to assume that, when news of Abraham's preparations for battle to protect his wells reached Abimelech, he considered it both necessary and desirable to try to defuse an increasingly volatile situation that might draw him into an unwanted conflict not only with Abraham but also with an Amorite alliance. Because a man of Abraham's stature was the aggrieved party, and surely remembering the painful consequences of his previous encounter with Abraham in the matter of Sarah, Abimelech decided to reach out to him directly and cautiously.

Abimelech's approach to Abraham clearly reflected that the king had not forgotten the awesome dream about a god most favorably disposed toward Abraham and his wife, and concluded that prudence dictated that he act toward Abraham in a manner that clearly showed deference to that deity. Once having gotten past that point, Abimelech's approach was to remind Abraham that although he had been given free access to the lands in which he continued to sojourn, he did owe a debt of gratitude for this to the city-state of Gerar that permitted it. What Abimelech now asked for in this regard was that Abraham commit to what amounted to a non-belligerency pact that would remain in effect for an indeterminate period far into the future. Bearing in mind that Abraham deliberately still lived in a tent because he had been told that the land, over which he had been given a divine deed, would not come into his personal possession during his lifetime and into the hands of his descendants only some four centuries later, in accord with the divine revelation he had received earlier, he had no objections to Abimelech's request that he enter into a long-term pact with him.

However, Abraham made sure, the pact was to be reciprocal, and he demanded similar assurances from Abimelech, pointing out that people acting in Abimelech's name had committed a violation of his rights that he would not permit to happen again. Abimelech, perhaps honestly, perhaps disingenuously, claimed that whatever was done was done without his knowledge, suggesting that he fully disapproved of the sort of confiscation that Abraham had suffered. Having thus cleared the air between them, and observing traditional practices appropriate to such an occasion, Abraham and Abimelech agreed to enter into a non-belligerency pact.

Immediately thereafter, Abraham insisted that Abimelech acknowledge before witnesses that the well at which they were now convened was in fact one that was dug by Abraham and by customary law was his property. Abimelech had no choice but to so stipulate to Abraham's ownership and they both swore to uphold the pact to which they had agreed. *Wherefore that place was called Beer-sheba; because there they swore both of them*, that is, it was called the "well of the oath," to commemorate what had taken place there.

With the crisis averted, Abimelech and Phicol returned *into the land of the Philistines*. This geographical reference appears to be an anachronism introduced by the biblical author that is difficult to explain. Historically, the Philistines do not appear as such in the land until several centuries after Abraham, and their location was along the coastal lowland, the Shephelah, and not as far inland as described here. However, some scholars speculate that there may have been earlier immigrations of Philistines into the area centuries prior to the main intrusions of the Sea Peoples into the region in the thirteenth century B.C.E., and that the Gerar of the biblical narrative may have been a city-state established by those earlier Philistines who subsequently were absorbed into the general Canaanite population.[309]

In any case, after concluding the treaty, Abraham continued to sojourn in the general area for many years to come. Moreover, the biblical writer informs us, *Abraham planted a tamarisk-tree in Beer-sheba, and called there on the name of YHVH, El Olam*. Abraham not only marked the occasion of the conclusion of a treaty with Abimelech by planting a tree, expected to last for generations, to symbolize his assertion of a right to Beersheba; the tree also served as a reminder that the pact with Abimelech had been sworn in the name of the eternal God, who would forever remain a witness to the agreement.

Abraham's planting of a tamarisk in Beersheba may also be understood as reflecting the expectation that, as Abraham aged, there eventually would come a time when he would have to cease living as a semi-nomad and settle in a fixed place, essentially leaving the pastoral life behind and taking up that of an agriculturist. As will be seen later, he does ultimately settle in Beersheba, his tamarisk perhaps serving as the first of such plantings intended to provide a windbreak against the sandstorms that would otherwise ravage the fruit orchards he would cultivate.[310]

11

Abraham's Greatest Trial and Its Aftermath

As pointed out in the introduction to this study, the pattern and sequence of the episodes in the life of Abraham that are presented to us by the biblical writer may be understood as intending to portray a series of tests or trials of the patriarch's moral fortitude and growing commitment to act in the faith that continued to deepen during the course of his mature life. What occurs next is generally considered by most but not all traditionalists to be his last trial, albeit that it is the only one specifically identified as such by the biblical writer. It was, in any case, the greatest challenge to faith and morals to which he was subjected during the course of his long spiritual odyssey.

> *22.1 And it came to pass after these things, that Elohim did prove Abraham, and said unto him: "Abraham"; and he said: "Here am I." 22.2 And He said: "Take now[311] thy son, thine only son, whom thou lovest, even Isaac, and get thee into the land of Moriah; and offer him there for a burnt-offering upon one of the mountains which I will tell thee of."*

Having been instructed earlier to send away his older son, Abraham heard himself now being asked to do away with his younger son and thereby effectively erase the possibility of the actualization of the divine promise that the commitments made to Abraham under the covenant would be fulfilled through Isaac and his descendants, something that simply did not make any sense. The biblical writer does not tell us the reason for this horrendous demand, or indeed what it was intended to demonstrate, leaving students of the texts to ponder these questions and to suggest possible answers, each of which provides a sometimes radically different perspective on what the narrator seeks to convey to us through this unsettling story. A few examples of the arguments made by some traditional commentators over many centuries will indicate something of the range of such perspectives.

It has been suggested that the purpose of this last trial is to create the circumstances under which Abraham may bring about his ultimate active intellectual perfection. Through this trial, Abraham will complete his transformation from a natural philosopher into a man of supreme faith.[312] In this view, Abraham, in effect, makes an existential leap into the absurd, sacrificing the demands of reason on the altar of faith. Another approach suggests that the distinguishing feature of this final test is that it probed an aspect of Abraham's personality left essentially untouched by his previous trials. His previous ordeals focused primarily on testing the extent of his compassion for others; this final test was necessary to observe how he would act when called upon to act dispassionately with regard to others, including even his own son, when required by divine command.[313] A somewhat different although not unrelated approach argues that, in all his previous trials, Abraham's responses to the various challenges were all consistent with the demands of reason. In this case, however, the act he is commanded to perform transcends and opposes reason, placing him in the unenviable position of having to choose between faith and reason. Although Abraham chooses faith, he does so ambivalently, unable to abandon reason entirely. As is evidenced later by the secretive manner in which he proceeds, Abraham appears to be ashamed of carrying out even a divine command that violates the norms of conduct that he himself has advocated.[314] In this same regard, it has been suggested that it was in anticipation of this supreme test that Sarah was taken to his harem by Abimelech prior to the birth of Isaac. According to this perspective, this was necessary so that Abraham should have a natural disincentive for sacrificing Isaac for any reason other than as an act of pure faith, since the sacrifice of Isaac would cause people to speculate that perhaps he did so because Isaac was really the offspring of Abimelech, conceived when Sarah was held captive.[315]

Another approach to the problem suggests that, in all his previous trials, Abraham managed to overcome a variety of externally imposed adversities. This last supreme test was to see if he also was capable of overcoming himself. All of Abraham's hopes for the future rested on his son Isaac, through whom all the divine promises to the patriarch were to be fulfilled, thereby giving meaning to his long troubled life. Now Abraham is being asked, as a test of his faith, to slaughter his son and thereby negate all that he had striven for. To carry out this divine command required that Abraham consciously subordinate everything dearest to his heart. He had to conquer himself and commit an act out of absolute faith that would surpass his own self-sacrifice had it been demanded of him.[316] A related commentary suggests that the intent of the test was not to see if Abraham would actually sacrifice his son, an act that clearly was not desired, but whether he would complain or challenge God about the apparent reversal of His explicit promise that Abraham's seed would be realized through Isaac, something that could not happen if Isaac were sacrificed. By not even raising the issue, Abraham made it clear that he was prepared to act beyond reason if faith demanded it of him.[317] However, effectively negating this argument, if one considers the likelihood, as discussed below, that Isaac was already a mature man at the time of the *Akedah*, it has been suggested that it is quite possible that Isaac may already have had relations with a woman and have sired a son or daughter. In such case, it would have been possible to fulfill the promise that Abraham's seed would be realized through Isaac, even if the latter were now to be sacrificed.[318]

One medieval commentator, suggesting that the text does actually provide a significant clue to the correct answer, takes a rather radical position on the issue. He observes that the passage opens with the statement, *And it came to pass after these things*, and asserts, providing numerous corroborating instances in Scripture, that whenever this phrase is employed in the text it indicates that the event to come is directly related to that which immediately preceded it in the narrative. In this case, the immediately preceding event was Abraham's entering into a multigenerational pact with Abimelech, the king of Gerar, which effectively meant that Abraham formally acknowledged the legitimacy of his dynasty as rulers of the territory they claimed. The commentator then goes on to argue that, by entering into this pact, Abraham had in effect unilaterally, albeit unintentionally, abrogated the covenant with God, in accordance with which the land in question was given to him and his descendants in perpetuity for all time. In other words, Abraham had no right to enter into a legal arrangement that alienated any portion of the land that was granted to him as an integral part of the covenant, even though his descendants would not actually take control of it until some time in the distant future. Accordingly, it was divine displeasure at Abraham's effrontery in this regard that precipitated this harsh divine reaction in the form of a punishing test.[319]

Another medieval commentator suggests that the original sin of Adam in the Garden of Eden, which in effect placed materialism ahead of spirituality, cast a stain on succeeding generations that led to the decline of humanity until the advent of Abraham, whom God considered worthy of a new covenant. However, it was essential first to remove the stain on mankind through a redeeming act of sacrifice that would negate the materialism. Since the primary manifestation of the appetite leading to materialism is in the sexual drive, it was necessary that the nature of the redemptive sacrifice be such that would symbolically expiate Adam's sin, and this would be a sacrifice of the direct product of man's sexual drive.[320] That is, by his readiness to sacrifice the product of his own sexuality, his beloved son Isaac, Abraham would make clear to future generations that the spiritual must properly take priority over the material, and thereby bring the people closer to God.

Finally, and reflecting a more modern but in my view anachronistic perspective, it has been argued that the attempted sacrifice was necessary to establish a clear basis for discontinuance of the long-standing religious practice.[321] Because child-sacrifice was a well-established ritual of many primitive religions, it would have been insufficient merely to outlaw the practice. Had Abraham simply not been willing to carry it out, it would have been interpreted by many as a deliberate affront to the gods and therefore misunderstood. What was required was a dramatic demonstration that God does not want such human sacrifice. Abraham, as leader of the new faith, was put to the test solely to see how he would respond. It was never intended that the actual sacrifice of Isaac be carried through.[322]

Whatever the answer to this most difficult conundrum, the final theophany that Abraham would experience, which presumably came to him in a dream if not as a nightmare, must have left him thunderstruck. The same divine voice that had set him on his course so many years ago by demanding, *Lekh-Lekha* or *Get thee* (Gen. 12:1) away from family and country, was now making an ultimate demand of him, *Lekh-Lekha* or *Get thee* (Gen. 22:2) to Moriah and sacrifice your son and heir. The compound Hebrew term *Lekh-Lekha* is found only in these two verses in Scripture, which have been viewed as bookends, so to speak, of the saga of the trials of Abraham.[323] God was demanding not Abraham's life, which would have closed a chapter of the past, but the life of his son and heir, which would shut off the future and essentially render his entire life meaningless. As one writer puts it, the relationship between Abraham and his son was unique in at least one dramatic respect. Although many give lip service to the idea, few people are truly concerned about their future descendants, "nonexisting persons over whom one has no control and at whose mercy one will be. The dead are delivered into the hands of the living, in whose power it is to give meaning to the lives of those who came before them or to deprive them of all meaning by the choices the living make." The relationship between the generations tends to work the other way; people are apt to think about their forebears, those who came before and serve as a source of inspiration and strength for them as they face an uncertain future. In this case, however, the divine promise to Abraham concerning his descendants presupposes a unique relationship of trust and identification that begins with Isaac, and which Abraham expects to be honored by those to come after him. Because of this, and far exceeding normal paternal affection for one's children, "Abraham's love for Isaac is so great that a divine promise of something good for him is of far greater interest to Abraham than his own welfare."[324]

The demand being made on him was unambiguous; he was to offer up *thy son*, not another's, *thy only son*, not Ishmael but his only remaining son, the son *whom thou lovest*, specifically, *Isaac*. The biblical author thus indicates the growing intensity of the drama, in which Abraham is led step by step to the realization that what he had heard was no mistake, a slip of the tongue so to speak. But what was he to make of such a demand? Aside from its self-evident cruelty, what purpose would it serve? By clearly indicating that *Elohim did prove Abraham*, that is, put him to a test, the biblical writer is telling us quite clearly that it was not necessarily something that God actually wanted him to carry out to the letter. The actual slaughter and immolation of Isaac was neither the purpose nor the desired outcome of the ordeal; its sole intent was to see how Abraham would cope with the challenge that the divine instruction presented.[325] But, what was the specific aim of the test? Was it intended to test Abraham's faith that, despite the fact that carrying out the demand would seem to negate the divine promise to him, somehow everything nonetheless would turn out as God promised? Was it a test to see if Abraham had reached the point in his spiritual odyssey where faith would completely overshadow reason when the two seemed to be in conflict? Was it a test of his love for God, as some have suggested?[326] Was he being asked to make what later commentators would describe as a leap of faith, a leap into the absurd?[327] And what of his highly developed sense of righteousness and justice? What had Isaac done to deserve to have his life snuffed out? Was it morally comprehensible to murder one person in order to demonstrate someone else's degree of faith? Could it be that Abraham believed human sacrifice to be morally wrong, but was willing to suspend that moral judgment on the basis of his faith in the God who demanded it?[328] Can one truly claim in this regard, as did one writer, that Abraham's attempted sacrifice of Isaac represented a "teleological suspension of the ethical," if such a thing is even conceivable from a biblical perspective?[329] Would not slaughtering Isaac and immolating him as a burnt offering constitute an obvious reversion to the primitive human sacrifice practices of the paganism that Abraham had rebelled against throughout his life? Would he not be shedding innocent blood, thus becoming a murderer in the eyes of all who did not believe in the sacral value of human sacrifice, many of who presumably had come to such a view under Abraham's direct influence? Moreover, was there any assurance that Isaac would simply allow himself to be slaughtered by his aged father, without a murmur, without demanding a satisfactory response to the question of why Abraham wanted to do this to him? Was this just a test of his willingness to sacrifice his beloved son, something that would never actually be allowed to take place, especially if Isaac refused to play his assigned role in the affair?

Some modern commentators offer the somewhat radical suggestion that Abraham understood the demand made on him as providing a means of penance for what he had done to Ishmael so many years earlier.[330] That is, even though he did not want to disown Ishmael and only did so because God told him to acquiesce to Sarah's demand, his guilt over the affair had never ceased to haunt him. Viewed from this perspective, Abraham would have seen the sacrifice of Isaac, for whom he had sacrificed Ishmael in a figurative sense, as a sort of punishment in kind. That is, expiation of his guilt demanded that he now reprise with Isaac what he had previously and without cause inflicted on Ishmael, namely cutting him off from his heritage.[331] This, arguably, would account for Abraham's conspicuous and resounding silence in face of what he was told to do. Against this view of the episode as one describing Abraham's neurotic guilt over what he had done to Ishmael, it is difficult to imagine what purpose the narrative serves since providing a vehicle for Abraham's catharsis can hardly be construed as the test that the biblical writer has already told us was taking place. Accordingly, even though such a psychological theory has some appeal to contemporary sensibilities, it does not have much explanatory power in the context of the biblical narrative.

Another question that begs for a response is why he was he being told to do this deed on an initially unspecified mountaintop in the land of Moriah. One possibility is that since it would take several days to get there on foot, as it evidently did, given that only one ass seems to have been taken for the four people who made the trek, the delay would provide more than adequate time for Abraham to deliberate on the consequences of what he was planning to do. If he were to go through with it, it would not be an act that he undertook in the euphoria of the immediate afterglow of a divine vision, but one undertaken after rationally considering its enormity. Moreover, if the traditional commentators are correct and Moriah is identical with the area in Jerusalem where the Temple of Solomon would later be built as the central shrine of Abraham's descendants, the sacrifice of Isaac was to be carried out in the territory of Melchizedek, the venerable priest-king of Salem.[332] But Melchizedek, the priest of *El Elyon* (Gen. 14:18), possessed of a spirit compatible with Abraham's, surely disapproved of and rejected the pagan practice of human sacrifice, yet Abraham was directed to do just that in

Melchizedek's domain, thus making Abraham appear as a hypocrite in the latter's eyes, if he were to become aware of what Abraham was planning to do.

These may have been but a few of the highly troubling thoughts that raced through Abraham's mind as he contemplated the implications of the act he was being commanded to carry out. But what should he do? Earlier, he had pleaded quite aggressively, albeit unsuccessfully, to prevent the annihilation of Sodom and Gomorrah. Should he now attempt to do the same on behalf of Isaac, or would that appear to be too self-serving? For Abraham, this was clearly the ultimate test of his faith and he felt compelled by that faith to obey the command he heard, even though it seemed to defy reason. The demand for Isaac's life must have struck him as so bizarre that, even if he was inclined to do so, he would not know how to argue with God against it. What rational argument could he make against something that was so inherently irrational? All he could do was to obey and place his complete trust in God that somehow everything would turn out for the best. Once again, just as he did when he was first commanded *Get thee*, so did he now with regard to what would be the final command that he would receive, he *went* (Gen. 12:4, 22:3) without demurrer or argument.

> 22.3 *And Abraham rose early in the morning, and saddled his ass, and took two of his young men with him, and Isaac his son; and he cleaved the wood for the burnt offering, and rose up, and went unto the place of which Elohim had told him.* 22.4 *On the third day Abraham lifted up his eyes, and saw the place afar off.* 22.5 *And Abraham said unto his young men: "Abide ye here with the ass, and I and the lad will go yonder; and we will worship, and come back to you."* 22.6 *And Abraham took the wood of the burnt-offering, and laid it upon Isaac his son; and he took in his hand the fire and the knife; and they went both of them together.* 22.7 *And Isaac spoke unto Abraham his father, and said: "My father." And he said: "Here am I, my son." And he said: "Behold the fire and the wood, but where is the lamb for a burnt-offering?"* 22.8 *And Abraham said: "Elohim will provide Himself the lamb for a burnt-offering, my son." So they went both of them together.*

Immediately after recovering from the shock of his horrific dream, and determined to carry out the divine instructions, Abraham arose early to make the necessary preparations for the mission. Two of the things he did may strike one as odd. First, he *saddled his ass*. The provision of this detail suggests that the biblical writer is indicating that he did this chore personally. But, why did the aged Abraham not have one of his household do this for him? This creates the impression that he may have done so himself in order to leave his encampment with as little fanfare as possible, getting himself ready for the trip first and only then awakening Isaac and *two of his young men*, who were to go along, presumably for the purpose of making the unexpected departure of Abraham and Isaac seem less suspicious, and possibly also to provide some security along the way. Why would Abraham follow such a procedure? It seems likely that he wanted to leave the camp before everyone was awake, especially Sarah.[333] He would not wish to be put in a position where he had to lie to her about where he was going and for what purpose, and he did not dare tell her the truth, something that would likely have caused her to consider him mad. This way he and Isaac could slip away unchallenged, merely leaving word that something had suddenly come up and that they would be gone for at least six days, enough time for the roundtrip. It seems likely that it was not unusual for Abraham to make such trips, and his sudden departure this time would not have caused any undue anxiety to Sarah, even though she may have been puzzled by his having taken only one ass for four people.

The second thing that seems somewhat strange is that *he cleaved the wood for the burnt offering*, before he left. Once again we are left with the image of the aged Abraham going out to the woodpile at the crack of dawn or even earlier and chopping enough wood for a sacrificial fire, the need for which would surely have raised questions, especially from Sarah. Why was it necessary for Abraham to take wood with him? Was there none to be found where he was going? One possible explanation might be that Abraham wanted to be fully equipped for his mission upon his departure, to make any question-raising interactions with others along the way as unnecessary as he would have found them undesirable. Even though Abraham as a man of faith may have seen himself on a divine mission, as a man of reason he may well have been rather ashamed at what he was about to do.

The trip to Moriah took three days, which surely gave Abraham plenty of time to ruminate on and struggle with himself over what he was planning to do. Why did it take such a long time to make the journey? Was it, as suggested above, so that Abraham, after extended and agonizing deliberation, would be certain of why he was going to do such a horrendous act to his beloved son, and thus do so only after careful consideration rather than as a spontaneous but not carefully thought through response to the divine demand? Was it to ensure that the trip would take three days that Abraham took only one ass even though there were four people in the entourage, ensuring slow going since, assuming that the aged Abraham rode on the animal, the other three would have to walk the entire distance? Whatever the reason, after three days Abraham and his small entourage arrived within sight of the hill that was his specific destination in *the land of Moriah*, the location of which he was somehow made aware even though the biblical writer does not indicate how this came about. At that point, *Abraham said unto his young men: "Abide ye here with the ass, and I and the lad will go yonder; and we will worship, and come back to you."* Abraham clearly did not want the young men accompanying him to be witnesses to what was about to take place, nor did he want them to be confronted with the moral dilemma of whether or not to attempt to intervene and prevent him from sacrificing Isaac. He therefore instructed them both to remain behind with the ass, as well as the supplies for the return trip, while he and Isaac ascended the designated hill to perform an act of worship, before rejoining them.

The question that challenges us at this point is what was going through Abraham's mind when he told the young men, *we will worship, and come back to you*? Did he expect to slaughter Isaac and then see him miraculously come back to life so that they could both return to his men and then home to Sarah? Or, did he sincerely believe that God would not permit him to actually slaughter his only son and heir to the covenant, and that God was merely testing him to see how far he was prepared to go on the basis of faith alone, a question to which Abraham himself probably did not know the answer?

In any case, Abraham proceeded on the basis that, one way or another, there was going to be a sacrifice, and he therefore had Isaac carry the wood for the fire while he carried a vessel containing burning embers to light the sacrificial fire, as well as a knife with which to carry out the slaughter. As they approached the sacrificial site, Isaac, who apparently had no knowledge of what Abraham had planned for him, naively observed, *Behold the fire and the wood, but where is the lamb for a burnt-offering?*[334] Remarkably, Abraham responded, *"Elohim will provide Himself the lamb for a burnt-offering, my son."* What did Abraham mean by this? Was he being deliberately disingenuous, implying that what was about to take place was a joint divine-human ritual in which God would supply the sacrificial animal and Abraham would slaughter and immolate it? Moreover, what would be the significance of God providing an animal for Abraham to sacrifice? The whole concept of sacrifice is predicated on the idea that one voluntarily gives up something of personal value for a higher purpose. God has asked Abraham for his son. In what conceivable manner could an animal provided by God serve as a substitute for Isaac, unless one makes the highly dubious assumption that Abraham is telling Isaac, in effect, that what God wants from Abraham is a burnt-offering, the slaughter and consumption by fire of a living being, and not necessarily an offering that would represent a personal sacrifice for him in the strict sense of the term?

It is at this point in the narrative that the biblical writer abandons us completely to our imaginations. Once they actually arrive at the designated spot, how is Abraham going to proceed with the sacrifice of his son? The answer to this question depends on what we assume about the age of Isaac at this juncture in his life. Although Abraham's and Isaac's ages at this point in the story are not given, many commentators suggest and I assume so as well, that it was the shock of this incident that precipitated the death of Sarah, once she learned that her husband had been prepared to slaughter her only son.[335] As reported later (Gen. 23:1), Sarah was 127 years old when she died, making Isaac 37 years old at the time since Sarah was 90 when he was born. At the same time Abraham must have been 137, the century difference in age between father and son making it unlikely that Abraham would have been able to overpower Isaac and carry out his sacrifice if the latter were unwilling to die in such a manner. To assume as many commentators do, that Isaac was actually quite young at the time, making any objections he might have had to what was being done to him moot, raises other seemingly insoluble problems, such as why Sarah evidently separated from Abraham shortly before her death, when she had to be over a hundred and twenty years old at a minimum, and where a very young Isaac disappeared to after the incident, issues that will be discussed later. Moreover, it would require, as some commentators suggest, that the story be understood as having occurred out of its given sequence.[336] In my view, however, such an approach is both inappropriate and unwarranted because it is not required to make sense of the biblical narrative. Apparently adopting a mid-position on the question of Isaac's age, one ancient writer claims he was twenty-five years old at the time, which solves the second problem, but not the first, which he does not address at all.[337]

It is tempting, particularly from an apologetic standpoint, to effectively remove Isaac from the decision process by assuming him to be a child, thus focusing the entire story on Abraham's immersion in blind faith to the point where it entirely overrides reason and paternal feelings. However, I have become convinced that this approach reflects a serious misreading of what the biblical writer wishes us to understand from the account. Accordingly, I take the view here that Isaac is indeed a grown man and fully capable of preventing Abraham from slaughtering him, if he so chose. As will be seen, by making this basic assumption regarding Isaac's age, the story takes on some rather different aspects and outcomes.

Returning to the narrative, it must be asked, is the aged Abraham going to be able to physically overpower his adult son, bind and slaughter him, and then immolate him on what would be his funeral pyre? Or does the loving father, his heart being torn apart by grief at the expected demise of his son at his own hands, seek to explain to Isaac the circumstances that have brought them to this critical point in both their lives. In other words, is Abraham going to try talking his son into allowing himself to be put to death? It seems clear from what follows that Abraham must have selected the latter approach, making what happens next depend entirely on Isaac's reaction to what his father has revealed to him.

Isaac could have concluded that Abraham had become deranged and simply have refused to participate in the bizarre ritual. Or, Isaac might have concluded that, even if Abraham could justify to himself what he was proposing to do, he was under no obligation to allow himself to be slaughtered and therefore could refuse to participate voluntarily in the planned sacrificial act. This approach might have provided an optimum solution to Abraham's dilemma. After all, it was Abraham who had received the divine instruction to slaughter his son; Isaac had not been privy to a theophany that demanded that he permit himself to be slaughtered. Accordingly, Abraham would have demonstrated his readiness to ritually slaughter his son, which was physically possible only if his son was willing to be slaughtered. The only other way would be to murder him surreptitiously, a method that was unlikely to be considered an appropriate form of ritual sacrifice. And, since Isaac was under no moral or covenantal obligation effectively to commit suicide, he could simply refuse to be Abraham's burnt offering. If it were Abraham's intention and readiness to sacrifice his son because God asked him to do so that was being tested, he surely would have passed muster. After all, man can only attempt to do what he believes he must, but cannot be held accountable for those things that interfere with his intentions that are beyond his control.

Alternatively, Isaac could have concluded from what his father had told him that he too, in a sense, was being tested as well, even though in his case the test was by no means explicit.[338] Presumably, he had been raised to believe that his purpose in life was to carry on Abraham's mission, to keep alive the inspired belief in the covenant in his descendants until the point in history when the divine promises of nationhood for the seed of Abraham would be fulfilled. If Abraham had been told to sacrifice him and thereby assure that the fulfillment of the divine promise would be fulfilled in some miraculous rather than in a natural manner, then his life served no further purpose. It has been suggested, in explanation of Isaac's seemingly enigmatic personality, that he suffered from a problem common to the children of great men who dramatically overshadow their heirs. They tend to be both intimidated by the achievements of the parent and burdened by the sense of obligation to preserve those achievements for the future; their own individuality and sense of self become of secondary importance, if considered at all.[339] Accordingly, if Abraham was obligated to sacrifice him, Isaac's sense of filial obligation may have demanded that he not oppose his father in this essentially incomprehensible act. And, it would appear, this was the approach taken by Isaac—he would indeed voluntarily be the sacrificial lamb provided by God.

> 22.9 *And they came to the place which Elohim had told him of; and Abraham built the altar*[340] *there, and laid the wood in order, and bound Isaac his son, and laid him on the altar, upon the wood.* 22.10 *And Abraham stretched forth his hand, and took the knife to slay his son.* 22.11 *And the angel of YHVH called unto him out of heaven, and said: "Abraham, Abraham." And he said: "Here am I."* 22.12 *And he said: "Lay not thy hand upon the lad, neither do thou any thing unto him; for now I know that thou art an Elohim-fearing man, seeing thou hast not withheld thy son, thine only son, from Me."*

There is a certain irony in what now occurred, which is in a sense anticlimactic. The point at which Abraham told Isaac what he was planning to do to him was actually the high point of the drama. Imagine the heartbreak Abraham must have experienced in telling his only remaining son, the embodiment of all his hopes and aspirations, that he had no choice but to slaughter him because his faith in God outweighed all rational considerations. That was the point at which he had demonstrated that he was indeed *an Elohim-fearing man*, one who would not withhold his only son from being sacrificed to God. He had, in effect, shown his readiness to sacrifice his reason on the altar of faith, the most that could conceivably be demanded of any person. It surely was this consideration that led the divine voice to say to him, *now I know that thou art an Elohim-fearing man*.

But what is it that God knows now that He didn't know before? Was not Abraham a God-fearing man long before this most severe trial? It has been suggested that what is at issue here is what it means to be God-fearing. Abraham, notwithstanding his faults and lapses, which the biblical writer does not hesitate to expose in the narrative, is nonetheless portrayed as a relative paragon of virtue, an outstanding humanitarian, and a true man of faith, attributes fully consistent with his personality and intrinsic character. The question is how he would fare if he were required to do something because of his faith that was intrinsically repulsive to him, completely inconsistent with his nature. It is one thing to act meritoriously when what is required fits one's natural disposition; it is quite another to do so when what is required of a person violates his every instinct. It was relatively easy for Abraham to be just and merciful. Would he be capable of injustice and cruelty if God asked it of him? The story of the *Akedah* demonstrated that he could go against both his reason and his instincts if faith demanded it of him. It was his conscious and clear-headed willingness to perform such a totally irrational act that led to the remark, *now I know that thou art an Elohim-fearing man*. Until Abraham had been tested in this regard, because he was granted freedom of will, his reaction could not be known for certain.[341] His willingness to do what under other circumstances he would consider inconceivable provided the answer. The actual act itself was neither required nor desired. Accordingly, as one commentator put it, "Abraham was not blessed for correctness in his conception of God's will; he was blessed because when he thought he knew God's will, he was willing to obey it to the limit."[342]

However, things got out of hand because of Isaac, who caused a secondary drama to ensue. God had not spoken to Isaac, commanding him to lay down his life. His readiness to be sacrificed in the absence of a revelatory experience demanding it was essentially irrational. The fact that Abraham had received such a revelation was irrelevant. Isaac was expected to use the rational faculty with which he was endowed by his Creator to make reasoned judgments, and not to deal with ultimate matters such as life and death capriciously. Indeed, it would appear that this was the reason why Abraham *bound Isaac his son*. Some traditional commentators have suggested that the binding of Isaac was done at his own request to assure that he did not bolt at the last moment, and thereby nullify the ritual act.[343] It seems reasonably clear that Abraham would not have been able to manhandle Isaac in such a manner if the latter was unwilling. The implication is that Isaac, who was not commanded to participate in an act of ultimate self-sacrifice to complement Abraham's charge to sacrifice him, was concerned that his belief that he was doing what God wished may not have been strong enough to overcome his natural inclination to survive. Once bound, the voluntary aspect of his submission was no longer an important consideration. As a result, it became necessary for divine intervention to prevent a travesty from taking place. Once having passed the test of intention and readiness, actually carrying out the act of human sacrifice was something that could not be countenanced and was to be prevented. In effect, Isaac had unknowingly created a situation that now truly placed Abraham in moral jeopardy.

As a result, it became necessary to instruct Abraham to desist from proceeding with the sacrifice of his son. He is told, *Lay not thy hand upon the lad, neither do thou any thing unto him*. There appears to be a redundancy here that needs clarification. If Abraham is not to lay his hand on his son, what does the additional injunction, *neither do thou any thing unto him*, add? It has been suggested that, even though Abraham was now told not to go forward with the slaughter, he found himself in a quandary. By direct divine revelation, he had been told to sacrifice Isaac and now, through another divine voice, he is told to desist. To which voice is he to listen? As one contemporary writer puts it, "It is here, with the knife poised in the air, as the painters and sculptors of the event have understood, not when Abraham stretches out his hand to take the knife, that the crisis comes."[344] Abraham must choose, alone and at once. The decision to go ahead with the sacrifice of Isaac was one that he came to after careful deliberation over a three-day period; the decision to let him live was made in an instant. Given the choice between the conflicting divine imperatives, he chose life for Isaac. However, he nonetheless may have felt a need to bring closure to the awesome event by some concrete act as a tangible manifestation of his unconditional obedience to the will of God, and he perhaps thought that symbolically drawing a little blood from Isaac might serve such a purpose.[345] However, this was both unnecessary and inappropriate from the divine perspective; his demonstrated willingness to sacrifice Isaac was quite sufficient to show that he was *an Elohim-fearing man*. Any deliberate mutilation of Isaac at this point would have been pointless as well as counterproductive because Abraham had not been instructed to carry out any such ritual act.

Abraham evidently had passed the test imposed on him by demonstrating his willingness to sacrifice his only son if God desired it; however, it was never intended that he actually commit such an abominable act. Indeed, some early commentators went so far as to assert that Abraham misunderstood what he was being told to do in the first place. According to this view, he was not told, as the translation has it, to *offer him there for a burnt-offering*, but rather just to "take him up" to the mountain, which is a literal meaning of the Hebrew term translated as *offer him*. In other words, he was only told to take Isaac with him to the designated mountain and perhaps to sacrifice a burnt offering there, but not that Isaac was to be that sacrifice.[346] The argument then, is that it was Abraham who erroneously inferred from this statement that it was Isaac who was to be sacrificed.[347] Why would Abraham make such a faulty inference? Presumably because human sacrifice was still a rather common religious practice among the peoples of Cisjordan, and he may have thought it was a test to see whether he would be willing to do something that was so irrational simply because God wished it.

A contemporary writer who treats the interaction between God and Abraham as an exercise in game theory provides an interesting perspective on the *Akedah* episode, analyzing it exhaustively as a deadly serious game in which both players essentially have two basic strategic choices. Abraham has the choice of offering Isaac or not offering him, while God has the choice of reneging on his demand if Abraham does offer Isaac and relenting on it if he does not, or, refusing to renege or relent regardless of what Abraham does. The first option for God implies that, irrespective of the choice Abraham makes, as far as God is concerned it is merely a test that He does not wish to see actually carried out. The second option implies that God actually wants Abraham to slaughter and immolate Isaac. The first move in this game is Abraham's, and he must make the fateful strategic choice: obey blindly or refuse to comply.

> To obey God blindly is, in fact, to act *as if* one has a dominant strategy—an unconditionally best choice—that requires no detailed preference information about the other player, much less an anticipation of what strategy he might choose. On the other hand, when a character's faith in God is not blind, he needs to make more sophisticated calculations to ascertain how to act rationally. Although his strategy choice may be the same in either case, the logical process needed to arrive at it in the second case will be more demanding in terms of both the preference information required and the sophisticated need to process this information.

The basic question this analysis seeks to answer is whether Abraham acted in blind faith or whether his choice was rational. To argue that Abraham made a rational choice in proceeding with the sacrifice of Isaac, he would have had to know or at least to have some inkling of God's preferences. Accordingly, given the repeated promises by God to Abraham regarding his descendants, promises that would be negated if the sacrifice of Isaac were to be carried out, it seems reasonable to assume that Abraham thought he had good reason to believe that God would most likely adopt the first strategy option and renege on His demand, should Abraham proceed to offer Isaac as a sacrifice. The author of the analysis concludes that the demand that Abraham offer up Isaac does not really test the "blindness" of Abraham's faith. "Thus, although God's harrowing test of Abraham succeeds in establishing that Abraham will obey His command—however ghastly—Abraham may well have done so for reasons other than faith. Hence, God's test does not assuredly dispel doubts about Abraham's faith, given Abraham knows God's preferences and is rational."[348]

Despite attempts to put a best face on the episode by emphasizing the depth of Abraham's faith, there are aspects of the story that remain extremely troubling, and it may be that the biblical writer has incorporated a sub-text that demands further exposition. All would agree that it surely would have been a great personal tragedy for Abraham to take the life of his beloved son. The critical question is, how did he dare accept responsibility for committing such an act as a consequence of his faith in God's ultimate justice—it was not *his* life that was to be snuffed out? It was Isaac, an innocent, who was to be killed, and the justice of this cannot simply be accepted as a matter of faith. Abraham should have challenged God in this instance just as he did with regard to Sodom and Gomorrah, notwithstanding that it might appear self-serving, something that is hardly sufficient justification for his thundering silence. Why did he remain silent in this instance, the greatest challenge of his life?

One possible answer is that his silence was a more effective challenge on behalf of Isaac than anything he could have said. God had gone to great lengths to mold Abraham into the sort of person who could father the civilization He desired to see on earth, and to provide him with an appropriate heir, Isaac, to carry on with the task after him. Now God demanded that Abraham make it impossible for God to fulfill His promises under the terms of His own covenant by killing Isaac, and thus put an end to the entire divine experiment in human engineering, so to speak. By not challenging this demand, Abraham may be understood, in effect, as turning the tables on God, making the sacrifice of Isaac a test for Him as well as one for himself. In other words, the whole matter of the *Akedah* was an issue between God and Abraham; the fact that the life or death of Isaac hung in the balance was a secondary consideration at best, which may help explain why Abraham didn't tell him about what he had in mind from the outset of their trip to Moriah. Abraham, acting on his supreme and unquestioning faith in God, was prepared to carry through the slaughter of his son as demanded of him by God. This presupposes that Abraham was convinced that God had for some reason decided to rescind the promises made to him regarding Isaac, and that Abraham accepted that decision without equivocation as a reflection of his absolute faith. This approach argues that it was not as some claim that Abraham believed that no matter what he did, somehow everything would turn out all right in the end. For if Abraham truly believed that he could proceed with the sacrifice of Isaac and that God would ultimately prevent it from being carried out, his act would not have been one of absolute faith but something of a charade.[349] No! It was essential that Abraham truly believe that the death of Isaac at his hands would put an end to everything he had striven for throughout his adult life. The question, to which Abraham did not know the answer, was whether God was prepared to allow this to happen. Again, the answer is—no! And so, the biblical writer tells us, God relented at the last moment, and Abraham emerged from the struggle of wills, so to speak, victorious, a conclusion consistent with the traditional reading of the story as a test of Abraham's faith, which he passed with flying colors.[350]

However, it must also be observed that, although there is a divine acknowledgement that Abraham is a God-fearing man, the biblical narrative nowhere actually states that Abraham passed the ultimate test set for him, implicitly suggesting that this biblical story of the testing of Abraham may have possibly long been misread and misunderstood. Perhaps the story should be read instead as a contest between Abraham's sense of justice and his faith, a test the patriarch ultimately *failed* by subordinating the search for justice to blind faith. This counterintuitive point is clearly reflected in an anecdote about a person who offered the following response to the question of why God, who asks Abraham to sacrifice Isaac, also sends an angel to stop it. "God was fed up with Abraham; when He asked him to sacrifice his son—that was the test—He wanted Abraham to say no!"[351] What this response argues, in effect, is that man is given free will and is expected to use it in the pursuit of justice, even if it seems to him that he has received a divine communication which he interprets as commanding him to do what he knows is an immoral and unjust act. Seen from this perspective, the test given to Abraham was whether he could reason his way through the moral complexities implied by the divine instruction to sacrifice Isaac, and ultimately reject blind obedience in favor of reasoned moral choice.[352]

Put simply, the lesson of the biblical story may well be that it is unacceptable to God as well as to man to subordinate the obligation to do justice to a blind faith that would cause man to pervert justice in practice. As one contemporary writer put it, "The message of the end of the *Akedah* is quite plainly that God does not want even his God-fearing adherents to go so far as to murder in God's name or even at God's command."[353] Perhaps this is the reason that God no longer speaks directly to Abraham—it is an angel who stays his hand from slaughtering Isaac, possibly as a sign of divine dissatisfaction that Abraham had once again made direct intervention necessary.[354] As one writer put it: "God does not like man to come to him through resignation. Man must strive to reach God through knowledge and love. God loves man to be clear-sighted and outspoken, not blindly obsequious."[355] He wanted Abraham to challenge Him.

Regardless of how the story of the *Akedah* is interpreted and explained, it is clear that although Abraham may have erred in his judgment regarding the best way to respond to the divine demand, his actions were done out of pureness of heart and a total faith in the justice of God's ways; there was no question of any benefit to be gained by Abraham doing away with his most precious possession. Accordingly, once the attempted sacrifice of Isaac was halted, Abraham's diversionary but unknowingly prophetic remark to his son, "*Elohim will provide Himself the lamb for a burnt-offering, my son*," came true. God had in fact provided a suitable animal for the burnt offering. Abraham had but to open his eyes, figuratively speaking, to find a suitable substitute for his son.

> ^{22.13} *And Abraham lifted up his eyes, and looked, and behold behind him a ram caught in a thicket by his horns. And Abraham went and took the ram, and offered him up for a burnt-offering in the stead of his son.* ^{22.14} *And Abraham called the name of that place YHVH jireh; as it is said to this day: "In the mount where YHVH is seen."*

Although this appears to be a neat solution to the incident, it raises a rather significant question that the biblical writer seems to ignore entirely. To be willing to offer his son, whom Abraham sired and nurtured to be his successor, as a burnt offering in response to a divine command surely represents an extreme sacrifice on his part. And, in lieu of that son, given all that occurred, an animal might be a suitable offering if it represented a sacrifice on Abraham's part. But what is the significance of offering a wild ram, which is not Abraham's property, as a sacrifice, assuming that the notion of sacrifice is that one voluntarily gives up something of value to another, the greater that value the greater the sacrifice? To give up something that is not yours to begin with is a not a sacrifice at all. In this instance Abraham did not even have to go to the bother of hunting an animal, he found one at hand entangled in a thicket waiting for him. In other words, it would seem that Abraham went through the ritual of sacrifice without actually sacrificing anything, something that makes us wonder what the biblical writer is hinting at by providing this vignette of the sacrifice that wasn't.[356] Is it to suggest that the psychological and emotional ordeal Abraham had just undergone had taken a tremendous toll on him, such that he was no longer thinking straight, at least for the moment? Indeed, if he had not been overcome by the experience would he under normal circumstances have performed such a meaningless act as to offer as a burnt offering something that represented no value and therefore no loss to him? Or, could it be that Abraham was so relieved that he did not have to go through with the sacrifice of his son that he felt an irrepressible obligation to make some overt demonstration of his gratitude, even though he was unable, as a practical matter to offer anything that would actually constitute a sacrifice. Accordingly, he may have concluded that the ceremonial offering of a snared ram, being the best he could do under the circumstances, would suffice to symbolize his gratitude, which he registered for posterity by naming the place *YHVH jireh*, that is, *the mount where YHVH is seen*, a site that presumably later became a "holy place" to which people came to pray. Given these considerations, it is interesting to observe how the biblical author describes the reception of this 'non-sacrifice'.

> 22.15 *And the angel of YHVH called unto Abraham a second time out of heaven,* 22.16 *and said: "By Myself have I sworn, saith YHVH, because thou hast done this thing, and hast not withheld thy son, thine only son,* 22.17 *that in blessing I will bless thee, and in multiplying I will multiply thy seed as the stars of the heaven, and as the sand which is upon the sea-shore; and thy seed shall possess the gate of his enemies;* 22.18 *and in thy seed shall all the nations of the earth be blessed; because thou hast hearkened to My voice."*

The biblical writer pointedly observes that, for a second time, the voice Abraham hears is not that of God, but of one of His messengers; God no longer deigns to communicate directly with Abraham, whose status may be seen as having been reduced following the need to intervene to prevent him from killing Isaac. Nonetheless, he is praised by God *because thou hast done this thing, and hast not withheld thy son, thy only son.*

This message raises some difficult questions. What is *this thing* that Abraham has done? We know what he was prepared to do, as well as what he did not do, but not what he did do that merited such praise. Moreover, what does it mean to say *thou…hast not withheld thy son*? In the end, Isaac was withheld. Could "this thing" refer, as one writer put it, to the consideration that "Since you made no exception of your son to the command of goodness, and did not accept the ghastly but ready notion that the gravest enormity would be the greatest gift, for that reason you are blessed."[357] That is to say, as I understand the author, although Abraham was prepared to sacrifice Isaac at the demand of God, he never for a moment saw this horrendous act as something that elevated his spirit to the highest possible point for a mere human. And, when the opportunity to desist came at the voice of an intermediary, he did not hesitate for an instant to halt the slaughter. Confronted by conflicting demands, his conscience demanded that he listen to the divine voice that would spare his son. Only afterward did he learn that he had made the choice that God desired. "His reward is not for blind obedience, then, but for (and through) moral insight."[358]

Accordingly, both for his essential moral revulsion regarding the command to sacrifice Isaac and his selfless readiness to sacrifice his reason on the altar of his faith, which caused him to set aside his moral judgment and thereby necessitated divine intervention, the divine message reaffirms the promises made earlier. In other words, even if Abraham is understood as having failed to meet the test imposed on him in the way desired, his accumulated merit is nonetheless such as to be rewarded with the fulfillment of all the commitments made to him earlier. The ultimate point of the story appears to be the recognition that even Abraham, the best of all men since Adam, remains a flawed human being, a conclusion critical to understanding the subsequent course of the biblical narrative.

Abraham was intended to be, so to speak, a new Adam, the founder of a moral and just civilization, something that his primeval ancestor failed to accomplish, producing instead civilizations that were ultimately destroyed in the great Deluge in the days of Noah. Those ancient civilizations were replaced by a civilization that reached its zenith in the Tower of Babel and all that it implied. In the episode just concluded, the biblical author indicates that although Abraham was able to climb to the heights of individual human capacity to serve God with all one's heart, it was an insufficient basis for founding the desired civilization, one that must be designed for normal humans and not for saints. Such a civilization would have to be predicated on a system of divinely ordained and inspired law and justice that transcended the foibles of individuals, no matter how great or profound. The guidelines for such a system would eventually be revealed to the descendants of Abraham, but this would not take place for a number of generations. In the meantime, Abraham had essentially fulfilled the most that could be expected from a single great but nonetheless imperfect human. His covenantal role would now be assumed by his son Isaac, notwithstanding the latter's traumatization by his near death experience at the hands of his father, something that evidently was not really the divine intention in the test of Abraham that went awry.

22.19 *So Abraham returned to his young men, and they rose up and went together to Beer-sheba; and Abraham dwelt at Beersheba.*

The episode at an end, Abraham went back to the waiting young men he had brought with him and then returned to Beersheba. But what happened to Isaac? The biblical writer implicitly suggests that Isaac did not return together with Abraham, and it is not clear that he returned to his home even later. Perhaps his recent flirtation with death had a sobering effect on him and he needed some time to himself to reflect on and assess the significance of what had occurred. Perhaps, as has been suggested, the entire incident had a remarkable liberating effect on Isaac who had spent his entire life up to this point in the shadow of the overwhelming personality of Abraham, and who, as a result of the trauma of his experience at Moriah, now suddenly freed himself from that thralldom to become an autonomous person for the first time.[359] In any case, it is clear that the next time we hear of Isaac he is to be found deeper into the Negev region than Beersheba, at the site where Hagar had her first visionary encounter with an angel, Beer-lahai-roi, between Kadesh-barnea and Bered (Gen. 16:14).

The biblical writer also provides an interesting bit of information indicating a significant change in Abraham's attitude. For the first time, he tells us, *Abraham dwelt at Beersheba.*[360] That is, after many years of highly disruptive "sojourning," for the reasons discussed earlier, Abraham now evidently wanted the stability he had previously denied himself and ceased his semi-nomadic existence, deciding to settle into a permanent residence where he would spend his remaining years. What brought this about? Perhaps Abraham learned from the experience at Moriah that it was not the divine intent that man should live by blind faith, but rather by rational faith. The divine promise of nationhood in the land in which he had been sojourning for decades was going to be fulfilled in the generations to come; he had no doubt about that. In the meantime, he had continued to view himself as a stranger in the very land for which he already had the deed, so to speak, even though its formal occupancy by his descendants was to be deferred for several centuries. But why did he behave in this manner? God had not told him to live as a vagabond. There was no valid reason for him to deny himself and his family and household the stability they surely craved. Abraham may have come to realize that pursuing his spiritual odyssey did not require that he deliberately deny himself the morally responsible benefits that life had to offer, depending on objective circumstances. And so, at long last, Abraham established a permanent residence in Beersheba, perhaps even trading in his tent for a house.

What the biblical writer does not tell us directly is what the impact of all this had been on Sarah. Once Abraham returned to Beersheba without Isaac, he had no alternative but to tell her what had happened at Moriah. It is not too difficult to imagine her reaction to the news that her husband had planned to slaughter her son as though he were a sheep, Isaac being saved only by divine intervention. It surely must have shattered Sarah, and the next thing we are told about her is that she died.[361]

> 23.1 *And the life of Sarah was a hundred and seven and twenty years; these were the years of the life of Sarah.* 23.2 *And Sarah died in Kiriath-arba—the same is Hebron—in the land of Canaan; and Abraham came to mourn for Sarah, and to weep for her.*

There is a curious disjunction in the narrative. We were just told that Abraham had settled in Beersheba, and now we find that Sarah died, not in Beersheba but in Kiriat-arba or Hebron, in those days a not inconsiderable distance to the north. What was Sarah doing in Hebron when Abraham was in Beersheba? Did the near tragedy of the attempted sacrifice of Isaac cause an irreparable rupture between husband and wife? How would one expect the usually levelheaded Sarah to react to such an event? It is virtually inconceivable that she would have agreed to Abraham's intended sacrifice of Isaac, and it was for this reason that he almost certainly did not inform her of it. It is quite understandable that her reaction after the fact was to view Abraham as having lost his mind and, at a minimum, to need some separation from him to recover her composure. Is it possible that she died thinking that Abraham may have agreed to sacrifice Isaac because he himself was uncertain about whether Isaac was actually his son? It has also been suggested that Sarah may have felt that she had now received the full brunt of divine judgment for her not entirely selfless treatment of Hagar and Ishmael.[362] Accordingly, she may have felt a desire to return to the terebinths of Mamre, at Hebron, where she first came to believe that she would actually give birth to a son in her ninetieth year. All we are told is that she went to visit or live in the Hebron area, where she may have known people from their earlier stay there. In any case, it was there that she succumbed.

Word was sent to Abraham in Beersheba, *and Abraham came to mourn for Sarah, and to weep for her.*[363] It is noteworthy that Isaac does not appear to have come for the funeral. Surely he knew that Sarah had no part in his near-death experience, and did not feel estranged from her. Was he out of reach, and therefore unaware of what happened? Or was there some other reason for his absence? Traditional commentaries attempt to provide a variety of possible answers, none of them particularly compelling or even plausible in some instances. Once again we are left to speculate on something that could easily have been made clear. What we can assert with some confidence is that with the death of Sarah, an era had come to an end. Although the biblical author does not elaborate much on Sarah's role in the enterprise undertaken by Abraham, it was undoubtedly considerable starting with the gathering of disciples in Haran before their great adventure began, and ending with her clearing the way for Isaac's uncontested succession. His only indirect tribute to Sarah is the mention of her age at her death, which while not seeming particularly significant is in fact notable because it is the only time in the biblical text that the age of any of the matriarchs of Israel is given.

12

Abraham's Odyssey Comes to an End

Sarah's death surely struck Abraham very hard; they had loved much and endured much together, and now she was gone, their differences resulting from the affair of the *Akedah* remaining unreconciled. Abraham, however, could not allow himself to be immobilized by grief; he had to deal with the matter of a proper burial for his beloved wife, which he wanted to do as soon as possible out of respect for her remains. If, as we suppose, Sarah left Beersheba because it from there that Abraham had taken her son to be slaughtered, Abraham surely thought it inappropriate to bring her back there for burial. Instead, he sought to obtain a suitable place of interment in the vicinity of Hebron, where Sarah was first told that she would conceive a son, a place that represented a happier time in her life, and Abraham turned to the leaders of the Hittite community for assistance in that regard.

> [23.3] *And Abraham rose up from before his dead, and spoke unto the children of Heth, saying:* [23.4] *"I am a stranger and a sojourner with you; give me a possession of a burying-place with you, that I may bury my dead out of my sight."* [23.5] *And the children of Heth answered Abraham, saying unto him:* [23.6] *"Hear us, my lord: thou art a mighty prince among us; in the choice of sepulchers bury thy dead; none of us shall withhold from thee his sepulcher, but that thou mayest bury thy dead."* [23.7] *And Abraham rose up, and bowed down to the people of the land, even to the children of Heth.* [23.8] *And he spoke with them, saying: "If it be your mind that I should bury my dead out of my sight, hear me, and entreat for me to Ephron the son of Zohar,* [23.9] *that he may give me the cave of Machpelah, which he hath, which is in the end of his field; for the full price let him give it to me in the midst of you for a possession of a burying-place."*

Because he was a renowned chieftain, the Hittites graciously offered to allow him to bury Sarah in any of the family or communal vaults they possessed. Abraham, however, had something else in mind. He wanted an exclusive burial site in which to bury Sarah, where he would be assured of being able to join her when his time came. He evidently had been made aware of such a suitable site, but before he could purchase land in Hebron he needed the consent of the local authorities. And so, *Abraham rose up, and bowed down to the people of the land*, the "people of the land" being a technical term employed by the biblical writer for a communal council, in this instance the local council of the Hittites, whose approval of his proposal was essential.[364] Because he was anxious to bury Sarah as soon as possible, he also asked the council to intercede with the owner of the property he wished to purchase to expedite the transaction, foregoing the normal bargaining process, which would be too time-consuming for his purposes. Accordingly, Abraham made it clear that he did not wish to haggle and was prepared and willing to pay whatever was the owner's initial asking price.

> 23.10 *Now Ephron was sitting in the midst of the children of Heth; and Ephron the Hittite answered Abraham in the hearing of the children of Heth, even of all that went in at the gate of his city, saying:* 23.11 *"Nay, my lord, hear me: the field I give thee, and the cave that is therein, I give it thee; in the presence of the sons of my people give it I thee; bury thy dead."* 23.12 *And Abraham bowed down before the people of the land.* 23.13 *And he spoke unto Ephron in the hearing of the people of the land, saying: "But if thou wilt, I pray thee, hear me: I will give the price of the field; take it of me, and I will bury my dead there."* 23.14 *And Ephron answered Abraham, saying unto him:* 23.15 *"My lord, hearken unto me: a piece of land worth four hundred shekels of silver, what is that betwixt me and thee? bury therefore thy dead."* 23.16 *And Abraham hearkened unto Ephron; and Abraham weighed to Ephron the silver, which he had named in the hearing of the children of Heth, four hundred shekels of silver, current money with the merchant.* 23.17 *So the field of Ephron, which was in Machpelah, which was before Mamre, the field, and the cave which was therein, and all the trees that were in the field, that were in the border thereof round about, were made sure* 23.18 *unto Abraham for a possession in the presence of the children of Heth, before all that went in at the gate of the city.* 23.19 *And after this, Abraham buried Sarah his wife in the cave of the field of Machpelah before Mamre—the same is Hebron—in the land of Canaan.* 23.20 *And the field, and the cave that is therein, were made sure unto Abraham for a possession of a burying-place by the children of Heth.*

The question that urges itself on us is why we are presented with this elaborate discussion about the purchase of the field and cave, which could have been condensed into the simple statement that Abraham had arranged to buy a field with a cave in it to bury Sarah. Perhaps it is to demonstrate that despite the trauma of the affair of the intended sacrifice of Isaac and the subsequent death of Sarah,

Abraham had not lost any of the shrewdness that had enabled him to become a powerful and respected figure in an alien society.

Abraham is clearly extremely anxious to bury Sarah as soon as possible, presumably so that she is interred before significant decay sets in. The people of Hebron understand and appreciate this, and are prepared to allow him, a stranger, the privilege of burying his wife in one of their sepulchers. If Abraham had agreed, the burial could have taken place immediately. However, Abraham rejects their generous offer. He wants to bury Sarah in a site to which he holds title, in a place in which he does not reside. This raises an entirely different problem; he has to get the council of the Hittite city to agree to permit the sale of Hittite property to a stranger who will become in effect an absentee landlord, an arrangement that must have been unusual to say the least. Would they agree to this? And why would Abraham risk delaying the burial by raising such a formal request of the council? After all, he knows that all the land will eventually become the property of his descendants, property to which he already has the deed in the form of a divine commitment, so why is he insisting on purchasing the cave at Machpelah? The most straightforward answer is that he wants to make sure that he will be buried alongside his beloved, perhaps as a symbolic reconciliation that they had not managed to achieve before Sarah's demise, and the only way he can be certain of that is if he holds exclusive rights to the site. However, it has also been suggested that Abraham wishes to begin the process of formalizing his presence in the country by acquiring property and the legal status that property-ownership entails. His days of wandering had come to an end, and he was determined to establish permanent and acknowledged roots in the land.[365]

Aware that his request might engender delays, Abraham seems to have taken certain precautions. Meetings of the council were public affairs, and were held at the entrance to the city gate where all significant public and private business was conducted. He also understood that a meeting at which a petition from a prominent foreign sheikh was to be considered would attract most if not all of the prominent citizens and landowners to the audience. He thus had reasonable assurance that Ephron, from whom he wished to purchase the site, was present at the meeting. In his petition, he asked that the council not only approve his request, but that for the sake of acting quickly, while his dead wife lay unburied, they intervene with Ephron on his behalf to expedite matters. Even before the council could respond, once publicly identified by name, Ephron felt compelled to speak up and in a gratuitous gesture offer to simply give Abraham the plot, knowing full well that Abraham was willing to pay his initial asking price. Once Ephron had made this offer, the council's acquiescence was pro forma; since Ephron had already agreed to give Abraham the land; the only question was whether it would be given gratis or be paid for. Abraham, of course, refused the offer of the site as a gift and insisted on paying for it. At that point, Ephron stated his asking price, probably inflated from the site's true value but not high enough to be seen as an obvious attempt to fleece an unsuspecting buyer, which Abraham promptly paid in *current money with the merchant*, that is, in exchangeable currency. The biblical writer then indicates that Abraham's deed to the site, whose parameters were specifically stipulated, was publicly acknowledged, and that Abraham proceeded to bury Sarah *in the cave of the field of Machpelah before Mamre—the same is Hebron—in the land of Canaan. And the field, and the cave that is therein, were made sure unto Abraham for a possession of a burying-place by the children of Heth.*

One is struck by the repeated emphasis on Hebron in this narrative, in which the field of Machpelah becomes the first site in Cisjordan that is actually owned in accordance with the common law of the land, and in a sense occupied in perpetuity, by Abraham. Hebron thus becomes part of the territorial heritage of Abraham centuries in advance of the fulfillment of the divine promise that his descendants will inherit the land of Cisjordan after they return from their period of exile. Without getting into a discussion of when this parenthetical passage was actually written, it certainly took on great significance later when Hebron also became the first capital of the kingdom of Judah under David.

With the death and burial of Sarah, Abraham underwent the last of the series of trials and tribulations in his long spiritual odyssey. He was already well advanced in age and perhaps more important, with Sarah now gone, he felt old and tired and believed that his end was near as well. However, there remained one significant task that he needed to accomplish before he succumbed to the ravages of age, namely, to assure that the line of succession to the divine covenant continued beyond Isaac. And, toward this end, he was particularly concerned about ensuring not only that Isaac married before Abraham's death, but that his heir not marry a Canaanite woman. Accordingly, it was to be an arranged marriage between Isaac and a bride from a people Abraham deemed more suitable, and his own trusted servant, most probably the aging Eliezer of Damascus, who was his chamberlain, was assigned to play the role of marriage broker.

> 24.1 *And Abraham was old, well stricken in age; and YHVH blessed Abraham in all things.* 24.2 *And Abraham said unto his servant, the elder of his house, that ruled over all that he had: "Put, I pray thee, thy hand under my thigh.* 24.3 *And I will make thee swear by YHVH, Elohei hashamayim veElohei haaretz [the God of heaven and the God of the earth], that thou shalt not take a wife for my son of the*

daughters of the Canaanites among whom I dwell. [24.4] *But thou shalt go unto my country, and to my kindred, and take a wife for my son, even for Isaac."*

Abraham entrusted his loyal servant, who was earlier identified as the overseer of Abraham's estate, with the mission of seeking out an appropriate bride for Isaac. However, uncertain that he would be able to fulfill this charge before Abraham's demise, the patriarch asked his loyal servant to take an oath to the effect that he would carry out his mission even if Abraham passed from the scene before it was accomplished. Following what was evidently an ancient procedure symbolizing fealty, the servant was to place his hand under his master's thigh while making his vow. The implication of this procedure was, since the *yerekh* or thigh or loin was the source of one's progeny, current or still to be born, violation of the oath would also be a hostile act against them as well and the violator might be subject to retribution at their hands.[366]

Although Abraham insists that his servant follow the traditional procedure that affirms one's fealty to his master, he does not demand the profession of his personal obligation of fealty to assure that his wishes will be carried out, but makes his servant swear by God that he will do so. This suggests that Abraham was fully confident that his most trusted servant, despite his not being of the seed of Abraham and therefore not a party to the covenant, continued to believe in the God of Abraham and would consider an oath taken in His name to be a sacred obligation even greater than personal fealty that he must fulfill to the letter. It is noteworthy that the oath that his servant is to make is not to find a wife for Isaac, because this may not be possible for him to do. What Abraham is demanding is that his servant take an oath that under no circumstances will he arrange a marriage for Isaac with one of *the daughters of the Canaanites among whom I dwell*. The servant is to proceed to Abraham's family in the area of Haran as his emissary, and to find a bride for Isaac among his countrymen, preferably but not necessarily from among his extended family. This qualification seems to be implicit in his charge to his servant to *go unto my country, and to my kindred*, suggesting that although a bride from among his kindred might be most desirable, such endogamy was not an absolute requirement.

This demand raises a number of questions. Why is the thought of Isaac marrying a Canaanite so unacceptable to Abraham? If he has so much contempt for the Canaanites, why does he live among them? He could have continued to live in relative isolation, distant from them. For example, he might have relocated to the lands of the city-state of Salem, under the control of Melchizedek or his descendants, which he might have found more culturally congenial, especially since that is where his last experience of a theophany took place. Moreover, if it is because the Canaanites are polytheists, what benefit in this regard does he expect to reap by turning to his family in Mesopotamia who are also polytheists? After all, it was to break away from those very connections that he left Haran and his family in the first place so many decades earlier.

With regard to the last question, it would seem that there is no significant difference between Canaanite and Mesopotamian polytheism, and from that standpoint alone it is difficult to understand why Abraham would prefer one to the other. There are, however, two other considerations that may explain Abraham's attitude. Were Isaac to marry a Canaanite woman, and having no living kin of his own in the land, his household would inevitably be influenced by his Canaanite wife's relatives, creating what Sarah would have considered an inappropriate environment within which Isaac would have to raise his children. Indeed, it was over such a concern that she forced Abraham to send Hagar and Ishmael away. However, the danger would be significantly reduced if Isaac's wife were from a distant land, without local connections of her own. Such a wife would be more likely to conform to her husband's wishes regarding the home environment. But, in this case, he could have sent his servant to Egypt, which was closer, to achieve the same end, a fact that suggests another and more significant reason for wanting a wife for Isaac from among his cousins. He evidently hoped this would be possible because he had recently been informed that his brother Nahor, who had married his dead brother Haran's orphaned daughter Milcah (Gen. 11:29), had at least one unmarried granddaughter, Rebekah, although there may have been others as well, as indicated in the biblical citation, omitted earlier, that interrupted the flow of the narrative linking Sarah's death to Isaac's near sacrifice at the hands of Abraham.

> 22.20 *And it came to pass after these things, that it was told to Abraham, saying: "Behold, Milcah, she also hath borne children unto thy brother Nahor:* 22.21 *Uz his first-born, and Buz his brotherm and Kemuel the father of Aram;* 22.22 *and Chesed, and Hazo, and Pildash, and Jidlaph, and Bethuel."* 22.23 *And Bethuel begot Rebekah; these eight did Milcah bear to nahor, Abraham's brother.* 22.24 *And his concubine, whose name was Reumah, she also bore Tebah, and Gaham, and Tahash, and Maacah.*

God had made it clear that Abraham's heir with regard to the covenant was to be the child of both Abraham and Sarah, who were close relatives besides being husband and wife. Abraham may have considered it to be equally desirable that Isaac and his spouse have a similar relationship, so that Isaac's successor would be of the same family as both Abraham and Sarah, and Rebekah, or possibly other unnamed young women from the large extended family deriving from Nahor and Milcah, who perfectly matched this criterion, would therefore be an ideal match for Isaac, if she or they were still available and willing.[367] This would suggest further that Abraham had no greater problem with living among the Canaanites than he would have had if he had continued to live among his polytheistic family in Haran. This was clearly exemplified by his longstanding close relations with the Amorite clan of Mamre, Aner, and Eshkol.

The question was whether arranging the marriage for Isaac that Abraham wanted was practicable.

> [24.5] *And the servant said unto him: "Peradventure the woman will not be willing to follow me unto this land; must I needs bring thy son back unto the land from whence thou camest?"* [24.6] *And Abraham said unto him: "Beware thou that thou bring not my son back thither.* [24.7] *YHVH, Elohei hashamayim [the God of heaven], who took me from my father's house, and from the land of my nativity, and who spoke unto me, and who swore unto me, saying: Unto thy seed will I give this land; He will send His angel before thee, and thou shalt take a wife for my son from thence.* [24.8] *And if the woman be not willing to follow thee, then thou shalt be clear from this my oath; only thou shalt not bring my son back thither."* [24.9] *And the servant put his hand under the thigh of Abraham his master, and swore to him concerning this matter.*

His trusted servant sought further clarification from Abraham concerning his mission. Before he was prepared to undertake it, making the sort of binding commitment to it that Abraham demanded, his servant wanted to know what he should do if he found the right woman, but she was unwilling to make such a drastic relocation on the word of a servant. In that case, he asked, should he return to get Isaac and then bring Isaac to Abraham's former homeland in Mesopotamia, presumably to finalize the arrangements for bringing his spouse back to Cisjordan? Abraham again stated most emphatically that under no circumstances was Isaac to return to Abraham's earlier homeland, and indicated his conviction that since such an endogenous marriage was desired by God, He would intervene by sending an angel to make sure that everything worked out according to plan. However, it appears that Abraham may have second thoughts about this assertion; there was no actual indication of any divine intention to intervene in this matter, which effectively would have amounted to coercing the woman identified as a suitable spouse for Isaac to become his wife, something that would hardly establish the basis for a harmonious relationship. No, Isaac's wife would have to enter into marriage with him as an act of free will. Accordingly, Abraham essentially discarded his first statement of assurance to his servant and told him that, if the woman by her own free-willed decision was unwilling to follow him back to Cisjordan, he would be absolved of any responsibility for the failure of his mission. But, again, under no circumstances was Isaac to travel to Abraham's earlier homeland. With the matter clarified to his satisfaction, the servant swore an oath to this effect, following a procedure designed to emphasize his obligation of fealty to Abraham.

Upon reflection, there is something particularly strange about this whole discussion between Abraham and his servant concerning Isaac. Why didn't Abraham instruct Isaac, who was already a mature man, not to leave Cisjordan under any circumstances, and not to marry a Canaanite unless his servant emissary failed to find a bride for him among his cousins that was willing to go to a strange country to meet her future husband, who for some unspecified reason could not come to her? Why was Abraham so insistent that Isaac should not depart from the territory of Cisjordan, even temporarily, as he himself had done? Was Abraham concerned that Isaac was perhaps weak-willed and subject to manipulation, and that he might be induced to remain abroad permanently? Was this perhaps Abraham's reaction to the fact that Isaac had been convinced that it was his obligation to be sacrificed because God told Abraham to do so, even though he had not received any such demand? Presumably, if Isaac were prepared to lay down his life only because he wanted to please his father, would he not also be subject to abandoning the land his descendants were to inherit under the covenant under pressure from a woman he might desire to wed? Abraham had received no divine vision in this regard, and it was evidently his judgment that it was essential that his seed maintain a presence in the land promised under the covenant, at least until some point in the future when circumstances would compel them to leave for the exile of which he was foretold. Until that time came, they were to remain in the land; leaving it even temporarily was considered too risky and Abraham evidently did not feel that Isaac was sufficiently steadfast for him to be convinced that he would return to the land once he left it.

The story of the mission undertaken by Abraham's servant, narrated at what appears to be excessive length and detail, would appear to be rather tangential to the intense interest in Abraham shown by the biblical author until now, notwithstanding that it is of great importance for the story of Isaac and Rebekah. However, I will suggest that it is inserted at this point, even though it interrupts the flow of the narrative, because it relates directly to Abraham, albeit in an oblique manner.

24.10 *And the servant took ten camels, of the camels of his master, and departed; having all goodly things of his master's in his hand; and he arose, and went to Aram-naharaim, unto the city of Nahor.*

Abraham's trusted servant undertook the mission assigned to him, within the parameters set for it by his master, but exercised full discretion about how to carry out what probably seemed from the first to be one destined for failure. His stratagem for enticing a member of Abraham's extended family in Mesopotamia, or possibly from another family if Rebekah or another cousin were unavailable or unsuitable, to agree to a marriage and residence in comparatively remote and provincial Cisjordan was to make a conspicuous display of his master's wealth, something that would make such a match attractive to a prospective bride's family, if not to the young woman herself. Toward this end, he decided it would be best to arrive in Haran, the domicile of the extended family of Nahor, at the head of a sizeable caravan including ten camels, some of which were presumably laden with gifts, the animals subsequently to be used to convey the bride and her retinue back to Cisjordan.

In describing this, the biblical writer makes the curious remark that he *took ten camels, of the camels of his master.* Specifying that the servant took animals belonging to his master for the purpose of his mission seems quite superfluous; surely no one would expect him to take animals of his own, even if it were conceivable that Abraham's servant possessed a personal herd of as many as ten camels, a most unlikely situation. What is it that this detail was intended to convey? In the absence of any clue to its import in the text, a question that most commentators simply do not address at all, it has been suggested that the statement was intended to reflect the notion that there was something very special about the camels of Abraham that might assist his servant in accomplishing his mission, namely, by illustrating the extraordinary moral standards maintained by the house of Abraham that even extended to the behavior of his animals. According to this imaginative homiletic interpretation, Abraham's camels were trained to travel muzzled so as not to graze in the fields of others, which would be the equivalent of appropriating their property without prior permission.[368] Presumably, awareness of the high standards of ethical conduct maintained in the house of Abraham would make the prospect of marrying Abraham's heir even more attractive to a young woman with the moral fiber desirable in a wife for Isaac, who would also become the second matriarch of the future nation.

The text also asserts that the servant had *all goodly things of his master's in his hand,* the meaning of which is ambiguous. Is it telling us that since he was the overseer of Abraham's domain, and therefore had access to all the wealth of his master, he decided what gifts to bring to the prospective bride and her family? Perhaps it is reflecting the idea that because there had been no prior inter-familial negotiations, Abraham's surrogate had to be in a position to pay whatever bride price was demanded, without having first to return to obtain Abraham's agreement, and that much of that wealth, presumably in gold and silver bullion or artifacts as well as other items of value, was contained in the loads borne by at least one or more of the camels. Or, as some commentators suggest, is it saying that the servant had *all* the wealth of Abraham in his hands? That is, is the text suggesting that the servant was carrying a copy of Abraham's will or deed of gift assigning all his worldly possessions to Isaac as a means of assuring the family of the prospective bride that the match was in their interest, in that their child would become very wealthy.[369]

With the preparations for the venture completed, Abraham's servant departed for Haran. One of the things left unstated or even alluded to in the biblical narrative is that it might have taken as much as a month for a caravan to make its way from Beersheba to Haran. Another is that Abraham's servant could hardly have made the trek, bearing a highly valuable cargo, alone. We must assume that, at the least, a sizeable contingent of armed men accompanied him to assure his safety and that of Abraham's valuable goods that he was taking with him, as well as to provide a security escort for the prospective bride should his mission be successful, in which case some of the camels may have been carrying necessary supplies of food and water for the long journey.

Abraham's servant and emissary knew exactly who he was to look for first, but it was left for him to determine if she was suitable for the critical role she would have to play in assuring the continuity of Abraham's line and heritage. It would not do to simply go to the family home of Abraham's brother and nephews and propose a marriage between Rebekah or another cousin and Isaac, even though they would most likely support such an arrangement for the economic benefits it might bring. The emissary's primary concern was to be convinced that the prospective bride had the qualities necessary to assume the matriarchal role in Isaac's household that Sarah did in Abraham's. He wanted to obtain assurance of this before he revealed on whose behalf he had come to Haran. The question was how he would make such a determination since there was no acceptable way for him, especially as a foreigner, to meet a prospective bride and interview her. Moreover, speech can be deceptive and not necessarily indicative of what one really thinks or would behave. The only practical approach to assessing a candidate's suitability for Isaac was to contrive to meet her in an informal way and to determine both whether she was visually attractive and whether or not she possessed at least one highly desirable character trait, one that could easily be tested. The singular characteristic that he chose to be the determining factor was possession of a good heart. Sensitive to the tribulations through which Isaac had passed, he decided that what Isaac most needed was a life companion whom he could cherish, one who above all else was compassionate. To make such a determination, Abraham's emissary concocted a scheme that he put into play once he arrived at the outskirts of Haran.

> 24.11 *And he made the camels to kneel down without the city by the well of water at the time of evening, the time that women go out to draw water.* 24.12 *And he said: "O YHVH, the God of my master Abraham, send me, I pray Thee, good speed this day, and show kindness unto my master Abraham.* 24.13 *Behold, I stand by the fountain of water; and the daughters of the men of the city come out to draw water.* 24.14 *So let it come to pass, that the damsel to whom I shall say: Let down thy pitcher, I pray thee, that I may drink; and she shall say: Drink, and I will give thy camels drink also; let the same be she that Thou hast appointed for Thy servant, even for Isaac; and thereby shall I know that Thou hast shown kindness to my master."*

The scheme was predicated on the assumption that Rebekah or another perhaps available cousin would be among the young unattached women who routinely came to the well to fill a pitcher just before evening set in. The emissary evidently was aware that this practice was as much social for some as it was utilitarian for others. That is, whereas some needed to draw water for the needs of their families, others from wealthy families that had servants to perform such chores, such as was the case with Rebekah's family, nonetheless came primarily to socialize with their unmarried peers. Accordingly, the emissary expected the young women to come to the well unless they were unwell or, in a worst case, unsociable, the latter perhaps being a sign that one was unsuitable as a wife for Isaac.

The plan itself was quite simple. The emissary, covered with the dust of the road and appearing as a weary traveler, would stand by the well with his string of camels and, as each attractive young woman filled her pitcher, placed it on her shoulder, and began to return home, he would ask if he might have a drink of water from her pitcher. There were three possible responses to his request. He could be ignored; he could be told to draw water for himself; or, seeing him as a tired traveler, the young lady might feel sorry for him and take the trouble to give him a drink from the pitcher, which she would then have to refill. Any of the attractive young women who chose the latter course of action would demonstrate the trait he sought, that of compassion. However, the exemplar among the latter would be the good-hearted young woman who would not only give water to a tired traveler but also volunteer to provide water for his weary and thirsty animals as well. He then prayed to the God of Abraham that He *let the same be she that Thou hast appointed for Thy servant, even for Isaac*; that is, that the exemplary young woman who acted in such a manner be the one destined to marry Isaac, and that it would be a true kindness to Abraham if that young woman turned out to be a member of Abraham's extended family, and thus fulfill his master's sincerest wishes.

What is particularly striking about this passage is the substance of the emissary's prayer. At the beginning of his prayer, Abraham's servant pleads for God to *show kindness unto my master Abraham*, and at its end he asserts that if his plan proves successful, *thereby shall I know that Thou hast shown kindness to my master*. Isaac's getting an appropriate bride seems to be a secondary consideration here, the main focus is on what this will mean for Abraham. What is the subtext that the biblical author is implicitly setting forth here? Assuming that the servant in this passage is Eliezer or someone else who has been very close to Abraham for a long time and in a position to witness and assess his state of mind, he would have known that Abraham was surely greatly distressed by the complete absence of any communion with God since the traumatic episode of the *Akedah*, not even during the period of his mourning for Sarah. Given this context, Abraham's loyal servant and confidante would seem to be suggesting, in effect, that the success of his bride-acquisition mission would be taken by Abraham as a sign that he had not lost favor with God, in the absence of any further communication, permitting him to live the rest of his life in spiritual serenity.[370] It is this that makes this seemingly unrelated episode a critical element in the conclusion of Abraham's spiritual odyssey.

> *24.15 And it came to pass, before he done speaking, that, behold, Rebekah came out, who was born to Bethuel the son of Milcah, the wife of Nahor, Abraham's brother, with her pitcher upon her shoulder. 24.16 And the damsel was very fair to look upon, a virgin, neither had any man known her; and she went down to the fountain, and filled her pitcher, and came up. 24.17 And the servant ran to meet her, and said: "Give me to drink, I pray thee, a little water of thy pitcher." 24.18 And she said: "Drink, my lord"; and she hastened, and let down her pitcher upon her hand, and gave him drink. 24.19 And when she had done giving him drink, she said: "I will draw for thy camels also, until they have done drinking." 24.20 And she hastened, and emptied her pitcher into the trough, and ran again unto the well to draw, and drew for all his camels. 24.21 And the man looked steadfastly on her;*

holding his peace, to know whether YHVH had made his journey prosperous or not.

Even before he finished his prayer for success on behalf of both Abraham and Isaac, the divine response was given in the form of a young woman, who happened to be Rebekah, approaching the well, pitcher on her shoulder. A quick glance revealed that she was beautiful, and, the narrator adds, *a virgin, neither had any man known her.* Although this description seems redundant, the Hebrew word translated as "virgin" does not necessarily carry a sexual connotation and may be used to refer to a young girl of marriageable age,[371] although one is left wondering why this statement is made here at all.[372]

Putting his scheme into play, Abraham's emissary waited until she had filled her pitcher and only then proceeded to ask if she would give him a drink from her pitcher. To his delight, she immediately responded affirmatively and lowered her pitcher, saying *Drink, my lord.* It has been suggested that addressing him in this honorific manner, not knowing who he was, was a clear indication that she was a person highly respectful of others, regardless of station.[373] When he finished drinking, she spontaneously offered to provide water for his camels as well, *until they have done drinking.* This exceeded anything he had hoped for from even the most good-hearted of young women. Camels consume enormous amounts of water, and unless Abraham's camels had very recently been watered, providing enough water to sate ten camels from a pitcher would be a Herculean task.

Abraham's emissary *looked steadfastly on her*, that is, he must have stood dumbfounded as the young woman ran to and from the well to the trough until she provided for all the camels. As he watched her, he said nothing but pondered whether she would make the ideal bride for Isaac, *whether YHVH had made his journey prosperous or not.* He may have wondered if he should rest satisfied that he had found the right person, whether she was Rebekah or not, or to wait and see if others, among them perhaps Rebekah, would act in a similar fashion. Although her identity was unknown to the emissary at that moment, the narrator makes it explicitly clear that not only was she Rebekah but that she was the granddaughter of Nahor and Milcah, and not the progeny of one of Nahor's concubines. Presumably, this was deemed worthy of mention here because Milcah was the daughter of Abraham's brother Haran and was herself Abraham's niece, and nothing would please Abraham more than to have Isaac marry completely within his extended family.

> ^{24.22} *And it came to pass, as the camels had done drinking, that the man took a golden ring of half a shekel weight, and two bracelets for her hands of ten shekels weight of gold;* ^{24.23} *and said: "Whose daughter art thou? Tell me, I pray thee. Is there room in thy father's house for us to lodge in?"* ^{24.24} *And she said unto him: "I am the daughter of Bethuel the son of Milcah, whom she bore unto Nahor."* ^{24.25} *She said moreover unto him: "We have both straw and provender enough, and room to lodge in."* ^{24.26} *And the man bowed his head, and prostrated himself before YHVH.* ^{24.27} *And he said: "Blessed be YHVH, the God of my master Abraham, who hath not forsaken His mercy and His truth toward my master; as for me, YHVH hath led me in the way to the house of my master's brethren."*

Evidently concluding that it made more sense to take advantage of the opportunity at hand than to forego it in the hope that another and even better one might emerge, Abraham's emissary decided to pursue the possibility of obtaining this extraordinary young woman as a bride for Isaac, whether or not she was Rebekah. Both as a reward for her kindnesses and perhaps also to impress her, he gave her valuable personal gifts on the spot, at the same time inquiring about who she was and whether it would be possible for him to lodge at her home while he remained in Haran, a step that would greatly facilitate negotiations with her family. Her response to the latter was affirmative.

Her response was also surprising, in that it indicated that the valuable gold ornaments he had given to her did not especially impress her. Had it been otherwise, she surely would have answered that there was indeed room for him at her home, and that his animals could be accommodated as well. Instead, she said: *We have both straw and provender enough, and room to lodge in*, giving her first thoughts to the needs of the animals, clearly indicating that she was raised in a culture in which one was obligated to see to the needs of the animals for which he was responsible before one saw to his own needs. But most important was her response to his inquiry about her identity. Abraham's emissary was astounded to learn that this young woman was the daughter of Bethuel, that is, she was in fact Rebekah. It was now absolutely evident to him that even though he had been prepared to choose someone other than from Abraham's relatives, there had indeed been a divine intervention in Abraham's behalf that brought Rebekah to him at that moment. Once Abraham received his report, he too would take it as a clear indication that he still found favor with God. He prostrated himself in prayer, exclaiming: *Blessed be YHVH, the God of my master Abraham, who hath not forsaken His mercy and His truth toward my master*. All that remained to be done was to negotiate and conclude the arrangements with Rebekah's family.

24.28 And the damsel ran, and told her mother's house according to these words. 24.29 And Rebekah had a brother, and his name was Laban;[374] *and Laban ran out to the man, unto the fountain.*[375] *24.30 And it came to pass, when he saw the ring, and the bracelets upon his sister's hands, and when he heard the words of Rebekah his sister, saying: "Thus spoke the man unto me," that he came unto the man; and, behold, he stood by the camels at the fountain.* 24.31 *And he said: "Come in, thou blessed of YHVH; wherefore standest thou without? For I have cleared the house, and made room for the camels."* 24.32 *And the man came into the house, and he ungirded the camels; and he gave straw and provender for the camels, and water to wash his feet and the feet of the men that were with him.*[376] 24.33 *And there was food set before him to eat; but he said: "I will not eat, until I have told mine errand." And he said: "Speak on."*

Rebekah ran to the women's quarters to tell her mother about what had happened, and word of it came to her brother Laban as well. Laban, who emerges here and appears again later in the biblical narrative as an unsavory character, is introduced, according to some, in an unexpected manner, *And Rebekah had a brother, and his name was Laban*. It has been observed that it appears to be a convention of biblical writers to introduce persons of virtue by "his name was," followed by the name, such as in *his name was Boaz* (Ruth 2:1), and to introduce unsavory persons with the formula "such and such was his name," as in *Nabal is his name* (1 Sam. 25:25). By implication then, Laban is to be seen in this passage as a man of virtue. Although the text does not clearly indicate why this should be the case, it may be inferred that Laban is being described as a man who is concerned about protecting the honor and person of his immediate family. No sooner does he hear that a stranger had the effrontery to accost his sister, and that she returned home with gifts, possibly implying payment for some nefarious service rendered, his immediate reaction is to seek out and punish the offender, *and Laban ran out to the man, unto the fountain*.[377] This should be understood as saying that he *began* to go out to confront the stranger over the affront to his sister.

However, we are then told that the valuable gold ornaments bestowed on Rebekah by the stranger who, according to her account, was a representative of their wealthy granduncle Abraham, intrigued Laban. His righteous indignation promptly abated and Laban, sensing opportunity, now proceeded to the well, where the emissary had remained, to personally invite him as well as his entourage to lodge in his home. It is also noteworthy that it was actually the household of Laban's father Bethuel, who was evidently held in some disdain by his son, who arrogated his father's role. It is also noteworthy that the biblical author has Laban, who surely did not share Abraham's beliefs and who later invoked *the God of Nahor* (Gen. 31:53), the pagan god of his grandfather, nonetheless refer to

Abraham's emissary as *thou blessed of YHVH*, perhaps as an indication of Laban's desire to ingratiate himself with the stranger in the hope of reaping some benefit from him later. This is also reflected in the textual statement, *and he ungirded the camels; and he gave straw and provender for the camels, and water to wash his feet and the feet of the men that were with him*, the "he" in this most likely referring to Laban, who was evidently going out of his way to make his guests feel indebted to him for the unexpected services being rendered to them.

Once they had taken care of their animals and had cleaned themselves from the dust of the road they were invited to share some food, in accordance with the prevailing rules of hospitality, before they got down to the question of what the man was doing in Haran. It has been observed that in Middle Eastern tribal societies, it is considered a breach of hospitality to inquire about the identity of one's guests before they have something of the host's food to eat, in case there is some cloud hovering over the guest's presence such as a blood feud between tribes or clans. Once having eaten, such considerations are put aside for as long as one is a guest. However, Abraham's emissary, who surely was familiar with the custom, refused to eat anything until he made clear who he was and why he had come. The implication being that if there were any outstanding issues between the family of the host and the master he represented that might impede his mission, it would be inappropriate for him to impose on their hospitality any further.

Why does Abraham's emissary make such an unprecedented step, thereby violating longstanding norms of hospitality and social intercourse? The reason is hinted at by the text, which suggests that Laban's offer of hospitality and subsequent overly generous behavior occurred only after *he saw the ring, and the bracelets upon his sister's hands*. Abraham's emissary sensed, either by direct observation or surmise, that, notwithstanding Rebekah's exemplary behavior, the household from which she came was ethically suspect, something that would become quite clear years later. Accordingly, the emissary deemed it appropriate to seize control of the situation from the outset by taking this socially bold step.

Taken aback by the emissary's directness, a surprised Laban urged him to speak his mind, which he proceeded to do.

> 24.34 *And he said: "I am Abraham's servant.* 24.35 *And YHVH hath blessed my master greatly; and he is become great; and He hath given him flocks and herds, and silver and gold, and men-servants and maid-servants, and camels and asses.* 24.36 *And Sarah my master's wife bore a son to my master when she was old; and unto him hath he given all that he hath.* 24.37 *And my master made me swear, saying: Thou shalt not take a wife for my son of the daughters of the Canaanites, in whose land I dwell.* 24.38 *But thou shalt go unto my father's house, and to my kin-*

dred, and take a wife for my son. ²⁴·³⁹ *And I said unto my master: Peradventure the woman will not follow me.* ²⁴·⁴⁰ *And he said unto me: YHVH, before whom I walk, will send His angel with thee, and prosper thy way; and thou shalt take a wife for my son of my kindred, and of my father's house;* ²⁴·⁴¹ *then shalt thou be clear from my oath, when thou comest to my kindred; and if they give her not to thee, thou shalt be clear from my oath."*

Abraham's emissary makes a brief presentation that he hopes will find favor with his audience and bring about the results he wants. He begins by identifying himself as a servant of Abraham, who in the many years since he left Haran had become a very powerful and wealthy sheikh, an assertion designed to capture their full attention. He then goes on to say that Abraham's late wife Sarah, who presumably was the butt of much gossip in the extended family because of her childlessness in the years that Abraham and she lived alongside his brothers in the household of their father Terah, had finally given birth to a son late in life, and it was this son that was the heir to all of Abraham's fortune. At this point, they may already begin to surmise what he is getting at, the point which he makes in his very next statement, in which he deliberately misquotes his master's charge. Abraham had instructed him, *thou shalt go unto my country [artzi], and to my kindred [moladeti,* better translated as "homeland"*], and take a wife for my son*. However, in his presentation to Rebekah's family, the emissary states, *thou shalt go unto my father's house [bet-avi], and to my kindred [mishpahti], and take a wife for my son.* Although the distinctions are not clear in English translation cited here, they are quite significant in the Hebrew text. Whereas Abraham's principal charge to his servant was to bring back a suitable bride for Isaac from his place of origin, primarily to preclude his son from taking a Canaanite wife, Abraham's emissary cites his master as having instructed him to bring back a wife from his clan (*bet-avi*) and family (*mishpahti*).³⁷⁸ The point the emissary is making here, to help sell the idea of the proposed alliance, is that Abraham wants his fortune to remain within the extended Terahide family, and to that end has ordered his servant to seek out the family of Nahor, whose son Bethuel has an unmarried daughter, and to propose a marriage between Rebekah and Abraham's son and heir, Isaac. This, he avers, is the mission that he has come to them to carry out.

Moreover, Abraham's shrewd servant implicitly makes clear, this should not be misinterpreted as a sign that Abraham is desperate that this mission be fulfilled under any and all circumstances, something that would give Bethuel enormous leverage in any negotiations over bride price and dowry. Abraham, of course, recognizes that Rebekah may not wish to leave her ancestral home to the turbulent territory of Cisjordan, where his wealth in lands and herds is based, but he hopes that with divine help this problem will be overcome. But, if she nonetheless is unwilling, *then shalt thou be clear from my oath, when thou comest to my kindred.* That is, Abraham has no desire to create a situation in which the bride of Isaac is effectively coerced into the marriage. The clear implication of this is that Abraham's emissary has been charged to seek out Rebekah and propose a marriage to Isaac. If the young woman demurs, this aspect of the emissary's obligation is fulfilled and he is free to seek another candidate. Also implied in the recitation of Abraham's charge to him, although Abraham never explicitly discussed the possibility, is the consideration that it may not be feasible to come to a mutually satisfactory arrangement with Rebekah's family, in which case he had been told by his master: *if they give her not to thee, thou shalt be clear from my oath.* In other words, serving as his master's advocate, Abraham's emissary is making clear that he has not been instructed to make a deal for Rebekah at any or all costs; he is empowered to negotiate and to exercise his own judgment as to whether a mutually acceptable arrangement can be arrived at. In effect, the emissary is telling Bethuel and his family that Abraham is giving them the first right of refusal and not the equivalent of a sword to hold over his head.

Having concluded his opening remarks, he continued with a detailed description of the events that brought him into their home.

> 24.42 *"And I came this day unto the fountain, and said: O YHVH, the God of my master Abraham, if now Thou do prosper my way which I go:* 24.43 *behold, I stand by the fountain of water; and let it come to pass, that the maiden that cometh forth to draw, to whom I shall say: Give me, I pray thee, a little water from thy pitcher to drink;* 24.44 *and she shall say to me: Both drink thou, and I will also draw for thy camels; let the same be the woman whom YHVH hath appointed for my master's son.* 24.45 *And before I had done speaking to my heart, behold, Rebekah came forth with her pitcher on her shoulder; and she went down to the fountain, and drew. And I said to her: Let me drink, I pray thee.* 24.46 *And she made haste, and let down her pitcher from her shoulder, and said: Drink, and I will give thy camels drink also. So I drank, and she made the camels drink also.* 24.47 *And I asked her, and said: Whose daughter art thou? And she said: The daughter of Bethuel, Nahor's son, whom Milcah bore unto him. And I put the ring upon her nose, and the bracelets upon her hands.* 24.48 *And I bowed my head, and prostrated myself before YHVH, and blessed YHVH, the God of my master Abraham, who led me in the right way to take my master's brother's daughter for his son.* 24.49 *And now if ye will deal kindly and truly with my master, tell me; and if not, tell me; that I may turn to the right hand, or to the left."*

In his slightly altered recapitulation of the events of the day, the emissary repeats those aspects that will lead his listeners to conclude that Abraham's primary concern was with the qualities of the prospective bride and only secondarily with her provenance. This again made it reasonably clear that, while obtaining Rebekah for Isaac was highly desirable, other options remained. Accordingly, he effectively demanded an immediate response, favorable or otherwise, and quickly received the one he had hoped for.

> 24.50 *Then Laban and Bethuel answered and said: "The thing proceedeth from YHVH; we cannot speak unto thee bad or good.* 24.51 *Behold, Rebekah is before thee, take her and go, and let her be thy master's son's wife, as YHVH hath spoken."* 24.52 *And it came to pass, that, when Abraham's servant heard their words, he bowed himself down to the earth unto YHVH.* 24.53 *And the servant brought forth jewels of silver, and jewels of gold, and raiment, and gave them to Rebekah; he gave also to her brother and to her mother precious things.*

The reply was favorable. The emissary is told to take Rebekah to be a bride to Isaac, and the emissary, basking in the success of his mission, does not forget to render praise to God who made it successful, and immediately distributes precious gifts to all involved. Yet, a carefully reading of the text suggests that all was not as clear and smooth as the emissary was initially led to believe.

It seems clear that Bethuel, Abraham's nephew, is not the effective decision-maker in his own household, for reasons that have been withheld. His son Laban, with his wife playing a secondary role, has essentially arrogated that role, as indicated by his taking the lead in offering a response to the emissary. The actual statement he makes, seconded by Bethuel, should in itself have raised some concern in that it was self-evidently disingenuous. The fact that Laban and Bethuel, both pagans raised in a pagan household, should ascribe what took place to the God of Abraham, saying *The thing proceedeth from YHVH*, a God they did not believe in, followed by their assertion that *we cannot speak unto thee bad or good*, that is, that because of divine intervention they are rendered neutral in the matter, should have aroused some suspicion. In other words, they did not agree to anything at all; they simply stated that the matter was not in their hands and that the emissary was free to take Rebekah with him if he so chose, *as YHVH hath spoken*, an assertion that *they* did not consider divine and therefore authoritative. The implication of this soon became apparent once the initial euphoria and celebration came to an end.

It is also worth noting that they may have been disappointed with the largesse the emissary was distributing, especially to them. The text states: *And the servant brought forth jewels of silver, and jewels of gold, and raiment, and gave them to Rebekah; he gave also to her brother and to her mother precious things.* The translation of the latter clause may in fact overstate the matter. The biblical text actually states that after the emissary gave precious jewels to Rebekah, he gave Laban and her mother *migdanot*, which may be understood as confections or sweetmeats, or at best unspecified gifts. This might well account for later efforts to extract more from the emissary before the matter was finally concluded, as discussed below.[379]

> [24.54] *And they did eat and drink, he and the men that were with him, and tarried all night; and they rose up in the morning, and he said: "Send me away unto my master."* [24.55] *And her brother and her mother said: "Let the damsel abide with us a few days, at the least ten; after that she shall go."* [24.56] *And he said unto them: "Delay me not, seeing that YHVH hath prospered my way; send me away that I may go to my master."* [24.57] *And they said: "We will call the damsel, and inquire at her mouth."* [24.58] *And they called Rebekah, and said unto her: "Wilt thou go with this man?" And she said: "I will go."* [24.59] *And they sent away Rebekah their sister, and her nurse, and Abraham's servant, and his men.* [25.60] *And they blessed Rebekah, and said unto her: "Our sister, be thou the mother of thousands of ten thousands, and let thy seed possess the gate of those that hate them."*

Whereas, Abraham's emissary thought that all his business had been concluded, thus occasioning an evening of festivities, the morning quickly brought him back to the realities of Rebekah's family. In fact, not much had been concluded, notwithstanding the precious gifts that had already been bestowed upon Rebekah, Laban, and her mother, presumably as the bride price, in part or in whole. Rebekah's brother and mother now wished to delay her departure for *yamim o asor*, translated here as *a few days, at the least ten*, a Hebrew idiom that had also been understood by ancient translators as "one year or ten months."[380] The proposed delay probably had less to do with their reluctance to see Rebekah depart her home perhaps never to be seen again, as some commentators suggest, than with the hope that the emissary might be forthcoming with additional gifts to procure their agreement. In other words, all that had been concluded the previous day was that they interposed no objection to the match, which did not include any commitment to facilitate it.

The text is silent with regard to what the emissary may have done at this point to procure Rebekah's immediate release; it only records the emissary's sense of urgency and request that his departure with Rebekah not be delayed any further. Once having overcome their initial call for a delay, presumably by providing an appropriate inducement, the emissary was confronted by another unanticipated problem: the entire agreement would be void if Rebekah herself did not wish to leave her homeland with him, a consideration that obviates the suggestion that they wanted a delay because of their reluctance to let her leave them. Once they had gotten as much as they could from the emissary, it appears that they left it up to Rebekah to decide her fate; if she wanted to go with him immediately she was free to do so.[381] It is noteworthy, however, that Rebekah is not actually asked if she agrees to the marriage but only if she is willing to go with the servant. Indeed, she is asked, *wilt thou go with this man*, not with Abraham's servant or emissary, indicating according to some a sense of disdain, perhaps intended to sway her answer toward the negative. That is, she may merely have been asked if she is willing to go with the servant or does she prefer to wait until the prospective groom comes for her, perhaps with additional gifts for the family. As it turns out, Rebekah, whose values differed so substantially from those of her brother, who was de facto head of the household, evidently had no qualms about leaving her home with the emissary for that of Abraham and his son and heir Isaac. Once her decision was made, she received a blessing for prosperity from her family and along with her longstanding nurse and caregiver departed her home with Abraham's emissary and retinue.[382]

> [24.61] *And Rebekah arose, and her damsels, and they rode upon the camels, and followed the man. And the servant took Rebekah, and went on his way.* [24.62] *And Isaac came from the way of Beer-lahai-roi; for he dwelt in the land of the South.* [24.63] *And Isaac went out to meditate in the field at the eventide; and he lifted up his eyes, and saw, and, behold, there were camels coming.* [24.64] *And Rebekah lifted up her eyes, and when she saw Isaac, she alighted from the camel.* [24.65] *And she said unto the servant: "What man is this that walketh in the field to meet us?" And the servant said: "It is my master." And she took her veil, and covered herself.* [24.66] *And the servant told Isaac all the things that he had done.* [24.67] *And Isaac brought her into his mother Sarah's tent, and took Rebekah, and she became his wife; and he loved her. And Isaac was comforted for his mother.*

As suggested earlier, it appears that Isaac had gone into the desert to live an almost monastic life, spending much time in meditation, presumably trying to comprehend the meaning of all that had happened to him. There is no indication whatever that Abraham was anywhere nearby, or that the servant brought Rebekah to meet Abraham first, before going deeper into the Negev to Isaac. Moreover, we do not know if Isaac had any inkling of what his father was arranging for him; there is a good chance that he knew nothing until Abraham's servant, who presumably was their go-between, told him about it now when he arrived with the prospective bride. It is especially noteworthy that Isaac had kept Sarah's tent with him, presumably removing it from Abraham's household, which suggests that he may have blamed his father for precipitating his mother's demise, his moroseness at this compounded further by his own failure to attend her burial. Isaac duly married Rebekah, who appears to have given him a new lease on life, and he soon came to love her as she occupied his mother's tent.

This tangential episode in the broader saga of Abraham ends with the enigmatic statement, *And Isaac was comforted for his mother.* In what way was he comforted? Did his wife Rebekah also become as a mother to him, taking Sarah's place and thus comforting him for the loss of his biological mother? From what occurs later in the story of Isaac, it becomes quite clear that Rebekah becomes the dominant figure, manipulating Isaac to assure that Abraham's heritage and the divine covenant associated with it passes to the son most fit to bear it, much as Sarah did with regard to Abraham, only more so.

With Isaac appropriately married, Abraham's historic role essentially comes to an end. Even though he will have outlived Sarah by some thirty-eight years, we are told nothing of him during that long period other than that, notwithstanding his advanced age, he lived comfortably for the rest of his years (Gen. 24:1), and, in effect, began an entirely new life.

> 25.1 *And Abraham took another wife, and her name was Keturah.* 25.2 *And she bore him Zimram, and Jokshan, and Medan, and Midian, and Ishbak, and Shuah.* 25.3 *And Jokshan begot Sheba and Dedan. And the sons of Dedan were Asshurim, and Letushim, and Leummim.* 25.4 *And the sons of Midian: Ephah, and Epher, and Hanoch, and Abida, and Eldaah. All these were the children of Keturah.* 25.5 *And Abraham gave all that he had unto Isaac.* 25.6 *But unto the sons of the concubines, that Abraham had, Abraham gave gifts; and he sent them away from Isaac his son, while he yet lived, eastward, unto the east country.*

Although it is not certain that Abraham waited until after Sarah's death to take a second wife, it seems quite likely, given his earlier experience with Hagar. It is not at all clear that Sarah would have tolerated any such thing, and it is quite clear that Sarah had a powerful influence over the affairs of Abraham's household. In any case, Abraham, at a very advanced age, showed remarkable virility, siring no less than six sons by his second wife Keturah, definitively putting to rest the malicious gossip about his not being the father of Isaac because of his alleged impotency, an allegation that surely continued to haunt Sarah ever since she gave birth. By contrast with Hagar, we are told nothing of Keturah's origins and must presume she was a Canaanite, demonstrating clearly, as suggested above, that Abraham's objection to Isaac marrying a Canaanite had little or nothing whatever to do with either their ethnicity or their paganism.

It also seems quite clear that Abraham himself viewed this second marriage as being distinct in every respect from his marriage to Sarah, which reflected a sense of purpose and mission that was missing here. This marriage surely was intended to provide him with companionship throughout his remaining days, the children that it produced perhaps an unintended but acceptable consequence of the conjugal relationship that he enjoyed with Keturah in his declining years. The biblical writer makes it quite clear that Abraham did not consider them as his sons or heirs in the same sense as Isaac filled that role. Everything he owned was left to Isaac, who was to be his sole heir, except for the gifts that he bestowed on these later children, whom the biblical writer designates as *the sons of the concubines*, as well as on his first son, Ishmael, further indicating the difference in status between Sarah and the two secondary wives, Hagar and Keturah. Moreover, to assure that his legacy to Isaac would not be subject to challenge by these half-siblings, he did exactly what Sarah had insisted he do with Ishmael. He sent them away out of the country to settle in the lands to the east, just as Ishmael settled in the wilderness region to the south. And, to make sure that his will prevailed in this matter, Abraham ensured that their permanent emigration from Cisjordan took place while he still lived.

Having secured his legacy to Isaac to the extent feasible, Abraham's long troubled but fruitful life came to a natural end.

> *25.7 And these are the days of the years of Abraham's life which he lived, a hundred threescore and fifteen years. 25.8 And Abraham expired, and died in a good old age, an old man, and full of years; and was gathered to his people. 25.9 And Isaac and Ishmael his sons buried him in the cave of Machpelah, in the field of Ephron the son of Zohar the Hittite, which is before Mamre; 25.10 the field which Abraham purchased of the children of Heth; there was Abraham buried, and Sarah his wife. 25.11 And it came to pass after the death of Abraham, that Elohim blessed Isaac his son; and Isaac dwelt by Beer-lahai-roi.*

Abraham thus dies thirty-eight years after his only true wife Sarah, and was buried by his sons Isaac and Ishmael in the burial place Abraham had purchased in Hebron so that he could be buried near her when his time came. The fact that Ishmael came to bury Abraham clearly indicates that whatever hurt he may have felt at being forced to leave his birthplace was overcome by the success he subsequently experienced in life. It has also been suggested that Ishmael ultimately may have forgiven his father for flouting primogeniture and sending him away, thus making it unnecessary for him to have undergone the trauma of the *Akedah* experienced by his half-brother Isaac.[383] Similarly, Isaac also put aside the trauma of his near death experience at the hands of his father and had become reconciled to him, presumably, before Abraham's death, although the biblical author is silent in this regard.

Finally, we are told, that upon Abraham's passing away, *Elohim blessed Isaac his son*. What had been a matter of grave concern to Abraham and Sarah throughout their later years had been successfully resolved; the spiritually legacy to Isaac remained intact and in effect. With God's blessing, the biblical writer assures us, Isaac became the beneficiary of the divine covenant in place of his father, and the bearer of the monotheistic idea and its corollary implications for the creation of a civilization predicated on the ideals of justice and righteousness that would ultimately serve as the reason for being of the people and nation of Israel.

However, the saga of Abraham would not be complete without an accounting of the divine promises to Hagar regarding Ishmael.

> 25.12 *Now these are the generations of Ishmael, Abraham's son, whom Hagar the Egyptian, Sarah's handmaid, bore unto Abraham.* 25.13 *And these are the names of the sons of Ishmael, by their names, according to their generations: the firstborn of Ishmael, Nebaioth; and Kedar, and Adbeel, and Mibsam,* 25.14 *and Mishma, and Dumah, and Maasa;* 25.15 *Hadad, and Tema, Jetur, Naphish, and Kedem;* 25.16 *these are the sons of Ishmael, and these are their names, by their villages, and by their encampments; twelve princes according to their nations.* 25.17 *And these are the years of the life of Ishmael, a hundred and thirty and seven years; and he expired and died; and was gathered unto his people.* 25.18 *And they dwelt from Havilah unto Shur, that is before Egypt, as thou goest toward Asshur: over against all his brethren did he settle.*

And so, Abraham's story concludes with an unelaborated genealogy of the twelve descendants of Abraham's firstborn son, each of which became a prince in his own right, and the saga of Isaac and Rebekah and their sons begins.

Selected References

Abravanel, Isaac (1437-1508). *Perush haTorah*. 5 Vols. in 1. Warsaw: Levenson, 1862.

Ahai of Shabha (680-752). *Sheiltot deRav Ahai Gaon*. 3 Vols. Commentary by Naftali Zvi Berlin. Jerusalem: Mossad Harav Kook, 1986.

Albo, Joseph (c.1420). *Sefer Ha'Ikkarim*. 5 Vols. Edited and Translated by Isaac Husik. Philadelphia: Jewish Publication Society, 1946.

Albright, William F. *The Biblical Period from Abraham to Ezra*. New York: Harper and Row, 1963.

———. *Yahweh and the Gods of Canaan: A Historical Analysis of Two Contrasting Faiths*. Garden City: Doubleday, 1968.

Almosnino, Moses (c. 1515-c. 1580). *Pirkei Moshe*. Jerusalem: Torah Shlemah Institute, 1970.

Alshekh, Moses (d. after 1590). *Torat Moshe*. 2 Vols. Warsaw, 1879; Reprint, New York: Klulat Yofi, 1966.

Alter, Robert. *Genesis: Translation and Commentary*. New York: W.W. Norton, 1996.

Arama, Isaac (c.1420-1494). *Akedat Yitzhak*. 6 Vols. Israel, 1974.

Arieti, Silvano. *Abraham and the Contemporary Mind*. New York: Basic Books, 1981.

Augustine (354-430). *The City of God*. New York: Random House, 1950.

The Babylonian Talmud. 18 Vols. Translated under editorship of I. Epstein. London: Soncino Press, 1978.

Bahya ben Asher (13th cent.). *Biur al haTorah*. 3 Vols. Edited by Charles B. Chavel. Jerusalem: Mossad Harav Kook, 1966.

Bat-Halevi, D. *Derekh haAvot el haMonoteizm: Perush leSefer Bereshit*. Jerusalem: R.H. Hakohen, 1970.

Bekhor Shor, Joseph (12th cent.). *Perush Rabbi Yosef Bekhor Shor al haTorah*. Edited by Yehoshafat Nebo. Jerusalem: Mossad Harav Kook, 1994.

Berkovits, Eliezer. *Man and God: Studies in Biblical Theology*. Detroit: Wayne State University Press, 1969.

Berlin, Naftali Zvi Judah (1817-1893). *HaAmek Davar*. 5 Vols. New York: Mercaz HaSefarim, 1952.

Berman, Louis A. *The Akedah: The Binding of Isaac*. Northvale: Jason Aronson, 1997.

Bodoff, Lippman. "The Real Test of the *Akedah*: Blind Obedience Versus Moral Choice." *Judaism*, 42:1, Winter 1993, pp. 71-92.

———. "The Binding of Isaac: Religious Paradoxes, Permutations, and Problems." *Midstream*, November 2001, pp. 25-28.

The Book of Jasher. Translated from the Hebrew by Mordecai Manuel Noah. New York: Hermon Press, 1972.

Boteach, Shmuel. *Wrestling with the Divine: A Jewish Response to Suffering*. Northvale: Jason Aronson, 1995.

Bowie, Walter. "Testing of Abraham (22:1-19)." In George A. Buttrick, ed. *The Interpreter's Bible*. New York: Abingdon Press, 1952, Vol. 1, pp. 642-646.

Brams, Steven J. *Biblical Games: A Strategic Analysis of Stories in the Old Testament*. Cambridge, MA: MIT Press, 1980.

Brown, Francis, S.R. Driver, and Charles A. Briggs, Eds. *A Hebrew and English Lexicon of the Old Testament*. Oxford: Oxford University Press, 1972.

Buber, Martin (1878-1965). *Israel and Palestine: The History of an Idea*. London: East and West Library, 1952.

―――. *On the Bible: Eighteen Studies*. Edited by Nahum N. Glatzer. New York: Schocken Books, 1968.

Calvin, John (1509-1564). *Genesis*. 2 Vols. in 1. Edinburgh: Banner of Truth Trust, 1979.

Cassutto, Moses David [Umberto] (1883-1951). *Perush al Sefer Bereshit*. 2 Vols. in 1. Jerusalem: Magnes Press, 1969.

Charlesworth, James H., ed. *The Old Testament Pseudepigrapha*. 2 Vols. New York: Doubleday, 1985.

Cohen, Jack J. "'Is This the Meaning of My Life?' Israelis Rethink the *Akedah*." *Conservative Judaism* 43:1, pp. 50-60.

Crescas, Hasdai (c.1340-1410). *Or Adonai*. Ferrara, 1555; Facsimile edition Jerusalem: Makor Publishing, 1970.

Daube, David. *Studies in Biblical Law*. New York: Ktav Publishing House, 1969.

David ben Abraham Maimuni (1222-1300). *Midrash Rabbi David haNagid: Sefer Bereshit*. Translated by Abraham I. Katz. Jerusalem: Mossad Harav Kook, 1964.

Davidson, Benjamin. *The Analytical Hebrew and Chaldee Lexicon*. Peabody: Hendrickson Publishers, 1990.

Davidson, Robert. *Genesis 12-50*. Cambridge: Cambridge University Press, 1979.

Davies, W.D. *The Territorial Dimension of Judaism*. Berkeley: University of California Press, 1982.

Delaney, Carol. *Abraham on Trial: The Social Legacy of Biblical Myth*. Princeton: Princeton University Press, 1998.

Dershowitz, Alan M. *The Genesis of Justice: Ten Stories of Biblical Injustice that Led to the Ten Commandments and Modern Law*. New York: Warner Books, 2000.

De Vaux, Roland. *Ancient Israel*. 2 Vols. New York: McGraw-Hill, 1965.

Dillmann, August (1823-1894). *Genesis: Critically and Exegetically Expounded.* 2 Vols. Translated by Wm. B. Stevenson. Edinburgh: T. & T. Clark, 1897.

Driver, Samuel R (1846-1914). *The Book of Genesis.* 14th Edition. London: Methuen, 1943.

Ehrlich, Arnold B (1848-1919). *Mikra kiFeshuto.* 3 Vols. Berlin: Poppelauer's Buchhandlung, 1899.

Ehrlich, Avi. *Ancient Zionism: The Biblical Origins of the National Idea.* New York: Free Press, 1995.

Eldad, Israel. *Hegyonot Mikra.* Jerusalem: Sulam, 1958.

Elijah ben Solomon Zalman of Vilna (1720-1797). *Kol Eliyahu.* Pieterkov: N.N. Kronenberg, n.d. Reprinted in Israel, 1961.

Emmanueli, Yitzhak Moshe. *Sefer Bereshit: Hesberim veHe'arot.* Tel Aviv, 1978.

Encyclopaedia Judaica. 16 Vols. Jerusalem: Keter, 1973.

Ephraim Solomon of Luntshits (1550-1619). *Perush Kli Yakar haShalem.* 2 Vols. Jerusalem: Horev, 1999.

Etheridge, J.W. *The Targums of Onkelos and Jonathan ben Uziel on the Pentateuch.* 2 Vols. in 1. New York: Ktav Publishing House, 1968; Reprint of 1862 Edition.

Etz Hayim: Torah and Commentary. New York: Rabbinical Assembly/United Synagogue of Conservative Judaism, 2001.

The Fathers According to Rabbi Nathan. Translated by Judah Goldin. New Haven: Yale University Press, 1955.

Firer, Ben-Zion. *Hegyonah shel Torah.* 5 Vols. Tel Aviv: Sifriyati, 1967.

———. *MeAdam ve'ad Avraham: Sippur Mikra'i.* Tel Aviv: Sifriyati, 1971.

Fleischman, Yosef. "Garesh haAmah haZot ve'et B'Nah." *Beit Mikra*, No. 157, Jan-March, 1999, pp. 146-162.

Fox, Everett. *The Five Books of Moses: A New Translation with Introductions, Commentary, and Notes*. New York: Schocken Books, 1995.

Frankel, Ellen. *The Five Books of Miriam: A Woman's Commentary on the Torah*. New York: HarperCollins, 1996.

Freedman, H. *Jeremiah*. London: Soncino Press, 1970.

Friedman, Richard Elliott. *Commentary on the Torah*. New York: HarperSanFrancisco, 2001.

Ganzfried, Solomon (1804-1866). *Apiryon*. Israel, n.d.

Gelman, Yehuda. "And Sarah Died." *Tradition* 32:1, 1997, pp. 57-67.

The Genesis Octapla: Eight English Versions of the Book of Genesis in the Tyndale-King James Tradition. Edited by Luther A. Weigle. New York: Thoman Nelson & Sons, 1965.

Gerber, Israel J. *Immortal Rebels: Freedom for the Individual in the Bible*. New York: Jonathan David, 1963.

Gerondi, Jonah (c. 1200-1263). *Derashot vePerushei Rabbenu Yonah Gerondi leHamishah Humshei Torah*. Edited by Shmuel Yerushalmi. Jerusalem: Vagshal, 1988.

Gerondi, Nissim ben Reuven [Ran] (c. 1310-c. 1375). *Perush al haTorah*. Edited by Leon A. Feldman. Jerusalem: Makhon Shalem, 1968.

Gibschtein, Joshua. *Daat Torah: Biur al haTorah beDerekh haHigayon*. Pieterkov, 1932; 2nd Facsimile Edition: Tel Aviv: Moreshet, n.d.

Ginzberg, Louis (1873-1953). *The Legends of the Jews*. 7 Vols. Philadelphia: Jewish Publication Society, 1968.

Glueck, Nelson (1900-1971). *The River Jordan*. Philadelphia: Jewish Publication Society, 1946.

Gordis, Robert (1908–). *Judaic Ethics for a Lawless World*. New York: Jewish Theological Seminary of America, 1986.

Goitein, S.D. *Iyyunim beMikra: Behinato haSifrutit vehaHevratit.* Tel Aviv: Yavneh, 1967.

Goodman, Lenn E. *God of Abraham.* New York: Oxford University Press, 1996.

Gordon, Cyrus H. and Gary A. Rendsburg. *The Bible and the Ancient Near East.* 4th Edition. New York: W.W. Norton, 1997.

Gordon, Samuel Leib (1865-1933). *Hamishah Humshei Torah.* 5 Vols. in 1. Tel Aviv: S.L. Gordon, 1952.

Greenberg, Moshe. "Hab/Piru and Hebrews." In Benjamin Mazar, ed., *The World History of the Jewish People*, Vol. 2, *Patriarchs.* New Brunswick, NJ: Rutgers University Press, 1970.

Gunkel, Hermann (1862-1932). *Genesis.* Translated by Mark E. Biddle. Macon: Mercer University Press, 1997.

Haberman, Joshua O. *The God I Believe In.* New York: The Free Press, 1994.

Hackett, Jo Ann. "Rehabilitating Hagar: Fragments of an Epic Pattern." In Peggy L. Day, ed. *Gender and Difference in Ancient Israel.* Minneapolis: Fortress Press, 1989, pp. 12-27.

Hamishah Humshei Torah (Mikraot Gedolot). 2 Vols. Tel Aviv: Schocken, 1958.

Harari, Raymond. "Abraham's Nephew Lot: A Biblical Portrait." *Tradition* 25:1, Fall 1989, pp. 31-41.

Hartom, A.S. *Bereshit.* 2nd Revised Edition. Tel Aviv: Yavne, 1975.

Hayyun, Joseph (d. 1497). *Millei deAboth.* Printed in *Perushei Rishonim leMassekhet Aboth.* Jerusalem: Torah Shlemah Institute, 1973.

Herford, R. Travers (1860-1950). *Pirke Aboth. The Ethics of the Talmud: Sayings of the Fathers.* New York: Schocken Books, 1962.

Hertz, Joseph H. (1872-1946), Ed. *The Pentateuch and Haftorahs.* 2nd Edition. London: Soncino Press, 1997.

Hezekiah ben Manoah (mid-13th cent.). *Hizzekuni: Perush haTorah.* Edited by Charles B. Chavel. Jerusalem: Mossad Harav Kook, 1982.

Herzog, Chaim and Mordechai Gichon. *Battles of the Bible*. New York: Random House, 1978.

Hirsch, Samson Raphael (1808-1888). *The Pentateuch*. 5 Vols. Translated from German into English by Isaac levy. 2nd Edition. New York: Judaica Press, 1971.

Hoffmann, David Zvi (1843-1921). *Bereshit*. 2 Vols. Translated from German into Hebrew and edited by Asher Wasserteil. Bnei Brak: Netzah, 1969-71.

Horowitz, Isaiah (c. 1565-1630). *Shnei Luhot haBrit*. 2 Vols. Israel, n.d.

Ibn Ezra, Abraham (1089-1164). *Perushei haTorah leRabbenu Avraham ibn Ezra*. 3 Vols. Jerusalem: Mossad Harav Kook, 1976.

Jacob, Benno (1862-1945). *The First Book of the Bible: Genesis*. Abridged and edited by Ernest I. and Walter Jacob. New York: Ktav Publishing House, 1974.

Jacob ben Asher (c 1270-1340). *Perush haTur haArokh al haTorah*. Jerusalem: Beferush uveRemez, 1969.

Jacobson, B.S (Issachar). *Meditations on the Torah*. Tel Aviv: Sinai, 1956.

Janzen, J. Gerald. *Abraham and All the Families of the Earth: A Commentary on the Book of Genesis 12-50*. Grand Rapids: William B. Eerdmans, 1993.

Josephus: Complete Works. Translated by William Whiston. Grand Rapids: Kregel, 1960.

Judah Loew ben Bezalel [Maharal] (c.1525-1609). *Gur Aryeh*. In *Otzar Perushim al haTorah: Arbah Perushim al Rashi*. 2 Vols. New York: A.I. Friedman, 1965.

Halaveh, Judah (c. 1420). *Imre Shefer: Biur al Sefer Bereshit*. Edited by Hayyim Hirschler. Jerusalem: Makhon Harav Hirschler, 1993.

Keller, Werner (1909–). *The Bible as History*. 2nd Revised Edition. Revised by Joachim Rehork. New York: William Morrow, 1981.

Kierkegaard, Soren. *Fear and Trembling* and *The Sickness unto Death*. Translated by Walter Lowrie. Garden City, NY: Doubleday, 1954.

Kimhi, David [Radak] (c.1160-1235). *Perush Radak al haTorah*. Edited by Abraham Ginzberg. Pressburg, 1842; Facsimile Edition: Jerusalem, n.p., 1968.

———. *Sefer haSharashim*. Berlin: n.p., 1847; Facsimile Edition: New York, 1948.

Kugel, James L. *The Bible As It Was*. Cambridge, MA: Belknap Press, 1997.

Leibowitz, Nehama. *Iyyunim beSefer Bereshit: BeIkvot Parshanenu haRishonim vehaAharonim*. 3rd edition. Jerusalem: Histadrut haTzionit haOlamit, 1971.

Levi ben Gershom [Gersonides-Ralbag] (1288-1344). *Perushei haTorah leRabbenu Levi ben Gershom*. 5 Vols. Edited by Yaacov Leib Levi. Jerusalem: Mossad Harav Kook, 1992-2000.

Luzzatto, Samuel David [Shadal] (1800-1865). *Perush Shadal al Hamisha Humshei Torah*. Tel Aviv: Dvir, 1971.

Maimonides, Moses [Rambam] (1135-1204). *The Guide of the Perplexed*. Translated by Shlomo Pines. Chicago: University of Chicago Press, 1963.

———. *The Commentary to Mishnah Aboth*. Translated by Arthur David. New York: Bloch Publishing, 1968.

Malbim, Meir Leibush (1809-1879). *HaTorah vehaMitzvah*. 2 Vols. Jerusalem: Pardes, 1956.

Marcus, Aaron (1843-1916). *Keset haSofer: Perush al Tanakh uMishnaiot*. Vol. 1. 2nd Edition. Tel Aviv, 1971.

Mecklenburg, Jacob Zvi (1785-1865). *HaKtav vehaKabbalah*. 2 Vols. Jerusalem: Am Olam, 1969.

Meir Simhah haKohen (1853-1926). *Meshekh Hokhmah*. Jerusalem: Eshkol, n.d.

Meiri, Menahem (1249-1316). *Bet haBehirah: Massekhet Aboth*. Edited by Abraham Shoshana. Jerusalem: Makhon Ofek, 1994.

Menora, Shlomo. *Peshat veHigayon baMikra: BeIkvot haRishonim.* Tel Aviv: Or, 1978.

Midrash haGadol. 5 Vols. Edited by Mordekhai Margaliot. Jerusalem: Mossad Harav Kook, 1975.

Midrash Lekah Tov al Hamisha Humshei Torah. 2 Vols. Edited by Salomon Buber. Vilna: Romm, 1880; Facsimile Edition: Jerusalem: Vagshal, 1986.

Midrash Rabbah. 10 Vols. London: Soncino Press, 1983.

Midrash Seder Olam. Podgorze: S.L. Deutscher, 1898; Reprinted, Israel, 1971.

Midrash Seder Olam. Analysis and Notes by Ber Ratner and Samuel K. Mirsky. New York: Moznaim Publishing, 1988.

Mikraot Gedolot. 5 Vols. New York: Lyon Press, n.d.

Mikraot Gedolot. 2 Vols. Tel Aviv: Schocken Publishing House, 1958.

Moskowitz, Moshe. "Towards a Rehumanization of the *Akedah* and Other Sacrifices." *Judaism* 37:3, Summer 1988, pp. 288-294.

Moore, Carey A. *Judith: A New Translation with Introduction and Commentary.* Garden City, NY: Doubleday, 1985.

Munk, Elie (1900-1981). *The Call of the Torah.* 5 Vols. Translated from the French by E.S. Mazer. New York: Mesorah, 1992-97.

Murray, David A. *The Real Meaning of Genesis.* Boston: Stratford, 1930.

Nahmanides [Moses ben Nahman-Ramban] (1194-1270). *Perushei haTorah.* 2 vols. Edited by Charles B. Chavel. Jerusalem: Mossad Harav Kook, 1959.

Nahshoni, Yehudah. *Sefer Hagut beFarshiot haTorah.* 2 Vols. Bnei Brak: Sifriyati, 1989.

The New Jerusalem Bible. New York: Doubleday, 1985.

Notes on the New Translation of the Torah. Edited by Harry Orlinsky. Philadelphia: Jewish Publication Society, 1970.

Och, Bernard. "Abraham and Moriah—A Journey to Fulfillment." *Judaism* 38:3, Summer 1989, pp. 293-309.

Peli, Pinchas H. *Torah Today: A Renewed Encounter with Scripture*. Washington, DC: B'nai B'rith Books, 1987.

———. "A Society which Lived for Itself." *Jerusalem Post International Edition*, November 7, 1987, p, 22.

Pesikta Rabbati. 2 vols. Translated by William G. Braude. New Haven, CT: Yale University Press, 1968. (BM517)

Pirkei de Rabbi Eliezer. Translated and Annotated by Gerald Friedlander. New York: Sepher-Hermon, 1981.

Pitzele, Peter. *Our Fathers' Wells: A Personal Encounter with the Myths of Genesis*. New York: HarperCollins, 1994.

Plaut, W. Gunther, ed. *The Torah: A Modern Commentary*. New York: Union of American Hebrew Congregations, 1981.

Porto (Rafa-Rappaport), Abraham Menahem (1520-after 1594). *Minhah Belulah*. Verona, 1594; Reprinted, Jerusalem, 1972.

Pritchard, James B., ed. *Ancient Near Eastern Texts: Relating to the Old Testament*. Second Revised Edition. Princeton: Princeton University Press, 1955.

Rad, Gerhard von. *Genesis: A Commentary*. Revised Edition. Philadelphia: Westminster, 1972.

Rashi [Solomon b. Isaac] (1040-1105). *Perush Rashi al Massekhet Avot*. Printed in *Perushei Rishonim leMassekhet Avot*. Jerusalem: Torah Shlemah Institute, 1973.

———. *Perushei Rashi al haTorah*. Edited by Charles B. Chavel. Jerusalem: Mossad Harav Kook, 1983.

———. *The Torah: With Rashi's Commentary Translated, Annotated, and Elucidated by Yisrael Isser Zvi Herczeg*. 5 Vols. New York: Mesorah, 2000.

Robertson Smith, W (1846-1894). *The Religion of the Semites: The Fundamental Institutions*. New York: Meridian Books, 1956.

Rosenblatt, Naomi H. and Joshua Horwitz. *Wrestling with Angels: What Genesis Teaches Us About Our Spiritual Identity, Sexuality, and Personal Relationships*. New York: Dell Publishing, 1996.

Sacks, Robert D. *A Commentary on the Book of Genesis*. Lewiston, NY: Edwin Mellen Press, 1990.

Samuel ben Meir [Rashbam] (c.1080-1158). *Perush haTorah*. Edited by David Rosin. Breslau, 1882; Facsimile Edition: New York: Om Publishing, 1949.

Sarna, Nahum M. *The JPS Torah Commentary: Genesis*. Philadelphia: Jewish Publication Society, 1989.

———. *Understanding Genesis*. New York: Schocken Books, 1966.

Schatz, Elihu A. *Proof of the Accuracy of the Bible*. Middle Village, NY: Jonathan David, 1973.

Scherman, Nosson. *The Chumash* (Stone edition). New York: Mesorah, 2000.

Schorsch, Ismar. *Weekly Torah Commentary*, "Parashat Lekh Lekha," Jewish Theological Seminary, October 15, 1994.

Scullion, John J. *Genesis: A Commentary for Students, Teachers, and Preachers*. Collegeville, MN: Liturgical Press, 1992.

Seidman, Hillel. *Die Sedrah fun der Voch: Bereshit*. New York: Belle Harbor Publishing, 1964.

The Septuagint Version of the Old Testament and Apocrypha with an English Translation. Grand Rapids: Zondervan Publishing House, 1972.

Sforno, Obadiah (c. 1470-c. 1550). *Biur al haTorah*. Edited by Zev Gottlieb. Jerusalem: Mossad Harav Kook, 1980.

Shkop, Esther M. "And Sarah Laughed…" *Tradition* 31:3, 1997, pp. 42-51.

Sicker, Martin. *Reading* Genesis *Politically: An Introduction to Mosaic Political Philosophy*. Westport: Praeger, 2002.

Sifre: A Tannaitic Commentary on the Book of Deuteronomy. Translated with Notes by Reuven Hammer. New Haven: Yale University Press, 1986.

Sofer, Moses (1762-1839). *Torat Moshe.* 2 vols. New York: Grossman, 1960.

Speiser, E.A. *Genesis.* Garden City: Doubleday, 1964.

————. *Oriental and Biblical Studies: Collected Writings of E.A. Speiser.* Edited by J.J. Finkelstein and Moshe Greenberg. Philadelphia: University of Pennsylvania Press, 1967.

Spero, Shubert. "The Akedah: *Machloket L'Shem Shamayim. Jewish Bible Quarterly* 28:1, 2000, pp. 56-59.

Spiegel, Shalom. *The Last Trial: On the Legends and Lore of the Command to Abraham to Offer Isaac as a Sacrifice: The Akedah.* Translated from the Hebrew by Judah Goldin. New York: Pantheon Books, 1967.

Steinberg, Joshua. *Millon haTanakh: Ivrit veAramit.* Revised Edition. Tel Aviv: Yizrael, 1960.

Steinsaltz, Adin. *Biblical Images: Men and Women of the Book.* Translated by Yehuda Hanegbi and Yehudit Keshet. New York: Basic Books, 1984.

Stigers, Harold G. *A Commentary on Genesis.* Grand Rapids: Zondervan Publishing House, 1975.

Talmud Yerushalmi. 3 Vols. Jerusalem: Torah Mitziyon, 1968.

Tanakh: A New Translation of the Holy Scriptures According to the Traditional Hebrew Text. Philadelphia: Jewish Publication Society, 1985.

Tarlow, Peter E. and E. Cleve Want. "Bad Guys, Textual Errors, and Wordplays in Genesis 21:9-10." *Journal of Reform Judaism,* Fall 1990, pp. 21-29.

Teubal, Savina J. *Sarah the Priestess: The First Matriarch of Genesis.* Athens, OH: Swallow Press, 1984.

————. *Hagar the Egyptian: The Lost Tradition of the Matriarchs.* San Francisco: Harper and Row, 1990.

Tosefta. Edited by Moshe S. Zuckermandel. New Edition. Jerusalem: Wahrman, 1970.

The Tosefta: Translated from the Hebrew with a New Introduction. Translated by Jacob Neusner. 2 Vols. Peabody: Hendrickson Publishers, 2002.

Uzzieli, Israel Joseph (1837-1917). *Binah beMikraot ubeMeforshim: Sefer Bereshit*. Jerusalem: Hayyim Lifshutz, n.d.

Van Seters, John. *Abraham in History and Tradition*. New Haven and London: Yale University Press, 1975.

Vawter, Bruce. *On Genesis: A New Reading*. Garden City: Doubleday, 1977.

Vermes, Geza. *The Complete Dead Sea Scrolls in English*. New York: Allen Lane Penguin, 1997.

Wacholder, Ben Zion. "How Long Did Abram Stay in Egypt?" *Hebrew Union College Annual*, Vol. 35 (1964), pp. 43-56. Essay also found in Ben Zion Wacholder, *Essays on Jewish Chronology and Chronography*. New York: Ktav Publishing House, 1976, pp. 45-58.

Westermann, Claus (1909-2000). *Genesis: An Introduction*. Translated by John Scullion. Minneapolis: Fortress Press, 1992.

————. *Genesis: A Practical Commentary*. Translated by David E Green. Grand Rapids: William B. Eerdmans, 1987.

Wiesel, Elie. *Messengers of God: Biblical Portraits and Legends*. New York: Random House, 1976.

Wyschogrod, Michael. *The Body of Faith: Judaism as Corporeal Election*. New York: Seabury Press, 1983.

Xenophon. *Xenophon's Anabasis or Expedition of Cyrus and the Memorabilia of Socrates*. Translated by J.S. Watson. London: George Bell & Sons, 1891.

Zornberg, Avivah Gottlieb. *The Beginnings of Desire: Reflections on Genesis*. New York: Doubleday, 1995.

The Zohar. 5 Vols. 2nd Edition. Translated by Harry Sperling and Maurice Simon. London: Soncino Press, 1984.

About the Author

Dr. Martin Sicker is a writer and lecturer on the Middle East and Jewish history and religion. His is the author of 25 previous books including *The Rise and Fall of the Ancient Israelite States, Reading Genesis Politically, Rabbinic Political Theory, Between Man and God: Issues in Judaic Thought, The Political Culture of Judaism*, and *The Moral Maxims of the Sages of Israel*.

Endnotes

1. Although the patriarch will be referred to as Abraham in this introductory chapter, he will subsequently be referred to as Abram until his name is actually changed to Abraham, according to the biblical narrative.
2. William F. Albright, *The Biblical Period from Abraham to Ezra*, pp. 1-2.
3. W.D. Davies, *The Territorial Dimension of Judaism*, pp. 8-9.
4. See Martin Sicker, *Reading Genesis Politically*, pp. 129-37.
5. Martin Buber, *On the Bible*, pp. 25-26.
6. Samson R. Hirsch, *The Pentateuch: Genesis*, p. 236.
7. Jubilees 17:17-18. In James H. Charlesworth, ed., *The Old Testament Pseudepigrapha*, vol. 2, p. 90.
8. Ibid., 19:8.
9. R. Travers Herford, *Pirke Aboth* 5:4, p. 126. Herford notes: "The Scripture does not say that there were ten trials, and the commentators differ in the way in which they make up the number. But from the point of view of the haggadist there is no importance in the number; it is merely a convenient aid to memory, the fact to be remembered being that Abraham endured many trials and bore them all" (Ibid.).
10. *The Fathers According to Rabbi Nathan*, ch. 33.
11. M.D. Cassutto, *Perush al Sefer Bereshit*, vol. 2 supplement, pp. 202-3.
12. *Pirke de Rabbi Eliezer*, ch. 26-31.
13. *Pseudo-Philo* 6, in James H. Charlesworth, ed., *The Old Testament Pseudepigrapha*, vol. 2, pp. 310-12. According to Jonah Gerondi, this episode constitutes the first of Abraham's trials (*Derashot vePerushei Rabbenu Yonah Gerondi leHamishah Humshei Torah*, p. 41). Menahem Meiri also considers this to be the first trial and is one of the very few commentators to consider the second trial to be that of the divine revelation that Abraham's descendents would be outcasts for four centuries, which clearly

appears to be out of sequence with the order of events presented in the biblical text. However, Meiri apparently accepts the theory that Abraham received this revelation immediately after his departure with his father from Ur but before he subsequently left Haran for Canaan (*Bet haBehirah: Massekhet Aboth* 5:3, pp. 223-25, and note 27, p. 224).

14. Among the major medieval rabbinic commentators, Rashi is perhaps the only one who adopts the scheme set forth in this midrashic work in its entirety. By contrast, the first two trials identified by *Pirke de Rabbi Eliezer* are completely omitted by both Maimonides and Joseph Hayyun.

15. See *Midrash haGadol* on Gen. 12:1, pp. 215-216. Maimonides also considers the demand that Abraham become a stranger in a strange land to be his first trial (*The Commentary to Mishnah Aboth*, 5:3, p. 94). Joseph Hayyun similarly considers the essence of this first trial to be the requirement that Abraham turn his back on home and family (*Millei deAboth*, p. 229), as does Cassutto (*Perush al Sefer Bereshit*, vol. 2 supplement, p. 201). Jonah Gerondi lists this as the second trial.

16. According to Maimonides, Hayyun, and Cassutto, the famine in the land promised to Abraham and the consequent need to abandon it, even temporarily, represents the second trial. Jonah Gerondi considers this to be the third trial.

17. Maimonides considers the episode of Sarah being taken to Pharaoh to be the third trial, whereas Cassutto lists Abram's split with Lot as the third trial. Jonah Gerondi considers it to be the fourth trial. Maimonides and Hayyun consider the fifth trial to be Abraham's coming under pressure to marry Hagar at Sarah's insistence. Cassutto sees the fifth trial as the need to send the pregnant Hagar away in order to keep the peace in his household.

18. In Maimonides' enumeration, as well as that of Cassutto, this represents the fourth trial, which Hayyun describes as the need to go to war against the superior forces of the Mesopotamian kings. Jonah Gerondi considers this to be the fifth trial; the sixth trial, in his scheme, being the necessity of taking Hagar at an advanced age because of the failure to produce an heir through Sarah. Maimonides, Hayyun, and Cassutto consider the sixth trial to be Abraham's circumcision at an advanced age, which Jonah Gerondi counts as the seventh.

19. This is omitted in Maimonides' and Hayyun's list of the trials. Both Maimonides and Hayyun consider the seventh trial to be that of Sarah's abduction by Abimelech, king of Gerar (Gen. 19:2), which Jonah Gerondi and Cassutto consider to be the eighth trial. Cassutto considers the seventh trial to be Abraham's concern about the safety of Lot in connection with the destruction of Sodom. As noted earlier (note 13), Meiri considers this to be the second trial.

20. *Midrash Rabbah: Genesis* 44:19.

21. Although some editions of Rashi's commentary on *Avot* list circumcision as the eighth trial, in the critical edition of the work (*Perush Rashi al Massekhet Avot*), he omits circumcision as the eighth trial and substitutes the incident of Sarah's abduction by Abimelech.

22. Maimonides and Hayyun consider the need to send Hagar away at Sarah's insistence to be the eighth trial. According to Maimonides, Jonah Gerondi, and Cassutto, the ninth trial was the need for Abraham to send his son Ishmael away, something that troubled him deeply, as indicated in the biblical text. By contrast, Hayyun, like Jubilees, considers the ninth trial to be that of the *Akedah*.

23. This is the generally accepted view of most commentators. However, as indicated, Jubilees considers the tenth trial to be concerned with the death of Sarah, but does not explain in what way. Hayyun, who also adopts the position of Jubilees, considers the tenth trial as related to Abraham's desire to find an appropriate site in which to bury his beloved Sarah. Even though the land was promised to Abraham, he nonetheless had difficulty in obtaining a suitable burial place, and this in itself presumably constituted a test of his faith in the divine promise.

24. Cassutto suggests that the tradition of ten trials finds its roots in the device of numerical harmony employed by the biblical writer. That is, just as there were *ten* generations between Adam and Noah, and *ten* generations between Noah and Abraham, so did Abraham undergo *ten* trials or stages of development in his lifetime (*Perush al Sefer Bereshit*, vol. 2 supplement, p. 201).

25. Moses Almosnino, *Pirkei Moshe*, p. 177.

26. Buber, *On the Bible*, p. 36. See also Cassutto, *Perush al Sefer Bereshit*, vol. 2 supplement, p. 203.

27. *Babylonian Talmud* (henceforth *B.T.*): *Gittin* 43a.

28. *B.T. Kiddushin* 49a.

29. Robert Alter, *Genesis*, p. xii.

30. *B.T. Yevamot* 24a; *B.T. Shabbat* 63a.

31. In this regard, see John Van Seters, *Abraham in History and Tradition*, pp. 65-103.

32. Cyrus H. Gordon and Gary A. Rendsburg, *The Bible and the Ancient Near East*, p. 111.

33. Elihu A. Schatz, *Proof of the Accuracy of the Bible*, p. 29.

34. Jubilees 11:14-15. Alternatively, a later source gives the name of Abram's mother as Amathlai or Emtelai, the daughter of Karnabo (*B.T. Baba Batra* 91a).

35. M.D. Cassutto, *Perush al Sefer Bereshit*, vol. 2, p. 183.

36. For discussion of this period in the biblical narrative, see Sicker, *Reading Genesis Politically*, pp. 131-37.

37. This is the view argued by Nahmanides, *Perushei haTorah* on Gen. 12:1.

38. Cassutto makes a strong case for their not being the same, but fails to suggest why the name of the father of Milcah and Iscah is of any particular consequence that caused it to be recorded by the text (*Perush al Sefer Bereshit*, vol.2. p. 189).

39. There is an ancient Jewish tradition that Iscah and Sarai are one and the same. That is, Iscah was the name given to her by her father Haran, but after his death she was adopted by Terah as the latter's daughter, and it was Terah who gave her the name Sarai (Shlomo Menora, *Peshat veHigayon baMikra*, p. 110). This notion is already reflected in the first century writing of Josephus, wherein he identifies Sarai as the sister of Milcah (*Antiquities of the Jews* 1:6:5). Similarly, one of the sages of the Talmud observed: "Iscah was Sarai, and why was she called Iscah? Because she foresaw [the name Iscah being derived from an Aramaic root meaning to gaze or to look] by holy inspiration" (*B.T. Sanhedrin* 69b). This of course would make Sarai Abram's niece and not a true half-sister, and thus avoid the implication of incest in Gen. 20:12, given that the Mosaic Law later specifically proscribes such sibling marriage, even though the event would have long predated the enactment of the prohibition. In addition, there

have been numerous commentators through the centuries who have asserted that the Haran who is the brother of Abram and the father of Lot is not the same Haran who is the father of Milcah and Iscah (Sarai), and that it is for this reason that Haran is not identified as the father of Lot, Milcah, and Iscah. This would even further distance the blood relationship between Abram and Sarai, but does not adequately account for the statement in Gen. 20:12. And so, the questions remain unresolved.

An alternate and somewhat radical approach to the issue is taken by Savina J. Teubal, who argues that although incest taboos certainly existed during the period in which these stories take place, the understanding of what constituted incest depended on whether the society in question was patrilineal or matrilineal, and asserts that the context of the Abram-Abraham story is a matrilineal society. "In Sarah's society, however, patriliny was not the custom. Sarah is introduced to us as Terah's daughter-in-law, not as his daughter. In matriliny, descent is traced through the mother; and since, as Abraham explained, he and Sarah had different mothers, they would not be considered siblings, or in any way blood relatives. It is for this reason that they were permitted to be married." In other words, these biblical episodes took place during "a period in which the union of nonuterine siblings was not regarded as incestuous" (*Sarah the Priestess*, pp. 14-15.

40. Nahum M. Sarna suggests that this omission is extraordinary and must therefore be deliberate. "The Narrator withholds information so as not to ruin the suspense in chapter 20 when Abraham, in order to extricate himself from an embarrassing predicament, reveals that Sarai is his half sister" (*The JPS Torah Commentary: Genesis*, p. 87, note 29). Alternatively, E.A. Speiser suggests, "The likeliest solution under the circumstances would seem to be that Sarah was Terah's daughter by adoption, which is why the relationship was not duly recorded in Genesis 11" (*Oriental and Biblical Studies*, p. 78).

41. Speiser, *Oriental and Biblical Studies*, pp. 77-78.

42. Yitzhak M. Emmanueli, *Sefer Bereshit*, p. 239.

43. See note #39.

44. According to some scholars the Hebrew term *akarah*, translated as "barren" is understood as meaning "childless" but not necessarily infertile (Sarna, *The JPS Torah Commentary: Genesis*, p. 87, note on 11:30). This

understanding of the term is helpful in accounting for Sarah's later pregnancy in non-miraculous terms. However, it is unlikely that this is the actual meaning or intent of the term as used by the biblical author. The root of the word, *akar*, means to root out, to destroy, making a man who is an *akar* or a woman who is an *akarah* a person who is infertile. See Benjamin Davidson, *The Analytical Hebrew and Chaldee Lexicon*, p. 612.

45. According to Robert Davidson, "the name Canaan, which first appears in texts of the fifteenth century B.C., probably signified originally the Phoenician coast" (*Genesis 12-50*, p. 22, note 5). Because of the uncertainty as to what actually constituted Canaan as far as the biblical author is concerned, throughout this study I will use the geographic descriptor Cisjordan in place of "land of Canaan," which should be understood as the territory west of the line of the Jordan River reaching from Lebanon to the Gulf of Aqaba.

46. For discussion of this see Sicker, *Reading Genesis Politically*, pp. 133-36.

47. Haran, about 550 miles from Ur, lay at the strategically important intersection of the main east-west route from Nineveh to Carchemish with that of the north-south route to Damascus.

48. Buber, *Israel and Palestine*, p. 21.

49. Xenophon identifies the Chaldeans, "a free people, and warlike," as part of the forces blocking the Greek expeditionary force from entering Armenia (*Anabasis* 4:3-4).

50. Harold G. Stigers, *A Commentary on Genesis*, pp. 133-34.

51. *Pirkei de Rabbi Eliezer*, ch. 26, p. 189.

52. It is noteworthy that Augustine, to reconcile an obvious contradiction between the New Testament Book of Acts and the chronicles of Eusebius, suggests that the length of Abraham's stay in Haran was less than one year (*The City of God*, 16:16, p. 541).

53. The apocryphal book of Judith records, in this regard: "These people are descended from the Chaldeans. At one time they settled in Mesopotamia because they did not want to worship the gods of their ancestors who were in Chaldea. They had abandoned the ways of their ancestors and worshipped the God of Heaven, the god they had come to know. When the Chaldeans drove them out from the presence of their gods, they fled to

Mesopotamia and settled there for a long while" (Carey A Moore, *Judith* 5:6-8).

54. According to the understanding proposed by Eliezer Berkovits, wherever the divine name *YHVH*, the Tetragrammaton, appears in Scripture it refers to God in His aspect of sovereign over nature and history (*Man and God*, p. 22).

55. Pinchas H. Peli wrote: "For the people of Israel, the immanence of God in this world is inextricably linked with the Land. The call addressed to Abraham to go to the Land is so meaningful that anything which happened in his life up to this point (and on which Jewish Midrashim and the Islamic Koran elaborate) is totally ignored" (*Torah Today*, p. 12).

56. M.D. Cassutto, *Perush al Sefer Bereshit*, vol. 2, p. 102 and vol. 2 supplement, p. 206.

57. Adin Steinsaltz wrote in this regard: "Idolatry…is, therefore, not the first or the most primitive stage of religion. It is a later development…a transition from the primal belief in an unknown God to a worship of tangible and comprehensible gods…Polytheism is thus a complicated and sophisticated system of worship springing from the need to establish a 'rational' and direct contact with the Divine" (*Biblical Images*, p. 16).

58. Josephus, *Antiquities of the Jews*, 1: 7: 1.

59. This notion may also be seen reflected in Peter Pitzele's observation that "most of Abraham's ordeals are ordeals of the imagination that take place between the lines and behind the words of the story" (*Our Fathers' Wells*, pp. 83-84).

60. Hillel Seidman, *Die Sedrah fun der Voch*, p. 38. Seidman suggests that this test was of such significance that everything that preceded it was considered as comparatively irrelevant, and was therefore omitted from the biblical narrative.

61. The order of the command, *Get thee out of thy country, and from thy kindred, and from thy father's house*, appears to reflect an illogical sequence of events, since the order of actually departing would be the reverse. Accordingly, Jacob Zvi Mecklenburg suggested that what is being described is a spiritual rather than merely a physical withdrawal that begins with the peripheral and concludes with severing ties with the core" (*HaKtav vehaK-*

abbalah on Gen. 12:1). For a similar interpretation, see Richard Elliott Friedman, *Commentary on the Torah*, p. 49.

62. Much ink has been expended on trying to reconcile the fact that Abram is told to leave his homeland, which was originally Ur, after he had already left it and is residing in Haran. Both traditional and modern critical commentators have attempted to deal with this, all rather unsuccessfully. There is one ancient tradition (recorded by Stephen in the Book of Acts 7:2) that asserts that the divine message to Abraham was given prior to his having arrived at Haran but after having already left Chaldea. Some other later commentators have asserted that the message was received in Ur, and was therefore that which precipitated the relocation to Canaan, which was disrupted by Terah's decision to remain in Haran instead. Critical scholars have sought to resolve the problem by asserting, not on the basis of any textual evidence but simply because it appears to resolve the issue, that two distinct literary sources are involved here; one asserting that Abram came from Ur, and the other that he came from Haran in the first place. However, all this is based on the questionable assumption that the Hebrew term *moledet*, which literally means "birthplace," is always used in that literal sense, an assertion that is categorically rejected by Cassutto (*Perush al Sefer Bereshit*, vol. 2 supplement, p. 213). According to A.S. Hartom, in biblical usage *moledet* refers to the place where the family resides (*Bereshit*, on Gen. 11:28, p. 49). Moreover, those who make the literal assumption do not seem to consider that one may adopt a new homeland as though it were their birthplace. It is worth noting in this regard, that Jewish immigrants to modern Israel have no difficulty whatever in referring to their adopted homeland as their *moledet*, and there are ancient references in which the term is used in this sense as well (Emmanueli, *Sefer Bereshit*, p. 184).

63. Naomi H. Rosenblatt and Joshua Horwitz write: "In order to realize spiritual goals, we need to live in the world with our feet planted firmly on the ground. The promised land is not a blank canvas empty of human life, because a new community or a new nation isn't built in a vacuum. We have to work within the existing political realities. Though Abraham is a spiritual pioneer, he understands that he must navigate in the real world" (*Wrestling with Angels*, p. 103).

64. Menora, *Peshat veHigayon baMikra*, p. 112.

65. Samson Raphael Hirsch, *The Pentateuch* on Gen. 12:5.

66. There is a midrashic interpretation that deals with the problem by employing a play on words, asserting that the term *areka*, "will show you," may be read as *arayikh*, meaning "I will show myself to you." Read this way, the verse would be instructing Abram to proceed to the land in which God would eventually reveal Himself to him (*Midrash haGadol: Bereshit*, vol. 1, p. 217).

67. This notion is elaborated upon, including a recapitulation of several traditional commentators who interpret the relevant passage in this way, in Avivah Gottlieb Zornberg, *The Beginnings of Desire*, pp. 74-76.

68. It is especially noteworthy that the command to Abram, "*Lekh-Lekha*" translated variously as "*Get thee out*," or "*Go for yourself*," or any of a number of other possible variations, is repeated when Abraham is told to set out on another trek to an unspecified location in connection with his last trial, which is to involve the sacrifice of his heir Isaac (Gen. 22:1).

69. Speiser notes the significance of the biblical use of the term *goy* rather than *am* or "people." "Unlike *am*, *goy* requires a territorial base, since the concept is a political one" (*Genesis*, p. 86, note 2).

70. The notion of a polyethnic nation is conceivable in contemporary times only by incorrectly using the term "nation" as a synonym for "state," a usage which is both widespread and highly misleading, especially when it also equates nationalism with patriotism.

71. This interpretation draws on the thought of Hirsch, who considers the divine promise as meaning: "I would make you into a nation to which other nations have only to look to become conscious of what their task is, and this task, which you are to accomplish, in contrast to the efforts of all the nations, is 'to become a blessing!' All others strive, not to be a blessing, but to be blessed...self-aggrandizement and ruthless extension of their own well-being the deciding goal for all their efforts." By contrast, the people of Abraham are "to dedicate themselves with all devotion to the divine purpose of bringing happiness to the world and mankind, thereby as models, to re-establish Man to its original pure calling" (*The Pentateuch* on Gen. 12:2).

72. J. Gerald Janzen observes: "Abram will become a great nation with a great name. The 'name' echoes the concern for a name in Gen. 11:4, just as 'great' (Heb. *Gdl*) echoes the tower (*mgdl*, literally 'great structure') in 11:4...There is a vivid contrast between God's opposition to human

attempts to make a name for themselves and God's intention to give Abram a great name." Moreover, "The separation from familiar place and faces, which the people in 11:4 see as filled with danger, is a separation that to Abram is filled with promise" (*Abraham and All the Families of the Earth*, pp. 15-16).

73. David Kimhi, *Perush Radak al haTorah* on Gen. 12:2, p. 35b.

74. Cassutto, *Perush al Sefer Bereshit*, vol. 2 supplement, p. 215.

75. Hirsch wrote, "In these two words [become a blessing] the whole moral task is summarized the accomplishment of which is the condition for the fulfillment of God's wish...and this task, which you are to accomplish, in contrast to the efforts of all other nations, is 'to become a blessing'" (*The Pentateuch*, on Gen. 12:2, p. 227).

76. Hermann Gunkel, *Genesis*, p. 164. John Calvin wrote in this regard: "Here the extraordinary kindness of God manifests itself, in that he familiarly makes a covenant with Abram, as men are wont to do with their companions and equals. For this is the accustomed form of covenants between kings and others, that they mutually promise to have the same enemies and the same friends" (*Genesis*, vol. 1, p. 347).

77. Calvin, ibid., p. 348.

78. Nissim Gerondi, *Perush al haTorah*, p. 155.

79. Cassutto suggests that this may be an allusion to the universality of the basic concepts of Israelite belief that is given greater expression in the later teachings of the prophets (*Perush al Sefer Bereshit*, vol. 2 supplement, p. 215).

80. Benno Jacob, *The First Book of the Bible*, p. 87.

81. Rashi understands the phrase, *in thee shall all the families of the earth be blessed*, to mean that the name of Abram will be used as an exemplar that men will aspire to emulate, and gives the example of a father urging his son to be like Abram (*Perushei Rashi al haTorah* on Gen. 12:3). Janzen writes in this regard: "All human families, however much their speech may differ, will have in common this one word 'Abram' when they use it to ask God's blessing upon themselves. Thus they will begin to receive through this common word what through common speech they earlier sought to sustain but in fact lost. They will find a unity, a solidarity, that cannot be shattered by being scattered across the face of the earth. The

benefit that is to come through Abram, then, has to do with two basic aspects of human life—biological descent and social interrelatedness (or nature and politics)" (*Abraham and All the Families of the Earth*, p. 18).

82. As Jonah Gerondi points out, Abram's decision-making process was out of line with that which was pervasive in his society and culture (*Derashot vePerushei Rabbenu Yonah Gerondi leHamishah Humshei Torah*, pp. 31-32).

83. Kimhi, *Perush Radak al haTorah* on Gen. 12:5, p. 36a.

84. Cassutto cautions that, although Abraham's age serves as useful data for harmonizing the timeline of his saga, the number of his years should not necessarily be taken at face value. He points out that not only in antiquity, but even to this day, especially among older people in the Middle East, ages are sometimes given in estimated numbers that do not necessarily correspond to reality, simply because of inadequate or non-existent birth records. Moreover, the ages cited in the ancient records, as is the case here, tend to be given in multiples of five, and in some instances in multiples of seven (*Perush al Sefer Bereshit*, vol. 2 supplement, p. 217).

85. August Dillmann points out that in the phrase *makom Shechem*, translated as *place of Shechem*, the term *makom* does not merely refer to a district, "but a place where worship is offered, the seat of a cultus" (*Genesis*, vol. 2, p. 13).

86. The Hebrew term *elon*, translated here as "terebinth," has also been translated by some as "oak," a tree that closely resembles the terebinth, both being quite common in Cisjordan. However, as pointed out by Samuel R. Driver, most scholars accept that *elon* refers to a terebinth, where as *allon* refers to an oak. The distinctive difference between them is that the oak tends to grow in clumps or forests, whereas the terebinth is usually found alone, thus making it more likely to take on a religious significance (*The Book of Genesis*, p. 147).

87. Josephus writes, "Abram, having no son of his own, adopted Lot, his brother Haran's son, and his wife Sarai's brother" (*Antiquities of the Jews*, 1:7:1, p. 32). This is clearly based on the traditional assumption that Sarai is the same person as Iscah, the daughter of Haran, and that the same Haran is also the father of Lot.

88. Levi ben Gershom [Gersonides], *Perushei haTorah*, vol. 1, "*Toelet #3*," p. 102.

89. Nissim Gerondi, *Perush al haTorah*, pp. 155-56. This represents Nissim's view of the simple meaning of the biblical text, and is echoed in the commentary of Judah Halaveh, *Imre Shefer* p. 109. Nissim does, however, also offer a radically different and contradictory interpretation based on one resolution of a chronological problem that was of concern to the sages of the Talmud.

90. The translation of the Hebrew word *asu* as "gotten" has led some to believe that the reference is to the servants and slaves Abram may have purchased in Haran. However, the term may perhaps more correctly be translated as "made," that is, "converted," and taken, as I take it, to refer to those persons Abram and Sarai (Kimhi suggests that it refers to Lot and not Sarai) successfully convinced to reject polytheism and who were willing to follow them wherever they led. In this latter regard, a talmudic sage asserted, "He who teaches Torah to his neighbor's son is regarded by Scripture as though he had fashioned him, as it is written, *and the souls which they had made in Haran*" (*B.T. Sanhedrin* 99b). This was clearly how the early Aramaic paraphrasers of the text understood the clause, Onkelos rendering it as *veyat nafshshata deshaabidu le'oraita* "the souls whom they had made subject to the law," and Jonathan ben Uziel as *veyat nafshata di gayeru* "the souls they had proselyted" (J.W. Etheridge, *The Targums*, vol. 1, pp. 58, 193). The Aramaic texts can be found in most standard Hebrew editions of the Rabbinic Pentateuch such as *Hamishah Humshei Torah (Mikraot Gedolot)*, listed in the references.

91. Werner Keller, *The Bible as History*, p. 70.

92. David Zvi Hoffmann notes in this regard, that the biblical passage indicates "that the Canaanites emigrated to the land in a rather late period. It appears that the land was originally settled by Semitic tribes that were subsequently compelled to withdraw slowly because of the Canaanites" (*Sefer Bereshit* on Gen. 12:6, p. 209), who were considered Hamites. It is assumed by some that the Canaanites had only recently moved north from their original area of settlement near the Red Sea.

93. After Shechem's destruction in the first century during the wars of the Roman emperor Vespasian, the city was rebuilt under the name of Flavia

Neapolis, the latter term Arabized to yield Nablus, which remains the Arabic name of the city.

94. W. Robertson Smith notes, "The famous holy tree near Shechem, called the tree of soothsayers in Judg. ix.37, and the 'tree of the revealer' in Gen. xii. 6, must have been the seat of a Canaanite tree oracle' (*The Religion of the Semites*, p. 196). He also observes, "Oracles and omens from trees and at tree sanctuaries are of the commonest among all races, and are derived in various ways, either from observation of phenomena connected with the trees themselves, and interpreted as manifestations of divine life, or from ordinary processes of divination performed in the presence of the sacred object" (Ibid., p. 195).

95. Cassutto notes that it is only after Abram is in the land promised to be his patrimony that God appears to him; previously, and outside the land, he only hears the divine voice (*Perush al Sefer Bereshit*, vol. 2 supplement, p. 234). The implication of this is that the biblical author, in effect albeit not explicitly, is thereby setting forth the basis for the belief in the special sanctity of what will later be called the Holy Land. Buber makes this same point, arguing that the promise "is first given not in Haran but in Canaan itself—only when God can say to His chosen one: 'Unto thy seed will I give *this* land'" (*Israel and Palestine*, p. 21).

96. Cassutto suggests that the term *mizbeah* or altar, as employed here, is not meant in its literal sense as a place where sacrifices are carried out, there being no mention whatever of such activity at this time. Instead, the term is being used figuratively to designate a marker or memorial to commemorate the divine appearance to Abram at that location and as a religious-national marker to indicate the dedication of the land, later to be conquered by his descendants, to the service of God (ibid).

97. Jonah Gerondi make the significant observation that this is but the first of four altars that Abraham builds in four places that will play key roles in Israel's subsequent history: Shechem, between Bethel and Ai, Hebron, and Moriah, which is later identified with Jerusalem. The implication of this is that the biblical writer is drawing direct connections between the acts of the first patriarch and those of his descendants in the land (*Derashot vePerushei Rabbenu Yonah Gerondi leHamishah Humshei Torah*, p. 32). Janzen makes the same point when he notes that the altar that Abram builds serves as a symbol of his eventual possession of the land (*Abraham and All the Families of the Earth*, p. 22).

98. Meir L. Malbim contends that Abram never gave serious thought to holding God to account for His promise, "because he viewed himself as too insignificant to warrant divine intervention into the course of nature on his account. Therefore, he placed no reliance on miracles to assure his survival of the famine. Instead, he sought a natural solution" (*HaTorah vehaMitzvah* on Gen. 12:10).

99. This approach is clearly reflected in the later biblical admonition to phenomenal imitation, *Go to the ant, thou sluggard; consider her ways, and be wise; which having no chief, overseer, or ruler, provideth her bread in the summer, and gathereth her food in the harvest* (Prov. 6:8).

100. David ben Abraham Maimuni, *Midrash Rabbi David haNagid: Sefer Bereshit*, p. 58; Ben Zion Firer, *MeAdam ve'ad Avraham*, p. 84.

101. There has been a tendency among commentators both classical and modern to envision Sarai as a raving beauty, which makes it difficult to reconcile with her supposed age of 65 at the time. This has led numerous commentators, such as August Dillmann, to depict the passages relating to her beauty and to her age to different literary traditions (*Genesis*, vol. 2, p. 18), thereby explaining the discrepancy but not why they were not reconciled in the final text. It might be more useful to think of Sarai as a very attractive woman, notwithstanding her age, perhaps not as strikingly gorgeous as a thirty or forty-year old beauty but still beautiful, something that is not all unlikely, and therefore possibly still quite desirable, especially to older men, who may admire the freshness and vitality of youth but may nonetheless feel more comfortable with someone closer to their age for a variety of reasons, as the study of gerontology indicates. Another consideration is the biblical writer's perspective; given that Sarah is reported later to have lived to the age of 127, at 65 she would be middle-aged and therefore not necessarily too old to be considered still very attractive. Moreover, it is important to bear in mind that it is not the narrator who is telling us of her beauty, but Abram who speaks to his wife about it; and to him, beauty being in the eye of the beholder, she may still have been as beautiful as ever, despite the passing years.

102. "A papyrus tells of a Pharaoh who…sent armed men to fetch a beautiful woman and make away with her husband. Another Pharaoh is promised by his priest on his tombstone that even after death he will kill Palestinian sheiks and include their wives in his harem" (Joseph H. Hertz, *The Pentateuch and Haftorahs*, p. 47, note 12).

103. The following discussion of the ruse developed by Abram, with Sarai's cooperation, is based in large measure on the commentary of Isaac Abravanel (*Perush haTorah*, "*Bereshit*," p. 37b), whose analysis of the relevant texts seems to best comport with the general context of the story and what occurs afterward.

104. The Hebrew particle *na*, translated here as *I pray thee*, indicates by its use that what follows is a logical consequence of the prevailing circumstances, and is not an arbitrary request or demand. By its use, Abram is signaling to Sarai that what he is asking of her is necessary, and her silent acquiescence reflects that she understands why that is so.

105. Driver notes, "The 'soul' in Heb. Psychology, is the seat of feeling and emotion, hence in poetry, or choice prose, 'my (thy, his, &c.) soul' becomes a pathetic periphrasis for the personal pron.,—often, indeed, in poetry interchanging with it in the parallel clause" (*The Book of Genesis*, p. 149).

106. An explanation of this aspect of the story is provided in the *New Jerusalem Bible*, p. 31, note 12e: "A custom prevalent in Upper Mesopotamia has been adduced in explanation of this. Among the Hurrian aristocracy of Haran (Abraham's 'native land') a husband might legally adopt his wife as his sister, and the latter enjoyed greater protection and higher social status. Such seems to have been the case with Sarai, and Abram appears to have boasted about this to the Egyptians, who misunderstood what he meant. The biblical author, relating the traditional story, evidently did not understand its true significance either." For further consideration of this issue see E.A. Speiser, *Genesis*, pp. 92-93. As pointed out in an earlier study by Speiser, "Hurrian family practices contain certain features which have no counterparts in any other contemporary Near Eastern society. This is especially true of the pervasive role of the brother, as a result of an underlying fratriarchal system which the encroachments of patriarchy managed to restrict but could not entirely eliminate" (*Oriental and Biblical Studies*, p. 68).

107. As Claus Westermann put it, "An insignificant man at the mercy of the powerful has only his wits for a weapon" (*Genesis: A Practical Commentary*, p. 103).

108. Hermann Gunkel wrote in this regard: "Ancient Israel regarded the lie much more mildly than we. If no particularly foul intention is associated

with it, it was not considered dishonorable…How should a poor *ger* [alien] in a strange land get by without lies?" (*Genesis*, p. 169.)

109. The half-sibling relationship between Abram and Sarai is affirmed in Gen. 20:12, and, as suggested earlier, their marriage evidently did not constitute incest in Mesopotamian society, in which kinship was "metronymic, in contrast to patronymic which considers children born of the same father as members of the family. Traces of a metronymic society appear in various parts of the Bible" (W. Gunther Plaut, *The Torah*, p. 99, note 1).

110. *Genesis Apocryphon* XIX, in Geza Vermes, *The Complete Dead Sea Scrolls in English*, p. 454.

111. David A. Murray, *The Real Meaning of Genesis*, p. 158.

112. Judah Halaveh, *Imre Shefer*, p. 117.

113. Firer, *MeAdam ve'ad Avraham*, p. 89.

114. *Genesis Apocryphon* XX, in Geza Vermes, *The Complete Dead Sea Scrolls in English*, p. 455. Ben Zion Wacholder points out that the Hellenistic Jewish writers, some of whom lived in Alexandria, were fascinated by the story of Abram's encounter with the Egyptian pharaoh, with the *Genesis Apocryphon* weaving a romance around the episode ("How Long Did Abram Stay in Egypt?" p. 46).

115. This perspective is based on that presented by Aaron Marcus (*Keset haSofer* on Gen. 12:16). According to this interpretation of events, what Abram gained financially from the affair was the opportunity to replace the losses he had incurred because of his delayed departure from Cisjordan. As such, the gifts he received from the pharaoh did not significantly augment his already considerable wealth.

116. Ephraim of Luntshits argues persuasively that if the pharaoh was unaware that Sarai was already married, what transgression had he committed that he should be punished in advance of his having forced her into a compromising relationship, given that he thought she was Abram's sister? "Therefore, it seems to me that even though she publicly declared herself to be his sister, she in any case told Pharaoh the truth, that she was Abram's wife, thinking that a king sitting on the throne that dispensed justice would not commit such an immoral act. But Pharaoh paid no heed to her, saying that he took her at her first declaration" (*Kli Yakkar* on Gen. 12:17).

117. Abraham Menahem Porto (Rafa-Rappaport), *Minhah Belulah*, p. 18a.

118. Naomi H. Rosenblatt and Joshua Horwitz, *Wrestling with Angels*, p. 110.

119. Arnold Ehrlich, *Mikra KiFeshuto*, vol. 1, p. 34, commentary on Gen. 12:20.

120. An analysis of these various sources and chronologies can be found in Ben Zion Wacholder, "How Long Did Abram Stay in Egypt?", pp. 43-56.

121. Menora suggests that the notice about Lot is introduced here to emphasize that Pharaoh's expulsion order was directed specifically at Abram and Sarai, and did not apply to Lot, who therefore evidently followed Abram voluntarily. He suggests further that this notice was included because at the time that the story was promulgated among the Israelites, which was after the later exodus from Egypt, when they were about to confront the descendants of Lot, the Moabites and Ammonites, as they passed through their territory in Transjordan during their circular route to Canaan. Presumably, it was desired that the Israelites look upon them favorably, because their ancestor Lot was a loyal follower of Abram and that the Israelites should therefore be careful not to offend them during the passage through their territories (*Peshat veHigayon baMikra*, p. 118). Although this explanation is plausible, it does not fit very well with what actually occurs later in the narrative, as will be seen in the chapter that follows.

122. Nissim Gerondi, *Perush al haTorah*, p. 172.

123. Menora, *Peshat veHigayon baMikra*, p. 119.

124. Ibid.

125. Abraham Menahem Porto (Rafa-Rappaport), *Minhah Belulah*, p. 18a.

126. Raymond Harari, "Abraham's Nephew Lot: A Biblical Portrait," p. 33.

127. Avi Ehrlich, *Ancient Zionism*, p. 27.

128. Obadiah Sforno points out that Lot's choice was neither of the options recommended by Abram (*Biur al haTorah* on Gen. 13:11, p. 39).

129. As argued by Nehama Leibowitz: "The order of the words in a biblical sentence is not accidental." Shades of meaning, reflecting approval or disapproval, closeness or distance, and other opposite relationships, "are not expressed by verbosity, or by lengthy psychological explanations, or extensive analyses of moods and inner thoughts, but through subtle hints in

minute changes of style, one of them being the order of words in a sentence" (*Iyyunim beSefer Bereshit*, p. 89).

130. Following his exploration of the history and archeology of the Jordan Valley, Nelson Glueck concluded: "Our recent explorations in the Jordan Valley have shown beyond doubt that it was once densely inhabited...[Lot] was certainly right when it came to describing the Jordan Valley. It is true that his description was meant only for its lower part, including the entire Jericho area and the Plains of Moab, but it applies equally well to almost all the rest of the Jordan Valley" (*The River Jordan*, p. 73).

131. D. Bat-Halevi writes: "Lot is a captive to what his eyes see." The description in the text of the lushness of the plain "is to emphasize Lot's impressionability. In this manner he is sharply contrasted with Abram" (*Derekh haAvot el haMonoteizm*, p. 61).

132. Ehrlich, *Ancient Zionism*, p. 28.

133. Although it has long been commonly assumed that Sodom and Gomorrah were located near the southern end of the Dead Sea, there is no conclusive evidence to date that this was the case. The biblical text itself would appear to be equally if not more compatible with locating the sites at the northern end of the Dead Sea, where the Jordan flows into it.

134. The Aramaic targum (paraphrase) of Onkelos renders the verse as, "And the men of Sodom were wicked in their riches, and guilty in their bodies before the Lord greatly." Jonathan ben Uziel elaborates further, "And the men of Sodom were depraved in their wealth with one another, and they sinned in their bodies; they sinned with open nakedness, and the shedding of innocent blood" (J.W. Etheridge, *The Targums*, vol. 1, pp. 60, 196). Both Aramaic paraphrases suggest that the city was wealthy and that it misused its wealth, presumably against those less fortunate, internally as well as abroad, while the latter also pictures Sodomite society as morally depraved as well as tyrannical.

135. Firer, *Hegyonah shel Torah*, vol. 1, pp. 58-61.

136. Calvin considers the divine command to Abram to travel the land until he knows it well as a trial of faith, "that he may more clearly perceive himself to be a stranger; and that, being exhausted by continual and fruitless disquietude, he may despair of any stable and permanent possession. For

how shall he persuade himself that he is lord of that land in which he is scarcely permitted to drink water, although he has with great labour dug the wells?" (*Genesis*, vol. 1, p. 376.)

137. It is noted by Menora that the wording of the relevant text, *And Abram moved his tent, and came and dwelt by the terebinths of Mamre, which are in Hebron*, seems to be out of sequence. He therefore suggests that it is intimating that Abram went there first along with some aides and *moved his tent* there, established his camp, and then *came and dwelt by the terebinths of Mamre* along with his entire retinue and possessions (*Peshat veHigayon baMikra*, p. 122).

138. Jacob notes that the names of the kings of Sodom and Gomorrah, Bera and Birsha, appear to be derived from the Hebrew words for evil [*ra*] and wicked [*rasha*] (*The First Book of the Bible*, p. 94). This may be taken as an early allusion to the corruption that will cause their destruction later.

139. According to Werner Keller, the road got its name from the inhabitants of that stretch of territory who preserved the memory of the expedition of the four kings (*The Bible as History*, p. 86). In much later Roman times, the road was known as Trajan's Road (*Via Traianus*), linking the Gulf of Aqaba to Damascus and beyond.

140. Various scholars have attempted to correlate the names given in the biblical text to known historical figures of the general period in which these stories are assumed to have taken place, and in doing so have generated significant chronological problems that are of only marginal importance to the central thrust of the Abraham saga, and will not be pursued here. Thus, some identify *Amraphel* with Hammurabi, the great Amorite king of Babylonia; *Arioch king of Elisar* with Eriaku, king of Larsa, and *Tidal king of Goiim* with Tudghula, a king of the northern Mesopotamian "hordes," presumed to be Kurds. Some understand *Goiim* as the Hebrew form of Gutium or Kurdestan. No one appears to have as yet come up with a similar identification for *Chederlaomer*. Whether or not these identifications are valid is really of relatively little consequence for the biblical narrative under consideration here, which cannot be treated as a historical document in the modern sense. For a full discussion of the problem of identifying the Mesopotamian kings, see Driver, *The Book of Genesis*, pp. 156-58.

141. The approach taken here to understanding what the biblical writer is actually telling us about the conflict was suggested in large part by Nissim Gerondi, whose primary concern was to explain the significance of the repeated identification of the *vale of Siddim* in the narrative (*Perush al haTorah*, pp. 176-79).

142. Ibid., p. 176-77.

143. The possible relationship and significant differences between Hebrew and Hapiru are discussed in depth by Moshe Greenberg, "Hab/Piru and Hebrews," pp. 188-200.

144. Levi ben Gershom [Gersonides], *Perushei haTorah*, commentary on Gen. 12:5, vol. 1, p. 101; Samuel L. Gordon, *Hamishah Humshei Torah*, vol. 1, p. 47.

145. The specificity of the number of men is surprising, suggesting that the text is preserving the memory of an actual count, perhaps reflecting the idea that Abram mobilized every man he could spare for the expedition.

146. In their military analysis of the campaign, Chaim Herzog and Mordechai Gichon wrote: "While the northern allies…swept down the King's Highway east of the Jordan to establish control over the route leading to Eilat and the Red Sea, Abraham was free to move on a parallel line west of the Jordan. Using the watershed road on the central mountain massif, he moved in a direction opposite to that of the northern kings and arrived in good time to lay an ambush not far from Damascus on the road to Hobah, the area of the eastern foothills of the Hermon…The site of the nocturnal ambush was of course somewhere near the convergence of the two highways which was near Damascus proper. It is tempting to suggest the Barada gorge northwest of Damascus, an ancient highway and scene of many an ambush, as the setting for Abraham's battle" (*Battles of the Bible*, p. 18). However, it is unclear why these writers conclude that the Mesopotamians were moving south at the same time that Abram was moving north, something for which I see no indication whatever in the biblical narrative.

147. Driver considers the possibility that the name *El Elyon* may be actually that of an ancient Canaanite deity, "whom his worshippers recognized as the *highest*, in opposition to other, inferior deities, and who could consequently be more readily identified with Jehovah." But, he speculates, "it may also have been merely chosen by the narrator as a name which on the

one hand would not be unsuitable for a Canaanite to use, and on the other hand was capable of being referred to Jehovah, and so fell in with his evident desire to represent Melchizedek as a worshipper of the true God" (*The Book of Genesis*, p. 165).

148. The interpretation adopted here differs somewhat from traditional approaches to these texts, which tend to fail to draw any reasonably acceptable connections between the behavior and the statements of the three actors in the scene. The most suggestive of the many commentaries consulted is that of Isaac Arama wherein he attributes particular significance to the consideration that Melchizedek is both priest and king. As such he is in a position to declare that Abram "is entitled to all the property and captives, both under the law of heaven as well as that of the kingdom, and that for this reason Abram gave him the tithe of all just as one tithes that which one obtains new in the first instance" (*Akedat Yitzhak* 16:15 on Gen. 14:20).

149. The suggestion that Abram adopted this terminology and the theology it reflected from Melchizedek is already found in the comment of the early medieval (geonic) scholar, Ahai of Shabha: "From where did Israel derive this term for God? From the blessing with which Melchizedek blessed them there" (*Sheiltot deRav Ahai Gaon*, #145, Vol. 3, pp. 203-4).

150. This point is emphasized by the sages of the talmudic era: "Until Abraham came into this world, the Holy One, blessed be He, reigned, if one dare say such a thing, only over the heavens…but when Abraham came into the world, he made Him king over both the heaven and the earth" (*Sifre*, Piska 313, p.319). It is noteworthy, however, that the Septuagint omits the inclusion of the Tetragrammaton in this verse.

151. The sage, R. Levi said, "Abraham was filled with misgiving, thinking to himself, Maybe there was a righteous or God-fearing man among the troops which I slew" (*Midrash Rabbah: Genesis* 44:4, p. 362-63).

152. Ibid., p. 363.

153. Sforno, *Biur al haTorah* on Gen. 15:1, p. 41.

154. Jacob suggests that Abram may have given the name Eliezer, which is Hebrew for "God helps". to his Damascene servant (*The First Book of the Bible*, p. 99).

155. Samuel D. Luzzatto points out that the verb *holekh*, translated as *go hence*, is employed several times in Scripture as a euphemism for "dying" (*Perush Shadal al Hamisha Humshei Torah*, on Gen. 15:2, p. 68).

156. E.A. Speiser, *Genesis*, p. 112.

157. Albright suggests that by adopting Eliezer, "Abraham contracted to assign his property to the former in case of his own decease. This custom doubtless originated at a time when real property was treated as inalienable, i.e., it was not allowed to be sold to an outsider. In this way he could obtain credit in order to buy donkeys, equipment, and supplies for caravaneering or related activities" (*Yahweh and the Gods of Canaan*, p. 66).

158. Sforno, *Biur al haTorah* on Gen. 15:3, p. 42.

159. Luzzatto points out that the use of the Hebrew form *ve-he-emin*, for "and he believed," indicates that that he had already maintained this belief earlier and not that it was a belief that was now occasioned (*Perush Shadal al Hamisha Humshei Torah*, on Gen. 15:6, p. 68).

160. See for example, Sforno, *Biur al haTorah* on Gen. 15:6, p. 42.

161. Eliezer Berkovits, who also takes the pronoun as referring to God, argues that the term *tzedakah*, translated as "righteousness," may be understood in some cases as "an act of kindness, of help, based on respect and acknowledgement of another person," which in this case is God. "To believe in God's word against all reason and all nature is like an act of helping kindness toward God. It is like it; it is not it, for God is never in any need. It is for this reason that the Bible says of Abraham's faith that God 'counted it to him for *s'daqah*.' While no man can act with *s'daqah* toward God, Abraham's act of faith was counted to him as if he had performed an act of *s'daqah* toward God" (*Man and God*, pp. 296-97).

162. Luzzatto suggests that, because of the repeated promises that had not yet begun to become transformed into reality, Abram may have thought that it was some test that he had to go through first, and that he may have been asking what he needed to do to satisfy the prerequisites for the promises to be fulfilled (*Perush Shadal al Hamisha Humshei Torah*, on Gen. 15:8, p. 69).

163. Yehudah Nahshoni, *Hagut beParshiot haTorah*, vol. 1, p. 45.

164. Hertz observes: "The ancient method of making a covenant was to cut an animal in half, and the contracting parties to pass through the portions of

the slain animal. Thereby the parties were thought to be united by the bond of a common blood" (*The Pentateuch and Haftorahs*, note on Gen. 15:10). This notion of a formalized ritual of this kind for enacting a covenant derives primarily from the words of the prophet Jeremiah, *And I will give the men that have transgressed My covenant, that they have not performed the words of the covenant which they made before Me, when they cut the calf in twain and passed between the parts* (Jer. 34:18). H. Freedman, commenting on the prophet's statement, notes, "This was the ancient manner of making a covenant. Its significance was probably that of an implied oath: may the person who breaks the covenant be cut in two even as the calf is divided (*Jeremiah*, p. 234).

The medieval philosopher Joseph Albo wrote in this regard: "The reason for this practice in making a covenant is because a covenant is a permanent bond between the two parties for the purpose of cementing and binding their friendship that they should be like one body and each should take care of the other as of himself. For this reason they cut an animal in two and pass between the parts, as a sign that just as those two parts formed one body in the animal when it was alive and each felt the pain of the other...so the two parties making the covenant are to be as one body while living and nothing but death shall part them" (*Sefer Ha-Ikkarim*, 4:45, p. 442).

165. The meaning of the Hebrew term *meshuleshet*, translated in the text as "three-year old," is obscure and the subject of wide controversy. The medieval grammarian and biblical commentator Kimhi offers two alternate meanings to the term: three-year old or third-born (*Sefer haSharashim*, p. 391). However, in his commentary on Genesis he asserts that it is impossible to translate the term as used in the text as "three-year old," preferring the interpretation offered by the Aramaic Targum which renders it as "three" or a triple number (*Perush Radak al haTorah*, p. 41a), that is, three of each kind, an interpretation maintained by some commentators. Luzzatto, however, prefers the second of Kimhi's definitions in the latter's grammatical work, and renders the biblical text as meaning "third-born" (*Perush Shadal al Hamisha Humshei Torah*, pp. 69-70). Jacob also renders the term as "third-born," based on the idea proffered by a number of medieval commentators to the effect that "Thirdborn animals were regarded as particularly strong and fat" (*The First Book of the Bible*, p. 101). I have adopted this interpretation here because it is the one

that requires the least ancillary interpretation as to what the significance of triples of each animal might be or the significance of three-year old animals.

166. B.S. Jacobson, basing his commentary on that of Jacob in connection with 15:16 (a commentary that is not included in the abridged version cited in the bibliography), writes: "Three generations will be cut to pieces by thralldom and toil, persecution and oppression. The fourth generation, however, is likened to a bird, who throughout the Bible represents the symbol of liberty. They will be integrated and go out free to return to the Land of the Fathers" (*Meditations on the Torah*, p. 14). Ehrlich similarly considers the three animals to symbolize the three generations that will be subjected to servitude (*Mikra kiFeshuto*, vol. 1, p. 40).

167. This interpretation is suggested by Hertz, who considers the appearance of the birds of prey as "symbolically foreshadowing the obstacles in the way of taking possession of the land" (*The Pentateuch and Haftorahs*, note on Gen. 15:11).

168. Augustine asserts, "All these things were said and done in a vision from God" (*The City of God* 16:24, p. 546).

169. Joshua Gibschtein, in offering this explanation makes the case that even in modern times there are still nomadic and semi-nomadic peoples, such as Gypsies, that resolutely resist a sedentary and stable existence (*Daat Torah*, p. 28). Even in contemporary Israel this remains a serious problem with regard to the Bedouin.

170. Abravanel offers this explanation as an alternative to a variety of traditional interpretations that view the Egyptian exile as punishment for sins committed by the patriarchs or during their lives (*Perush haTorah* on Gen. 15:13-15, vol. 1, p. 41).

171. Scholars have long debated when this period of four hundred years was to have begun, and where it is supposed to have taken place. It should be noted, however, that the promise to Abraham did not specify that his descendants would live as strangers in Egypt for 400 years, as is commonly assumed, but rather in a land not theirs, which might well include Cisjordan itself. This point was already addressed by Augustine, who argued that it did not mean "that this people was to be in that servitude under the oppressive Egyptians for 400 years, but it is foretold that this should take place in the course of those 400 years" (*The City of God* 16:24,

p, 547). Indeed, a careful calculation, based on the biblical genealogies and confirmed by most ancient rabbinic sources, indicates that the actual period of Israel's sojourn in Egypt was no more than 210 years. Assuming that this later figure of 210 years for the period Israel actually spent in Egypt is correct, the figure of 400 years for the overall period of homelessness can be accounted for if we consider the calculation to have begun with the birth of Isaac, who was 60 when Jacob was born (Gen. 25:26). The latter descended to Egypt, according to the biblical record, when he was 130 years old (Gen. 47:9). In this way 190 years are accounted for prior to the period of the actual sojourn and subsequent bondage in Egypt, which lasted for 210 years, yielding a grand total of 400 years. Moreover, it seems reasonable to assume that the count would begin with the birth of Isaac, since he will be the first of Abraham's descendants. Although some suggest that the count should begin from the "covenant between the pieces," some obvious problems in reconciling the number years result from the fact that we are not told Abraham's age at the time that the theophany took place.

The chronological problem is further compounded by the assertion later, *Now the time that the children of Israel dwelt in Egypt was four hundred and thirty years* (Ex. 12:40). Although there is no explicit support for the theory in Scripture, Abraham ibn Ezra proposes a plausible scheme to account for the additional 30 years by asserting that the count of 430 began when Abraham left Ur, supposedly at the age of 70, and who then spent five years at Haran before departing for Canaan, enabling the text to state that he was 75 when he departed Haran, which was 25 years before the birth of Isaac (*Perushei haTorah* on Ex. 12:40, vol. 2, p.84). It would appear that the calculation given in *Midrash Seder Olam* 5 is based on the same assumption that Abraham left Ur at the age of 70, thereby accounting for the extra five years needed to make up the 430-year figure. For further examination of these chronological issues, see Elihu A. Schatz, *Proof of the Accuracy of the Bible*, pp. 39-40.

172. Hoffmann, *Genesis*, vol. 1, p. 243.

173. Sarna writes, in this regard: "In the days of the patriarchs the measure of the pagan sin was not yet complete and Israel would have to wait—and suffer—until God's time was ripe. Divine justice was not to be strained even for the elect of God, and even though its application related to the pagans" (*Understanding Genesis*, p. 124).

248   The Trials of Abraham

174. Nahshoni reviews this and other theories regarding the question of the "four generations" in his commentary (*Hagut beParshiot haTorah*, vol. 1, pp. 50-51). See also Schatz, *Proof of the Accuracy of the Bible*, pp. 41-42, on the significance of the term "generation' in this biblical text.

175. Jacob comments: "The fiery apparition passing through means that the living God passes through the times of oppression and unites those who are separated...The birds, however, are not cut in two. A bird is a symbol of freedom. Therefore, the undivided birds symbolize the generation of liberation from Egyptian bondage, the fourth generation. The three other animals must represent the three generations of oppression, expressed by their being cut to pieces. The bird of prey descending on the carcasses is the oppressor who would devour the people" (*The First Book of the Bible*, p. 103).

176. It is noteworthy that there are a number of different boundary notices given in the biblical writings, of which this is merely the first.

177. This ancient practice is reflected in one of the Mesopotamian legal documents from Nuzi, wherein it specifies: "Kelim-ninu has been given in marriage to Shennima. If Kelim-ninu bears (children), Shennima shall not take another wife; but if Kelim-ninu does not bear, Kelim-ninu shall acquire a woman of the land as wife for Shennima, and Kelim-ninu may not send the offspring away" (James B. Pritchard, ed., *Ancient Near Eastern Texts*, p. 220).

178. This seems the most likely explanation of how Hagar the Egyptian came to be a personal servant of Sarai. One early source goes even farther, suggesting: "Hagar was Pharaoh's daughter. When Pharaoh saw what was done on Sarah's behalf in his own house, he took his daughter and gave her to Sarah, saying, 'Better let my daughter be a handmaid in this house than a mistress in another house'" (*Midrash Rabbah: Genesis* 45:1).

179. The Hebrew term *shifhah*, translated here as "handmaid," actually means a "female slave," a chattel servant not to be confused with referring to some sort of employee, as the English term may suggest.

180. Ehrlich raises the question of why Hagar is identified by her place of origin, twice in this passage, when neither of the handmaids of the wives of Jacob, Bilhah or Zilpah, are so identified. He suggests that because Egypt was the most advanced civilization of the period, the biblical author wanted to indicate that Ishmael was the product of Abram and someone

who could contribute something from the best of the nations of the time (*Mikra kiFeshuto*, vol. 1, pp. 40-41).

181. Speiser notes that the Hebrew term *ishah*, like its Akkadian cognate, may mean either wife or concubine (*Genesis*, p. 117). However, taking the term to actually mean wife here, Israel J. Gerber suggests that the implication of the verse is that Sarai rejected the option of ordering Hagar to Abram's bed. "Any arrangement to produce an heir to Abraham would require the full consent of all concerned. To persuade Hagar to agree to this arrangement without coercion, Sarah made a sweeping concession. Sarah told Hagar that she would not assume the role of concubine, but would become a true wife of Abraham, with all privileges" (*Immortal Rebels*, p. 52). This interpretation is based on the assertion in *Midrash Rabbah: Genesis* 45:3, p. 381, to the effect that Hagar was given to Abram as a wife and not a concubine.

182. Scripture describes a second wife as a *tzarah*, meaning rival or adversary, to the first. *And her rival [tzaratah] vexed her sore, to make her fret, because the Lord had shut up her womb* (1 Sam. 1:6). The implication is that introducing an additional wife into the household is bound to create tensions that will disturb the tranquility of the home. A further implication is that polygamy is inherently undesirable although not specifically forbidden by biblical law. The Talmud suggests that it falls into the category of those things that are allowed by the Torah, "to provide for human passions" (*B.T. Kiddushin* 21b). That is, since a man who desires another woman is likely to pursue her regardless of his marital status, it is best to allow him to marry her and thereby channel his desire in a more restricted and responsible manner.

183. Hartom suggests that the Hebrew *ibaneh mimenah*, translated here, *I shall be builded up through her* because the word *banah* or "build" is imbedded in the phrase, may actually be a play on the word *ben*, meaning "son." In this case the phrase might be translated *I shall have a son through her*, which would make her meaning much clearer (*Bereshit* on Gen. 16:2, p. 62).

184. As Teubal writes: "It was obviously not necessary that the mother of the child Sarah was to acquire belong to her bloodline. It may in fact be possible that the concept of *blood* as the medium to transmit the line of descent came at a much later date. The concept of a bloodline can only have served elitist groups who envisioned themselves as divinely endowed, as

evidenced in the dynastic succession of warrior aristocracies. On the other hand, clan status was inherited directly from the mother" (*Hagar the Egyptian*, p. 47).

185. Nahmanides wrote, "His intent was merely to do Sarai's will so that she might build a family from Hagar, for she will find satisfaction in her handmaid's children" (*Perushei haTorah* on Gen. 16:2, p. 96).

186. Ellen Frankel envisions Sarai as explaining her pique as follows: "I was motivated solely by my vision of the future: Abraham needed an heir. But Abraham mistook my gesture, thinking that I was giving him a mistress, not a son. Thus he failed to honor my act, so blinded was he by the joy of fatherhood. Had he acknowledged my pain and sacrifice, shielding me from Hagar's shaming, Ishmael might have received the birthright" (*The Five Books of Miriam*, p. 19).

187. Judaic scholars have long been divided over how to understand the relationship between Abram, Sarai, and Hagar. If Hagar was a slave that Sarai acquired in Egypt, then, according to ancient legal tradition, "whatever a woman acquires belongs to her husband" (*B.T. Gittin* 77a). In this case, Hagar would have been the joint property of Abram and Sarai, and not the latter's exclusively. Other commentators cite another tradition, which describes Hagar as "a handmaid of 'plucking' whom he [Abram] was bound to support but might not sell" (*Midrash Rabbah: Genesis* 45:1). "Plucking," or *melog*, in the sense used here, is a technical term that refers to the portion of a wife's dowry, the usufruct of which the husband may enjoy without any responsibility for its loss or deterioration. In other words, "plucking" or *melog* represents a category of property wherein the husband may enjoy the benefits but the principal belongs to the wife, and only she can dispose of it. In this case, Abram could enjoy the usufruct of Hagar, her child, but she would remain the property of Sarai. However, for this theory to hold, it becomes necessary to argue that Hagar the Egyptian was actually a slave given to her by Sarai's father as part of her dowry.

188. Jo Ann Hackett, "Rehabilitating Hagar," p. 21.

189. The Code of Hammurabi provides that in a case where a woman gives "a female slave to her husband and she has then borne children, if later that female slave has claimed equality with her mistress because she bore children, her mistress may not sell her; she may mark her with the slave-mark

and count her among the slaves" (Pritchard, ed., *Ancient Near Eastern Texts*, #146, p. 172).

190. The approach taken here in interpreting this story follows Maimonides' caution against taking the occurrences of angels in Scripture literally. "We have explained that wherever it is mentioned that an *angel* was seen or had spoken, this has happened only *in a vision of prophecy* or *in a dream* whether this is explicitly stated or not...From what we have set forth before regarding the necessity of preparation for prophecy and from what we have mentioned regarding the equivocality of the term *angel*, you should know that *Hagar the Egyptian* was not a prophetess...For the words that they heard or that occurred to their mind were similar to the *voices*, which the *Sages* constantly mention. This is a state that accompanies an individual who is not prepared for prophecy. It is only the equivocality of the term that occasions errors as to this" (*The Guide of the Perplexed*, 2:42).

191. As Davidson notes: "We must not think of the angel of the Lord in this narrative as some heavenly, winged creature distinct from God...The angel of the Lord is simply one of the forms in which the Lord appears. He is the Lord himself, graciously reaching out to touch the life of Hagar in her hour of need" (*Genesis 12-50*, pp. 51-52). Gerhard von Rad goes farther and suggests that the term "angel" is misleading in that the word, as used in the Hebrew Scriptures designates either a human or divine messenger, "just as the Greek *angelos* in the New Testament does not mean 'angel' only. (The Latin *angelus* was the first to become a fixed term for heavenly beings)" (*Genesis*, p. 193).

192. The literal meaning of the Hebrew name Ishmael is "God hears."

193. The Hebrew text translated as "*Behold, thou art with child*" has also been translated as "*Behold, you will conceive.*" The latter translation implies that Hagar was pregnant and had miscarried before she ran away. Now she is being informed that, if she returns to Abram, she will conceive once again, and carry the child to term (Nosson Scherman, *The Chumash*, Gen. 16:11-12).

194. Von Rad observes: "He will be a real Bedouin...eagerly spending his life in a war of all against all—a worthy son of his rebellious and proud mother! In this description of Ishmael there is undoubtedly undisguised

sympathy and admiration for the roving Bedouin who bends his neck to no yoke" (*Genesis*, p. 194).

195. There is little consensus among commentators about what this clause actually means, although none seem to take it literally as referring to his half-brothers, which would presuppose that Abram would have other sons, as he indeed does later on.

196. Nissim Gerondi, *Perush al haTorah*, p. 213.

197. Israel J. Uzzieli notes that in relating the birth of Isaac in Gen. 21:3, *And Abraham called the name of his son that was born unto him, whom Sarah bore to him, Isaac,* the wording used is markedly different than that employed here. The implication being that Ishmael is more closely identified with his mother Hagar, whereas Isaac, whose mother is Sarah, is linked more closely to Abraham (*Binah beMikraot ubeMeforshim* on Gen. 16:15).

198. Hartom suggests that the repeated use of Abram's name in the text implies that upon Hagar's return and after Ishmael's birth, Abram dealt with both intimately (*Bereshit*, on Gen. 16:16, p. 64).

199. The Hebrew word *tamim*, translated here as "wholehearted," may also be translated as "complete." Nissim Gerondi suggests that *tamim* may have the second meaning here, in the sense that Abram is about to be told to circumcise his foreskin, an act which might be perceived as making the body incomplete, and is therefore assured that what might seem as deleterious actually will lead to greater completeness (*Perush al haTorah*, p. 214).

200. The particular meaning and significance of the use of the name *El Shaddai*, often arbitrarily translated as "God Almighty," is uncertain, and numerous theories have been put forth by biblical scholars over the centuries, most of which deal with theological implications that appear peripheral to the main thrust of the narrative. Hartom observes that it is most frequently employed to emphasize divine intervention in matters relating to fertility and procreation (*Bereshit*, on Gen. 17:1, p. 64).

201. The name was translated in the Septuagint as *pankrator*, and in the Vulgate as *omnipotens*, and therefore subsequently as *almighty* in English. Some scholars have also noted the affinity with the Arabic word *shadad*, meaning mighty.

202. Israel Eldad, *Hegyonot Mikra*, pp. 39-40.

203. Jacob suggests "the image is taken from the shepherd who walks behind his herd directing it by his calls (Gen. 48:15), or from the father under whose eyes the child walks. It is more than the walking 'with' God of Enoch and Noah who were practically led by the hand" (*First Book of the Bible*, p. 109).

204. According to the understanding proposed by Berkovits, wherever the divine name *Elohim* appears in Scripture it refers to God in His aspect of divine guide and protector, reflecting a providential relationship (*Man and God*, p. 50).

205. In addition to the Israelites and the Arabs, who are presumed to be descendants of Ishmael, the textual reference is widely assumed to relate to those putative nations mentioned in Gen. 25:1-8.

206. Jacob, *First Book of the Bible*, p. 111. While this perception may have been true for the ancient world generally, it is disputed in 1 Sam. 8 as inappropriate for Israel, which is intended to follow a different model of governance.

207. Luzzatto, *Perush Shadal al Hamisha Humshei Torah*, on Gen. 17:6, p. 73.

208. "At first he became a father to Aram only, but in the end he became a father to the whole world" (*B.T. Berakhot* 13a).

209. The term *raham* does not appear as such in Hebrew, although it does in Arabic, leading some scholars to conclude that *raham* was an archaic Hebrew term whose use was discontinued by the time the Genesis story was written down, thus necessitating the inclusion of the explanatory "*father of a multitude*" for the benefit of those unfamiliar with the meaning of the *raham* portion of the name of Abraham. Some scholars, attempting to find a Hebrew etymology for the name appropriate to the biblical context, suggest that the *ham* of Abraham is an abbreviated form of the word *hamon*, meaning multitude, and that the name Abraham is actually *Abir* (chief)-*ham* or "chief of multitude" (Francis Brown, S.R. Driver, and Charles A. Briggs, eds., *A Hebrew and English Lexicon of the Old Testament*, p. 4). It has also been suggested that *raham* is nothing more than an embellishment of the word *ram* intended to further exalt the bearer of the name (Joshua Steinberg, *Millon haTanakh*, p. 8).

210. "This restriction intentionally excludes the practice of clitoridectomy, or female circumcision, found in many parts of the world" (Sarna, *The JPS Torah Commentary: Genesis*, p. 125, note10). Similarly, Ehrlich, *Mikra kiFeshuto*, vol. 1, p. 44.

211. Buber, *On the Bible*, p. 39.

212. "In ancient Egypt, circumcision appears to have been practiced from the earliest dynasties—that is, more than 6,000 years before the present—and is thought to have been of independent invention there (though the proximity of areas such as those known today as the Sudan and Chad, where mutilation appears to have been long established, may raise a doubt as to its independent invention). In any event, what makes Egyptian circumcision especially interesting is that the scholarly evidence indicates that, no matter where and upon whom it was practiced, it represented a sign of affiliation to the cult of sun god, Amon-Re, chief deity and creator of all things. Part of the Egyptian cosmogonic myth suggests that Amon-Re mutilated his genitals in some way. From Classical Greek sources, we know that the surgery appears to have been a privilege of the priestly castes" (Ashley Montagu, "Mutilated Humanity," paper presented at The Second International Symposium on Circumcision, San Francisco, CA, April 30-May 3, 1991).

213. Luzzatto, *Perush Shadal al Hamisha Humshei Torah*, on Gen. 17:10, p. 73.

214. Roland de Vaux wrote in this regard: "It is difficult to determine the extent of the practice of circumcision in the ancient East, for the available evidence is uncertain and contradictory. In Egypt, bas-reliefs bear witness to the custom from the third millennium B.C., texts mention it, Herodotus speaks of it, and yet some of the mummies are not circumcised. It certainly seems to have been obligatory for the priests" (*Ancient Israel*, Vol. 1: *Social Institutions*, p. 46).

215. The Hebrew term *orlah* is used in the Talmud to refer to the prohibited fruit of trees during the first three years after their planting, in accordance with the biblical injunction of Lev. 19:23. The fruit of immature trees is not considered suitable as a first-fruit offering to God, and is therefore also considered unsuitable for human consumption. The prophets also allegorically applied the related term, *arel* or "uncircumcised," to the

rebellious heart (Ezek. 44:7, 9), the dulled ear (Jer. 6:10), and the *uncircumcised in the heart* (Jer. 9:25).

216. Ismar Schorsch writes: "The significance of the eighth day is illuminated by a singular prohibition in Leviticus: 'When an ox or a sheep is born, it shall stay seven days with its mother, and from the eighth day on it shall be acceptable as an offering by fire to the Lord (Lev. 22:27).' In other words, no sacrificial animal is to be removed from its mother for the first seven days of its life…Similarly, circumcision is delayed to the eighth day, as if to say that it is the very first time when the male child may symbolically be dedicated to the service of God" (*Weekly Torah Commentary*, "Parashat Lekh Lekha," Jewish Theological Seminary, October 15, 1994).

217. Kimhi, *Perush Radak al haTorah* on Gen. 17:14, p. 45a.

218. As will be seen later, matrilineal descent continued to be considered important to Abraham when it came to the marriage of his son Isaac, with regard to whom he gave clear preference to endogamous as opposed to exogamous marriage.

219. Nissim Gerondi suggests that the reason why the text is so abrupt with regard to Sarai's change of name compared to the more elaborate explanation of Abram's name change is that Sarai was a more complete person than Abram from the perspective of the divine. Accordingly, Abram merited the name change to Abraham only after he perfected himself through circumcision, whereas Sarai did not have to undergo any comparable ordeal—she was already at such a higher stage. Her change of name merely had to await his, because her change of status was contingent on his (*Perush al haTorah*, p. 219).

220. Everett Fox, *The Five Books of Moses*, comment on 17:16, p. 73.

221. R. Isaac, one of the sages of the Talmud, taught: "Four things cancel the doom of a man, namely, charity, supplication, change of name and change of conduct…Change of name, as it is written *'As for Sarai thy wife, thou shalt not call her name Sarai, but Sarah shall her name be*; and it continues, *And I will bless her, and moreover I will give thee a son of her* (B.T. Rosh Hashanah 16b). Thus, the change of name is linked to her new ability to conceive.

222. Fox, *The Five Books of Moses*, comment on 17:1, p. 71.

223. Menora, *Peshat veHigayon baMikra*, pp. 138-39.

224. Ibid., p. 152.

225. It is clear that the idea of ideological "conversion" to Judaism is one that appears much later in history, although it clearly seems to be foreshadowed here.

226. An early medieval rabbinic document asserts: "All heathens who come to Israel are circumcised by their own freewill and with their consent, and in fear of Heaven are they circumcised...But slaves are circumcised both by their freewill and with their consent as well as without their consent, and no confidence is placed in slaves. Likewise with all the slaves who were circumcised with our father Abraham, they did not remain true (converts) in Israel, neither they nor their seed...Why did he circumcise them? Because of purity, so that they should not defile their masters" (*Pirkei de Rabbi Eliezer*, ch. 29, p. 208).

227. "What became of these proselytes? No further mention is made of them for they dispersed when they saw that Abram's children no longer showed them hospitality and charity to the same extraordinary degree that the 'father of peoples and believers' had" (Elie Munk, *The Call of the Torah: Bereishis* on Gen. 12:5, p. 157).

228. As Jacob suggests, that this followed shortly after the preceding events is indicated by the assertion that God appeared *unto him*, rather than stating "unto Abraham," implying a certain continuity in the story (*The First Book of the Bible*, p. 116). There is a rabbinic tradition that this occurred on the third day following his circumcision, a time when the discomfort from the procedure is thought to be at its highest (*B.T. Baba Metzia* 86b). The idea that the third day is the most painful is derived from the story of the rape of Dinah, *And it came to pass on the third day* [following the circumcision of the men of Shechem], *when they were in pain, that two of the sons of Jacob...took each man his sword, and came upon the city unawares, and slew all the males* (Gen. 34:25).

229. Abraham Menahem Porto (Rafa-Rappaport), *Minhah Belulah*, p. 23a.

230. "One angel does not perform two missions, nor do two angels together perform one mission" (*Midrash Rabbah: Genesis* 50:2).

231. The general idea is found in *B.T. Baba Metzia* 86b, with some differences. In the talmudic version one angel comes to heal Abraham and later res-

cues Lot, the second announces the forthcoming birth of Isaac, and the third brings about the destruction of Sodom.

232. This is the position taken by Maimonides, who asserts, "wherever it is mentioned that an *angel* was seen or had spoken, this happened only *in a vision of prophecy* or *in a dream* whether this is explicitly stated or not" (*The Guide of the Perplexed*, 2:42).

233. Kimhi, *Perush Radak al haTorah* on Gen. 18:1, p. 46b.

234. There is a debate in the Talmud over whether the word *Adonai* in this passage refers to God or to one of the visitors who is being addressed as "my lord," which, of course affects the interpretation of the entire passage (*B.T. Shevuot* 35b). It should be noted, however, that the Masoretic text of the Bible, which supplied the standardized diacritical marks to facilitate proper pronunciation, places a *kamets* under the penultimate letter of the word which, according to the medieval commentator Bahya ben Asher, indicates clearly that the Masoretes considered the term to apply to God and not to man (*Biur al haTorah* on Gen. 18:3). As Elie Munk summarizes Bahya's lengthy argument, "nouns formed with a *kametz* indicate the absolute state whereas those with the *patach* are in the construct. Consequently, the word [*Adonai,* pronounced the same with either mark in the Sephardic pronunciation but differently in the Ashkenazic pronunciation] written with a *kametz* designates God, but when formed with a *patach* it refers to men" (*The Call of the Torah: Bereishis*, p. 232).

235. "Rab Judah said in Rab's name: Hospitality to wayfarers is greater than welcoming the presence of the *Shechinah* [the Divine Presence], for it is written, *And he said: My Lord, if now I have found favor in Thy sight, pass not away, etc.* R. Eleazar said: Come and observe how the conduct of the Holy One, blessed be He, is not like that of mortals. The conduct of mortals [is such that] an inferior person cannot say to a great[er] man, Wait for me until I come to you, whereas in the case of the Holy One, blessed be He, it is written, *And he said: My Lord, if now I have found, etc.*" (*B.T. Shabbat* 117a). Rashi also acknowledges this as an alternate explanation of the text, and explains further that this is not precluded by the order of the verses in the text, which are not necessarily sequential in terms of the events they describe (*The Torah* on Gen. 18:3).

236. Abravanel suggests that Sarah had gone into seclusion because she was depressed by not having any children, let alone grandchildren, of her own;

something that made her extremely self-conscious and uncomfortable with people from outside the immediate household (*Perush haTorah* on Gen. 18:9, p. 45d).

237. Emmanueli, *Sefer Bereshit*, p. 270.

238. Esther M. Shkop, "And Sarah Laughed...," p. 43.

239. *Midrash Rabbah: Genesis* 38:6.

240. This interpretation is implicit in the commentary of Sforno. *Biur al haTorah* on Gen. 18:21, p. 49.

241. *Midrash Rabbah: Genesis* 49:6.

242. Commentators through the ages have been concerned about the fact that only two of the "men" go to Sodom, no indication being given regarding what happened to the third. Luzzatto suggests that the entire conversation purportedly taking place with God actually takes place with the third man or angel, the divine emissary who remains behind, who is the one with whom Abraham engages in a colloquy (*Perush Shadal al Hamisha Humshei Torah* on Gen. 18:22, p. 79).

243. Shmuel Boteach writes: "For a human being, who is not all-knowing, to accept that something dreadful is happening in Sodom and not have this bother him because he has faith in God, is an insufficient and flawed response. As far as faith, his faith is perfect, but where is his pursuit of justice? God may have his reasons and thus for God it is just to afflict Sodom.... [But] God's commandment to man is to establish justice, and always to promote life, not to trust that God is just. The question of God's justice is a non sequitur. Of course He is just. But this is not the issue. Are we just? is the real question...God created us with a mind and a heart and told us to pursue justice until we actually achieve justice. God did not instruct us to believe that He is just. When it comes to issues of life and death God wishes for us to affirm life and challenge those who would deny it" (*Wrestling with the Divine*, p.196).

244. *Midrash Rabbah: Genesis* 49:9.

245. Meir Simhah haKohen, *Meshekh Hokhmah*, commentary on Gen. 18:24, p. 16. This approach is predicated on the earlier biblical observation that *Noah was a man in his generations a man righteous and whole-hearted* (Gen. 6:1). The implication of the text is that Noah was righteous *in his generations*, but would not necessarily have been considered as such at another

time. In other words, righteousness is not an absolute but an attribute relative to the prevailing circumstances.

246. David Daube, *Studies in Biblical Law*, p. 155.

247. Munk, *The Call of the Torah: Bereishis*, p. 241. Munk bases his view on a pertinent passage in the Talmud, which relates that R. Meir was incensed by the conduct of some lawless men and invoked Psalm 104:35, *Let sinners cease out of the earth, and let the wicked be no more*, as his prayer. His wife Beruria, a noted scholar in her own right reproved him, arguing that the Hebrew text *yitamu hatta'im*, translated as *Let sinners cease*, with a hardly perceptible change of vocalization, would yield *Let sin cease*. "Since the sins will cease, there will be no more wicked men! Rather pray for them that they should repent, and there will be no more wicked. He did pray for them, and they repented" (*B.T. Berakhot* 10a).

248. *Midrash Rabbah: Genesis* 49:9.

249. *Notes on the New Translation of the Torah*, pp. 92-93. Davidson similarly argues, "It is best to stress the legal background to the Hebrew words, and translate 'innocent' and 'guilty'" (*Genesis 12-50*, p. 70), a position also taken by Robert Alter (*Genesis*, p. 81).

250. *The Genesis Octapla*, pp. 50-51.

251. In an otherwise engaging examination of the discussion between Abraham and God, Alan M. Dershowitz, writing from a juridical perspective, tends to use the terms law and justice as well as righteousness and innocence interchangeably, thus confusing the issue and, in my view, missing some of the essential points of the interchange (*The Genesis of Justice*, pp. 69-93).

252. For an in-depth discussion of the biblical concept of communal responsibility, see Daube, *Studies in Biblical Law*, chapter 4. It is noteworthy that, in his discussion, Daube, writing from the perspective of a jurist, seems to have entirely missed the critical distinction being made here between righteousness and innocence, and their political as opposed to jurisprudential implications.

253. *Etz Hayim: Torah and Commentary*, note on 18:24, p. 103.

254. *Midrash Rabbah: Genesis* 49:9.

255. Dershowitz, while seeming to acknowledge the classical argument that "without a core number of righteous people, it will not be possible to influence the multitudes of wicked, as evidenced by Noah's inability to change his generation of sinners," immediate lapses into his own explanation, again equating the terms righteous and innocent, and unconvincingly arguing that "ten, although an arbitrary number, suggests an approximate balance between convicting the innocent and acquitting the guilty" (*The Genesis of Justice*, p. 88).

256. Silvano Arieti, *Abraham and the Contemporary Mind*, p. 118.

257. Speiser notes that this must have been the evening of the day following their visit with Abraham, which must have lasted until the late afternoon. Given that the presumed location of Sodom is approximately forty miles from Hebron, a trip that would normally take about two days in antiquity, they would not have arrived at Sodom until the evening of the following day, at the earliest (*Genesis*, p. 138).

258. According to Sforno, the Hebrew term *mishteh*, translated as "feast," refers to a meal at which wine is consumed as a major component of the meal (*Biur al haTorah* on Gen. 19:3).

259. *Midrash Rabbah: Genesis* 50:5.

260. Plaut, *The Torah*, p. 135.

261. As Von Rad suggests: "The surprising offer of his daughters must not be judged simply by our Western ideas. That Lot intends under no circumstances to violate his hospitality, that his guests were for him more untouchable than his own daughters, must have gripped the ancient reader, who knew whom Lot intended to protect in this way" (*Genesis* p. 218).

262. This possibility is suggested as one dispassionate approach to understanding Lot's dilemma by Frankel: "If we look at the problem through the lens of the social scientist, we discover political and economic reasons behind Lot's choice: hospitality cements social bonds, incurs reciprocal obligation, balances power among potential rivals. Thus, when the wicked Sodomites call for Lot's guests...he must choose among several competing pressures: to placate his neighbors, safeguard his guests, or protect his daughters. Since his daughters lack the power to either jeopardize or strengthen his position, it is no wonder that Lot chooses to sacrifice their

future marriageability rather than dishonor his guests or provoke his neighbors. Such a move is certainly politically expedient" (*The Five Books of Miriam*, p. 25).

263. Isaiah, declaiming against the wickedness he saw, compared it to that of Sodom and Gomorrah, and focused particularly on the Sodom-like corruption of the judicial system in favor of the powerful and wealthy. He exhorted: *Learn to do well; seek justice, relieve the oppressed, judge the fatherless, plead for the widow* (Isa. 1:17). Jeremiah, declaiming against the false prophets of Jerusalem, complains: *They commit adultery, and walk in lies, and they strengthen the hands of evil-doers, that none doth return from his wickedness; they are all of them become unto Me as Sodom, and the inhabitants thereof as Gomorrah* (Jer. 23:14)

264. Peli, "A Society which Lived for Itself," *Jerusalem Post International Edition*, November 7, 1987, p, 22.

265. The Hebrew term employed in the text, *sanverim*, is found again only in 2 Kings 6:18, and is generally understood by traditional commentators to refer to a temporary blindness. Brown, Driver, and Briggs define it as "sudden blindness" (*A Hebrew and English Lexicon of the Old Testament*, p. 703).

266. Josephus suggests that Lot had but two daughters, who were betrothed but not yet married (*Antiquities* 1:12:4). However, there is a midrashic tradition that insists that he had at least four daughters. This conclusion is arrived at by a variant reading of the biblical text as stating, "And Lot went out, and spoke unto his sons-in-law, *and those who would marry* his daughters" (*Midrash Rabbah: Genesis* 50:9). There is also a tradition that Lot had yet another daughter named Paltit, who was earlier slain by the Sodomites for showing compassion to a beggar (*The Book of Jasher* 19:24-35, p. 53).

267. *Midrash Rabbah: Genesis* 50:11.

268. This hesitancy is emphasized for readers of the vocalized Hebrew text by the placement over the word "lingered" of the *shalshelet*, a musical notation signifying a rarely used trebled note sung when chanting the Torah in the synagogue,.

269. *Tosefta: Sanhedrin* 14:4.

270. "Because of Abraham...you are being given the opportunity to escape" (*Pesikta Rabbati*, Piska 3:3).

271. As Rashi put it, "You do not deserve to see their punishment, while you are being saved" (*Perushei Rashi al haTorah*, on 19:17).

272. This seems to be implied by the psalmist in Ps. 52:8, 54:9, 92:12, and 118:7.

273. Thus, a later biblical writer will caution: *Rejoice not when thine enemy falleth, and let not thy heart be glad when he stumbleth; lest the Lord see it, and it displease Him* (Prov. 24:17-18).

274. Because in the Hebrew text Lot is told to go "to *the* mountain," it is conjectured by some that the mountain in question is the dwelling place of Abraham, either at Hebron, which is at a considerable height above the Jordan plain, or to where Abraham lived before Lot separated from him, a high point in the hill country between Beth-el and Ai.

275. This Zoar is not to be confused with the Egyptian frontier fortress mentioned in Gen. 13:10. It is named Zoar because Lot describes it as *mitzar* or "little." Some have identified the site as the town of Bela, mentioned earlier in connection with wars between the kings of the Jordan plain and the Mesopotamian alliance described in Gen. 14 (Joshua Steinberg, *Millon haTanakh*, p. 725).

276. Josephus suggests that it was a thunderbolt that set the city ablaze (*Antiquities* 1:12:4).

277. Sarna attributes the origin of the salt tradition to the base of Mount Sodom (Jebel Usdum), which consists of a ridge of rock salt that extends for about five miles (*The JPS Torah Commentary: Genesis*, p. 138, note on 11:26).

278. Evidently citing Abraham De Sola (1825-1882), author of works on scriptural botany, zoology, and medicine, in this regard, Hertz observes, "a similar fate befell lingering refugees at Pompeii" (*The Pentateuch and Haftorahs*, p. 68, note on 19:26). Josephus claims to have seen the pillar of salt (*Antiquities* 1:12:4), although one suspects that more than one such salt-based formation was labeled as *the* "pillar of salt" over time.

279. Jacob ben Asher, *Perush haTur haArokh al haTorah*, on Gen. 19:26, p. 42.

280. That Zoar was spared is clear by implication in Deut. 29: 22, which lists Sodom, Gomorrah, Admah, and Zeboiim, as the cities overthrown by God in His anger, a list in which no mention is made of Zoar, which was the fifth city of the Sodomite confederation in the Jordan plain (Gen. 14:8).

281. *Midrash Rabbah: Genesis* 51:8.

282. Nissim Gerondi, *Perush al haTorah*, pp. 256-57.

283. This interpretation cited by Kimhi in the name of an eleventh century scholar, Joseph Kara (*Perush Radak al haTorah* on Gen. 19:31).

284. Firer, *Hegyonah shel Torah*, vol. 1, p. 87.

285. Refer to Note 266 above.

286. Not trusting Lot to act in their best interests, as Frankel puts it: "They barter their own maidenheads for security, each obtaining from Lot a son to support her in her old age. For with their old world in flames and their mother petrified, what other options do they have (*The Five Books of Miriam*, p. 26)?

287. *B.T. Nazir* 23a; *B.T. Horayot* 10b; *The Fathers According to Rabbi Nathan*, ch. 34, p. 138.

288. Levi ben Gershom, *Perushei haTorah*, vol. 1, p. 139.

289. Munk writes in this regard: "For even if Sarah had only been Abraham's unmarried sister, is it right that every female foreigner entering the country should be at the disposal of the prince for his pleasure? And even if the customs of Gerar sanctioned such action, they were nonetheless still sins before God, and it was up to the prince to sanction only those customs that complied with ethical conduct" (*The Call of the Torah: Bereishis*, p. 261).

290. *B.T. Makkot* 9a.

291. The translation of *Elohim* here as God has been seen by some as problematic because the verb form associated with it is in the plural form, suggesting that it is being used in this verse not as a divine name but in a secular sense as referring to "authorities," specifically those authorities who forced Abraham into exile from Ur of the Chaldees, and not God who inspired him to leave Haran. Thus, it is noted in the Talmud, that this is the only

place in the saga of Abraham where *Elohim* is not used as a divine name (*Talmud Yerushalmi: Megillah* 1:9, near end).

292. It has been observed that the term *fear of Elohim* has a somewhat different connotation that the more usual formulation, *fear of YHVH*, the former reflecting an external concern, namely, the fear of punishment by the God of justice, whereas the latter refers to fear permeated with reverence and veneration of the God of love and mercy. Accordingly, as Isaiah Horowitz wrote, Abraham's words to Abimelech should be understood as saying, not only is there no *fear of YHVH* in this place, there is not even any *fear of Elohim* here (*Shnei Luhot haBrit*, "Assarah Maamrot," 3, p. 37, col. b). It is noteworthy that this exposition, in a posthumous work first published in 1649, explains the shift in the names of God here from *YHVH* to *Elohim* without need of recourse to the documentary hypothesis to account for it.

293. There is some scriptural evidence that such marriages were still considered acceptable centuries later, in the period of the early monarchy (2 Sam. 13:13). However, as noted in the first chapter of this book, it has been argued that Sarah may have been a granddaughter of Terah, whom he adopted as his daughter after the death of her father Haran, making her Abraham's wife, sister, and niece all at once.

294. Naftali Zvi Judah Berlin (*HaAmek Davar* on Gen. 21:6) takes note that in this passage Sarah refers to God as *Elohim*, the epithet traditionally held to suggest, in the words of Shkop, "the manifestation of the divine quality of judgment rather than compassion" ("And Sarah Laughed…", p. 47). That is, Sarah saw Isaac's birth as a mixed blessing, something necessary for the divine plan irrespective of the pain it might also cause to those directly involved.

295. Ishmael's age at this point in the narrative is uncertain. We know only that he was about fourteen when Isaac was born, and that this incident took place following the time Isaac had finished being weaned, a period the duration of which is unknown to us with any certainty but most likely was between two or three years at a minimum. Sarna notes, "because lactation delays the onset of menstruation, the prolongation of nursing was widely used as a contraceptive technique" (*The JPS Torah Commentary: Genesis* on 21:8, p. 146).

296. That is, even if Ishmael was the son of a slave, he would still be entitled to share equally in the inheritance in accordance with the customary Mesopotamian law as recorded in the Code of Hammurabi #170 and #171, which indicates that if the father ever acknowledged the children of a slave-woman as his sons, they would be so entitled (Prichard, ed., *Ancient Near Eastern Texts*, p. 173).

297. *The Tosefta: Sotah* 6:6, vol. 1, p. 857; *Sifre*, Piska 31, p. 56; *Midrash Rabbah: Genesis* 53:11.

298. Peter E. Tarlow and E. Cleve Want, "Bad Guys, Textual Errors, and Wordplays in Genesis 21:9-10," p. 27.

299. Munk, *The Call of the Torah: Bereishis*, p. 270.

300. The Lipit-Ishtar Law Code, par. 25, stipulates, "If a man married a wife (and) she bore him children and those children are living, and a slave also bore children for her master (but) the father granted freedom to the slave and her children, the children of the slave shall not divide the estate with the children of their (former) master" (Prichard, ed., *Ancient Near Eastern Texts*, p. 160). However, Yosef Fleischman, challenges the application of this rule to the present situation on legal grounds, in terms of ancient Mesopotamian law ("Garesh haAmah haZot ve'et B'Nah," p. 151). Similarly, Teubal argues against the application of the law in this case because here the slave and child belong to Sarah and not Abraham, whereas the law of Lipit-Ishtar concerns the slave and child of the husband (*Hagar the Egyptian*, p. 121).

301. For a discussion of the critical personality differences between Abraham and Sarah leading to very different spiritual orientations, see Yehuda Gelman, "And Sarah Died," pp. 60-65.

302. The sages of the Talmud understood the phrase, *in Isaac*, to indicate prophetically, "in" but not "all," thus excluding Esau, one of Isaac's two sons, from the covenantal legacy ultimately bequeathed to Jacob (*B.T. Nedarim* 31a).

303. Calvin, *Genesis*, vol. 1, p. 548.

304. Through what can only be a misreading and consequently a mistranslation of the somewhat awkwardly worded Hebrew text, the Septuagint renders the relevant clause regarding Ishmael as, "and he put the child on her shoulder," creating the image of Hagar being sent out into the wilder-

ness carrying a small amount of food and water and a small child, a widely accepted image that clearly does not comport with the unequivocal information that Ishmael was thirteen years old when he was circumcised, prior to Isaac's conception and subsequent birth, and therefore was at least sixteen or seventeen years old when this incident takes place. In corroboration of this, we are told explicitly in Gen. 16:16 that Abraham was eighty-six years old when Ishmael was born, and in Gen. 21:5 that he was one hundred when Isaac was born.

305. Fleischman, "*Garesh haAmah haZot ve'et B'Nah,*" p. 150.

306. *Midrash Rabbah: Genesis* 53:13, p. 472.

307. One such legend describes how Abraham attempts repeatedly, after three-year intervals, to visit Ishmael but never manages to see him. However, he does leave messages with Ishmael's wife that he loves and misses him, in effect bringing about a partial reconciliation, which accounts for Ishmael's later participation in the burial of Abraham (*Pirkei de Rabbi Eliezer*, ch. 30, pp. 218-19).

308. This name of God has been variously translated as "Everlasting God" as well as "God of the Universe." There is no indication in the text as to which is more theologically apropos in the given context. Among the classical Jewish commentators, Maimonides prefers the former interpretation, while Nahmanides prefers the latter one. According to Maimonides, time itself is a divine creation and the creation of the world, therefore, could not have had a temporal beginning, a consideration that he considers essential to true monotheism. And in this regard, he wrote: "It was Abraham our father, peace be on him, who began to proclaim in public this opinion to which speculation had led him. For this reason, he made his proclamation in the name of *YHVH, El Olam*" (*Guide of the Perplexed* 2:13, p. 282). As the translator of Maimonides points out, the correct translation is "God of Eternity," even though the word *olam* also means "world" in modern Hebrew. Nahmanides acknowledges Maimonides' argument but contends that Abraham's purpose here is to make Abimelech aware of the temporal power of God in the universe (*Perushei haTorah* on Gen. 21:33), and prefers to understand the term *olam* in the more modern sense, which was already in common use in talmudic times.

309. Sarna suggests that "the 'Philistines' of patriarchal times may have belonged to a much earlier, minor wave of Aegean invaders who founded

a small city-state in Gerar long before the large-scale invasions of the Levant, which led to the occupation of the Canaanite coast…At any rate, the Philistines of patriarchal times adopted Canaanite culture and lost their separate identity" (*The JPS Torah Commentary: Genesis*, Excursus 15, p.390). Gordon and Rendsburg similarly argue, "The fact is that the wave of Sea Peoples, which included the Philistines, around 1200 B.C.E. was only a late migration in a long series of migrations that had established various Aegean folk in Canaan long before 1500 B.C.E. By the Amarna Age their settlements had become linguistically Canaanitized so that interpreters are never needed to facilitate relations between Hebrews and Philistines" (*The Bible and the Ancient Near East*, p. 118).

310. Plaut, *The Torah*, p. 143-44. There is a view expressed in the Talmud that Abraham actually planted an orchard in Beersheba (*B.T. Sotah* 10a).

311. The Hebrew particle *na*, appended to the verb "take" and translated here as *take now*, and in other passages as *I pray thee*, indicates by its use that what follows is a logical consequence of the prevailing circumstances, and is not an arbitrary request or demand. However, it is not clear what those circumstances are, or what Abraham understands them to be. One of the sages of the Talmud asserted: "*na* can only denote entreaty. This may be compared to a king of flesh and blood who was confronted by many wars, which he won by the aid of a great warrior. Subsequently he was faced with a severe battle. Thereupon he said to him, 'I pray thee, assist me in battle, that people may not say, there was no reality in the earlier ones.' So also did the Holy One, blessed be He, say unto Abraham, 'I have tested thee with many trials and thou didst withstand all. Now, be firm for My sake in this trial, that men may not say, there was no reality in the earlier ones'"(*B.T. Sanhedrin* 89b).

312. Arama, *Akedat Yitzhak: Sefer Bereshit*, ch. 21, pp. 168b-169a.

313. Moses Alshekh, *Torat Moshe al haTorah*, Part 1, pp. 115-116.

314. Malbim, *HaTorah vehaMitzvah* on Gen. 22:5.

315. Moses Sofer, *Torat Moshe al haTorah*, p. 11b.

316. Nissim Gerondi, *Perush al haTorah* p. 283 and Hoffmann, *Bereshit*, pp. 338 ff. Similarly, S.D. Goitein argues that the story should be understood as a story for the common man and not theologians or philosophers, the basic premise of which is that Abraham has repeatedly demonstrated his

faith and trust in God, but had not yet been forced to put that faith to an ultimate test. This story of his greatest test will demonstrate to those to whom the story is addressed that Abraham had reached the point where no considerations, no matter how awful, other than obedience to the divine will would determine his actions (*Iyyunim beMikra*, pp. 72-79).

317. Solomon Ganzfried, *Apiryon*, p. 11b. on Gen 22:1.

318. Hezekiah ben Manoah, *Hizzekuni: Perush haTorah* on Gen. 22:8.

319. Samuel ben Meir (Rashbam), *Perush haTorah* on Gen. 22:1, pp. 19-20.

320. Hasdai Crescas, *Sefer Or Adonai* 2:2:6.

321. According to the *Encyclopedia Judaica*, "The original intent of the narrative has been understood by the critics either as an etiological legend explaining why the custom of child sacrifice was modified in a certain sanctuary by the substitution of a ram (Gunkel) or as a protest against human sacrifice," (2:480-81). However, anthropologist Carol Delaney argues, "Despite the commonality of this type of interpretation, there are historical, anthropological, and theological reasons why such interpretations are untenable." (*Abraham on Trial*, p. 71).

322. Luzzatto, *Perush Shadal al Hamisha Humshei Torah* on Gen. 22:1. It is noteworthy that numerous contemporary biblical scholars have rejected the notion that the *Akedah* is essentially a diatribe against child sacrifice.

323. Buber, *On the Bible*, p. 41.

324. Michael Wyschogrod, *The Body of Faith*, p. 22.

325. Hermann Gunkel observed that the Hebrew term *nissah*, translated as "prove" or "test" means, "to see what condition someone or something is in," and, when used in a religious sense, is "whether someone will obey God's command or not" (*Genesis*, p. 233).

326. Albo observed that "This is why the patriarch Abraham was praised for this kind of love more than others...because he had no other purpose in mind than to do the will of God whom he loved...It seems clear from this that even though God commanded him, Abraham was not compelled to obey, seeing that he could have excused himself on good grounds if he had desired. But he did not do so. He suppressed a father's compassion for a son for the sake of his love for God" (*Sefer Ha'Ikkarim*, 3:36, vol. 3, p.332).

327. One extreme contemporary expression of this perspective is that offered by Bernard Och, who wrote: "When Abraham left Haran, he was sacrificing his past...now he is being asked to sacrifice his future, the God-promised future. These two commands symbolize Abraham's separation from the temporal and finite categories of human existence and his entrance into a new realm of being which is defined entirely by the will of God...With Abraham, command and response have merged in an expression of absolute trust and obedience; his response is no longer one possibility among the many, but the only possibility because it is the will of God. At this point, the word of God has become a part of Abraham's essential being and is now heard, not only as a voice from without, but, also, as the silent voice of his own inner self" ("Abraham and Moriah—A Journey to Fulfillment," p. 305).

328. Writing in a clearly apologetic tone, Robert Gordis argued, in this regard: "Abraham, living...in a world permeated by pagan religion, did not see himself confronted by a moral crisis when he was commanded by God to sacrifice Isaac, and he proceeded to obey. His faith was being subjected to the most painful test possible, but he was not being asked to violate the moral law as he understood it" (*Judaic Ethics for a Lawless World*, p. 108).

329. Soren Kierkegaard, *Fear and Trembling*, p. 67.

330. Samuel L. Gordon, *Hamishah Humshei Torah*, vol. 1, p.73.

331. This explanation of why Abraham was prepared to go forward with the sacrifice of Isaac without objection was proposed by David Polish in his *Eternal Dissent*, concluding: "Now, by joining the Ishmael and Isaac stories into a single narrative we learn that the *Akedah* is not only an account of unprotesting obedience and implicit faith of a test in submissiveness to God...The test is not so much of Abraham's loyalty to God but of his capacity...to push back the black tide of evil which he had once allowed to engulf him" (Quoted by Silvano Arieti, *Abraham and the Contemporary Mind*, p. 144). Arieti's own interpretation (pp. 146-59), while interesting, focuses primarily on how the *Akedah* theme has been reflected in subsequent history but does not satisfactorily answer the basic questions that have been raised.

332. The earliest association of Moriah with Jerusalem is found in the biblical book of Chronicles, which states, *Then Solomon began to build the house of the Lord at Jerusalem in Mount Moriah* (2 Chron. 3:1).

333. Josephus wrote in this regard, that Abraham "concealed this command of God, and his own intentions about the slaughter of his son, from his wife, as also from every one of his servants, otherwise he should have been hindered from his obedience to God" (*Antiquities of the Jews* 1:13:2).

334. The ambivalence of the early rabbinic commentators regarding the episode is reflected in the following brief diatribe attributed to Satan, who said to Isaac: "O thou hapless one, son of a hapless mother! How many fasts did thy mother fast, and how many prayers did she pray, until thou camest to her! And yet this old man, gone mad in his old age, is about to cut thy throat" (*Pesikta Rabbati*, Piska 40, p. 717).

335. According to perhaps the earliest of such interpretations, found in the Targum of Jonathan ben Uziel, Sarah was informed by Satan that Abraham had killed Isaac, "And Sarah arose, and cried out, and was strangled, and died from agony" (J.W. Etheridge, *The Targums of Onkelos and Jonathan ben Uziel on the Pentateuch*, vol. 1, p. 229).

336. Plaut, among others, argues that, "the story should be read not in chronological order but rather as an unrelated unit; here Isaac is a mere boy" (*The Torah*, note on 22:1, p. 146).

337. Josephus, *Antiquities of the Jews* 1:13:2.

338. This is the view of the matter taken by the author of the preeminent work of Jewish mysticism, the *Zohar*. "The text here is rather surprising, for instead of Abraham we should have expected here to read, 'God proved Isaac', seeing that he was already thirty-seven years of age, and no longer under his father's jurisdiction. He could thus easily have refused without rendering his father liable to punishment...But observe that although only Abraham is explicitly mentioned as being proved, Isaac, nevertheless, was also included in the trial, as is implied by the amplifying particle *eth* before 'Abraham', which indicates Isaac"(*Zohar* 119b, vol. 1, pp. 372-73). That is, the use of the particle *eth*, often translated as "with," in the Hebrew phrase *nissa eth Avraham* (*proved Abraham*) should be understood as indicating the testing of another along with Abraham, and that other could be none other than Isaac.

339. Steinsaltz, *Biblical Images*, pp. 31-33.

340. Gordon points out that the reference to "the" altar clearly suggests that the altar, the building of which is attributed to Abraham, was still in exist-

ence at the time the passage was composed (*Hamishah Humshei Torah*, vol. 1, p. 75).

341. Elijah ben Solomon Zalman of Vilna, *Kol Eliyahu*, #17, p. 7.
342. Walter Bowie, "Testing of Abraham (22:1-19)," p. 645.
343. *Midrash Rabbah: Genesis* 56:8.
344. Lenn E. Goodman, *The God of Abraham*, p. 21.
345. Munk, *The Call of the Torah: Bereishis*, p. 290.
346. *Midrash Rabbah: Genesis* 56:8; *Midrash Lekah Tov* vol. 1, p. 49a.
347. Offering a somewhat different but related approach to resolving the dilemma, the medieval commentator Bahya b. Asher suggests that Abraham was told to "offer" Isaac *in place* of a sacrifice, as evidenced by his later offering of a ram *instead* of Isaac. Presumably, what Bahya intends to say here is that Abraham was instructed to bring Isaac to the mountain, and instead of offering him as a sacrifice there, he was being asked to dedicate his son's life to divine service. Bahya's argument is based on a nuance in the biblical statement, *and offer him there for a burnt-offering (veha'aleyhu sham le'olah)*. However, he points out, if this was the actual intent of the statement, then the prefix of the last Hebrew word, *le*, is entirely superfluous. Therefore, the prefix, *le*, should be understood here, as it is in other biblical texts that he cites, as meaning, *instead of*, and the passage rendered as, *and offer him there instead of a burnt-offering* (*Biur al haTorah* on Gen. 22:2).
348. Steven J. Brams, *Biblical Games*, pp. 37-45.
349. Shubert Spero, "The Akedah," pp. 58-59.
350. Elie Wiesel thus suggests, with regard to Abraham's victory, "That was why God sent an angel to revoke the order and congratulate him; He Himself was too embarrassed" (*Messengers of God*, pp. 80-81).
351. Cited by Joshua O. Haberman, *The God I Believe In*, p.43.
352. This perspective is discussed at some length by Lippman Bodoff, in his article, "The Real Test of the *Akedah*: Blind Obedience Versus Moral Choice." However, Bodoff reaches the highly questionable conclusion that, because of his employment of delaying tactics in carrying out the divine command, Abraham clearly never intended to actually sacrifice Isaac, but was prepared to go through the process in the secure faith that

God would stop him from killing his son at the last moment, thus exhibiting proper moral judgment and total faith at the same time. Accordingly, in Bodoff's view, Abraham passed the test of blind obedience versus moral choice brilliantly. As he wrote in a more recent article, "Abraham passed the test of the *Akedah* when he showed God that he was prepared to proceed as God commanded *with faith that the God of justice and righteousness in whom he believed would never—and could never—let that sacrifice come to pass*" ("The Binding of Isaac: Religious Paradoxes, Permutations, and Problems," p. 27).

353. Bodoff, "The Real Test of the *Akedah*: Blind Obedience Versus Moral Choice," p. 71.

354. Jack J. Cohen wrote, in this regard: "Abraham sinned against his moral reason when he remained silent and placed his son upon the altar. Perhaps this is the reason…that God never again revealed himself to Abraham. Perhaps this, too, is a lesson of the *Akedah*—that man never play false to his finest instincts, lest he be added to the satanic powers in reality that delight in every sign of human hesitation and weakness" ("'Is This the Meaning of My Life?' Israelis Rethink the *Akedah*," p. 57).

355. Wiesel, *Messengers of God*, p. 80. Although I cite Wiesel because he precisely expresses my own view, I am not certain that he would agree with the context in which I quote him.

356. Early commentators were keenly aware of this problem and sought to resolve it by a variety of means, none very successfully. Moreover, it has been argued that the term *ayil* or "ram" normally applies to a domesticated male sheep, and not a wild one, raising the additional problem of how Abraham could avail himself of another's property, a problem that has troubled rabbinic commentators for many centuries. One midrashic solution to the complex of issues relating to the sacrifice of the ram proposes that the ram in question actually belonged to Abraham, and that it followed him on the trek from Beersheba to Moriah. It goes even farther and suggests that the ram in question was the leader of Abraham's flocks, which he, presumably affectionately, called Isaac. So Abraham sacrificed Isaac the ram in place of Isaac his son. (*Midrash HaGadol: Bereshit* on Gen. 22:13, p. 356). Of course, if this were indeed the case, then one might also assume that when Abraham was told to sacrifice Isaac, it was the ram named Isaac that was meant and not his son, a reasonable inference that is not openly hinted at in the rabbinic source.

357. Goodman, *The God of Abraham*, p. 22.

358. Ibid.

359. Plaut, *The Torah*, p. 152.

360. Although we were previously told that Abraham had *dwelt between Kadesh amd Shur*, the meaning of "dwelt" in that passage is quite unspecific, merely indicating that he had located himself in that general area, noting immediately, *and he sojourned in Gerar* (Gen. 20:1), which was the city-state that dominated that area.

361. The flow of the narrative is interrupted at this point, possibly to break the tension with regard to what happened next, to identify two generations of the descendants of Abraham's brother Nahor, some of whom, particularly Rebekah and her brother Laban (not named until later) will play important parts in the narratives concerning Isaac and his son Jacob and will be introduced at the appropriate point in the next chapter of this study.

362. Shkop, "And Sarah Laughed...," p. 50.

363. Judah Loew ben Bezalel (Maharal) explains that because the text states, *and Abraham came*, without specifying from where he came, we must assume it was from the location last mentioned, which, of course is Beer-sheba (*Gur Aryeh* on Gen. 23:2).

364. Hertz cites Meyer Sulzberger (*The Am-ha-aretz, the Ancient Hebrew Parliament*, Philadelphia, 1910) on the meaning and use of the term *am-ha-aretz*, translated as "people of the land": "The expression *am-haaretz* occurs 49 times in Scripture. In 42 of these instances it means neither the nation nor an individual boor [its usual meaning in post-biblical Hebrew], but is simply a technical term of Hebrew Politics and signifies what we would call Parliament" (*The Pentateuch and Haftorahs*, pp. 80-81, note on 23:7).

365. Nahshoni, *Sefer Hagut beFarshiot haTorah*, vol. 1, p. 75.

366. Hertz, *The Pentateuch and Haftorahs*, p. 82, note on 24:2; Speiser, *Genesis*, p. 178, note 2.

367. Abravanel, arguing from the standpoint of the rabbinic tradition that stipulates that "seed" or bloodline follows the mother, writes that since God promised the land to the seed of Abraham and Sarah, who were Semites,

Isaac's marriage to a Canaanite woman would make his descendants Hamites (*Perush haTorah* on Gen. 24:3).

368. *Midrash Rabbah: Genesis* 59:11 and Rashi, *Perushei Rashi al haTorah* on Gen. 24:10.

369. Ibid.

370. Zornberg writes, in this regard: "Implicit in the servant's prayers is the need to see a manifest indication of God's *hesed* to Abraham. His main criterion for the rightfulness of Rebecca's election is that he will sense *in her* the *hesed* that, since the Akedah, has been lacking from his master's experience. He prays to know, by means of her rightness, that *hesed* is being done to his master; not merely that God should be so kind as to make it happen that the girl he speaks to is the right one. The *hesed* he asks for, in other words, is not a means, but an end in itself (*The Beginning of Desire*, p. 140).

371. Sarna notes: "Hebrew *betulah*, like its cognates Akkadian *batultu*, Ugaritic *btlt*, Arabic *batul*, Syriac *bethultha*, does not by itself, without further definition, exclusively express virginity in the physical sense understood by the English word" (*The JPS Torah Commentary: Genesis*, p. 165, note 16).

372. It has been suggested by Andrew Schein ("The Test of Rebecca," pp. 28-32) that this information is of immediate relevance to Rebekah's suitability as a prospective bride for Isaac, and that the emissary must in fact already have had this information in hand before he approached her. Moreover, the whole test that he devised would not make much sense unless he had prior information about whom to approach with it. After all, a married or otherwise ineligible woman might pass it as well. This suggests that the emissary may have gone to the well sometime earlier during the day, the well serving as a highly frequented location for gathering information. Presumably, he may have made inquiries about Nahor's granddaughter's status and disposition and thus already knew that she was both suitable and available. Viewed from this perspective, the entire incident is more charade than actual test, the purpose of which is to make it appear that the divine hand is involved and thus make it easier to convince Rebekah's family to agree to her going off with a servant to a distant land to marry someone no one knows anything about. However, a critical problem with this otherwise plausible scenario is how the emissary can be certain that the young woman before him is Rebekah. He cannot know

this for sure until he engages her in conversation after she has passed the test he has devised.

373. Kimhi, *Perush Radak al haTorah* on Gen. 24:18.

374. It is assumed that Laban is named here because he was not identified as Rebekah's brother earlier (22:23).

375. This statement appears to be out of place here since it anticipates what is related in the next verse, and has been treated as such by most commentators. However, as will be seen, there is an alternate explanation for why the text is worded in this awkward manner,

376. As suggested earlier, it is inconceivable that Abraham's servant made the trip alone, and this is the first indication of this in the biblical text.

377. Hayyim ibn Attar, *Or haHayyim* on Gen. 24:29. For further discussion of Laban in this context, see Shlomo Riskin, "A Man to Copy, but Not to Follow," *Jerusalem Post International Edition*, November 16, 1998.

378. Arama, *Akedat Yitzhak*, vol. 1, p. 185a.

379. Alshekh, *Torat Moshe* on Gen. 24:55.

380. *The Targum of Onkelos*, ad loc. in J.E Etheridge, *The Targums of Onkelos and Jonathan ben Uziel on the Pentateuch*, Vol. 1, p. 236.

381. The Rabbis have taken the biblical report on this aspect of the episode as the prooftext for the ruling that a woman cannot be given away in marriage legally without her consent, although this may not actually be the sense of the text.

382. It is noteworthy that the blessing given to Rebekah has been adopted as part of the traditional Jewish wedding ceremony, and is recited by the groom when he places the veil over his bride's head in a ceremony preliminary to the actual marriage.

383. Gerber, *Immortal Rebels*, p. 72.

0-595-33753-8

Made in the USA
Columbia, SC
09 June 2025